CHOPIN PLAYING
From the Composer to the Present Day

CHOPIN PLAYING

From the Composer to the Present Day

by

JAMES METHUEN-CAMPBELL

A CRESCENDO BOOK

TAPLINGER PUBLISHING COMPANY

NEW YORK

I would like to thank the following London publishers for their co-operation in allowing me to use extracts from various sources for which they hold the copyright: J. M. Dent & Sons for the late Arthur Hedley's *Chopin*, the Oxford University Press for Edward Dent's *Ferruccio Busoni*, Kahn and Averill for Ronald Smith's *Alkan* and the Society of Authors for various short extracts from Bernard Shaw's musical writings.

First Printing
First published in the United States in 1981 by
TAPLINGER PUBLISHING CO., INC.
New York, New York

Copyright © 1981 by James Methuen-Campbell
Printed in the United States of America

Library of Congress Cataloging in Publication Data
Methuen-Campbell, James.
Chopin playing.

  "A Crescendo book."
  Discography: p.
  Bibliography: p.
  Includes index.

  1. Chopin, Frédéric, —1810-1849—Performances.
2. Piano music— Interpretation (Phrasing, dynamics, etc.) I. Title.
ML410.C54M48   786.3'041   81-8876
ISBN 0-8008-1511-4   AACR2

CONTENTS

CHOPIN PLAYING

From the Composer to the Present Day

PREFACE

I think that I must owe the deepest debt of gratitude for writing this book to my piano teacher, the composer and pianist, Frank Merrick, CBE. He was a pupil of Leschetizky, and through him, I became interested in those pianists who had studied under the great teacher, and this, allied to a deep love for Chopin's music, was the most tangible impetus for me to research this work. Mr Merrick's reminiscences of pianists, dating as far back as Sir Charles Hallé, who was an acquaintance of Chopin, were invaluable, and both he and his wife Sybil have always shown me the greatest kindness and hospitality.

The Polish pianist, Chopin scholar and authority on the folk song of his land, Adam Harasowski, has been of the greatest help. Miss Esther Fisher, Mrs Edith Smeterlin, the Rev. Eric Rees and Geoffrey Howard have all made material available to me that has been highly important. Dr Czesław Halski, Mme Natalia Karp, Guthrie Luke, Tamás Vásáry, Louis Kentner, CBE, Gordon Green, the late Vivian Langrish, Mme Marcella Barzetti, the Lady Ruth Fermoy, Ivor Newton, CBE, Sidney Harrison, Vlado Perlemuter, Jerrold Northrop Moore, Dr Anthony Polonsky, Eric Hughes of the British Institute of Recorded Sound, and my aunt, the historian Noreen Branson, have all been extremely helpful and friendly, furnishing me with many details and personal information, aside from in many cases welcoming me into their homes.

My visit to Poland in 1978 was also highly profitable, and I am extremely grateful to Mr Wiktor Weinbaum, the Director-General of the Chopin Institute in Warsaw, for arranging my visit there, and also for seeing that I met the most interesting Polish pianists and teachers. Among those who met and helped me there were Mme Halina Czerny-Stefańska, Roman Jasiński, Krystyna Kobylańska, Jerzy Żurawlew, Jerzy Lefeld, Mme Stefania Allinówna, the late Margherita Trombini-Kazuro and Jerzy Waldorff. Particular thanks are also given to my interpreter and friend, the young Polish pianist Krzysztof Słowiński, whose interest and patience were extremely useful, to Mme Janina Ohrt, the librarian at the Chopin Institute, who helped me over many linguistic hurdles, and lastly to Mme Barbara Drzewiecka, the widow of the pedagogue, Zbigniew Drzewiecki, who kindly made arrangements for my accommodation in Warsaw, and furnished me with many of her late husband's opinions.

I have also benefited from corresponding with the following: Jean-Jacques Eigeldinger, Gregor Benko, Emmett Ford, Harry L. Anderson, Miss Shulamith Shafir, Mme Gaby Casadesus, Peter Cowderoy and Gerald Stonehill.

Lastly, I would like to thank my friend Claire Seignior for making many kind suggestions to me during the early stages of the book. Margot Levy of Victor Gollancz has also been of indispensable help in preparing the book for publication.

London   J. M.-C.
June 1980

INTRODUCTION

GREAT MUSIC HAS a significance that transcends national boundaries, and Frédéric François Chopin is a composer whose music has played an especially significant role in drawing together musicians and music-lovers from all parts of the world. This book aims to describe the art of the great Chopin players, attempting to put their very widely different approaches into a historical and musical perspective and to illustrate the factors that have contributed to forming their styles of interpretation. I believe that Chopin's music is open to a wider variety of successful inter-pretations than that of any other great composer, with the possible ex-ception of J. S. Bach, and the comparison of performances of his music will, I hope, direct the reader towards certain points of particular interest in Chopin's writing as well as illustrating many aspects of pianism. Of course the listener's response to a performance will depend to some extent on his aesthetic constitution: there are those who are content to hear Chopin expressed in purely pianistic terms, and pianists such as Alexander Brailowsky and Josef Hofmann won special acclaim because of their success in this *métier*. But others require their pianist to reveal something of the musical essence of the composer, and although virtuosity is necessary to play many of Chopin's works, he is above all a composer of contrasts, and the ideal pianist has to be able to express his complex style with the utmost pianistic refinement.

Chopin himself was a great and highly original pianist, whose grasp of the capabilities of his instrument was unrivalled. He developed a unique style of composition which has lent itself to an enormous variety of in-terpretations, and the manner in which his works have been played since his death in 1849 has reflected the great changes which have taken place in public and private music-making, changes which have radically altered the way his music has been performed and received. The solo piano recital has supplanted the mixed salon performance, where music was often little more than an adjunct to conversation; piano technique has developed to a level unimagined in Chopin's day; the instrument itself has changed in a way which has entirely altered its capacities; the influence of the recording studio and the advent of broadcasting have significantly altered the approach of leading artists and their audiences, and there has been a similar interaction through the internationaliza-tion of the concert platform.

One can imagine the excitement of pianists of the last century dis-covering Chopin's music. My teacher Frank Merrick was the first pianist to play Debussy's works in Australasia before the First World War and took a great deal of pleasure in performing them, eagerly awaiting reactions; one critic described *Jardins sous la pluie* as an 'odd' composition. The same was true with Chopin's music – the early interpreters approached it with real discovery. It took many years for any 'tradition' or specified manner of rendering certain pieces, and these traditions usually had little to do with the way that Chopin himself played. Until the beginning of the present century, the piano virtuoso tended to emphasize the more sensational and sentimental aspects of music-making. Such pianists as Franz Liszt, Sigismund Thalberg, Carl Tausig and Anton Rubinstein were, above all else, superb bravura players, who in their own compositions delighted to stun their audiences with their note-spinning and crashing chords. They were also sentitive musicians who could play with real understanding, but it was not for this that their audiences adored them. Their style has been succeeded by many different approaches by succeeding generations of pianists, all of whom have been confronted by the problems of striking a balance between the different elements of Chopin's style; it is for the listener to determine which performance of any particular work he finds the most satisfying.

I do not believe that there is any one way of playing Chopin that is definitely 'right' or 'wrong', but there are particular traits which are the hallmark of good Chopin playing. These include the most subtle *legato*, the ability to sustain the purity of the melodic lines; contrasts in mood, textures and the balance between the parts; highly developed contrapuntal playing, and rhythmic flexibility. The phrasing must never sound stiff or fragmentary, and the musicality of the performer should always outweigh his pianism.

One of the most important elements in a performance of Chopin is the pianist's use of *rubato*. When applied with taste and perception this can bring the music to life in a way that the strictly academic observance of the note values can not. However, when misused, *rubato* can cripple the music, and reduce it to absurdity; this is more likely to arise in the case of pianists to whom Chopin's *rubato* does not come naturally and for whom it has to be learned, and it is broadly true that it is most easily grasped by pianists of Eastern European origin.

The word *rubato* has two meanings, one loose and the other more precise. When used in the former sense, it generally means the licence that the player can take with the rhythmic pulse of a piece, especially in relation to phrasing, thus adding to the natural flow of the music without obscuring its character. The other, more specific meaning of *rubato*, is the licence with which a pianist can treat the ornamented (usually right-hand) part of a piece while maintaining a steady tempo in the left-hand accompaniment (the hands are occasionally reversed). This type of *rubato* is highly disciplined, and it was a notable characteristic of Chopin's own playing, especially in the Mazurkas. When applied correctly it invests the music with life and movement, but if it is allowed to hold up the momentum of the piece – unless this has been specifically designated by the composer or is made essential because of the great many right-hand notes which have to be executed as the ornament to a left-hand accompaniment, in which case the right-hand part has been designed to delay the pace of the music – then the pianist is straying from the intended spirit of the music.

I believe that Chopin would have tolerated any imaginative performance of his works. He himself altered them in performing and teaching, varying the ornaments, improvising variants and altering dynamic markings; he never played any work the same way twice. Some pianists have in the past claimed that their performances of Chopin were 'authentic'. If this word is taken in its dictionary meaning 'of the original' or 'of the principal', then only those who had actually heard Chopin play could be relied upon to give 'authentic' performances. But since none of his pupils who survived him possessed a degree of talent approaching that of their master, they were unable to emulate his performances, and give 'authentic' renderings of his style. It is far more likely that pianists such as Cortot, Koczalski, Rosenthal, Michałowski and Pachmann, all of whom benefited from receiving the advice of the pupils and disciples of Chopin, but were themselves very great and gifted artists, were able to capture most closely the playing of the master. All these pianists knew Chopin's entire *oeuvre* and devoted a lifetime to the study of his music, and all who heard them play (this applies to Rosenthal in his maturity; in his younger days he was over-virtuosic) agreed that their Chopin had an authority which was lacking in others, and their discs bear this out.

The problem of achieving a satisfactory balance between the contrasting elements of Chopin's complex style will always present a challenge. It often happens that the pianist with the most highly developed technique fails to shape the melodic lines so as to allow them their direct appeal; superb technicians like Josef Hofmann and Shura Cherkassky, for example, have a tendency to emphasize so many of the contrapuntal details in the writing that the line of the music becomes confused – Hofmann in particular had a tendency towards making a melodic line out of an accompanying figure, a practice which can only be musically effective if the principal melody is not thereby obscured. And one can speculate on what Chopin's reaction might have been to hearing a pianist such as Emil Gilels play his B minor Sonata. His response might have been one of astonishment and delight, but it is possible that the constant search for new avenues, new meanings, new inflexions and new harmonic mixtures would not necessarily have won his approval, and he might have echoed Hallé's comments on Anton Rubinstein's playing: 'clever, but not Chopinesque'.[1]

The accounts of Chopin's own playing and his response to the performance of his works by other pianists indicates that he might have accepted a less than rigorous attention to his markings, and when one hears an exceptionally original pianist such as Guiomar Novaës, one accepts departures from the printed text, such as the practice of holding down the last quaver of each bar in the middle passage of the C sharp minor Waltz, Op. 64 No. 2, so as to create a tenor line. Whether Chopin himself intended this to be done is irrelevant if one sees the performer's role as 're-creator' of the music rather than merely that of 'conveyor of the notes'.

However, there are many points in Chopin's text which cannot be ignored without the loss of the shape and range of the original writing. For instance, the pianists who play the quaver section of the C sharp minor Waltz, Op. 64 No. 2, at double the speed of the opening bars are showing off how cleanly they can manage the passagework, rather than adhering to the spirit of the composition. Those who strengthen the textures by doubling up octaves to create a more powerful virtuoso impression (at the end of the B minor Scherzo, for example) are striving after an effect that would have not sounded particularly impressive on the pianos of Chopin's day and which alters the balance between the hands. Rachmaninov played the 'Minute' Waltz in D flat, Op. 64 No. 1, with a very slow, languorous tempo in the *sostenuto* middle section, and with an exaggerated *rallentando* that amounts to a clear meddling with Chopin's instructions – no change in tempo is marked.

Provided the performer carries out the instructions of the composer he is unlikely to stray far from the results which were originally intended, and if he does not care to do this, then he is no longer playing Chopin but imposing his own ideas on the music. Even the late Leopold Stokowski, in his orchestral transcriptions of piano works such as the D minor Prelude, Op. 28 No. 24, preserved the original dynamics written in by the composer; to do otherwise would have been to assume that the transcriber could render the composition more truly than its originator.

Chopin wrote a greater number of works that are in the concert repertoire, in proportion to his total output, than did any other composer – itself a testimony to his genius. From the time of the G minor Ballade, written when he was about twenty-one, all the works that he composed and published are considered to be masterpieces, with the exception of one or two simple Mazurkas and a few *genre* works. Over sixty opus numbers were published during Chopin's lifetime, but there is a substantial number of compositions which found their way into print after his death. These include the works with opus numbers 66–74, which were prepared for publication by his friend Julian Fontana. All the piano works in this latter category were composed during Chopin's early years, and among them there are some which are not of the same high standard as the compositions whose publication he authorized; only the *Fantaisie-Impromptu*, four of the Mazurkas and three of the Waltzes bearing these opus numbers can be compared in quality with the compositions whose publication Chopin approved.

The production of an '*Urtext*' of Chopin's works is fraught with difficulties. The problems arise because although Chopin prepared many of his compositions for publication with great care, he would when playing them himself vary the ornaments, improvise variants and alter the dynamics, and he often inserted alterations and variants into his pupils' copies when subsequently teaching. He frequently had new thoughts on a work already published, and would pencil these into a pupil's copy, and it may be true that he never envisaged the printed version of any of his works as a finally finished product. Krystyna Kobylańska's authoritative catalogue *Manuscripts of Chopin* demonstrates how many 'original' sources there are for Chopin's works, some of them even differing in respect of notation, and the second edition of Jean-Jacques Eigeldinger's *Chopin vu par ses élèves* shows in some detail the type of ornamentation Chopin himself used when playing his own works and the alterations he made in some of the harmonies. There are thus, in many cases, too many variants for any one version of Chopin's text to be pronounced 'authentic'.

Some pianists have tried to base their interpretations on the original manuscripts written in Chopin's own hand, rather than use editions deriving from his pupils' copies. This can lead to pedantry. The editions originating from Chopin's pupils – among them Mathias, Tellefsen, Mikuli and some lesser-known individuals who contributed copies of the music corrected in the composer's hand – contain much valuable material that cannot be ignored. In many cases they represent the composer's later thoughts on a published work, and his pupils' testimony and the documentary evidence of their copies of his music show that he did not regard the versions he sent off to his publishers as sacrosanct; he was always ready to improve them. Some of the authentic variants have been left out of subsequent editions only because they are difficult to perform.

Many of the best-established editions of Chopin's works derived from his pupils. These include an edition prepared by one of his favourite disciples, Thomas Tellefsen, published in Paris by Simon Richault in 1860; another by the French Chopin scholar Edouard Ganche, based on the notes made in the pupils' copies; the complete edition by Karol Mikuli, Chopin's pupil (Kistner, Leipzig, 1879), and the Peters edition (Leipzig, 1879) edited by Hermann Scholtz using editions corrected by Georges Mathias and Frau von Heygendorf, who had lessons with the composer. The Mikuli edition was used the longest, but in fact it contained a great deal more of Mikuli's ideas than many knew. Among Chopin's 'grandpupils', Michałowski, Debussy, Pugno and Cortot prepared editions of his works, Philipp wrote preparatory exercises for Chopin, and Huneker the introductory notes for Joseffy's edition for Schirmer.*

The most widely accepted edition to have been published since the Second World War is the Polish edition begun under the editorial chairmanship of Paderewski in 1937, and completed by Józef Turczyński in 1949. This 26-volume edition was prepared under the auspices of the Chopin Institute in Warsaw, and is more complete than any other; it is widely accepted as one of the most reliable and fair in existence. A so-called *Urtext* published by Henle Verlag, appeared in the 1960s, edited by Ewald Zimmermann, but this is of little more value than the Polish one. A new *Urtext* is currently being prepared in Warsaw by the Polish pianist and Chopin scholar Jan Ekier, but it is doubtful whether future editions of the composer's works will add anything new to the problem of interpreting his music.

The evolution of the piano over the past two hundred and fifty years – from an instrument which sounded much like a harpsichord to one having an identity entirely its own – has directly affected the way in which the instrument is played, and the writing of music for it. Chopin was of course the first great composer to devote himself almost exclusively to composing for the piano, but when he was young the piano was a very different instrument from what it is today: the frame over which the strings were stretched was made of wood, and the hammers that struck the strings were covered with leather, rather than felt. Although various companies began to use iron bars to strengthen the piano frame, it was some time before a cast-iron frame was used, and therefore the volume of sound was less than on the modern piano, and the tone was a good deal more mellow; the action was not especially strong. However, with various inventions that were patented in the 1820s, especially by the French firm Erard, the instrument became much more evenly regulated, with an action not dissimilar to that used today. Shortly afterwards, the power of the action was greatly increased, and iron rods were used to support the frame, so that the instrument became capable of standing up to dynamic virtuoso playing. These advances helped to inspire the creative minds of Liszt and Chopin.

At the beginning of the nineteenth century there were basically two types of piano, the Viennese and the English. The former possessed a brilliant treble but a light bass, the latter a heavier action with a more

---

* Tellefsen's edition of Chopin's complete works was published in 12 volumes, and excluded the songs. Edouard Ganche's edition of the complete works was published by Oxford University Press in 1932, and Mikuli's edition, in 17 volumes, was reprinted by G. Schirmer, New York.

profound bass. The English model had considerably more resonance than the Viennese, and was favoured by Beethoven, partly because it was capable of more volume. When Chopin came to Paris, the French piano makers had been recently experimenting with the action of the piano. Erard's instrument had a very brilliant treble and an evenly regulated action that created an immediately pleasant tone. Chopin owned such a piano, and played it regularly. However, a more interesting instrument was developed by the firm of Pleyel. This piano was better suited to Chopin's style, because on it the pianist could create his own tone quality, shape melodic lines in an individual manner, and achieve a far more subtle blend of harmonies than was possible on the Erard. Chopin used to say that when he was feeling weak he liked to play his Erard, because on this he had a readymade tone, but when he was well, he felt up to undertaking the more demanding Pleyel. He also owned an English Broadwood, which had a much better bass than the Erard, and was more clearly defined in tone than the Pleyel.

The Pleyel was ideal for expressing the most intimate side of Chopin's character, and the instrument undoubtedly inspired his writing: it was after owning a Pleyel that Chopin largely abandoned writing brilliant right-hand parts, which he had previously used for achieving effect. It is likely that in performance Chopin varied his interpretation according to the instrument on which he was playing. One can imagine that when playing the 'Revolutionary' Etude he would bring out the brilliancy of the right-hand part on the Erard, but emphasize the left-hand semi-quavers on the more sensitive Pleyel, where the ebb and flow of the figurations could be endowed with far more character.

Anyone who has heard Chopin's music on the pianos of his day will be aware of the very different emphasis in the sound of these instruments.* The whole character of the modern grand piano, as typified by the Steinway concert grand, is of clarity, with a rigidly controlled tone resulting from the initial impact of the action of hammer on string. The dampers act with the utmost effectiveness – once they return to the strings there is, on a first-rate instrument, no after-sound, and even when sustained by the right-hand pedal, the notes do not have very long duration, and die quickly – especially when compared with an Erard grand. The length of sustained tone produced on the pedalled notes of an 1840 Erard allowed the pianist to mix his harmonies and tonal palette in a way that is impossible on modern instruments, and the range of these pianos was correspondingly greater. Since the tension was not so great, the strings lay rather more slackly on the frame, and the action of the hammers could therefore be lighter. This allowed pianists to

* Francis Planté's performances on an Erard of the 1890s and Ernst Gröschel's discs on an Erard of the 1840s are discussed on pp. 80–83.

produce an almost unearthly *pianissimo* which is characterless on the modern grand. Furthermore, the use of the *una corda* pedal, which makes the hammers strike only one of the strings for each note, could assume a far more personal role, and the pianist could sound almost as if he were plucking the strings of a guitar or a harp. Thus the shaping of a melodic line could be far less clinical than on the modern grand; there was more room for nuance and expression because the strings were struck in a less uniform and mechanically controlled manner.

In addition, the fact that the hammers were covered with leather led to the sound produced having more of a 'tapping' effect than that of a felt-covered hammer, which strikes the string with a greater surface area of softer material; the leather hammer strikes the string more sharply, thus causing a different vibration. The best way in which this can be demonstrated in terms of modern instruments is on the cimbalom: it can either be struck with felt hammers, which produce a soft sound, or with leather ones, that produce a harsher sound on immediate impact, but have a greater range of harmonics. Since the damper action of the old pianos was less efficient, there was a far greater range of 'extraneous' noises from the unstruck strings, which often took the form of harmonics. The so-called 'sympathetic' strings of the viola d'amore, which lie under the fingerboard and are not struck or played, provide an idea of the role of these unstruck strings on the old pianos, and they added considerably to the resonance of the instrument. On the modern piano, the strings are so closely controlled by the dampers that they do not have the opportunity to contribute greatly to the quality of each sound; the Bösendorfer exploits this capability more than any other current make of piano.

A number of contemporary pianists perform Chopin's music on old pianos, and while recognizing this as a revealing musical document, I do not believe that this is the best way of performing his works today. In the first place, there are no pianos of the 1840s in their original working order; pianos deteriorate both with time and with use, and reconstructed or reconditioned pianos cannot be relied on to faithfully maintain the original sound. Secondly, such antiquarianism is contrary to Chopin's own approach to the instrument. He himself exploited the advances in piano manufacture which took place during his lifetime, and would have been likely to welcome subsequent improvements, though among modern pianos he might have inclined towards the Blüthner or Bösendorfer, and would not have felt much affinity with the thicker basses of the Steinway, which can radically alter the balance of his compositions unless applied with discretion.

The story of the recorded piano began when the boy Josef Hofmann made some cylinders for Thomas Edison in the late 1880s. Cylindrical recordings gave way to discs around the turn of the century, and these became a viable proposition in 1904. The piano fared especially badly on these early instruments, sounding rather like a banjo, but nevertheless by 1914 a number of pianists had made discs, and these included Edvard Grieg, Raoul Pugno, Alfred Grünfeld, Louis Diémer, Josef Hofmann and Cécile Chaminade. By this time the standard of recording had improved, but the sound waves were still captured by a horn being placed straight in front of the instrumentalist or singer. Since there was no electrical amplification of the sound waves in this 'acoustic' system, there was very little volume in these discs, and the bass range of the piano was virtually lost. The more concentrated sound of the human voice, or of the violin, fared much better – the 'instrument' could be aimed at the recording horn. The piano was too large for its sound waves to be channelled into such a small area.

While the early discs were still in a primitive state, another invention began to vie with the early gramophone, and superficially this seemed to be more dependable. This was the 'player-piano', for which a performance was recorded on a paper roll by a pneumatic device attached to the piano, which could perforate holes corresponding to the notes played. When this roll had been recorded it could be played back, either through another machine being attached to a piano which pneumatically depressed the keys corresponding to the holes cut, thus imitating the human finger, or by fitting the roll directly into a piano specifically designed to play back this system. The three best-known companies that marketed these devices and managed to attract famous musicians to record for them were Duo-Art, Welte-Mignon and Ampico, each company employing a system of its own. The last two were the most sophisticated, and nearly every pianist of note at the time recorded for them, including several still playing today, such as Jeanne-Marie Darré, Shura Cherkassky, Vladimir Horowitz, Artur Rubinstein and Robert Goldsand.

The progress of these machines was made redundant by the advent of the electrically recorded piano disc in the mid-1920s, and the advent of broadcasting at the end of the decade. Until the 1920s, it was impossible to record the performance of a large-scale work except by entirely primitive and unsatisfactory means (the early recording studios are described in the account of the playing of Raoul Pugno on page 76. The advent of electrically recorded discs made it possible to record any work satisfactorily, and for a recording company to profit by selling the results. The advent of the disc in the mid-1920s revolutionized performing standards, and helped both to make and to destroy various artists' reputations. Once pianists began to appreciate the importance of recording, the mechanical device began to exert an enormous attraction for them, an attraction which in some instances might be described as fatal, since many of the older pianists who made discs should never have done so; many elderly artists were undoubtedly tempted by the prospect of leaving a document for posterity, while there were other musicians whose recorded performances do not do them justice because they treated recording as a vogue which would disappear and the only tangible documentation of their playing today is a performance which they clearly did not undertake with sufficient care. Ignacy Paderewski was one of the casualties of the gramophone. Before the First World War he was one of the greatest pianists, but he was coaxed into the recording studio as an old man and made several discs, some of which are barely satisfactory and others disgracefully inaccurate for an artist of his high standing; the few recordings he made before the war, when in his fifties, are of a much higher calibre.

By 1931 both the Chopin piano concertos had been recorded, as had the two piano sonatas, the F minor Fantasy and the four Ballades, and there was avid competition among pianists for being attributed with the best disc of a particular work. The advent of the gramophone coincided with the death throes of a Golden Age of pianism, most of whose greatest proponents were recorded acoustically, and some electrically. Super-technicians like Josef Hofmann, Leopold Godowsky, Josef Lhévinne and Sergei Rachmaninov set down interpretations on wax that acted as a pinnacle of piano playing which others have aimed at but never reached. All these virtuosi were influenced by Anton Rubinstein and Liszt's pupils Emil Sauer and Moriz Rosenthal, and had little contact with the surviving members of Chopin's circle; they all lived in the United States and exerted a formative influence on the pianists of that country; all of them were supreme Chopin players, and any artist recording the works they put on wax has inevitably been compared with them. Their approach was quite different from that of the great French stylist Alfred Cortot, who by the mid-1930s had recorded a substantial proportion of Chopin's works.

Since that date, virtually every pianist of note has at one time or another recorded some Chopin, the only well-known pianists not to have been recorded in Chopin being Sir Clifford Curzon, Rudolf Serkin and the late Edwin Fischer, though they played his works in recital. By the mid-1950s most of Chopin's major works had been recorded by at least twenty pianists, and twenty years later, there were over a hundred different recordings of each of his piano concertos, and even more of the two piano sonatas. This has had an important influence on both performers and audiences. A pianist's reputation can be made or broken by the success of his records, but however far technology advances, a pianist will continue to sound different on disc from in the concert hall, because the human ear hears the direct sounds from the piano in a significantly different way from those from loudspeakers.

The growth of the recording industry and the advent of broadcasting have had the overall effect of raising standards of performance, since it is now easy for the listener to become acquainted with a very large proportion of Chopin's music played by the greatest pianists. However, the care with which discs are now produced has undoubtedly led to a decrease in spontaneity on the part of the artist. Since it is assumed that the prospective purchaser will want a 'perfect' recording which is not marred by wrong notes, the artist now comes to the recording studio fully, if not over-prepared. Any slips he may make are usually cut by the recording engineers and what is presented as 'a performance' of a particular work is often a mixture of different takes. The results of combining ten or fifteen takes to make a recorded performance are seldom satisfactory; most pianists prefer their discs to require as little editing as possible, because the combining of a variety of takes often destroys a stream of thought, and so they tend towards over-planning. As a result, discs originating from live performances often have a spontaneity and vitality which those made in the studio lack.

Another result of the repeated recording of Chopin's music has been the vogue for 'integral' or complete recordings of sets of works by a single pianist. It is now common for a leading pianist to record all the twenty-seven Etudes, all twenty-four Preludes, all four Ballades and Scherzos, and so on. This practice was virtually unknown in the concert hall before the beginning of the present century, although a few fool-hardy pianists in those days played all the Etudes as a sort of marathon; Anton Rubinstein played all the four Ballades in the Chopin programme of his 'Historical Concerts', but these were a special event. The performance of the complete twenty-four Preludes was popularized by Cortot and Busoni, and the Italian played the four Ballades in recital as well. Following their example, other pianists began to play Chopin's works in complete sets, and the practice has become common in the concert hall, some pianists even playing the four Ballades one after the other without pausing for applause. The results are seldom satisfactory. There is little to unite the four Scherzos or the four Ballades except their titles: they were composed at different dates and published separately, and were never intended by the composer to be played together. If they are played thus, the audience is invited to make false comparisons between these very individual compositions – it is when they are highlighted by another work that their full stature is appreciated. Furthermore, few pianists can play all four Scherzos and four Ballades with equal excellence; no pianist can play all the twenty-four Etudes equally well unless he has practised them every day of his life. None of the great technicians of this century – with the exception of Busoni, who possessed a transcendent technique – have treated Chopin in such a cavalier manner, and there were a number of Etudes that even Hofmann would not play in public.

In this study, I have first considered the playing of Chopin himself and the influence of the great teachers and pianists, Liszt and Leschetizky, and have then grouped pianists according to their countries of origin. Liszt's ideas about the interpretation of Chopin were presented to the public over a span of a hundred years, from his own performances in the 1840s to those of his last surviving pupils a century later, and his approach achieved far wider currency than that of Chopin because it was disseminated by his countless pupils. Leschetizky's influence was also of enormous importance because he was largely responsible for eliminating the bogus elements that had become typical of the piano virtuoso in the late nineteenth century, and his reverence for the text and systematic approach have become the leading characteristic of succeeding generations of musicians. Some of his pupils were more extravagant in their approach than Leschetizky himself would have allowed; he made his students think about the music they were playing, and left technical training to his capable assistants.

Another most important influence on modern pianists has been that of Anton Rubinstein, who not only set a previously unsurpassed level in terms of virtuosity, but demonstrated a unique tonal range and the ability to express his whole personality through his piano playing, an approach which though very different from Chopin's own enigmatically distant style, has strongly influenced Russian pianists ever since.

It is more difficult to gauge the influence of twentieth-century schools of pedagogy on the way that Chopin is played, and the advent of easy communication between all parts of the world has led to a greater number of promising young pianists receiving their training from the leading teachers from different countries. However, the influence of Alfred Cortot should be singled out in this context, because whereas French teachers had previously been concerned with technique rather than interpretation, the discovery of the inner core of the composition was central to Cortot's playing and teaching, and was more important for him than the pure mechanics of playing the notes properly. He is particularly important in the history of Chopin playing because it was he, above all others, who managed to convince other musicians and the critical public that Chopin was one of the very greatest composers.

Although I have adopted the convenient method of grouping pianists according to the countries where they were born or had their formative training, it would of course be mistaken to assume that all pianists of a particular nationality play in a similar way; there is no description of the 'Polish pianist' which could cover the very different styles of Turczyński, Małcużyński, Paderewski and Hofmann. However, there were up to the Second World War recognizable national characteristics in Chopin playing: the French favoured a rather shallow but beautifully shaded sound without great dynamic contrasts; the Italians developed a deep tone, the Hungarians spontaneity, the Germans academic weight, the English solid musicianship, the Russians temperament, and the Poles naturally rhythmic playing. Since the war, many of these characteristics of the European schools have disappeared, notably those of the French and Polish schools, and the pianists of these two countries, which were those where a distinctive tradition of Chopin playing is most likely to have been formed, have become as open to the influence of trends from other parts of the world as musicians anywhere else. The recording industry and the jet age have changed styles and standards of performance, and as artists have become more open to wider influences, national characteristics have been replaced by a more eclectic approach.

CHAPTER ONE

The Playing of Chopin and his Contemporaries

MANY MUSIC-LOVERS have a vision of poor Chopin simpering in the
fashionable salons of Paris, propped up by pillows and occasionally
venturing to play a few pieces on the piano in a delicate and effeminate
manner. This image is far from accurate. Chopin was consumptive, and
it could not be said that for most of his life his health was strong, but he
was not constantly plagued by illness. It was not until the fateful visit to
Majorca in 1838 that his health was permanently impaired – he
overstrained himself when battling against a violent wind, and the effects
were heightened by the primitive conditions in which he was living at the
Carthusian monastery at Valdemosa – but even then he often enjoyed
adequate health until the last two years of his life. During his last years,
when his strength was waning, he played a good deal more delicately
and with less animation than in his years of tolerable wellbeing, but
his physical condition was less important a component in his playing
than his mental constitution, and the available evidence suggests that
once he had reached maturity, his piano playing underwent few
changes.

Born in Warsaw in 1810, Chopin did not come from an outstandingly
musical family. His father, who was a French émigré and had come to
Poland to seek his fortune, was a fairly cultured man; his mother, who
was Polish, could play the piano well, and one of his sisters had some
talent, if nothing out of the ordinary. The boy showed his genius from
the earliest age, and when he was six he began lessons with an able musician, Adalbert Żywny. Żywny was of Bohemian origin, and gave Chopin
a training centred around the German keyboard classics of Bach and
Mozart, rather than current favourites such as Clementi and Cramer.
Żywny was principally a violinist, and knew little about the development
of virtuoso keyboard technique, but since Chopin was eager to learn and
full of intelligence, his master probably had little to do other than
demonstrate the basic principles of fingering and allow his pupil's
natural aptitude to develop. From a very early age the boy could improvise well, and Żywny equipped Chopin with the knowledge of Bach's
contrapuntal style that was to play such an important part in his compositions.

Chopin first appeared in public when he was eight, playing a concerto
by Gyrowetz; he had already written some polonaises by the age of

26

twelve, when he began three years of private study with the composer Józef Elsner, while attending the High School in Warsaw. Elsner was a very sound musician of real creative ability, and he recognized Chopin's genius at an early stage. He was principally a composer of religious music and opera (he had been appointed head of the Warsaw Conservatory with the special task of reviving Polish stage works), and he gave Chopin some valuable ideas about the use of melody in composition. But Chopin was not at all typical of Elsner's pupils who, following in his footsteps, wrote masses, string quartets and the like; from an early age he slipped into writing in a particular medium from which he virtually never strayed. Although he had a basic knowledge of orchestral writing and other forms, none of his mature compositions feature instruments other than the piano. (The Cello Sonata, one of his last works, was written jointly with his friend and confidant Auguste Franchomme.) Elsner was sensible enough not to impede Chopin's musical growth by attempting to divert him from keyboard composition, and he continued to encourage him after Chopin left Poland to live in Paris in 1831.

At the time of Chopin's musical development, Europe had just 'discovered' the piano and its capacity for brilliance. Many composers who were virtuoso pianists turned to writing works which would illustrate their capabilities, and they were so popular that the compositions of genius by Bach, Mozart, Haydn and Beethoven were neglected in favour of shallow studies and bravura pieces by Clementi, Moscheles, Kalkbrenner and the like. Some of the latter group of composers wrote a few works of quality, but those of their pieces that became most popular were of a lower creative level. Two Polish composers whose piano works achieved some popularity at this time were Prince Michael Ogiński (1765–1833) and Maria Szymanowska (1790–1831), a friend of John Field and a professional pianist who was favourably compared with Hummel. She wrote some Mazurkas, Rondos and Nocturnes (the latter deriving from Field, but not nearly so well-written), and Ogiński produced some attractive Polonaises. These composers' works have been recorded by the Polish pianist Regina Smendzianka for Muza Records, and although they contain moments of considerable sophistication, they are for the most part of fragmentary value.

However, Chopin had been brought up on the music of Bach and Mozart, who remained his models throughout his life, although he also loved Italian opera. The fourth influence in forming his compositional style was the folk music of his native country. Chopin's early bravura works show that he used the writing of Hummel, Field and Weber in finding the tools with which to express himself. In his two piano concertos, written when he was about twenty years old, there are piano figurations similar to those which occur in Hummel's works in the same form, and there are particularly striking similarities between the first subject of the first movement of Chopin's E minor Concerto and Hummel's A minor Concerto, and the piano part of the slow movement of these two concertos is also very similar. Much has been written about the relationship of Chopin's Nocturnes to those of the Irish composer John Field. Although Chopin may have picked up something of the idea of the Nocturne from Field's works in this form, his aims were very different – Field's music has a great deal of charm and considerable originality, but it was meant for the salon; Chopin achieved a much higher goal. From Weber, Chopin learned some of the exuberant effects that could be achieved in piano writing, and Weber's influence can be detected in his early Polonaises and in the *alla polacca* variation from the 'Là ci darem la mano' Variations for piano and orchestra which Chopin wrote in 1827.

The most profound influence on Chopin's compositional style was indubitably Bach. The great Polish piano teacher, the late Mme Trombini-Kazuro, told me that she aimed to teach her pupils to make their Bach 'sing' and their Chopin 'contrapuntal'. This statement may sound somewhat facile, but it correctly emphasizes that side of Chopin's writing that many pianists and musicologists have neglected. When Żywny inculcated the young boy who was his pupil with the music of Bach, he sowed a seed that came to fruition in works as diverse as the F minor Concerto, the C sharp minor Nocturne, Op. 27 No. 1, the Barcarolle and the F minor Ballade. Chopin's contrapuntal style was one of the most important characteristics of his compositions. Many composers of his day used counterpoint merely as an exercise to add variety to their writing; in Chopin, as in Bach, the different voices have a life of their own, and counterpoint is employed to achieve emotional contrast in the Preludes, Etudes, Nocturnes and Mazurkas, as well as the large-scale works. In the C sharp minor Nocturne, Op. 27 No. 1, for example, the entry of a middle voice at bar 20, to be played with the thumb of the right hand in the alto range, adds an unearthly quality to the music. This is no mere academic exercise, and when played by a master like Cortot, the effect is emotionally startling.

Elsner's influence on Chopin was also important, because he introduced him to Italian opera, showing him how he adapted the aria to feature in his Polish stage dramas. Żywny had earlier trained him to study Mozart's compositions, and Chopin grew up with a natural and unfussy approach to melodic writing. Like Dvořák later, Chopin had an extraordinary gift for conceiving melodies of great length and immense subtlety, and it is his accomplishments in melodic writing that have immortalized many of his compositions, such as the E major Etude, Op. 10 No. 3, the E flat Nocturne, Op. 9 No. 2, and the trio section of the *Fantaisie-Impromptu*.

In respect of the fourth element in Chopin's musical style – the folk music of Poland – it would be absurd to think of the young Chopin consciously planning to set a phrase of a song he might have heard in a particular way: had he done this, the effect would have been merely contrived. It is more probable that the boy naturally absorbed the melodies and rhythms he heard around him in the countryside where he was born, and later in the towns and villages; they were instilled in him from childhood. The combination of this image with an idea of the piano works being performed in Warsaw, and the influence of his teachers in respect of harmony and melodic line, can give one some understanding of Chopin's early musical development.

Most composers have taken up and developed existing modes of expression in a novel and original manner, but Chopin was among those great writers who have created something entirely new, something so original as to defy comparison with existing forms (Stravinsky's *Rite of Spring* is an obvious example). He both extended current forms and, especially in his large-scale works and the Mazurkas, broke new ground. One striking aspect of Chopin's creativity is that his style was fully developed by the time he was about twenty-five years old, and afterwards changed very little. It is almost uncanny that from the time he wrote the G minor Ballade and the 'Revolutionary Study', the Etude No. 12 from Op. 10, at the age of twenty-two, Chopin wrote nothing that was not a masterpiece for the rest of his life – or, rather, did not allow any of his works other than masterpieces to be published. It is as if having once chosen his medium, Chopin found no other modes of expression necessary, and whereas other composers have 'peaks' in their musical development, Chopin attained in his twenties a level of creative excellence from which he never faltered.

It can be assumed that Chopin's own playing reflected his admiration for Bach and Mozart. This is not to imply that he would have been determined to maintain a classical poise to the detriment of the free expression of the romantic ideas embodied in his writing, but that in his playing the overall contrapuntal and melodic structure of his compositions would have always taken precedence over virtuoso effect; Chopin never set out to stun his listeners with brilliant passagework for its own sake. Although he was capable of rising to the technical heights of Mendelssohn, Kalkbrenner or Herz, his aims did not lie in ever-accelerating pianistic display. He relished the more gentle sonorities of the piano, the soft nuances that one finds in compositions such as the Berceuse, the Barcarolle, and the D flat Nocturne, Op. 27 No. 2.

Chopin never played with a great volume of sound, and his style was therefore better suited to an intimate circle in a salon than to a large audience at a public concert, although he said on some occasions that he needed the stimulus of an audience to play at his best. He did of course object to the habit of audiences at that time of talking during a perform-ance – in the salons, the ladies could be heard discussing the pianist's appearance while he was playing, and in general audiences at that date were far less attentive and silent than they are now. Although early in his career Chopin played at public concerts in European cities, notably Vienna, he preferred, from the time he settled in Paris, to play to a select group of people who would readily appreciate his delicate touch and who were sympathetic to his nationalist ideals. He is said to have told Liszt that he disliked playing before people he did not know, or among whom he could sense hostility, and he envied Liszt's natural aptitude for winning public acclaim.[1]

Chopin's piano playing was largely self-taught, and he displayed some unconventional methods of fingering. He won great praise for his performances, and Cramer, whose reputation was based on his excellent studies, and who played throughout Europe for many generations, commented on the 'correctness' of Chopin's playing.[2] Others were deeply impressed by his unique musicianship and the extreme beauty of his touch, and he was praised not only for playing his own music but that of other composers, though he preferred only to play his own works in public. On his arrival in Paris, Chopin played to Friedrich Kalkbrenner, the most esteemed piano virtuoso of the day, renowned for the extreme accuracy and brilliance of his style. Kalkbrenner suggested that Chopin should undergo three years of study with him; he was an able teacher whose excellent pupils included Arabella Goddard, Marie Pleyel, Marie Blahetka, Edouard Silas, Camille Stamaty and Ambroise Thomas, and Chopin's playing probably lacked the finish that a methodical training in virtuoso technique might have provided. However, he did not aim to make his career as a pianist, and a course of training such as Kalkbrenner suggested would undoubtedly have wasted both his time and talent. Chopin's playing was based on natural ability rather than methodical tuition. He approached the piano in a spontaneous and im-provisatory manner entirely different from the style of the French pianists of his time. One of the most revealing descriptions of his playing was written by Charles Hallé, himself a pianist of note who later achieved fame as a conductor and founded the Hallé Orchestra:

> In listening to him, you lost all power of analysis; you did not think for a moment how perfect was his execution of this or that difficulty – you listened, as it were, to the improvisation of a poem, and were under the charm of it as long as it lasted. A remarkable feature of his playing was the entire freedom with which he treated the rhythm, but which appeared so natural that for years it had never struck me.[3]

The rhythmic freedom of Chopin's playing which so impressed Hallé was also remarked on by Ignaz Moscheles, the famous pianist and teacher, who commented that if most pianists were as free in their use of tempo and rhythm, the works they played would degenerate into disorder, but that Chopin could create anew whatever he played, and convince the listener of the overall discipline of the music – this paradox lies at the heart of the problem of *tempo rubato*.[4]

Few have agreed on Chopin's *rubato*, but more than one of his pupils (including Mikuli, Pauline Viardot-Garcia and Georges Mathias) described it as meaning that the left-hand accompaniment should keep strict time, allowing the right hand freedom in shaping the melodic line, along with all its ornamentation, above this.[5] It was this that must have impressed the fussy Moscheles – there was order in the freedom of Chopin's playing, with a sure foundation as regards tempo. When asked about Chopin's *rubato*, Liszt was said to have pointed to a tree blowing in the wind, another example of movement over a solid base.[6] This style of playing was very different from that of the German piano composers of this time, such as Mendelssohn, whose music in the main part requires a very disciplined approach to tempo, though in Field's Nocturnes there is a precedent for Chopin's use of the right-hand *reverie* around the left.

Chopin's remarkable touch commanded the immediate attention of his audience, and Mikuli described his tone as 'immense in *cantabiles*', and believed that only Field could equal him in this respect;[7] Chopin's tone was particularly remarkable because of the nature of the pianos of his day. Ferdinand Hiller, later a close friend of the composer, described one of Chopin's early performances in Paris in 1834: Hiller himself played, and was followed by Mendelssohn. Then came Chopin, the newcomer, and the audience was immediately enraptured by the delicacy and other-worldly quality of his playing.[8] Even when his health began to fail, Chopin could still command the closest attention, for if his playing lacked the energy remarkable in his early performances, he compensated for this with the most exquisite nuances. Hallé described a public recital in Paris in 1848, when, two years before his death, Chopin played the Barcarolle. Rather than allowing the music to reach its climax in the last pages through increasing the dynamics and momentum, he played *pianissimo* at the final return of the opening theme, thus altering all the markings in the text to suit his state of health; Hallé was nearly convinced that this version was preferable to the original![9]

Another musician who acclaimed Chopin was Robert Schumann, then a young music critic, in his famous article, 'Hats off, a genius!' This was written after Schumann had heard Chopin play his Variations on 'Là ci darem la mano' for piano and orchestra, Op. 2. These are typical of Chopin's youthful compositions – zestful, happy and brilliantly extrovert, revelling in the Weber-like dash which was then so popular. They are not, however, representative of his mature style, nor do they rank among his finest works. However, Chopin played them with such spontaneity and wit that they were considered highly original, and Schumann's article reflects the fact that Chopin's playing obviously possessed a rare authority. He captured his audience not merely through the charm with which he executed the filigree ornaments, but through a powerful force that captivated his listeners, and this is one of the characteristics that makes his music so exceptional.

Chopin's pupil Georges Mathias described his master's playing to Frederick Niecks, the composer's biographer, as 'absolutely of the old *legato* school, of the school of Clementi and Cramer. Of course he had enriched it by a great variety of touch; he obtained a wonderful variety of tone and nuances of tone . . . he had an extraordinary vigour, but only in flashes.'[10] In the preface to an edition of Chopin's works, Mathias wrote another interesting description of his playing:

Chopin pianiste? D'abord ceux qui ont entendu Chopin peuvent bien dire que jamais depuis on n'a rien entendu d'approchant. Son jeu était comme sa musique; et quelle virtuosité! quelle puissance! oui, quelle puissance! seulement cela ne durait que peu de mesures; et l'exaltation, et l'inspiration! tout cet homme vibrait! le piano s'animait de la vie la plus intense, c'était admirable à donner le frisson. Je répète que l'instrument qu'on entendait quand Chopin jouait n'a jamais existé que sous les doigts de Chopin; il jouait comme il composait.[11]

Although we can only guess at what Chopin's playing sounded like, we know from many written accounts that in everything he performed there was elasticity and communicativeness, but also a superrefinement, and a slight reserve. For sixty years after his death, any pianist who had studied with him claimed some 'secrets' of how his music should be played, but contemporary accounts show that Chopin himself did not play his pieces the same way twice, and there was never any fixed interpretation representing the composer's last words on the subject. His practice of adding ornaments and variants to the printed text is well-documented.

Chopin apparently disapproved of the liberties that Liszt took with his music, although he could admire interpretations of his compositions radically different from his own. Adolf Gutmann, for example, had a huge hand and could play very loudly (von Lenz said that Gutmann 'could knock a hole in the table' with a left-hand chord in the sixth bar of the C sharp minor Scherzo);[12] his style was entirely in contrast to Chopin's own, yet he was said to have been the composer's favourite pupil. Chopin could not have intended that his compositions should be played in any one particular way; he was not nearly as precise as Debussy in his manuscript markings, although what directions he gave are always adequate for the interpreter. The enormous divergencies in the manner of performing his works since his death might have appealed to his wit, though he might have found some renderings astonishing.

Chopin's Contemporaries

There was never a time when Chopin's music lacked advocates and admirers, and many pianists played his works in public during his lifetime. Moscheles, who was nearly twenty years older than Chopin, admired his compositions and used them for teaching purposes, and among Chopin's contemporaries, the pianists who played his music included Henri Herz, Anna Caroline de Belleville-Oury, Julius Benedict, and George Osborne (all born between 1800 and 1810). Among the leading pianists born between 1810 and 1820 who played Chopin were Liszt, Alkan, Thalberg, Hallé, Clara Schumann, Adolf von Henselt, Marie Pleyel, Marie Blahetka, Jacob Rosenhain, Alexander Dreyschock, Ferdinand Hiller, Ambroise Thomas, Robena Laidlaw and Henri Litolff – and the composer's pupils.

When Chopin died in 1849, the prevalent image of the pianist was not the romantic figure with long hair and eccentric lifestyle – this was chiefly the later invention of the Liszt circle. In the 1830s there were two distinct schools of piano playing – the German and the French; the Viennese tended to favour the French school, and the English the German. Those pianists who had passed through the exceptionally rigorous German system, or through the French training, laid great emphasis on finger technique and were equipped to tackle their instrument with the great bravura style that was the order of the day. However, keyboard technique was then in its infancy compared with the heights later reached by Liszt and Tausig and their successors. Moscheles, although a great technician for his time, was dumbfounded by the revolutionary fingering that Chopin's writing required, and took some time to assimilate this into his technique; a work such as the A minor Etude, Op. 10 No. 2, presented unprecedented problems.[13]

The greatest pianist of the time, apart from Chopin himself, was of course Franz Liszt, who had studied with Beethoven's pupil Carl Czerny, but was in all musical matters a law unto himself. Liszt represented a new breed of virtuoso who saw the piano as having a much wider range than that conceived by his lesser contemporaries such as Field, Kalkbrenner and Hummel. Their contribution to the development of piano-writing had been largely the creation of highly-ornamented figurations which achieved pleasant and graceful effects. (Weber had probed deeper, but his music was not very widely known at the time and it was Lenz who interested Liszt in Weber's sonatas in the 1840s.[14] As a pianist Liszt was not content just to please – he wanted to startle, to frighten, and to move people deeply by his playing. He had little in common with Felix Mendelssohn, whose piano music became so popular in Germany and England. Although fêted in the Paris salons, Liszt as an interpreter began to look for something more substantial, and he found much of what he was seeking after in Chopin. There were hints of jealousy in their personal relationship, but Liszt saw in Chopin the perfect marriage of an artistic personality – genius and its potent expression – and he idolized his music. He transcribed some of his songs for solo piano (the *Chants polonais*), dedicated the second version of his Berceuse to Chopin's friend and pupil, the Princess Marcelina Czartoryska, and his high regard for the composer is demonstrated in his flowery biography of Chopin (much of which was written by his mistress, the Princess Sayn-Wittgenstein), and is also described by H. R. Haweis in *My Musical Life*.

Problems usually arise when one great creative artist tries to interpret the music of another, because the performer has a tendency to make the music his own. Chopin is known to have objected to Liszt's tampering with his works, but he also praised some of Liszt's conceptions highly, since they revealed dimensions of the music he himself had not envisaged. He once wrote while listening to Liszt play, 'I should like to steal from him the way to play my own Etudes.'[15] It is obvious from Liszt's own style of composition that he could rise to the heroic side of Chopin's writing, and that Chopin would have admired this can be inferred from his approval of Gutmann's powerful treatment of the C sharp minor Scherzo. There have been many instances of composers who were themselves great pianists, preferring the interpretations of others to their own, like Rachmaninov and Horowitz, Debussy and Viñes.

Liszt found in Chopin's works the appropriate vehicle for his own pianistic aspirations, and he had no scruple in adapting them to achieve the effects he wanted. Chopin's influence on him was profound; Sacheverell Sitwell went so far as to suggest that Liszt 'was not free to assert his own individuality until Chopin was dead.'[16] This may be an overstatement, but Sitwell perceptively emphasizes Liszt's quick appreciation of Chopin's 'masculine strength' and of 'the architectural quality of his later works', which helped free him from the influence of Bellini. Liszt assimilated much of Chopin's poetic and communicative style into his own compositions, but in his more serious works he also showed an appreciation of Beethoven which Chopin lacked.

Liszt's appreciation of the subtlety and variety of Chopin's writing can be illustrated by his remark to the composer that it was necessary 'to harness a new pianist of the first rank' to play each of the Mazurkas; Chopin replied, 'Liszt is always right. Do you imagine that I am satisfied with my own interpretation of the Mazurkas? I have been satisfied a few times in those early concerts, when I could feel the appreciative atmosphere of the audience.'[17] Liszt's pupil Alexander Siloti recounts in his memoirs Liszt's description of an occasion when he challenged Chopin that he could play the F minor Etude, Op. 25 No. 2, better than he. The two played the work one after another in an adjoining room, and Liszt played first, but when the audience were asked which of the two was Chopin, 'they unanimously decided that Chopin had played first'.[18] It must be assumed that Liszt did not play with the reserve that was so often noted of Chopin's performances, and his playing on this occasion might well have been more overtly communicative than the composer's.

As a transcriber, Liszt seldom interfered with the original if he deeply admired its composer, as is witnessed by his transcriptions of Schubert's songs for piano, of his Waltzes as *Soirées de Vienne*, of the 'Wanderer' Fantasy for piano and orchestra, and of Bach's organ works for piano. Liszt held Chopin's music in the highest reverence; he may have departed from the printed text in playing Chopin's works, but he would have wished to maintain their original character. Lenz recounts that although when playing the Mazurkas, Liszt altered their harmonies and ornaments, he took the matter very seriously and never changed the text in a random manner.[19] As Liszt grew older, he very seldom played in public, and his style became more mature and less openly sensational, while still retaining its extraordinary inner conviction and spiritual quality. His appreciation of Chopin's works never diminished – Chopin remained for him the perfect model of the poet at the piano – and at the end of his life, when he agreed to play to an audience, Liszt would always turn first to Chopin's music.

Liszt's Chopin was, above all, re-creative; he made Chopin's music his own. This meant that he played Chopin with a greater degree of self-revelation than the composer himself would have allowed. Chopin's inner turbulence, which was only hinted at in his own playing, was given full vent in Liszt's, as the Hungarian virtuoso could express the facets in the composer's character that Chopin himself was too reserved a man to let loose. This is perhaps the reason why his playing made Chopin envious, but also drew his admiration: it confronted him with areas of his personality he did not realize he had revealed in his writing, and could not express in his own playing. Liszt's interpretation did not reflect the sick and negative side of Chopin's nature, but brought out its brave, nationalistic and boldly imaginative aspect. Liszt revealed all Chopin's creative energy, for he could project the music in a way that the composer could not.

Another member of Chopin's circle in Paris was the composer and pianist Alkan (Charles Henri Valentin Morhange). One of the most intriguing musical figures of his epoch, Alkan was a brilliant pianist, but played very little in public and lived the life of a recluse, writing some of the most original and fiendishly difficult piano music ever penned. A Hebraic scholar and a devout Jew, one would have expected him to have had little in common with the almost non-religious Chopin, but they became friends and were at one time neighbours. Ronald Smith writes in his excellent biography of Alkan:

> It is doubtful . . . if any musician was more familiar with Chopin's playing or more fully qualified to comment on it than Alkan himself. . . . 'Not only did Alkan answer my countless questions about Chopin's playing,' wrote Alexandre de Bertha (in 1909), 'but he played me all his immortal friend's masterpieces. He initiated me into most of the secrets of Chopin's playing which were lowered into the grave with him sixty years ago. . . . They compel one to the conclusion that Chopin should never be treated as a romantic or a revolutionary, but, on the contrary, as a staunch classicist who had involuntarily opened up new frontiers of his art which had lain dormant until his arrival. . . . Alkan would repeat again and again Chopin's own axiom that the left hand must act as conductor, regulating and tempering any involuntary inflictions [sic] of the right hand.[20]

This extract shows how sensitive Alkan was to the preservation of Chopin's musical intentions. When he emerged to give recitals in the mid-1870s, he included much of Chopin's music in his programmes: Polonaises, Ballades, Mazurkas, Nocturnes, the B flat minor Sonata and the Larghetto of the E minor Concerto in solo piano form.[21] Alkan shared Chopin's admiration for Bach and Mozart, although he also played a good deal of Beethoven, for which Chopin had a limited admiration; it is reasonable to suppose that his approach to the piano was essentially disciplined, both as regards regular tempos and the lack of blatant emotionalism – Alkan's piano works also have very few passages of indulgent writing.

It is difficult to trace whether Alkan was successful in passing on his thoughts about Chopin to either his pupils or other pianists: he communicated very little with the outside world. One of his pupils, Józef Wieniawski, the brother of the famous violinist Henryk Wieniawski, later went on to play a great deal of Chopin in recitals, and was widely admired, but the most likely inheritor of Alkan's precepts would have been Élie Miriam Delaborde, who was supposed to be his illegitimate son, and who was a well-known pianist and teacher. Amongst Delaborde's pupils who played Chopin were the American pianist, Olga Samaroff-Stokowski (Miss Hickenlooper), and the child prodigy Aline van Barentzen, who also had lessons from Leschetizky.

If Alkan's influence on the way that Chopin's music was played was negligible, that of Clara Schumann was enormous. The acceptance of Chopin in Germany was largely due to her advocacy, later cemented by Hans von Bülow, and she played his music from a very early stage. In 1833 she performed the first movement of the E minor Concerto at a Leipzig Gewandhaus concert, and in May 1834 gave the whole work and some Etudes.[22] In 1836 Schumann wrote to a friend from Paris: '[Chopin] played a number of new Etudes, Nocturnes and Mazurkas – everything incomparable. You would like him very much. But Clara is a greater virtuoso, and gives almost more meaning to his compositions than Chopin himself'.[23]

Clara Schumann heard Chopin himself play,[24] and her interest in his music was encouraged by her husband, who had acclaimed Chopin as a genius as early as 1831. She managed to blend a very finished technique with real emotional response, and was obviously a much deeper and more intellectual pianist than virtually every other female (and most male) pianist of the day. She included Chopin in her performing repertoire right up to her last concerts in the early 1890s, and her conceptions were always highly praised. Her playing contained a great deal more variety than that of most other German pianists of her time. Schumann contrasted her with another great lady pianist of the day, Anna Caroline de Belleville-Oury:

> They should not be compared. They are different mistresses of different schools. The playing of the Belleville is technically the finer of the two; Clara's is more impassioned. The tone of the Belleville caresses, but does not penetrate beyond the ear; that of Clara reaches the heart. The one is a poetess; the other is poetry itself.[25]

Belleville, eleven years Clara's senior, had studied with Czerny for four years, and this was probably the origin of her technical mastery. Her style was eminently suited to the fashionable salons, and she spent much of her long life in England, where she taught and composed salon music. As early as 1830 she had performed the 'Là ci darem la mano' Variations at a semi-public gathering,[26] and thus she was probably the first pianist of consequence other than the composer to play his works in public.

Very few of Clara Schumann's pupils ever centred their repertoire around Chopin. In later life Clara had a much greater affinity with her husband's music than with Chopin's, and a few critics complained that she played the works of the Polish composer too fast. Her influence on German pianists will be further discussed in Chapter Four.

Marie Pleyel also played Chopin's works during his lifetime; her husband Camille was a friend of the composer, and supplied him with his favourite pianos. The Op. 9 Nocturnes, published in 1832, are dedicated to Marie, and one can therefore assume that she was familiar with Chopin's compositions and would have played them in the salons from about this date. Antoine Marmontel, in *Les Pianistes célèbres*, gives this description of her Chopin playing:

> Ses doigts légers, souples improvisaient, pour ainsi dire d'eux-mêmes et sans l'effort de la moindre réflexion, ces traits aériens, aux allures vives, d'une ténuité transparente, qui Chopin aimait à placer dans ses Nocturnes, ses Ballades et ses Impromptus.[27]

This is a picture of a sensitive pianist with all the attributes of the French school at its best; Marie Pleyel's performances had little emotional depth, but her style was ideally suited to artistic renderings – perhaps her studies with Kalkbrenner had determined her priorities as a musician.

Another lady who came into contact with Chopin and played his music was Marie Leopoldine Blahetka. The exact contemporary of Marie Pleyel, she was also a pupil of Kalkbrenner, and had some lessons with Moscheles. Although not in the same class as Clara Schumann, she was a brilliant and well-finished, if shallow, artist. She was generally liked and Chopin, on his visit to Vienna in 1829, was much struck by her charms. (On the same visit he also met Carl Czerny, the great pedagogue, of whom he wrote, 'He is a good man, but nothing more.') Blahetka's career as a concert pianist did not last long, for she settled in Boulogne as a teacher and remained there until her death in 1887.

Although Thalberg and Herz, two arch-technicians, played a little Chopin, they mainly chose works that had a purely pianistic attraction. In the C sharp minor Waltz, Op. 64 No. 2, Thalberg is said to have played some of the single quaver notes of the *piu mosso* section in octaves.[28] Both Thalberg and Herz are reputed to have played the B flat minor Prelude, Op. 28 No. 16, with the utmost brilliance and effect, but the former was the greater artist of the two, as his own compositions show. Thalberg's music had a capacity for superficial communication, but lacked intellectuality, and his Chopin interpretations would have leaned heavily on the pianistic aspect of the writing for effect. Neither he nor Herz played the large-scale works, apart from the E minor Concerto.[29]

The German pianist Adolf von Henselt, a few years younger than the composer, and known as 'the German Chopin', played a great many of his works, but seldom in public.[30] Coming from the school of Hummel, he was intent on increasing the range of piano technique, and for many years his compositions were very highly regarded; pianists as recent as Godowsky and Moiseiwitsch used to play them. His F minor Piano Concerto, Op. 16, which has been recorded by the American pianist Raymond Lewenthal, has been much admired by Claudio Arrau, and is a work that taxes the capabilities of the most adept virtuoso. Henselt was renowned for his eccentric behaviour, but had a genuine skill for poetic writing. In 1838 he settled in St Petersburg as a teacher, and was appointed court pianist to the Czar.

Henselt's method was to develop a finger *legato* touch to the highest degree of perfection. He spent much time doing daily exercises to increase the stretch of his hand, so that he could play wide-ranging chords and swift arpeggios. His method yielded startling results; he excelled in powerful and brilliant passages, and had a unique depth of tone. He visited England in 1867, and the critic Alfred Hipkins, a Chopin enthusiast, wrote: 'His playing was glorious, faultless. For a German, Chopin is difficult . . . yet Henselt was a German, and Chopin never had a finer interpreter.'[31] Perhaps Henselt's interpretations were very different from Chopin's, because of his training and musical sympathies, but when he played a work that suited his technique, he was infallible. Lenz wrote in the 1870s:

> How I would have enjoyed watching Chopin's ecstasy could he have heard Henselt thunder, whisper, lighten through his A minor Etude. This rendering of Chopin by Henselt is so indescribably grand, so infinitely idealized, as if touched by the wand of Oberon, that I can find no words to adequately describe it.[32]

However, Lenz found Henselt's *rubato* in the Mazurkas inept, and thought his piano tone too great for these miniatures.[33] Henselt took Hummel's method to its zenith of technical accomplishment; although he taught a great deal, few of his pupils achieved fame, and the only other great pianist of a later generation to adopt the same technical methods seems to have been Tausig, although he was in all other respects much influenced by his teacher, Liszt. Both Henselt and Tausig used an abnormally high finger position, which was one source of their tone – they knew little about the relaxation of the wrist and forearm.

Few of the pianists who played Chopin's works in the mid-nineteenth century had much respect for the printed notes; Thalberg, Henselt and Herz had no hesitation in adding octaves and ornaments to the text. Apart from Liszt and Clara Schumann, there were few of Chopin's contemporaries who understood his genius, and the other pianists of this generation were of relatively little importance as interpreters. They were the products of the fashion of their time, which was for works which exploited the brilliant possibilities of the piano at a superficial level, rather than aiming to grasp the musical and intellectual avenues opened up by Chopin's works.

Chopin's Pupils

Chopin taught a great deal while he lived in Paris – he preferred to compose at George Sand's house at Nohant – but an exact list of his pupils is impossible to compile.* About 125 pupils' names are nearly certain, but of these only a small fraction became professional musicians. Chopin seems to have enjoyed teaching pupils of mediocre ability; it is possible that he did not feel secure or well enough to meet the challenge of one highly receptive pupil after another. Amongst the names of his pupils there are five princesses and about twenty other titled ladies. Many of these 125 may have only had a few lessons, though some stayed with him for four years or more.

Of all these pupils, the only ones who can be considered of any musical consequence were Charles Bovy-Lysberg, Otto Goldschmidt (Jenny Lind's husband, who bore the same name as Sarasate's secretary), Ignace Leyback, Georges Mathias, Karol Mikuli, Thomas Tellefsen, Anton Rée, Émile Decombes (who may only merit the description 'disciple'), Carl Filtsch, Friedericke Streicher (*née* Müller), Lindsay Sloper, Brinley Richards, the Princess Marcelina Czartoryska (*née* Radziwill), Mme Peruzzi (*née* Eustaphiew), Kazimierz Wernik, Adolf Gutmann, Mme Dubois (*née* O'Meara), Mme Rubio (*née* de Kologrivoff), Mme Antoinette Mauté de Fleurville, and the shadowy F.-Henri Péru, who caused considerable interest after the First World War. None of these pupils ever achieved international fame; some settled down as teachers, and a few played occasionally in public (Tellefsen, Mikuli, Princess Czartoryska, Mme Dubois, Mme Streicher, Gutmann, Wernik and Péru). The chief importance of those who taught is that their pupils, several of whom made discs, might have been the recipients of a style which had its foundation in Chopin's own playing.

There was one of Chopin's pupils whose talent might have blossomed – this was Carl Filtsch, of whom Liszt said, 'When this little one goes on the road, I shall shut up shop.'[34] Filtsch died in 1845 at the age of fifteen, having made a sensation in London and Vienna. He was a phenomenal prodigy: when he arrived in London to play Chopin's F minor Concerto he discovered that the orchestra did not have their parts, and, according to the music critic J. W. Davison, Filtsch wrote out all of them from

* See Appendix I, page 233.

memory.[35] Lenz recorded: 'He understood, and how he played Chopin! . . . Filtsch also played the E minor Concerto, which Chopin accompanied himself at the second piano, and insisted that Filtsch played it better than he.'[36] The boy became a friend of Leschetizky, who was his contemporary, and gave him an autograph copy of one of Chopin's Impromptus.*

After Filtsch's early death, it was the much less substantial talent of Adolf Gutmann that, among his pupils, pleased Chopin most, although Gutmann's approach to the piano was so different from his own. Gutmann began lessons with him as early as 1834, but made only one concert tour – at Chopin's recommendation – in 1846. Many years later Frederick Niecks, Chopin's biographer, sought out Gutmann in the Tyrol, but there was no piano at hand, and Niecks had therefore to rely for a description of Gutmann's playing on the information of Dr A. C. Mackenzie, who had heard him in Florence in the late 1870s. According to this source, Gutmann's performance was notable for 'beauty of tone combined with power'.[37] He taught a certain amount, but none of his pupils achieved a high reputation.

Chopin may have picked out Gutmann as his favourite pupil because he was attracted to a personality so different from his own, rather than because of his talent. But another pupil whose great ability has never been questioned was Princess Marcelina Czartoryska, Chopin's most faithful friend and confidante. Niecks somewhat ungraciously suggests that the acclaim she received owed more to her social status than to her pianistic talent,[38] but from two other sources there are accounts of her prowess. It is related in Alice Diehl's memoirs that Princess Czartoryska played the Polonaises 'with a startling, yet most beautiful originality, which the auditors who had heard the master himself declared to be the most perfect of all readings of the composer',[39] and Sowiński, in *Les Musiciens polonais*, describes her highly successful performance of the F minor Concerto at a charity concert in the early 1850s. After Chopin's death, Princess Czartoryska led a secluded life, and only played in public occasionally for charity, but a few pianists (the most famous being Natalia Janotha and Sigismund Stojowski) benefited from her advice.[40]

More influential were two pupils of Chopin who, while not startlingly talented pianists, were very successful and highly influential teachers – Georges Mathias and Karol Mikuli. Mathias, who was of German origin, was Professor at the Paris Conservatoire for twenty-five years, and was proud of his claim to be able to pass on some of Chopin's interpretations to his pupils. He began lessons with Chopin in 1840, when he was fourteen, and his descriptions of his master's playing have already

---

* This copy of the F sharp major Impromptu, Op. 36, is now in the Museum of the Chopin Institute in Warsaw.

been quoted.* Mathias described Chopin as a classicist,[41] and this idea may have been the foundation of the rather cold approach to Chopin's music that has been characteristic of the French school.

Mathias himself played in a manner which showed that his priorities were in the realm of delicate and sensitive nuances, such as had characterized Chopin's playing, and he told his American pupil Ernest Schelling at the end of the century that he thought modern pianos had less sonority than those of Chopin's day. Among Mathias's pupils, Ernest Schelling, Teresa Carreño and Raoul Pugno became noteworthy Chopin players; James Huneker wrote a biography of the composer and was assistant to the great Chopin player Rafael Joseffy; and Isidor Philipp became the most eminent piano teacher in France after the death of Louis Diémer in 1919. Mathias thus forms a link between Chopin himself and the modern French school.

Another such link was the pianist Émile Decombes, who may not have had lessons from Chopin, but was one of his disciples, and heard the composer play many times; he also played in a concert together with Chopin's pupils during the composer's lifetime. He was for many years in charge of the Infants' Class at the Paris Conservatoire, and through his hands passed Alfred Cortot (who was later taught by Diémer), Edouard Risler, Reynaldo Hahn, and Ernesto Berumen (who went on to have lessons with Leschetizky).[42]

Karol Mikuli was Polish, and had lessons from Chopin from 1844 until 1848. He toured in Russia, Rumania and Galicia, and settled in Lemburg (Lwów) where he was head of the Conservatory for thirty years; in 1888 he founded his own music school. His pupils included Moriz Rosenthal, Aleksander Michałowski, Jarosław Zieliński and Raoul Koczalski, all of whom were influential exponents of Chopin's music. Mikuli's edition of Chopin's works was widely used for many years, although it was strongly criticized because of its awkward fingering. Musicians have assumed that Mikuli was trying to reproduce Chopin's own fingering, particularly in the Etudes, but Aleksander Michałowski said that Mikuli never professed to do this because he considered Chopin's fingering too individual and wayward to be used by other pianists.[43]

The playing of all those of Mikuli's pupils who made recordings shows a beauty of tone and refinement of phrasing that may well bear the imprint of Chopin himself. The late Arthur Hedley, the leading English Chopin scholar, once said at a congress in Warsaw that Mikuli's knowledge of the composer was incomplete, since in his edition of the works he had failed to distinguish the manuscripts originating from Chopin's own hand from those of a copyist.[44] But it should be borne in

* See page 32 above.

mind that Chopin's copyists often tried to imitate the composer's hand when writing out a score, and that if this was well done, identification would have been difficult for anyone, however intimate with the composer. Mikuli's priorities were the accurate transmission of Chopin's ideas and pianistic style. He was himself a fine pianist, and three of his pupils – Koczalski, Michałowski and Rosenthal – were regarded as being among the most admirable and communicative Chopin-players of their time, an additional testimony to Mikuli's fidelity to Chopin's spirit and the authority of his interpretations.[45]

Koczalski made a disc of the E flat Nocturne, Op. 9 No. 2, as passed down to him from Mikuli, with the variants Chopin had used in his performance and pencilled into his pupil's copy.[46] This interesting evidence confirms that Chopin followed the nineteenth-century practice of introducing variants when he played his own works, and furthermore indicates that he was willing to pass these variants down in writing, so that he did not envisage that his pieces should always be played to the letter of the printed text. However, to a modern ear these 'improvements' make the work over-elaborate, and detract from its melodic form.

Two rather more obscure pupils of Chopin also demonstrate certain facets of the master's playing. Mme Antoinette Mauté de Fleurville, mother-in-law of the poet Verlaine, was Debussy's first teacher, and had a great influence on his piano-playing. Debussy later told Marguerite Long, author of *Au piano avec Claude Debussy*, that Chopin was his principal model and that the only two really fine pianists he had heard were Mme de Fleurville and Liszt.[47] Debussy made an edition of Chopin's works (published by Durand) which although interesting is of no great original value, since it was based largely on the ideas of the pianist Saint-Saëns which emanated from the singer Pauline Viardot-Garcia, a friend and pupil of Chopin.

The figure of F.-Henri Péru, Chopin's last-surviving pupil, is one of greater historical than musical interest. He emerged in 1914 as 'a pupil of Chopin', having never come to prominence before. With the exception of Mme Roubaud de Cournand, all the other Chopin pupils were dead by then, so that there was no one to refute his claim. Edouard Ganche, President of the Chopin Society in Paris, was unimpressed by Péru's claim; in his book *Dans le souvenir de Frédéric Chopin* he describes Mme de Cournand as Chopin's 'last pupil' and adds a footnote: 'From 1914 to 1922 there was a certain man who had the effrontery to call himself a pupil of Chopin, so as to gain charity from the public.'[48] Péru gave interviews to various magazines during these years and one of his pupils, Ludwika Ostrzyńska, wrote a pamphlet about him.[49] She knew him for eight years, and Péru told her that as a pupil of Kalkbrenner he had been so much struck by Chopin's music that he had sought lessons with him; Kalkbrenner (who had found him an impossible pupil) had readily agreed. Péru used to say that pianists of the early twentieth century generally played Chopin's work too fast – a criticism also made by Artur Rubinstein of Saint-Saëns's performances.[50] Péru gave a number of somewhat nebulous descriptions of Chopin's lifestyle, and played in public a little during the First World War, but he was by then very old and had stiff fingers and a bad memory. He continued playing until his death in 1922, and it was in his very last years that the New Zealand-born pianist Esther Fisher, a pupil of Philipp, heard him play some Nocturnes. She has recorded that Péru played with great aristocracy of phrasing, and that his performance left her with a favourable memory of a sensitive pianist. According to Jean Jacques Eigeldinger, author of *Chopin vu par ses élèves*, Péru was born in 1829, and so was still performing at the age of ninety-three!

Although few of Chopin's pupils were of more than mediocre talent, men such as Mikuli and Mathias were very influential as teachers, and were sufficiently able pianists to have been able to understand and communicate Chopin's style to their pupils. The relationship between teacher and student is usually of greatest interest when both have substantial musical talent and natural sympathy, and the quality of Chopin's pupils made them a less influential group of interpreters than might otherwise have been the case. But at the time of Chopin's death, there were many able pianists who had heard him play in the salons. It was chiefly through them that Chopin's style was transmitted to other musicians, and among Chopin's admirers the most influential and important was Liszt, the figure who dominated late nineteenth-century pianism.

CHAPTER TWO

The Pupils of Liszt, of Leschetizky and of Chopin's Pupils

The Pupils of Liszt

Liszt's influence on the way the piano is played today is as great as that of Chopin. His life can be conveniently divided into three periods: born in 1811, he was until 1847 chiefly a concert pianist; during the Weimar years (1848–61) he concentrated on composition; and from 1861 until his death in 1886, he divided most of his time between Rome, Weimar and Pesth, devoting much of his time to teaching, especially after 1870.

Liszt's pupils span several generations of pianists, ranging from those who were his contemporaries to those born in the 1860s, and among them were some of the greatest pianists of all time – Carl Tausig (1841–71), Hans von Bülow (1830–94), Emil von Sauer (1862–1942), Moriz Rosenthal (1862–1946), Giovanni Sgambati (1841–1914), Alexander Siloti (1863–1945), Bernhard Stavenhagen (1862–1914), and Eugen d'Albert (1864–1932). Among the earlier generation, the pianists who received Liszt's advice or took lessons from him included Mikhail Glinka (1804–57), who also had three lessons from John Field in St Petersburg; Wilhelm von Lenz (1809–83), Rudolph Viole (1815–67) and Pierre Robert Joseph (Alfred) Quidant (1815–93). His last generation of pupils, born in the 1860s, include d'Albert, Conrad Ansorge, Adele aus der Ohe, Richard Burmeister, Giuseppe Ferrata, Sauer, Rosenthal, Arthur de Greef and Stavenhagen. Thus although some of Liszt's pupils were over thirty when Chopin died in 1849, others were born fifteen years later. Nearly all of them played or performed Chopin's works, even though many of them were Germans, and the German temperament has little affinity with the Slav. Some of them (including Sauer, Rosenthal, Ansorge, Josef Weiss, Georg Liebling, Stavenhagen, and de Greef) left recordings of Chopin on disc or piano roll, though how much these performances reflect Liszt's thoughts on Chopin must be highly conjectural. As has already been described, Liszt idolized Chopin, and achieved something approaching the composer's ideal interpretation in his own performances, while seeking to convey the original intentions of the composer in his teaching and transcriptions.*
However sensational his early impact had been, Liszt's performances in his later years were noted for their lack of affectation and unnecessary

---

* See p. 35 above.

waywardness.[1] His last surviving pupil, Franz-Wald Erdody,[*] and many others have stated that Liszt often required his pupils to copy his own playing; this sounds very restrictive, though other famous teachers, such as Aleksander Michałowski, have done the same. But other evidence suggests that Liszt only resorted to this when his pupils had not formed a consistent interpretation of their own. His greatest pupils, who came to him when they had already formed their interpretative conceptions, had little need to rely on the master for a blueprint of a particular work. It was only the less-talented pupils, whose artistic foundations were either immature or inconsistent, who needed to copy their master's readings to convey the range of a particular work.

The imagination of any young musician who came into contact with Liszt seems to have been fired by his magnetic personality. It was this very attraction that could dangerously tempt aspiring artists to try to copy his performances, which was of course impossible: those aspects of a performance that can be imitated are usually only the superficial. All the evidence suggests that in playing Chopin with a richness that surprised the composer himself, Liszt was building upon the original, rather than attempting to alter its essence. That Liszt encouraged adulation is undeniable, but such was his hero-worship of Chopin that he would probably have corrected his pupils had they produced effects contrary to the spirit of the music.

Liszt's pupils were of a very different calibre to Chopin's. Whereas Chopin was content to teach a few talented pupils and a large number of titled ladies, Liszt only encouraged pupils if he thought they could advance their artistic development with him, and some very talented musicians who approached him were referred to other teachers. Unlike Chopin, Liszt studied with a number of great masters, including Carl Czerny and Antonio Salieri, the rival of Mozart, and was aware of the importance of a solid musical training. His own role was nearly always to attempt to add a new degree of insight to the playing of a pianist who had already shown sufficient ability to perform in public. His best pupils had already been to other masters – Friedheim had studied with Anton Rubinstein; Sauer and Siloti with Nikolay Rubinstein; Richard Hoffman, William Mason, Élie-Miriam Delaborde, Fritz Blumer and Rafael Joseffy with Moscheles; Agathe Backer-Grøndahl, Otto Bendix, Adele aus der Ohe and Emil Liebling with Kullak; and da Motta with Bülow. Sauer, Joseffy, Rosenthal and Backer-Grøndahl were finished artists when they came to Liszt, and had already begun successful concert careers. It would therefore be surprising if there had been any strong

---

[*] Although José Vianna da Motta (d. 1948) is usually recognized as having been Liszt's last surviving major pupil, this retired piano professor was discovered living in a home in the USA in the late 1950s.

similarities in their playing, except when they played works they had studied with the master.

Furthermore, Liszt (unlike Clara Schumann) never sought to persuade his pupils that, for example, one particular inner melody should always be emphasized, or that one particular interpretation should be regarded as definitive. He exercised the greatest care in altering Chopin's text, as is witnessed by Lenz's account of his discretion in adding to the left-hand accompaniment of the Mazurkas, which other pianists have attempted without much tact. This care for preserving the original text and spirit of the music can be observed in the playing of Liszt's best pupils; they did not play 'Chopin-Liszt', but Chopin released and sublimated by Liszt.

The greatest of Liszt's early pupils were Hans von Bülow and Carl Tausig. Bülow's musical roots were closest to those of Clara Schumann, and his Chopin playing is discussed together with that of other German pianists in Chapter Four. Tausig, who was of Bohemian origin, was born in Warsaw in 1841. His father Aloys was a competent pianist who had studied with Thalberg, and he had the vision to take the fourteen-year-old boy to see Liszt at Weimar. The young Tausig aroused great admiration on account of his 'extraordinary perfection' and youthful dash, and Liszt, who was usually reluctant to teach prodigies, immediately accepted him as a pupil. He made his debut in Berlin in 1858, and his knowledge and technique were such that he was said to be able to play every piece of music from the classical repertoire and those of contemporary composers from memory, also demonstrating a hitherto unimagined technical mastery. Liszt admitted that Tausig had greater manual resources than he himself possessed,[2] and it is noteworthy that Tausig is often described as playing without affectation, eccentricity or self-indulgence.

Like his master, Tausig worshipped Chopin, though he never met him.[3] He was the first great Polish pianist to play Chopin's music, and he gave recitals in Berlin devoted entirely to it. Following the conventions of his time, he did not hold back from making 'improvements' to the text if he thought them necessary; he re-orchestrated both the piano concertos, and would play the final unison semi-quavers at the end of the third movement of the E minor Concerto in interlocking octaves. Amy Fay, the perceptive American pianist who studied with Liszt and Tausig in their heyday and whose *Music Study in Germany* became a classic, wrote that Tausig possessed more 'delicacy of feeling' than either Bülow or Anton Rubinstein, and that it was only in Chopin's music that he managed to play with any warmth in the concert hall.[4]

Like all of Liszt's great pupils, Tausig seems to have found his conception of the capabilities of his instrument unleashed by his studies with the master, and he had a natural grasp of Chopin's idiom. The most detailed description of his playing was written by Wilhelm von Lenz, one of the very few pianists to have studied with both Chopin and Liszt:

> He played [the A flat Polonaise] and I have never heard this triumphal, stupendously difficult piece played so perfectly, and with such easy mastery – or rather, with such complete obliviousness of the technical difficulties. The trio section with the descending octaves in the left hand aroused an astonishment to which I gave unstinted expression. 'This is beyond anything,' I cried. 'How is it possible to play those octaves so evenly, so sonorously, and in that furious tempo? It goes from a murmuring *pianissimo* to a thundering *fortissimo!*'[5]

This work was one of Tausig's warhorses, and he had taken it to play for Liszt at his first lesson.[6] It is an interesting indication of the inferior technical standards of the day that Lenz considered this Polonaise 'stupendously difficult' – every self-respecting concert pianist today has it in his repertoire, and it is not thought of as particularly troublesome. Even if Lenz's own capabilities were mediocre, his comment suggests that anything more difficult than advanced Czerny was then thought of as exceptionally demanding, and it is likely that many of Chopin's pupils were so lacking in technical mastery that they could never have played his larger works.

Lenz wrote that Tausig played the Nocturnes 'just as Chopin played them'[7] – a comment he does not make about Liszt – which suggests that Tausig was a true master whose musicianship extended far beyond the realm of keyboard gymnastics. Tausig had the ability to immerse himself completely in Chopin's idiom, and his death at the age of only twenty-nine is one of the tragedies of musical history. However, he does not seem to have been an ideal teacher; he did not suffer fools gladly and could be devastatingly rude in lessons.[8] Aleksander Michałowski said that Tausig nearly ruined his technique by insisting that he practise with a very high finger position,[9] and Tausig's best-known pupils (Vera Timanov, Sophie Menter and Rafael Joseffy) all had lessons from Liszt.

The Norwegian pianist Agathe Backer-Grøndahl was six years younger than Tausig. A pupil of Hans von Bülow, who greatly admired her artistry, she had some instruction from Liszt at Weimar in the mid-70s. She was a composer of considerable originality and her chief assets as a pianist were said to be freshness of conception and an intuitive musical insight; unlike most female pianists of her time, there was nothing superficial in her art. She made her chief debut fairly late – in Berlin, when she was twenty-five – and quickly established a reputation as a refined artist; she chiefly played music from the romantic repertoire and performed a good deal of Chopin. She was unusually down-to-earth about her art, stating that as music was her profession she felt it essential to play her instrument as well as possible, and that she had learned much about piano playing from her housewifery![10]

In 1889 and 1890 she played in London, and won the highest admiration from Bernard Shaw, who was then music critic of *The Star*.[11] Shaw attended a dinner party after which Mme Backer-Grøndahl played the piano, and wrote:

> After the first two bars, I sat up. At the end of the piece (one of her own compositions) I said, 'Has anyone ever told you that you are one of the greatest pianists in Europe?' Evidently a good many people had; for, without turning a hair, she said 'It is my profession. But it is a bad instrument . . .'[12]

She rose to the heroic side of Chopin's writing and Shaw found her ideal in this sphere.[13] It has often happened that in the case of a naturally gifted musician, the performer's nationality, rather than leading to a lack of grasp of Chopin's Polish idiom, contributes a fresh and sympathetic outlook on the music because of the absence of preconceived ideas; such has also been the case with the Brazilian Guiomar Novaës, Rena Kyriakou from Crete, and Percy Grainger from Australia. Backer-Grøndahl played the large-scale works, such as the F minor Fantasy, and one adjective Shaw uses of her playing is 'floating', which is surely close to Marmontel's description of Chopin's own 'sonorous effects of various fluidity'[14] and Planté's 'floating tone'[15] – she managed to communicate melody with a rare buoyancy that is particularly apt in Chopin.

Other female pupils of Liszt played in a diametrically different manner. Whereas Backer-Grøndahl's playing was pre-eminently that of a musician, Sophie Menter, undoubtedly Liszt's greatest woman student, was described as approaching her instrument like a tornado. She had fingers of steel and a highly extravagant personality. Born in Munich in 1846, she became a child prodigy. She was for a time married to the famous cellist David Popper (the marriage ended in divorce), and lived until 1918, leaving some piano rolls of her playing, but unfortunately no discs. Her style was highly theatrical: she would walk on stage with a bag containing her jewels hanging from her waist, and throw some of them to the audience after a particularly successful concert. She travelled with as many as seventeen cats in her entourage, the favourite being 'Klecks' (Inkspot). She was said to have dressed a good deal better than most lady pianists of her day, although there was nothing feminine about her playing – the veteran pianist Francesco

Berger wrote of her, 'All is massive, majestic, masculine.'[16] Liszt's music was her speciality, and she excelled in compositions demanding stunning bravura playing. She could of course tackle such large-scale virtuoso works as the A flat Polonaise and the G minor Ballade, but her Chopin playing was said to lack intellect and feeling.*

Two other ladies who had lessons from Liszt made concrete reputations for themselves. One was Anna Mehlig, whose playing was technically strong – she was said to be Essipov's only rival in the E minor Concerto[17] and to have improved in stature when she retired from the concert platform shortly after her marriage to an Antwerp merchant. The other was an outstanding child prodigy, Vera Timanov, who could tackle the most taxing virtuoso works (the A minor Etude, Op. 25 No. 11, was a speciality)[18] and could have made a great reputation, but she settled in St Petersburg as a teacher, and although she lived until the Second World War, she left only a few piano rolls.

Eugen d'Albert is usually thought of as being solely a Liszt pupil, though he had previously received instruction from other teachers. After Tausig's death he became a particular favourite, and Liszt used to refer to him as 'my little Tausig'.[19] D'Albert's father was a musician of some standing, who had been brought to England by his mother as a boy, and had piano lessons from her and from Kalkbrenner. He achieved some eminence as a dance master, and published many pieces suitable to his profession. Eugen d'Albert was born in Glasgow, and trained with his father and the best teachers in London. When he was fifteen, an overture he had composed was performed at a students' concert in St James's Hall. He won the Mendelssohn Scholarship, which enabled him to study abroad first in Vienna and then with Liszt at Weimar, and in the 1880s he was performing at the most prestigious concerts in London. His technical mastery and 'titanic force of conception' were then remarkable, but in later years this dissolved into a mass of wrong notes, badly-controlled rhythms and the like. An arrogant man, d'Albert damaged an enviable career by playing in public when he no longer commanded a virtuoso technique. Not all pianists have long careers, and whereas some (such as Walter Gieseking) can retain their technique with very little practice, others, like Paderewski, have had to work desperately hard to present virtuoso works at the required standard. D'Albert's technique declined because in later life he devoted himself to composition, his most important work being the opera *Tiefland*, and he was not much concerned about his deteriorating reputation as a concert pianist. He made a number of discs which are now extremely rare.

---

* However, possibly the same critic wrote in the *Monthly Musical Record* a year earlier that her Chopin had 'much taste and refinement', but that oddly enough when playing the A flat Waltz, Op. 34 No. 1, she left out the last page of the work!

D'Albert's performances demonstrated the romantic school at its most romantic; he always played for overall effect rather than detailed point-making. He excelled in the big virtuoso works of Chopin that rely a great deal on gesture (the 'Winter Wind' Etude, Op. 25 No. 11, was a favourite, as were the Polonaises in A and A flat major); he responded at once to the grandeur to be found in Chopin, and was able to convey the structure of the music. In 1924 Alfred Einstein wrote that 'Although d'Albert no longer cultivates refinements of technique, he still maintains some of his former excellence.'[20] His recordings of Chopin are interesting: on an early Welte-Mignon piano roll, the A flat Polonaise receives a curiously 'straight' reading, but a disc of the A flat Waltz, Op. 42, from around 1923 demonstrates some powerful ideas although the playing is at times erratic. The reverse of this disc, which has the F sharp Nocturne, Op. 15 No. 2, is much more satisfying, with a highly sensitive opening; the whole reading is delicate and well-conceived. There are also discs of the two Etudes, Op. 25 No. 2 and No. 9 (the 'Butterfly'), in which d'Albert's fingers do not work very well, but his ability to maintain the line of the music can still be detected. Much of his reputation was built on his power in large works, and was lost in the recording studio, which then only allowed the artist to play miniatures, because of the limited amount of music that could be fitted on one side of a disc. Krehbiel wrote that d'Albert's Chopin was conceived on too large a scale, and deplored his lack of attention to detail.[21] However, one can assume that when his technique was comparable to Tausig's, d'Albert must have been a very impressive pianist, rising to Chopin's most demanding works.

Two years older than d'Albert, and born in 1862, Emil Sauer was a very different pianist, his art lying at the heart of the Viennese tradition of keyboard music. We are very lucky in possessing a number of Sauer's Chopin interpretations on disc, and most of these are magnificent testaments to a great pianist. If d'Albert followed in the tradition of Tausig, Sauer was closer to Alfred Grünfeld, a pianist who had stressed charm and aural appeal, and the type of light music that Grünfeld wrote was always very near to Sauer's heart. Sauer also had lessons with Anton Rubinstein's brother Nikolay, who was nearly as great a pianist, and from him he learned to play with temperament, inner conviction and a depth of spiritual commitment; he played to entice the ear as well as to move on a more serious plane, and was thus by temperament an ideal Chopin player.

Sauer's art embraced both large works and miniatures, and he excelled in all. He possessed one of the most polished techniques of any pianist, and his disc of the two Liszt piano concertos, although very slow (it was recorded when he was seventy-seven) transmits their spirit with uncanny power. His Chopin interpretation was ideally suited to works such as the B flat minor Sonata, in which he was supreme, the Barcarolle, the Impromptus, and the Waltzes. In a career that lasted sixty years he played as much Chopin as he did Liszt, and recorded the Etudes Op. 10 No. 3, Op. 25 Nos 7 and 12, the F sharp major Impromptu, the Berceuse, the *Fantaisie-Impromptu*, and the Waltzes Op. 34 No. 3 and Op. 42, and made Welte-Mignon rolls of such works as the D flat Nocturne, Op. 27 No. 2, and the 'Butterfly' Etude, Op. 25 No. 9. These reveal him as a pianist who had mastered Chopin's *rubato*, the emotional content of the music, and its technical problems, with far more than routine ability.

Sauer first played privately in England in 1882, but did not perform in public here till 1894, when he gave a series of eight recitals. He was a pianist whose tone never suffered whatever the dynamics (and of how few pianists can that be said), although some considered his style a little feminine.[22] He had many very distinguished pupils, the most famous of whom were Webster Aitken, Alexander Brailowsky, Stefan Askenase, Ignace Hilsberg, Maryla Jonas, Monique de la Bruchollerie and Helena Morsztyn, who sometimes used to deputize for him. When in his seventies he married Angelica Morales, a student of Brailowsky, and nearly fifty years his junior, and the couple were blessed with progeny. His widow is still active as a teacher and recitalist in the United States.

Sauer denied that Liszt had a great effect on his career, since Liszt was very old when he came into contact with him at Weimar in 1884, and Sauer was not greatly impressed by his playing, though he admired his music.[23] Sauer was strongly influenced by Nikolay Rubinstein, but his playing did not have many similarities with the Russian school. His style was one of the greatest moderation and emotional reserve, though not at all lacking in expression. His tone – as witnessed in his Chopin discs – was never diminished when he played rapidly, nor did he exploit virtuosity as an end in itself. A great Chopin stylist, his performance of the C sharp minor Etude, Op. 25 No. 7, is in my opinion one of the greatest recordings of this piece, showing a real grasp of the contrapuntal writing and a variety of dynamics which few are able to achieve. Sauer could also play with an air of improvisation, as in his disc of the F sharp major Impromptu, which shows a natural grasp of Chopin's idiom. Various similarities with the composer's own playing appear: both were capable of playing with an infinite degree of nuance, and both were reserved in their display of emotional expression. Of all Liszt's pupils, Sauer and Joseffy were the most refined, and also the most concerned with presenting Chopin's style without unnecessary subjectivism. A very attractive image of the old Sauer, described to me by Louis Kentner among others, is of his playing the piano to delight the young ladies, tossing off great feats of virtuosity with a twinkle in his eye!

If Sauer was one of the best exponents of Chopin among Liszt's pupils, there were also others who played his music with success. Conrad Ansorge, who was never a strong technician, managed to impress through the fervour of his character; de Greef through lucidity and intellectuality; Rosenthal through technique and refinement of emotion; Josef Weiss through his inborn talent; da Motta through his grasp of style and beauty of execution; Reisenauer and Schönberger through their tone and finish; Friedheim through his technique and temperament, and Stavenhagen on account of his balance and thoughtfulness – all of these were notable Chopin players. Benno Schönberger, one of the least known of Liszt's pupils, was certainly one of the best of them. Born in Vienna in 1863, he went to the most competent teachers of the day (Door, Bruckner and Volkmann) and later had lessons from Liszt in Pesth and Rome. From 1881 he was a favourite with London audiences, being particularly effective in large works, which he played with an unusually accurate finish. He was typical of the Viennese school; Shaw described him as 'a born player, if not a very deep one',[24] and his Chopin was apparently very musical and rather detached. There are no discs by which one can judge his playing, but he was an important player whose name must rank alongside the best of Liszt's pupils.

Of rather the same musical temperament, Arthur de Greef made a number of discs. He was a Belgian who toured extensively and had advice from Liszt at Weimar at the very end of the master's life. Famed for his playing of Grieg (the composer liked his reading of the Piano Concerto), he was also a dedicated teacher and was a professor at the Brussels Conservatoire for forty-five years. De Greef and Percy Grainger were the first pianists to make complete recordings of Chopin's B flat minor Sonata. De Greef's reading is disappointing, being a little wooden and uninteresting, but he was one of the first pianists to adopt a straightforward and totally unmannered way of playing Chopin, which his audiences apparently admired, but found a little boring. In his recording of the F sharp major Nocturne, Op. 15 No. 2, one readily admires his unfussy playing, and he displays real sympathy for Chopin's language. On the reverse of this disc, the A flat Waltz, Op. 42, is taken at a slower tempo than that favoured by most pianists of that day, and his emphasis is on form, leaving little to spontaneous expression. Shaw used exactly the same expression for de Greef's playing as he did for Schönberger's: 'not a very deep player.'[25]

Shaw's favourite amongst the Liszt pupils was Bernard Stavenhagen, born (as was de Greef) in 1862. He became a beloved pupil of Liszt, and stayed with him until the master's death in 1886. He consolidated a considerable reputation as a performer and a teacher (Edouard Risler and Ernest Hutcheson were his pupils) and he was a greatly admired Chopin player. According to Shaw, he drew affection from his audiences, and was noted for putting his hands in his pockets on stage when not placing them on the keyboard![26] Some said his Chopin was too German, and his playing showed much of the intellectuality of Bülow, but he could rise to a stupendous performance of the A flat Polonaise, in much the same vein as Tausig and d'Albert in his prime. Stavenhagen stood for all that was best in the German school – clarity, precision and directness. He made some piano rolls and a Pathé disc of the D flat Nocturne, Op. 27 No. 2 (unfortunately it remains lost), but one can only glean the superficial aspects of his art from these mechanical devices. He died aged fifty-two in 1914.

The later pupils of Liszt, such as Josef Weiss, Alfred Reisenauer, Frederic Lamond, José Vianna da Motta and Arthur Friedheim, all had their followers, but their reputations were not primarily based on their Chopin playing. Weiss, surely one of the oddest of pianists, seems to have combined genius and madness in his character, and died in an asylum. There is a very rare recording of his playing the A flat Waltz, Op. 42, which demonstrates some feeling for the music, but the whole effect is marred by eccentricity. Reisenauer and Friedheim also suffered from personal instability, and ended their days as alcoholics.

Reisenauer, born in 1863, studied with Liszt in Rome, and made his debut there in 1881, with his master conducting. He travelled widely, and his pupil Clarence Adler wrote that he was noted for his 'unparalleled tone production'.[27] According to the pianist Vladimir Cernikoff (who was himself a Chopin player, although his disc of the A flat Nocturne, Op. 32 No. 2, is abominable) Reisenauer was 'unsurpassable in Chopin's lyrical moods' and had 'a most beautiful touch, a luscious, sonorous *mezzo-voce*; only in *fortes* was he occasionally harsh'.[28] It is difficult to learn much of the character of his playing from his Welte-Mignon piano roll of the Berceuse, for no very definite artistic personality is transmitted, only an almost impressionistic approach to Chopin's writing. The tempo changes here are nearly inadmissible and, to use Cernikoff's description, the sounds 'come and go in torrents'. Since he excelled in displays of technique and ravishing pianistic effects, one can presume that although Reisenauer's playing was suited to certain works by Chopin, his performance of large-scale works would have been wanting in a sense of structure. He became a professor at the Leipzig Conservatory, where Clarence Adler and Sigfried Karl-Elert were among his pupils, but died as the result of alcoholism in his early forties.

Arthur Friedheim, another so-called 'favourite pupil' of Liszt, had previously studied with Anton Rubinstein. There appears to have been little of interest in his Chopin playing beyond his famed technical prowess, and there is a curious disc of his performance of the Funeral

March from the B flat minor Sonata – he breaks off at the end of the trio section and the performance fades out. He had some success as a conductor, and at the height of his powers as a pianist could play such works as the A flat Polonaise *à la* Tausig; one critic commented, 'He threshed Chopin's Polonaise in A flat so that grain and chaff went flying promiscuously' – a description that could also be applied to Anton Rubinstein's performance of the same work.

These last artists played Chopin in order to impose their personalities on the audience, to startle and surprise; they tended to leave the more serious repertoire to others, and consequently much of Chopin's music became misrepresented because it was badly played. However, Liszt also had many other late pupils with less flamboyant natures who settled down to long careers of scholarly performances and solid teaching, developing his study of Bach and Beethoven. This more serious side of Liszt's teaching, which leaned heavily towards the classics, is best represented in the playing of the Scottish pianist Lamond and the Portuguese da Motta; both were born in 1868 and died in 1948, and were the master's last surviving famous pupils. Frederic Lamond first made his name playing Liszt, but was later well-known as an interpreter of Beethoven, and recorded a number of his sonatas. He played a great deal of Chopin in a rather dry and detached manner, but with some very pleasant pianistic effects. Strangely, his only released disc of Chopin, the A flat Nocturne, Op. 32, chooses the least-known piece of the set (he also recorded two Mazurkas for Decca, but these were never released). The opening tempo of the Nocturne is very fast and the phrasing is slightly mannered, even affected. The middle section, which Arrau plays with such marvellous Latin warmth, is curiously lumpy, although the emotional gestures are made with real feeling and imagination; Lamond was not a pianist to linger over Chopin's exquisite phrases. Late in his career, he used to include a selection of ten Etudes in his programmes, which he apparently played in a rather dry manner with little pedal.[29] This latter characteristic is also evident in da Motta's performance of the A flat Polonaise on his only Chopin record. From the opening bars one can tell that this is going to be an emotionally reserved performance, the emphasis being on the structure rather than on the melodic line. His sympathies lay far more with the lyrical compositions of Liszt and those of his friend, Busoni.

Moriz Rosenthal, who could lay claim to being considered one of the very greatest pianists of all time, died in 1946. Born in 1862 in Lemberg (now Lwów), which was then in Austria, he showed his musical talent from a very early age and when he was nine began lessons with Chopin's pupil Karol Mikuli. His progress was so rapid that in 1876 he made his debut in Vienna with Chopin's F minor Concerto. He then spent two years as a pupil of Liszt at Weimar and Rome. He had a few lessons with Joseffy, but he is always thought of as a Liszt pupil, since his playing definitely bore traits of the master. Rosenthal's early success was largely based on his virtually unparalleled technical mastery – however, this did not satisfy all, and an early critic wrote:

> Unfinished musical students may think that they have witnessed the greatest triumph of piano-playing in Herr Rosenthal's heroic feats of execution, but every reasonable person will be thoroughly convinced that, beyond this outstanding performance, it is quite a different question when a serious position is to be taken up among real artists. The manner in which he played the shorter pieces of Haydn, Mendelssohn and Chopin, totally lacking in poetry, the proper effect being quite lost, only seems to show how unimportant his performances are in the aesthetic sense.[30]

Rosenthal, having followed Liszt to Rome, seems to have felt that he was not ready to embark on a solo career, and went to Vienna in 1880 to study philosophy, in which he completed a three-year course. In 1886 he was back at the piano and gave a sensational concert in Vienna. It was at this stage that people began to acknowledge his very deep musicianship and poetry – something which had hitherto given way to technical gymnastics. He made an extraordinarily successful American tour in 1888 and fifty years of concert-giving followed.

Rosenthal had studied with Mikuli, a pupil of Chopin, and had a natural affection for his music. Even Paderewski considered him the greatest Chopin player of his day[31] – he endowed the music with an aristocratic distinction different from Sauer's, his style having no hint of the salon. It was probably from Liszt that he learned to respect Chopin, and see in his music a vast range of colour. Rosenthal sometimes failed to overcome his natural revelling in bravura display, and up until the First World War his playing was still criticized in this respect; in 1906 the critic of *The Times* wrote, 'There are many musical qualities in his playing which are occasionally allowed to appear without being obscured by the tiresome exhibitions of dexterity by which he is distinguished.'*

In his prime Rosenthal played all Chopin from memory. Even such relatively obscure works as the *Allegro de Concert*, Op. 46, and the *Hexameron Variations* used to appear in his programmes. He was equally at home in large and small-scale works, and scored particular triumphs playing the F minor Ballade, the B minor Sonata, various brilliant

---

* This characteristic is nowhere to be found in Rosenthal's discs where everything is musically justifiable except the supplementing of the final unison runs in the last bars of the third movement of the E minor Piano Concerto.

Etudes and the best-known Waltzes. He also used to play a selection of the Preludes from Op. 28, and Arthur Hedley, the great English Chopin scholar, wrote: 'One hard-bitten music critic confessed that, as he listened to Rosenthal playing this Prelude (No. 13), he felt with emotion that it was the music of a vanished age, heard as in a shell that had been cast up on the shore of time.'[32]

It is extremely fortunate that Rosenthal left a number of discs and a few piano rolls that give us more than a glimpse of his art. He played a great deal of other music, but in his later years it was Chopin that especially featured in his programmes. One of his typical Chopin recitals included the *Allegro de Concert*, the E flat Nocturne, Op. 55 No. 2, two Mazurkas, five Etudes and some Preludes. In his last years he played the E minor Concerto, and this was recorded in 1931 with the Berlin State Opera Orchestra conducted by Frieder Weissmann. As was very common until recently, Rosenthal nearly always played the work with a cut in the opening orchestral introduction – this is featured in the recorded version – and his performance is both distinguished and subtle, despite a rather faint recorded sound. His Chopin performances captured on disc include the B minor Sonata, the Tarantelle, the Berceuse, four Etudes, eight Mazurkas, two Nocturnes, five Preludes, three Waltzes and some of the Liszt/Chopin *Chants polonais*.

One of Rosenthal's few piano rolls – made for Ampico, which was the most highly-developed system and a great improvement on both Duo-Art and Welte-Mignon – is of the famous Etude in thirds, Op. 25 No. 6. This demonstrates quite breathtakingly rapid *pianissimo* playing; the general effect is more subtle and less clinical than Josef Lhévinne's famous recording of the same work as there is more tonal colouring. Although one can only guess, it seems possible that the combination of Mikuli's and Liszt's teaching formed Rosenthal into the sensitive Chopin player that he became. His preoccupation with *pianissimo* shading was something very close to Chopin's own style of playing and cannot really be captured on modern pianos; the pianos of Rosenthal's early career were much more similar to those of Chopin's day than are those used nowadays. Another two Etudes that Rosenthal recorded on disc were Op. 10 No. 1, in extended right-hand arpeggios (Rosenthal recorded this twice, around 1927 and 1930) and Op. 10 No. 5 (the 'Black Key' Study), both of which were captured on disc before his technique began to diminish around the mid-1930s. The C major Etude, Op. 10 No. 1, has admirably light and clear textures, and the 'Black Key' is taken very fast with excellent articulation. A persuasively strong personality emerges; Rosenthal appears to have possessed substantial musical imagination and the full technical equipment to achieve his artistic ambitions.

As Rosenthal was a Pole, it is not surprising that he specialized in playing the Mazurkas. He revelled in the delicate nuances of Chopin and brought the music to life with great vividness – particularly beautiful are his discs of Op. 67 No. 1 (very little played, and here executed with marvellous gusto), Op. 63 No. 3 (a more sprightly reading than that of his fellow countryman, Aleksander Michałowski), Op. 33 No. 4 (with a greater economy of rhythm than in Friedman's famous reading) and Op. 50 No. 2, which is both thoughtful and expressive. Rosenthal was not a pianist to play Chopin's music with overwhelming emotional potency; in the D flat Nocturne, Op. 27 No. 2, there is very little concession to the almost sensuous writing – he takes a classical rather than a romantic approach. This tendency is also apparent in his recordings of the Waltzes in C sharp minor, Op. 64 No. 2, and the E minor work, Op. Posth.; these are lovely performances, which manage to present a very carefully-planned conception with unforced spontaneity.

I incline to the view that of all Liszt's pupils, the Chopin of Sauer, Joseffy and Rosenthal was probably the most convincing and natural. The three of them played a vast cross-section of Chopin's works and they appear to have grasped something of the essence of Liszt's genius as a pianist – this genius was the ability to re-create a piece anew at each performance. Sauer and Rosenthal never allowed their playing to become sentimental or slight, and both were masters of the finer points of pianism. They had a great depth of culture and a serious thoughtfulness, which set them apart from many of the other pianists of their day, and fitted them to be ideal interpreters of Chopin.

Leschetizky and his Pupils

The teaching career of Theodor Leschetizky has never been equalled. Born in Łańcut, Poland, in 1830, he began teaching when he was fifteen, and continued until his death at the age of eighty-five. A list of his outstanding pupils reads like a roll call of the leading pianists of the first half of the twentieth century: the names of Moiseiwitsch, Gabrilowitsch, Schnabel, Paderewski, Friedman, Brailowsky, Essipov, Hambourg, Śliwiński and Elly Ney indicate his success in producing first-class artists, though considering that at a conservative estimate 1,800 pupils passed through his hands it is perhaps not surprising that so many of them became well-known! Leschetizky was himself a great pianist, and could have pursued a successful career as a concert performer without much difficulty, but unlike so many fine pianists, he found teaching to be musically fulfilling in itself. He once said that he learned all he taught about the piano from his own master Czerny, who had been Beethoven's pupil, but he was probably being over-modest.[33] One aspect of his greatness as a teacher was that he did not rely on any one rigid method which he sought to impose on his students, but was always concerned with the individual. Some of his less talented pupils were reputed to have taught a 'Leschetizky method', but this can be dismissed without any serious consideration since he did not teach technique himself, but left this aspect of training to his assistants. The very variety of his pupils' talents precludes their having relied on a particular method.

Leschetizky was a man of wide culture; he claimed to have read Goethe and Schiller at the age of seven. He gave his first important concert when he was nine years old, playing a Czerny concertino under the baton of Wolfgang Amadeus Mozart II, the son of the composer, and became a pupil of Czerny two years later.[34] He played Chopin from childhood, and wrote of Czerny: 'He allowed me to play Chopin just as I pleased, and though he appreciated the great Polish writer, he sometimes said his compositions were sweetish.'[35]

Leschetizky was nineteen when Chopin died, and never heard the composer play, but he was a childhood friend of Carl Filtsch, and he met a number of Chopin's other pupils during his formative years. Being both a Pole and of a generation close to Chopin's, he was more concerned than were many teachers with preserving the original spirit of the writing. It would be misleading to suggest that he claimed to be able to pass on any 'secrets' about Chopin performance, but he grew up in a period when those who had known and studied with Chopin were in their heyday, and the conscious influence of such people on a receptive youth does not need to be spelled out.

As a concert pianist he was admired throughout Europe. He played to Napoleon's widow when a young man, and his concert career reached its peak in the 1870s. When he played in England in 1871 one critic commented, 'His mechanism is really miraculous.'[36] He lived in Russia for some time, and eventually settled in Vienna; he remained there for the rest of his life, and played the 'Emperor' Concerto there at his last concert in March 1887.

Leschetizky was a man of very strong character, who taught by using exaggerated examples and large gestures. Not that there was anything simple or crude about his teaching – quite the reverse – but he was able to communicate best by taking examples from everyday life and applying them skilfully to the performance of the piano. For instance, pupils who had problems with the basic rhythm of a piece were advised to think over the work when walking, and fit in the music with their steps – thus they had to maintain a regular pulse. His nationality and honest artistic temperament made him a conscientious proponent of Chopin's music, which was played in his classes as much as that of any other composer. Many of his pupils became world-famous Chopin players, and this was largely due to their master's painstaking efforts in giving them so much insight into the nature of the music. Unlike so many other teachers of the same generation, Leschetizky abhorred technical display *per se* and was always searching after the musical content of a work. He used a certain amount of demonstration in his classes, but not nearly as much as other teachers, such as Liszt and Michałowski. His teaching hinged on artistic sincerity, and the effective use of contrast in performance.

Before the First World War Leschetizky made a few piano rolls for the Welte-Mignon system, and these include the D flat Nocturne, Op. 27 No. 2, and one of the early Polonaises. In the Nocturne he introduces some variants in the right-hand ornamentation which by today's standards sound rather affected and do not appear to come from any particularly authentic performing tradition (that is, they were not so far as one knows passed down through Chopin's pupils); nevertheless, the performance shows him to have been a highly sensitive and poetic player. (Another legacy of Leschetizky's tendency to improve on Chopin's text can be found in his pupil Ignaz Friedman's edition for Breitkopf of the F minor Concerto, which gives an alternative version of a couple of bars in the first movement, though this is printed as an *ossia* rather than taking the place of the original.)

Leschetizky married four times: first, a singer, Mlle de Friedebourg, then the pianist Annette Essipov, next his secretary and pupil Eugenia Donnimirska Benislavska, and lastly another pupil, Marie Gabrielle Rozborska. Essipov was a great pianist and, together with Tausig, one of the first pianists to devote recitals entirely to Chopin's music. She was not afraid of presenting a programme which would defeat most pianists today: all twenty-seven Etudes and all twenty-four Preludes. She played virtually the whole of Chopin's *oeuvre*, and made her first important appearance at the Salzburg Mozarteum in 1869 with his E minor Piano Concerto. Her interest in Chopin's works increased when she went to study with Leschetizky in St Petersburg.

Essipov was acclaimed as one of the greatest pianists of her time, though opinions differed about her appearance: some said she looked masculine, others described her as 'attractive'.[37] She had very small hands, and Paderewski wrote that her playing was very feminine, contrasting her with Teresa Carreño, whom he thought 'a strong pianist, even too strong for a woman'.[38] Essipov, whose only fault was that she was always hungry,[39] could play with great delicacy of feeling, and her conceptions were emotionally moving. Her extraordinary clarity of technique added to the effect of simplicity and directness in her playing, and she was widely cultured and a good teacher. A number of her pupils were excellent Chopin players, among them Simon Barer, Leff Pouishnoff, Józef Turczyński, Leonid Kreutzer and Alfred Mirovitch; Schnabel also had lessons with her.

Essipov was one of the first of Leschetizky's pupils to gain wide acclaim, and from all accounts she was an ideal Chopin pianist. He also taught the elusive Fanny Bloomfield-Zeisler, a cousin of Moriz Rosenthal, who left an excellent Welte roll of the G flat Waltz, Op. 70 No. 1. Although born in Austria in 1863, she went to the United States in her early childhood and became one of the best pianists there. Unfortunately, at the height of her career she had a breakdown; her playing was always renowned for its highly-strung intensity, and the seeds of her illness became easily audible. She died in her mid-sixties in 1927. However, it was neither Essipov nor Bloomfield-Zeisler who really established Leschetizky's fame as a teacher, but his fellow-Pole, Ignacy Jan Paderewski.

Paderewski's reputation as a pianist has suffered a great deal through his playing during the last decades of his life: he died in 1941 at the age of eighty. Had he retired from the concert platform in the 1920s his reputation would probably have survived intact. That he was one of the very greatest pianists of all time is fully evident from the testimony of musicians and critics who heard him play at his best, and his discs undoubtedly fail to represent his art. When appearing before an audience he suffered from such terrible nerves that he very often could not eat on the day of a concert;[40] when making discs he may have suffered to an even greater extent, since he neither liked the recording studio nor the prospect of making 'a document for all time'. Harold Schonberg, in his excellent book *The Great Pianists*, suggests that it was Paderewski's lack of a thorough technical training when a child that led to his nervousness and unreliability during his maturity.[41] Before he went to Leschetizky, when twenty-four, Paderewski had had very little success. He had been appointed professor at the Warsaw Conservatory before he was twenty, at a time when he should probably have devoted his efforts to strengthening his pianistic equipment. Leschetizky at first discouraged him and told him that it was too late to accomplish much, since he had learned too many bad habits. However, Paderewski was not to be put off so easily, and through sheer determination managed to succeed.

Paderewski learnt a great deal from Leschetizky, in particular his extraordinarily communicative tone. Leschetizky used to tell his pupils that when he was young he had heard the pianist Julius Schulhoff, who had opened up a new world of tonal beauty for him;[42] he had learned that a pianist must be able to play a melodic line with the same expressiveness as the human voice. Leschetizky also used analogies of this type in teaching his students to phrase correctly – if one could imagine and hear inside one that the melodic line was being *sung*, then the right component of the performance had been grasped. Paderewski at his best had a hypnotic tone that immediately created a hushed atmosphere, whatever he was playing. Although he had begun to achieve international fame when he played for the first time in Paris in 1888, it was during his American tour of 1891 that his name became a household word. This tour came about when Steinway's representative asked Leschetizky to recommend a pupil whom he thought would be a success in the New World; Paderewski was chosen, and thus it was his master's decision that was instrumental in launching his extraordinary career.

Nothing came easily to Paderewski, and he had to practise for up to seventeen hours a day during his American tour.[43] Chopin's music was in his blood, but he still had to practise for many hours what another pianist might have assimilated in a few minutes. Comparing his working schedule with that of Walter Gieseking, for example, shows an immense contrast: the one could sightread a Scriabin sonata and play it perfectly,[44] the other had to study and re-study pieces that had been in his repertoire for years. Some might suggest that this confirms that Paderewski was not a great pianist, but this view cannot be substantiated, since he achieved results attained by no other pianist since Liszt and Anton Rubinstein, and this is attested by members of his own profession as well as the general public. He was, from all accounts and photographs, an attractive man – he had the small, hooded eyes typical of the Slav, with a mane of golden hair that turned white in later life, and the bearing of an aristocrat. All this was combined with a personal charisma that extended to both his platform manner and his playing; the ladies would go wild at his concerts.

Paderewski's numerous discs have to be treated very selectively. He did not come to the recording studio until he was fifty-one, and earlier in his career he had enough technique to impress Shaw, who wrote in 1889:

> He plays as clearly as von Bülow, or as clearly as is desirable, and he is much more accurate. He has not enough consideration for the frailty of his instrument; his fortissimo, instead of being serious and formidable, like that of Stavenhagen, is rather violent and elate. He goes to the point at which the piano huddles itself up and lets itself be beaten instead of unfolding the richness and colour of its tone. . . .
> His playing of [Chopin's] Etudes – three of them – was by far the best thing he did. The other Chopin pieces were not especially well-played.[45]

It is interesting that Paderewski always preferred to play on an Erard piano (of course, on his American tour he had to play a Steinway), the instrument Chopin himself had preferred when his health was weak. Later on in Paderewski's career, it was his tone that was his strength, and the Erard is a piano that presents the player with a readymade tone of brilliance and clarity. There is no doubt that his playing changed a great deal during his fifty-five years of concert-giving, and the discs that date from before the First World War are infinitely superior to those of the 1930s. There were certain works that he recorded a number of times, such as the Nocturne in F sharp major, Op. 15 No. 2, at four different dates from 1911 to 1939. His piano rolls are mostly disappointing, and it is only from some of the discs that one can obtain an impression of his playing at its best. Especially successful discs include the pre-1914 recording of the F sharp major Nocturne, in which the opening phrases are moulded with the utmost imagination and musicality. The mood here is one of a man reminiscing over intimate thoughts of particular poignancy – one can almost imagine that this is Chopin himself at the piano. There is also a magical version of the companion work to this Nocturne – the F major, Op. 15 No. 1. Here Paderewski plays with all his reputed magic – there is exquisite tone colour, and a restraint in the normally stormy middle section that is unusual and demonstrates an imaginative mind. Another work that emerges with particular success is the A flat Mazurka, Op. 59 No. 2 (this disc comes from the mid-1920s), where he shows his grasp of the miniature form. These performances are faultless, and had Paderewski allowed only these to be released, he would still be regarded as one of the supreme interpreters of Chopin – and without reservations.

Strangely, in Poland Paderewski's reputation as a Chopin player was never equal to that of his contemporaries, Aleksander Michałowski and Józef Śliwiński. Five years younger than Paderewski, Śliwiński was born in Warsaw and had the same kind of aristocratic bearing. He studied with Leschetizky for four years, and then went on to have lessons from Anton Rubinstein in St Petersburg. He taught for a time in Russia, at the Saratov Conservatory, and was famous as a propagator of 'weight' technique, which enabled him to produce a deep and moving tone; he toured successfully at the turn of the century. Śliwiński was especially effective in large-scale works, but became technically and musically unreliable in his later years. There are stories of his arriving at a concert and, after playing a few bars very badly, closing the piano lid and returning home. The Poles excused his behaviour because when on form he could play with the utmost expressiveness – and these occasions made the others bearable. His playing had great emotional potency, and he was ideal in the B flat minor Sonata, and in Schumann's large works.[46] The late Margherita Trombini-Kazuro, who heard Śliwiński several times, said he was a more soulful player than Michałowski, and that he could create a profound effect even on audiences who knew Chopin's music inside out.[47] His approach, she said, was basically simple, and unlike Michałowski, who occasionally altered the text and transcribed some works in the manner of Rosenthal, Śliwiński always adhered to the original. However, his playing did not exploit the heroic side of Chopin's writing.

None of Śliwiński's pupils became well-known, but Paderewski taught a number of noted Chopin players including Małcużyński, Niedzielski, Stojowski, Szpinalski, Szumowska, Schelling and Harold Bauer. Another Polish pupil of Leschetizky who achieved some fame – though not as a Chopin player – was Severin Eisenberger, who studied with him from 1896 to 1900.

The place of Ignaz Friedman in the history of Chopin playing is unique and unassailable. Born in Cracow, he studied there with Flora Grzywińska. In the late 1890s he went to Vienna to play to Leschetizky, who on first hearing him advised him to give up the piano as a career; fortunately Friedman did not follow this advice. Leschetizky accepted him as a private pupil, and after four years appointed him as one of his assistants. Friedman made his first concert tour in 1905, and settled in Berlin until he moved to Copenhagen during the First World War. He did not play in the United States until 1921, but from this date until his retirement over twenty years later, he almost invariably created a sensation wherever he performed. His last years were marred by crippling rheumatism in his hands.

There were certain works of Chopin in which Friedman was virtually an unrivalled master: the Mazurkas, some of the most taxing Etudes, the F minor Ballade, and many others, all of which he played with the same degree of technical brilliance as Hofmann and Lhévinne. His piano roll of the F minor Ballade, for instance, shows the same technical mastery as the recording of Josef Hofmann's famous Casimir Hall recital. I have met pianists who have said that Friedman could play the G sharp minor Etude in thirds, Op. 25 No. 6, with the same virtuosity as Lhévinne in his celebrated Victor disc of this work. Luckily, Friedman's recorded legacy of both piano rolls and discs is large, and most of these are a faithful testament to the talent of an exceptional craftsman. However, some of them are decidedly unimpressive, such as the Grieg Piano Concerto (his only record with orchestra), the A flat Polonaise and the A flat Ballade; the others are astounding.

Although he was unquestionably a great pianist, Friedman's appearance was unprepossessing, and the American critic Deems Taylor described him thus:

This stubby, grey man has a piano technique so utterly complete that his playing does not even seem effortless. He sits at the piano, exerting himself just about as much as would appear seemly in a good average player, and out of the instrument comes such sounds as it seems impossible for any pair of human hands to evoke – glittering scales that approach, flash by and disappear with the speed of lightning and yet are so cleanly fingered that every note is clear and round; runs in sixths, trills in thirds, chords that blare like trumpets, arpeggios that are like a caress, and never for a moment technique for its own sake.[48]

Friedman played and edited the greater proportion of Chopin's works, although his fingerings in the latter are rather fanciful (see Harry Neuhaus's comments in *The Art of Piano Playing*).[49] It seems from Friedman's case that Leschetizky was highly successful in curbing the excess of talent in some of the playing of his pupils – perhaps Mark Hambourg was an exception! Friedman's style would have been un-acceptable, had it not achieved a discipline and musical consistency; oc-casionally the less-organized aspects of his talent surface in his discs, and his generally high level of control was Leschetizky's legacy. Another characteristic of Friedman's playing that was developed by the Polish teacher was his unimaginable subtlety of tonal shading – his recorded performance of the E flat Nocturne, Op. 55 No. 2, has only ever been rivalled, in my experience, by a concert performance given by Shura Cherkassky. Friedman's mastery over the contrapuntal writing in this piece is complete (one is reminded of the fact that the nine-year-old Friedman could play all the Bach forty-eight Preludes and Fugues)[50] and the tonal resources of the instrument are exploited to the fullest extent. In the Mazurkas we are invited to an extravagant feast of extraordinary rhythmic pliancy and delicacy; the former being achieved by the use of fractionally tighter dotted rhythms than the written notes require, and the slightest delay in executing certain beats in the bar. The results, though highly effective, would have sounded mannered had they not been executed with emotional involvement, and Friedman is here revealed as an artist who has calculated every nuance with the greatest care. After repeated listening, his treatment of the Mazurkas may sound a little extravagant, partly because the same rhythmic formulas crop up in each performance, but when hearing a single performance at a time, I have been convinced that Friedman understood the rhythmic life of these pieces as few others have done; he portrays a humorous and athletic Chopin, and one is reminded that in his youth the composer had considerable physical litheness.

If Friedman's playing was far more brazen than, by all accounts, was Chopin's, there have been few pianists in the history of the instrument who have used rhythm to greater effect. However, this was not the only aspect of his art – his recordings of the C major Etude, Op. 10 No. 7, the C minor (the 'Revolutionary') Op. 10 No. 12, and of the G flat (the 'Black Key'), reveal a pianist whose stupendous technique has seldom been equalled and never surpassed. It is sad that many of his greatest interpretations, particularly some of the Etudes, were never recorded. One of his more rare discs is of particular interest: the Funeral March and Finale of the B flat minor Sonata reveal his unusual understanding of the capabilities of the sustaining pedal. It is a testament to his powers that his evocative artistry could make members of his audience weep; few have achieved this.

Friedman played more Chopin than the music of any other composer, but this was not true of all Leschetizky's pupils. Ossip Gabrilowitsch, Mark Hambourg and Benno Moiseiwitsch – all Russians – had the widest tastes in their repertoire. Gabrilowitsch was regarded by many as Leschetizky's greatest pupil, and he also took lessons from Anton Rubinstein, whose presentation of 'historical' cycles he adopted in his programmes. He married Mark Twain's daughter Clara Clemens (also a Leschetizky pupil) and had a successful career as a conductor. He gave his first public concert in Berlin in 1896 when he was eighteen, and toured America four years later. It is unfortunate that none of Gabrilowitsch's Chopin was recorded on disc, although one can gain some idea of his playing from his Duo-Art piano rolls. Few pianists are accurately reproduced on rolls, but Gabrilowitsch comes through with some vividness. The most notable feature of his playing was his tone, which reflected a rich and subtle imagination. He had that rare natural gift of always finding the right scale for a work, as is borne out by his performance on roll of the *Fantaisie-Impromptu*; there is passion in his playing, but it is always controlled, and technique is put to the service of the music.

Gabrilowitsch was never criticized as an artist. The same cannot be said about another of Leschetizky's Russian pupils, Mark Hambourg. His father was a distinguished music teacher, and his was one of those volcanic talents which always makes it difficult for the pianist to control his musical impulses. When Hambourg played at his best he was one of the outstanding pianists of the century, and Harold Schonberg, in *The Great Pianists*, criticizes him unnecessarily harshly[51] – many of Hambourg's discs are of undisputed quality and refinement. Although he played a nearly equal amount of Beethoven, Schumann and Liszt, Chopin's music was the cornerstone of his repertoire, and he was an excellent Chopin player. When he was young, his playing was said to be very similar to that of Anton Rubinstein, who spoke of him as his successor, and when Hambourg played to the almost blind Leschetizky shortly before the outbreak of war in 1914, the verdict of his former master was the same: 'You play more like Anton Rubinstein than any pianist I have ever heard.'[52] This was high praise, for Leschetizky admired Rubinstein's playing more than that of any other pianist of the same generation, and used to give his pupils graphic accounts of particular performances by the Russian.

Hambourg had a vast repertoire, which included the Chopin Concertos, and despite his grandiloquent style, he was often very successful in the miniature works. Many of his best discs are of Chopin, and his recordings of the A flat Waltz, Op. 42, and the G flat Etude, Op. 10 No. 5, demonstrate his virtuoso technique. This is surely the fastest performance of the 'Black Key' on record, and none of the notes are missing. Even at breakneck speed, Hambourg still manages to play the piece with some interesting *rubato*, and one of the strengths in his performances (a quality which so many pianists miss in Chopin) is that he always saw a piece of music as a whole and was never content to present either a merely pianistic or a superficially 'miniature' reading. The detailed point-making of a Cherkassky was anathema to him – it was the form of the work that mattered, the effect of its overall impact. The handling of a melodic line was another of Hambourg's attributes; in the E flat Nocturne, Op. 9 No. 2, he endows the melody with the degree of expression possessed by the human voice. The interplay between the two hands is exploited with the utmost sophistication and his sense of taste is absolutely convincing.

Hambourg's extraordinary use of tonal shading and dynamic range made his Chopin unfailingly interesting. His playing had a more ethereal quality than that of Gabrilowitsch, but was not nearly so consistent. Like Anton Rubinstein, he possessed the gift of playing with the greatest spontaneity and with emotional commitment. The Polonaise in B flat, Op. 71 No. 2, a youthful work of no mean virtuosity, receives a riveting performance in which the rhythms of the dance are kaleidoscoped into a few minutes of elated bravura playing. Hambourg's performances did not deteriorate with age – many of his discs from the 1930s are exceptionally fine examples of his art. On many occasions he played with greater taste and reverence for the music than did Friedman (the Waltzes in D flat, Op. 64 No. 1, and in G flat, Op. 70 No. 1, are good examples of this) and he usually kept closely to Chopin's printed text.

If Hambourg (perhaps unwittingly) preserved Anton Rubinstein's style of playing, another Leschetizky pupil, Benno Moiseiwitsch, was more restrained and controlled, though never less than fiery or poetic when the music required this. Moiseiwitsch, who lived most of his life in Britain, was one of the last of Leschetizky's pupils. Born in 1890, he went to Vienna to study with the master when fourteen, having already won acclaim as a prodigy. He made his debut in Reading in 1908, and his career was entirely successful. He made a great many discs as well as some piano rolls, and went on recording into the era of LPs, managing

– especially in Chopin – to present a very fine combination of modern discipline and romantic fervour, with largesse of gesture. His style had some similarities with Gabrilowitsch's, and he was essentially an emotionally warm player, who revelled in a full tone and lyrical expressiveness. He approached Chopin's music with a reverence learned from Leschetizky, and he was always intent on discovering the most economical way of performing it. Although many of the early discs show his interest in exploiting Chopin's inner lines, he found as he developed that he did not need to strive after 'interesting effects', and the peripheral aspects of his playing diminished with age.

Like all Leschetizky's great pupils, Moiseiwitsch had a great technique, and could produce an abundance of subtle nuance and tonal shading. But as he was an artist who aimed to exploit the potentialities of the modern grand piano, his playing was characterized by the drama arising from his use of the bass notes, rather than on the airy and subtly-shaded effects typical of the pianos of Chopin's day.

In his later years, Moiseiwitsch turned more and more to Chopin, and to the works of Schumann. A 1949 recording of the B minor Scherzo shows his preoccupation with the melodic rather than the angular aspects of Chopin's fast passagework. There were few jagged edges in his playing, and yet he was not suave in the manner of Sauer. The C sharp minor Scherzo, recorded at the same date, displays the utmost refinement, particularly in the last pages, while having all the urgency the work requires, and is a very rare performance. Moiseiwitsch (especially in his earlier discs) approached Chopin with an air of fantasy close to Chopin's own musical style, and far more compelling than the thin-toned French school of his time. He could vary his tonal palette to add variety to the music, and possessed a 'floating' right-hand singing touch, which lost none of its penetration in works requiring very rapid fingerwork. The 1926 disc of the B flat minor Scherzo, though full of fluffed notes, captures the work's spirit of caprice, yet never loses the melodic lines; there is a sense of excitement here which was surely inherent in Chopin's original creation.

Three other Chopin players who studied with Leschetizky before the First World War and began careers at around the same time were Mieczysław Horszowski (still playing as this is written), Alexander Brailowsky and Frank Merrick. Of the three Horszowski had probably the most amazing talent. Born in Poland in 1892, he went to Leschetizky as a boy, dressed in Polish national costume, and must by the only pianist to have played before a canonized saint (St Pius X) in the Vatican.* Heralded as 'the Mozart of his age', Horszowski is best-known today for his work as

* This was in 1906, when he was fourteen years old. In 1940 he also played before Pope Pius XII, whose cause for canonization has been introduced.

an accompanist, teacher and chamber musician: his long association with Casals is famous, and his enormous gifts as a solo artist in the works of Mozart, Beethoven and Chopin tend to be forgotten. He has played in public for over eighty years, having made his American debut in 1906, but so far as the recording industry is concerned, his is one of the largely unexploited talents. His only discs of Chopin – the E minor Concerto and the four Impromptus – are, to my mind, among the most musically satisfying discs of these works ever made. He settled in the United States in 1940, and has for many years been on the piano faculty of the Curtis Institute in Philadelphia. He brings to Chopin an intuitively serious insight that erases from the music any hint of brashness, and all that he plays emerges with a strong intellectual power. Horszowski's Chopin is unaffected, and – unlike Friedman's – never exaggerated; his playing is characterized by a gripping intelligence that is both pensive and direct, and by a musical honesty befitting his stature as one of the greatest Mozart players, virtually without peer among his generation. His Chopin seems to contain the gamut of human emotions, expressed with a lucidity that comes to him naturally.

A much more famous Chopin player was Alexander Brailowsky, whose warm personality endeared him to his audiences, though his exuberant playing alone does not explain his reputation. His name was always associated with Chopin's music, though he was not a Pole, but a Russian from Kiev. He went to study with Leschetizky in 1911, and soon became his star pupil, though there were some who said that his sister Lina* was an even better pianist (Jan Ekier and José Iturbi were also pianists who were unfavourably compared with their sisters!) and he made an extraordinary number of discs from the 1920s up to the 1960s. Although he performed the works of many other composers, he was always recognized as a specialist in Chopin. Brailowsky had one of the most exceptional memories in the musical world – he used to memorize train and air timetables, as does Cherkassky – and there was something almost compulsive about his music-making.[53] Brailowsky was not the first pianist to present the complete works of Chopin in a cycle of recitals (Risler and Lortat had done this earlier), but he performed this feat eight times: three times in Paris, twice in Buenos Aires (where each recital in one of these cycles was attended by 3,600 people) and in Brussels, Zürich, Mexico City and New York.[54]

In *Speaking of Pianists*, Abram Chasins describes how hard Brailowsky had to work in preparing his programmes.[55] There was never any question of his dedication, but his discs represent him as a rather prosaic artist who only occasionally performed with real insight. Over many years Brailowsky recorded the greater part of Chopin's works but few of

* Some sources give her name as Zena.

his discs, with the exception of the complete Nocturnes, are artistically satisfying – he always presented the bare bones of a composition without conveying much of its subtlety or depth. His recording career advanced largely because of his technical reliability, but there were some works, such as the E minor Concerto, which he always played well, and he recorded this three times. His 1928 recording, with the Berlin Philharmonic Orchestra conducted by Julius Prüwer, marked the first occasion that this work was committed to disc. Although the development section of the first movement is a little fast, the solo part is as a rule sensitively played, with many delightfully shaped phrases. There is a classical restraint here that has more in common with the French school than the usual approach taken by Leschetizky pupils, and it is significant that Brailowsky also had lessons from Planté.[56] His bravura is highly athletic, and his fingers never let him down however thrusting a tempo he demands. In the second movement, Prüwer shapes the introduction with real feeling, and Brailowsky's performance is a model of restraint and good taste. The technical mastery shown in the final movement fully explains the high reputation Brailowsky enjoyed at the time of this recording.

Another promising pianist who studied with Leschetizky before 1914 was a Welsh girl, Marie Novello-Williams, adopted daughter of one of the family of music publishers, who died in 1928 when in her early thirties. She made a number of discs which show her to have been a very strong technician, and played the Liszt Sonata particularly well.

Frank Merrick, the doyen of British pianists, was born in 1886. He went to Leschetizky as a boy in 1898, and in 1910 won a Diploma of Honour at the Rubinstein Competition in St Petersburg. He studied Chopin's works with Leschetizky, and played them throughout his career; in 1973 he performed the G minor Ballade at a recital celebrating the seventieth anniversary of his debut at the Wigmore Hall. He has always had a particular sympathy for Chopin's works, and edited them for Augener in the 1930s. His Chopin playing possesses the necessary range of moods – a disc of a recital recorded in the mid-1960s includes the F major Ballade, and portrays a composer whose extraordinary power is blended with delicate poetry. However, Merrick's very catholic approach to piano repertoire has prevented him from specializing in any particular composer, and Chopin's works have not been his most frequent preoccupation.

If Leschetizky's teaching inculcated anything into his pupils, it was an overall order in which musical expression was accorded priority over pianistic display. Nearly all his pupils seem to have played Chopin's music; even Schnabel used to play the twenty-four Preludes and the

Sonatas, and early in his career he made some Hupfeld piano rolls which include the *Bolero*, the Etude Op. 25 No. 2, the Nocturne Op. 15 No. 1, and the Prelude Op. 28 No. 23. In the history of piano teaching, Leschetizky represents a remarkably continuous tradition. He conveyed to his pupils some of Czerny's ideas which he said had derived from Beethoven himself. His ideas about the way Chopin should be played were formed in a close musical relationship with the composer, and he was able to transmit to his students ideas about Chopin's works which had their foundation in the playing of the composer's circle.

Pianists who Studied with Chopin's Pupils
The pianists who studied with pupils and disciples of Chopin, and left discs of the composer's music were Raoul Pugno (a pupil of Mathias); Moriz Rosenthal, Aleksander Michałowski and Raoul Koczalski (pupils of Mikuli); Natalia Janotha (a pupil of the Princess Czartoryska, who also encouraged Sigismund Stojowski and Ignacy Paderewski, both of whom recorded Chopin); Alfred Cortot, Lucien Würmser, André Benoist and Edouard Risler (pupils of Decombes, but only when they were young); and Victor Gille (who came under the influence of a number of Chopin's pupils living in Paris around the turn of the century). Michałowski had also studied with Moscheles, who had heard Chopin play on several occasions and who knew him. Francis Planté, who recorded in the late 1920s, had been a friend of the Princess Czartoryska, and of Franchomme, and had known Chopin's admirer Delfina Potocka,[57] while Louis Diémer, like Planté, was a pupil of Antoine Marmontel, who had heard Chopin play. Alongside these there were also a few pianists who were either associated with Chopin's pupils, or with those who had heard the composer play, and left only piano rolls but no discs of Chopin's music: Carl Friedberg (a pupil of Clara Schumann, who had both heard and played to the composer), Teresa Carreño (a pupil of both Mathias and of Gottschalk, the latter having heard the composer), and Ernest Schelling (a pupil of Mathias). Anton Rubinstein, who as a boy had heard Chopin play, must be discounted from these categories, since those pupils of the composer said that he 'took liberties' with Chopin's music.

It could not be justifiably claimed that these pupils were 'recipients' of a style of playing that was somehow 'authentic'. Nevertheless, aspects of Chopin's own playing were preserved in some of their performances, most notably those of Michałowski, Pugno, Koczalski, Schelling, Planté, and possibly Diémer. Michałowski, who was devoted to Chopin's music, sought out Mikuli to obtain from him as many hints as possible about Chopin's playing. Pugno used to play the F sharp major Nocturne, Op.

15 No. 2, in a much slower tempo than did any other pianist of the day, because his teacher Mathias had passed this instruction down to him. Planté too favoured slow tempos in many works that are today played very fast – this was something that derived from an acquaintance with Chopin's circle. Schelling's delicate and sensitive nature was very similar to Chopin's and, like Michałowski, in his most formative years he became friendly with a Chopin pupil – in his case, Mathias. Koczalski had no teacher other than Mikuli, who passed to him many variants that the composer himself had played. Diémer too came from a tradition that had been directly in contact with Chopin. The playing of Cortot, Risler, Diémer, Planté and Carreño will be discussed in the chapters on their countries of origin, because their links with the composer are relatively tenuous.

Although the name of Aleksander Michałowski is not well known in Western Europe, his reputation in Poland before 1914 was higher than that of Paderewski. Born in 1853, Michałowski studied with Moscheles, Coccius (his most profound influence) and Reinecke at Leipzig, and then with Tausig in Berlin.[58] In 1871, when he was eighteen, he became a friend of Chopin's pupil Mikuli, who passed on to him many of the composer's ideas about interpretation, and he also heard the Princess Czartoryska, who Sowiński says was Chopin's best pupil; she played some of the Mazurkas to him, and Michałowski always showed a great variety of styles in playing these works. In 1878 he visited Liszt at Weimar, and having been a student at the Leipzig Conservatory, he was at first received rather coldly. However, when Liszt heard him play the E minor Concerto, he told him that only a Pole could play Chopin so well, and advised him to devote himself to Chopin's music; Liszt also approved the variants which Michałowski introduced into Chopin's text.

As a young man, Michałowski regularly practised for ten hours a day, and built up a very large repertoire. He was a successful concert artist, but after 1906 (when he visited St Petersburg for the last time) he seldom left Poland, and preferred to concentrate on teaching and concert giving in Warsaw. From 1912 his sight began to deteriorate, and he rapidly became virtually blind. He then intended to abandon concert giving for teaching, but a speech trainer at the Conservatory, a Madame Ruszcz-ycówna, persuaded him to continue giving recitals, and unscrupulously coaxed him into sharing many of them with her.[59] In 1915 he gave over a hundred concerts, and in 1919 celebrated the fiftieth anniversary of his debut. As late as 1929, when he was seventy-six, he performed both the Chopin concertos in one programme.

Michałowski began teaching in 1875, and was appointed Professor at the Warsaw Conservatory in 1891. He remained there until 1918, when he moved to the Higher School of Music, and his best-known pupils included Wanda Landowska, Mischa Levitzki, Antoinette Szumowska, Jerzy Żurawlew (the initiator of the Chopin Competitions), Jerzy Lefeld (principally an accompanist), Bolesław Kon, Róża Etkin, and Józef Smidowicz; Harry Neuhaus and Vladimir Sofronitsky also had some lessons from him. Michałowski's particular emphasis was on instilling into his pupils a grasp of contrapuntal writing – he taught a great deal of Bach and other baroque keyboard works, especially during the first two years of study, and he helped to persuade his pupil Landowska to concentrate on the harpsichord – but he also helped them develop bravura playing and a sense of fantasy.[60]

Michałowski's playing was characterized by an immense technique and a particularly deep and communicative tone. When he died in 1938, he left behind him a considerable number of discs, which were recorded at three periods: around 1905, just at the end of the First World War, and in the 1930s. The first group were made for the Gramophone and Typewriter Company, the second for the same company in the Concert Record and Monarch series, and the third were all for Syrena. The best of these are of the D flat Waltz, Op. 64 No. 1, and the Polonaise in A, Op. 40 No. 1 (G & T); the C sharp minor Waltz, Op. 64 No. 2, and the Etude in E, Op. 10 No. 3 (Concert Record); and the B minor Scherzo, the E flat Etude, Op. 10 No. 11, the F sharp Nocturne, Op. 15 No. 2, and the C sharp minor Mazurka, Op. 63 No. 3 (Syrena). One particularly admires the rich and expressively full tone, which is especially effective in the Nocturne – the many spread chords here sound a little dated, but the general effect is limpid and graceful. The more virtuoso works show the technical mastery Michałowski preserved well into his old age; he played such demanding pieces as the Prelude in B flat minor, Op. 28 No. 16, and the E flat Etude, Op. 10 No. 11, demonstrating his command when he was over eighty. However, of all the discs that I have heard, the A major Polonaise is to my mind the best – Michałowski stresses the dance nature of the piece, treating the chords lightly and rhythmically and the only disappointments are that he mispedals in places. Michałowski suffered from extremely bad nerves before playing and had regularly to be forced onto the stage before a concert.

The first Polish pianist of note to take up a career as a teacher, Michałowski had the most profound influence on the way in which Chopin's works were played by succeeding generations of Polish artists. The late Zbigniew Drzewiecki, the famous Polish pianist and teacher, described his contribution thus:

As an interpreter of Chopin he created a certain style of rendering the composer's works which found many imitators. It consisted of the chiselling of swift passages and stressing their elegance in smoothing the edges of sharper expressive climaxes, in lending Chopin's works the air of almost drawing-room sentimentality. And yet this slight sentimentality was always under the strict control of moderation, instrumental purity and good taste.[61]

Drzewiecki uses the term 'sentimentality' as a criticism of Michałowski's playing, but Chopin's letters to his intimates show that he had a sentimental side; he lived, worked and taught in the milieu of the salon, and this was the setting in which Mikuli, who influenced Michałowski so much, studied with the master. Michałowski approached Chopin's music with an admiration amounting to reverence, and his performance was coloured by what Mikuli had told him. Michałowski's influence will be discussed in Chapter Four dealing with Polish pianists.

There can be little doubt of the profound effect of a 'Chopin tradition' on the playing of Raoul Koczalski who, unlike Mikuli's other famous disciples, Rosenthal and Michałowski, did not study with any other master. The many extant discs of his playing show Koczalski to have been one of the very greatest Chopin players. A child prodigy, he performed at a charity concert at the age of four, and was touring at seven. He appeared in London in 1893 when he was eight years old, and by the time he was eleven he had appeared in public over a thousand times.[62] When in his teens he was appointed court pianist to the Shah of Persia. He lived for many years in Berlin, but returned to Poland after the Second World War and died in Warsaw in 1948. Koczalski's substantial legacy of Chopin discs includes the four Ballades, the Berceuse (which he recorded three times), all twenty-seven Etudes, three Impromptus, some Mazurkas, five Nocturnes, two Polonaises, ten Preludes, a Scherzo, the Tarantelle and eleven Waltzes. Most of these performances date from the 1930s and were recorded for Polydor, and many of the works were recorded more than once. Koczalski's greatest strength was a natural and highly effective lyrical quality, expressed in one of the loveliest tones ever brought to the piano. Professor Drzewiecki described his playing as 'grounded in an instrumental *métier*, giving priority to the smoothness and flowing volubility or phrasing rather than to penetration into deeper layers of expression'.[63] However, his recordings paint quite a different picture – a pianist who could play the F minor Ballade with as much imagination (and far greater fluency) than Josef Hofmann. He had a very finished technique, that was ideally suited to a work such as the B flat minor Scherzo, in which his fingers ripple away with spontaneity and real musical feeling. He played the Mazurkas with a very great freedom of tempo even within a phrase, and the Nocturnes with a sense of spacious wonder that is entirely apposite, yet very rare. He immersed himself in Chopin's music as much as did Michałowski, and the results were outstandingly successful.

One of Koczalski's discs is particularly important in trying to define Chopin's own style of performing. This is the E flat Nocturne, Op. 9 No. 2, in a version including 'authentic' variants in the right-hand ornamentation which Chopin himself pencilled into Mikuli's copy of the work; Angela Lear has recently recorded this version for Pavilion Records. A modern listener may not find these variants any improvement on the original, but they give us a glimpse of the way in which Chopin himself improvised when performing his works. It is probable that Koczalski mastered Chopin's *rubato* as it was originally intended. His Chopin sounds inspired and poetic (except, surprisingly, in some of the Waltzes). In the F minor Ballade he adopts a fairly fast opening tempo and varies the way in which he executes the accompanying chords in the left hand, some being *legato*, others *staccato*. He rises to the climaxes in an entirely natural and unforced manner, and never allows his textures to be obscured by pedalling; his discs of the Etudes are also remarkable for the most economical use of the sustaining pedal. The performance of the Ballade is permeated with a sense of fantasy, and his immaculate technique adds finish to a near-perfect reading. It seems that the variety Koczalski could bring to Chopin in respect of tone, touch and poetry, was virtually limitless, and he conveys the impression that he had mastered the music so thoroughly that his performances are uncannily like what one would have expected of Chopin himself.

The career of Ernest Schelling is somewhat enigmatic. The first American-born pianist after Gottschalk to achieve a European reputation, he began playing the piano at four, and from 1882 until 1885 studied with Chopin's pupil Mathias at the Paris Conservatoire. From childhood he suffered from poor health, and Brahms remarked of him, 'What this boy needs is more oatmeal, more fresh air!'[64] He went on to have lessons with Leschetizky, Moszkowski and Paderewski. At the age of sixteen he was afflicted by crippling neuritis in his hands, and did not regain the use of his fingers fully for four years. It was then that he played to Paderewski, who was scathing about his ability, and commented, 'You have little technique, not much flexibility, but I still see a spark in you'[65] – it must have been deeply discouraging for a pianist who in his early teens had been hailed as 'the successor to Paderewski'. Schelling studied with Paderewski for three years, at a time when he was the great pianist's only pupil, and later went on to make a reputation as a composer and conductor. His concert career was often interrupted by his poor health and he made no discs,* but he is said to have been very much influenced by Mathias in performing Chopin, especially in regard

---

* The only recordings that exist of his playing (none of these has to my knowledge been issued commercially) are of a live performance of his own composition, *Impressions from an Artist's Life*, his *Nocturne a Ragaze*, Granados's Spanish Dance No. 10, and Paderewski's *Polish Fantasy* for piano and orchestra.

to adhering to the rigidly academic definition of *rubato*, that is, that the left hand should always remain in absolutely strict time.

A much greater and more distinctive pianist, another pupil of Mathias, was Raoul Pugno. He had a colossal musical talent, and was also a fine organist, and an enthusiastic accompanist who did much to help the soprano Maria Gay and the violinist Eugene Ysaÿe, among others. A most finished Mozart player, his style was very suitable to Chopin. He made a series of discs, some of them of Chopin's music, and the pianist Vladimir Cernikoff, writing in the *Monthly Musical Record* in February 1933, said that Pugno's style endowed his interpretations with 'spiritual communication'.[66] Unfortunately his discs were recorded on a slightly wavering turntable, but one can still detect an approach to the instrument not dissimilar to that of Saint-Saëns (also of course a great organist) in his recordings of his own music, though Pugno's playing has greater originality. He recorded the F sharp Nocturne, Op. 15 No. 2, the Funeral March from the B flat minor Sonata, the A flat Waltz, Op. 34 No. 1, the A flat Impromptu, Op. 29, and the Berceuse in Paris in 1903. These discs were made in the most primitive conditions: the studio was geared to singers, and the recording horn was fixed at the height of the average adult's mouth, being therefore too high for the piano. This was negotiated by mounting an upright piano on a platform to the level of the horn, and since Pugno was extremely fat, the process of installing him on the platform was very unwieldy. Fortunately, the basic character of his style was preserved.

Pugno's recording of the F sharp major Nocturne, Op. 15 No. 2, is the most interesting of his discs in regard to Chopin's possible intentions. He takes an extraordinarily slow tempo, a choice he justified in his book, *Les leçons écrites de Raoul Pugno*:

> Despite the metronome marking (crotchet=40), I think that this Nocturne is generally played too quickly. The tradition that was passed down to me by my master, Georges Mathias, who himself had played with Chopin, was that he impressed on me that the time signature for the opening section should have been 4/8, rather than 2/4. I play it at crotchet = 52, respecting the change necessary in the second part (i.e. double the time). This Nocturne, in a different tempo, loses all its character and intimate resemblance.[67]

Pugno's Welte-Mignon roll of the same work also uses this very slow tempo.

Unlike many French pianists of his generation, Pugno could play with considerable power, as is shown by his performance of the Funeral March. There are a few wrong notes, but the general effect is eerie in its intensity. Some of his other readings are very fast (the A flat Waltz, Op. 34 No. 1, and the A flat Impromptu, Op. 29), but this may have been dictated by the primitive reproducing machinery. Pugno also made rolls of the G minor Ballade and the Nocturne in G minor, Op. 37 No. 1, but these have not been transcribed onto LP. Pugno's Chopin was stylish and original – he had very supple fingers, and could thus execute infinite shades of delicate tonal colour. Admired for his playing of Mozart and Scarlatti, he had that sense of classical poise so necessary in Chopin's music, managing to combine strict discipline with deep lyricism, the discipline imposing an overall order on the compositions.

Pugno's master Mathias said in the 1890s that modern pianos did not possess the sonority of those of Chopin's day – presumably referring to tonal variety rather than depth of sound – and Pugno seems to have set out to compensate for this. Like Michałowski, Koczalski, Rosenthal and Isidor Philipp, Pugno's approach to sound was richly varied, and he could use the sustaining pedal in the most subtle way. The Erard pianos used by Chopin were particularly good at sustaining a pedalled note, and with long pedallings, very subtle harmonies could be blended; on today's rougher-sounding, more angular-toned pianos, these pedallings would only sound cacophonous. Pugno's very fleet technique was well-suited to the light and shallow action of the French pianos, and the 'whispering' effects found on his disc of the Berceuse are almost impossible to achieve on a modern grand. Through his unorthodox fingerings and cunning use of the sustaining pedal, Chopin undoubtedly achieved hitherto undreamed-of sonorities on the pianos of his day. Of course these could not be reproduced by all his pupils, but Mikuli and Mathias were able to convey something of their master's playing, and the performances of pianists such as Koczalski, Pugno and Michałowski may therefore reach an approximation of some aspects of Chopin's own performing style.

CHAPTER THREE

French Pianists and Chopin

WHEN CHOPIN DIED in Paris in 1849, French music was about to flourish in a hitherto unknown fashion. Berlioz was in his prime; Meyerbeer's *Le Prophète* had just received its premiere; César Franck was beginning his thirty-two-year term as organist of Sainte-Clothilde; Antoine-François Marmontel succeeded Pierre Joseph Zimmerman as head of piano at the Conservatoire, and was to teach such well-known pianists and musicians as Ambroise Thomas, Georges Bizet, Alkan, Józef Wieniawski, and Lefébure-Wély. A chapter in the history of the piano in France had ended in 1848 with the death of Louis Adam, father of the composer of *Gisèlle* and known as the founder of the 'French school' of piano playing, whose thesis on this subject became the established method of teaching the instrument.

The 1848 Revolution, fear of which had prompted Chopin to travel to Britain with his faithful pupil Jane Stirling, seems to have had an almost purgative effect on the approach to writing for the piano. The popularity of the shallow brilliance of such piano composers as Herz and Kalkbrenner was waning (though in the realm of opera there was of course much frivolity to come) and the composers who followed in their stead – Camille Saint-Saëns, Henri Ravina, Louis Lacombe, Sigismund Thalberg and Ambroise Thomas – were all influenced by Chopin; despite the light content of their music, they managed to exploit the range of the instrument with considerable imagination. The mature piano works of César Franck were not written until the 1880s, and it was later still that the Impressionist school of piano writing made its impact.

In the years following Chopin's death, his works were acclaimed in Parisian musical circles, and particular attention was paid to his pupils. These men and women treasured their association with the composer, and were much fêted. Others who had met him or remembered his playing claimed to keep alive a tradition of 'authentic' Chopin playing that became closely linked with the teaching at the Paris Conservatoire, where Chopin's music soon achieved a standing unequalled by the piano writing of any other master. His pupil Georges Mathias became a respected professor at that institution, and Chopin's heirs have dominated the piano faculty at the Conservatoire ever since; in addition to Mathias the piano professors there who had links with him include Pugno, Diémer, Risler, Decombes, Philipp, Marguerite Long and

Perlemuter, all of whom have played an important part in propagating Chopin's music through their teaching and performing careers.

Many of the self-styled *cognoscenti* who claimed some direct knowledge of the composer's playing survived until the beginning of the present century, and Parisian music-lovers were anxious to make the most of Chopin's French identity. Some went to absurd lengths in denying his Polish nationality: when in 1897 the Polish Literary and Artistic Society wished to erect a marble plaque at the entrance of the house at 12 Place Vendôme where Chopin died, the municipal council of the city of Paris objected to the proposed words 'célèbre musicien polonais'![1]

As a rule, the playing of French pianists has hinged on Chopin's non-Polish works. Cortot, for instance, gave many very convincing readings of the Mazurkas and Polonaises, but this music is not really in the blood of the Frenchman, as are the Waltzes and Impromptus. The earliest recordings made by French pianists (who include Diémer, Saint-Saëns and Planté) are however of particular interest because they were born round about the time of Chopin's death, and their musical environment was therefore close to the composer.

It is also most important that these pianists were trained on the same pianos that Chopin used, and these were of course very different to modern instruments. On the discs of Planté, Saint-Saëns, Risler and Diémer we hear pianists whose technique was founded on the requirements of an instrument which needed far less physical pressure, whose keys did not have to be pressed down so far, and which had a very restricted dynamic range compared with the modern concert grand. Chopin played chiefly on pianos by Erard, Pleyel and Broadwood, and these different makes varied in their possibilities; the Erard had a readymade tone, and though the tone of the Pleyel was more elastic, the pianist had to form and control it to a greater extent. The technical equipment of the pianists trained in the mid-nineteenth century therefore placed great emphasis on the production of tone. A further important distinction between these pianos and the modern concert grand lay in their capacity to sustain notes. On an Erard of the mid-nineteenth century a pedalled note, particularly in the middle register, had great staying power, and Chopin's accompaniments, both to Waltzes and Mazurkas, use a pedalled bass note at the beginning of the bar to serve as an harmonic framework until the next bar. Chopin's own pedal markings in the Nocturnes surprise some modern pianists because of their length, but on his pianos, long pedallings could be used to achieve a lovely blend of delicate and subtle harmonies. On the modern grand, unless the loudness of each note is calculated with the most delicate judgment, these harmonies disintegrate into a cacophonous jumble. The only way to make a low pedalled note sound throughout a long bar on the modern piano is to play it relatively loudly – and this loses the original intention of the composer.

However, although the early discs made by French pianists were on instruments similar to those that Chopin played, they were recorded under very adverse conditions. The first French pianist to record Chopin on disc was Raoul Pugno, the pupil of Mathias, in circumstances which have been described in the previous chapter: the recording horn was fixed at a height suitable for a singer, and to capture the sounds of a solo piano the instrument had to be mounted on a podium. With the exception of Planté, the pianists who made the early discs had to perform in these primitive conditions, and one result was that the bass range of the piano was virtually lost. To make matters worse, the Paris studio where the earliest discs were recorded had a faulty turntable that increased the distortion in the piano sound. Furthermore, each side of the disc could only capture a very limited amount of music, so only small works could be recorded. There are those who maintain that the piano rolls made by some of the most eminent pianists of the period, including Pugno, Risler, Diémer, Cortot, Planté and Saint-Saëns, are therefore more reliable, but these too have to be treated with great caution, since this method of reproduction had not yet reached the peak of its fidelity.

Francis Planté recorded some of Chopin's works on an Erard of the 1890s. The action of these instruments had been established at the beginning of the nineteenth century, and remained unchanged from the 1820s. But from that early date Erard began to use iron bars to support the tension of the strings, and the instrument used by Planté was more advanced than those of Chopin's day. It is therefore interesting to listen to a long-playing record of Chopin's music made in the early 1970s by Ernst Gröschel, playing an Erard of the 1840s. This disc gives one a very good idea of the sounds that French pianists were producing in the middle of the last century. It seems as if the instrument is in a good state of repair, and it is a piano such as Chopin himself might have played.

In the opening piece on Gröschel's disc, the *Fantaisie-Impromptu*, one is immediately struck by a certain amount of 'clatter' in the mechanism, especially in the more rapid passages. This is partly due to less sophisticated and harder hammers, which produce a more brittle tone than one is used to. The slow middle section of the piece is particularly effective because of the softer shades of the upper middle register. When the keys are struck softly the hammers lose their brittleness, and produce more subtle tones than the modern grand. There is a distinct lack of the profound bass notes that one hears on a Steinway of today, and therefore the C major Etude, Op. 10 No. 1, emphasizes the brilliant right-hand semi-quavers, rather than the usually thundering left-hand octaves; the balance of the work is thus shifted from the left hand to the right. The accuracy of rapid right-hand notes is more exposed here, and in a work such as the C sharp minor Etude, Op. 10 No. 4, which counter-balances rapid right-hand semi-quavers with the same figure alternating in the left hand, the brightness of the treble notes is startling; the work was written thus, with the light action of the instrument in mind. It is in the effect of rippling right-hand notes that sonorities are achieved on the pianos of this type – the G flat Etude, Op. 10 No. 5, the 'Black Key', contains far greater shades of tone on the Erard than one normally hears. The articulation of trills and shakes is crisper, and the greater definition in the treble is nowadays exaggerated by the sharp piano sound favoured by American recording technicians; fortunately that clinically unresonant timbre, which is the result of technology, rather than music, is absent here.

Planté's discs were recorded at his country estate at Mont-de-Marsan in the Pyrenees in 1928, and the tone of his Erard displays many of the same sounds one hears on Gröschel's disc. Perhaps the action of Planté's piano is a little more like that of today than Gröschel's, but it still preserves much of the character of the older instrument. The absence of a heavy bass on any piano at the time Chopin was writing had a definite effect on his piano figuration. He used various ploys to get round this, the most notable being unison trills such as one finds in the middle of the trio section of the A major Polonaise and in the bars leading into the coda of the F major Ballade.

Francis Planté, Edouard Risler and Alfred Cortot rank as the greatest French pianists. Unlike Risler and Cortot, Planté devoted himself almost exclusively to solo performance, though he did make a few arrangements,* and for a short time replaced Alkan in Franchomme's trio. His life revolved around piano playing, boar-hunting and religion, and he lived to be ninety-five. In a light-hearted mood he once remarked, 'It is more difficult to be a good hunter than a good pianist!'[2] Planté had begun to study the piano at the age of four, and played in public for the first time when he was seven. Three years later he entered Marmontel's class at the Paris Conservatoire, and won a first prize a year later. During the 1860s, Alice Diehl-Mangold met him as a visitor to the circle of Madame Erard, and many years later she recalled him in her memoirs as 'a slim, somewhat melancholy-looking youth, reserved, yet mild and modest. . . . His playing was of a most delicate and ethereal type, his touch bell-like and soft.'[3]

Planté's idols were Mozart, Schumann (whose music he popularized

---

* The most famous of these are of the Boccherini Minuet, of the 'Danse des Almées' from Joncières's *La Sardanapale*, and of the Gluck Gavotte, which was also arranged by Brahms.

in France), Liszt and Chopin. He knew the Princess Czartoryska, Chopin's friend and pupil, and also his close friend Delfina Potocka,[4] and he mixed in the circle of Chopin's devotees, thus hearing many accounts of the composer's playing. Planté had an eccentric streak. During recitals, he used habitually to talk to himself, to the audience and to his partner (often Saint-Saëns) in two-piano works, audibly admiring his 'exquisite shaping' of a particular phrase. He interrupted his career for two long periods when he left the concert platform to study – and to work off his indignation because the members of the audience talked to one another when he was playing. His death was mistakenly reported in 1898,[5] but in 1915 he re-emerged in Paris; he insisted on playing from behind a screen, thus fulfilling his vow never to 'appear' in public again.

For a French pianist, Planté had a very eclectic style. His musical contacts had included Liszt and Rossini,[6] and he was a keen student of the style of other pianists, not a man with a narrow vista about how the instrument should be played. He was also interested in modern music, and played over works by Stravinsky and Milhaud, which intrigued him.[7] He went on playing the piano for as much as eight hours a day into his nineties,[8] and Chopin's music was the cornerstone of his repertoire. In about 1930 Planté was visited at his home in the Pyrenees by Robert and Gaby Casadesus, and Mme Casadesus described to me how he played Chopin's Barcarolle for them, 'avec une sonorité exquise . . . une souplesse extrême'.[9] After the performance, Planté told them that he found this the most difficult of Chopin's works. At that meeting, he also played over the Mozart D minor Concerto with Mme Casadesus, and the Liszt A major with her husband. Through his unremitting exertions in practising, he maintained to the end a very good technique; it seems that pianists who have been child prodigies and played all their lives can preserve their basic craft into advanced age: Saint-Saëns, Artur Rubinstein, Wilhelm Kempff, Wilhelm Backhaus and Frank Merrick have all continued playing at the highest standard into their mid-eighties and beyond.

Planté's discs were made in 1928 when he was eighty-nine, and eight sides are of Chopin Etudes. These have all been reissued on long-playing record by the International Piano Library (now the International Piano Archives) and unfortunately some of the original quality has been lost in the transfer – the originals are more lifelike and have a greater dynamic and tonal range. Planté was of course past his peak when these discs were made, but he chose some Etudes which are particularly taxing from the technical point of view to be remembered by: Op. 10 Nos. 4, 5 and 7, and Op. 25 Nos. 2 and 11, and despite his advanced age he played them with complete assurance. The original discs convey the 'floating tone' which was the basis of his fame. I believe that when Debussy told Marguerite Long that in his music the piano should sound as if there were no hammers, he was asking for a quality embodied in Planté's playing. Planté achieved his 'floating tone' through a combination of perfect *legato* with a supple wrist, and he could make a melodic line sound as expressive as the human voice, soaring above an accompaniment and transcending the mechanism of the instrument, an effect I have sometimes heard achieved in the concert hall by Michelangeli, Małcużyński and Arrau. The famous organist Charles-Marie Widor once demonstrated this tone on the piano, saying that though he could only manage a few consecutive notes like that, Planté always played in this way.[10]

Like other performers of his generation, Planté always claimed that modern pianists played Chopin's music much too quickly, especially the A major Polonaise,[11] and in some of his performances of the Etudes (particular Op. 10 Nos. 4 and 5) the tempos are on the conservative side – this should not be attributed to his age. In the C major Etude, Op. 10 No. 7, he gives much attention to the detailed rhythms of the left hand. His playing was always strongly rhythmical, and one of his great favourites was the Tarantelle. He was once travelling in the French countryside when he came across a piano being transported on a trailer. On learning that he was a pianist, the men brought down the piano; Planté played the Tarantelle, and the men began dancing spontaneously in the road![12]

Planté's Chopin repertoire included the B minor Sonata, the F minor Ballade, the C minor Nocturne, Op. 48 No. 1, all the Études and Preludes, the A flat Polonaise and the *Andante Spianato and Grande Polonaise Brillante*.[13] The Polonaise was his *cheval de bataille*; he made a recording of it, but unfortunately the disc was never released. A comparison of Planté's performances with those of other pianists is revealing. In the 'Black Key' Etude, for instance, Planté is the slowest pianist out of ten others at 1·45 minutes; the next two slowest are Busoni's two versions (1·43 and 1·40 minutes respectively), then Horowitz at 1·34 (thus exploding the myth that great technicians play very fast). Ashkenazy, Uninsky and Gröschel all take 1·30 minutes, Levitzki 1·27, and the fastest is Novaës (1·25 minutes). Isidor Philipp, Novaës's teacher, was a friend of Planté, and her musical training was very similar to his, yet in respect of tempo their performances are at opposite ends of the spectrum. Nevertheless both are intent on bringing out the left-hand rhythms with a whimsical effect, and although Novaës is more polished, the general impression of her playing is similar to Planté's, and both showed a rare spontaneity. Even at an advanced age, Planté's style could never be attributed to anyone else; he was a natural performer, whose playing, like Cortot's, was generally richer than that of most other pianists. There was a directness and purity in his musicianship that made his Chopin deeply impressive; this was elegant playing at its best.

The composer Camille Saint-Saëns was another pianist who had come into contact with Chopin's circle. He knew the singer Pauline Viardot, who had been a friend of Chopin and had some piano lessons from him, and he owned an autograph copy of the F major Ballade which he donated to the Paris Conservatoire in 1919.[14] Debussy's edition of Chopin's piano works was largely based on Saint-Saëns's notes.[15] Although Saint-Saëns left some discs, they were only of his own works. Artur Rubinstein heard him play a Chopin Scherzo, and thought it was played too quickly.[16] Indeed, Saint-Saëns's discs display a very fluent technique, with rapid execution and a rather dry tone; it seems as if it was only in his compositions for violin and cello that he allowed emotional expression to come to the fore: neither in his piano music nor in his playing was there much depth of feeling.

Louis Diémer (1843–1919) established a reputation as a great pianist; the descriptions of his playing, and his disc of the D flat Nocturne, Op. 27 No. 2, suggest that he was a sympathetic and refined interpreter. Like Saint-Saëns, he was emotionally reserved in his conceptions; Mark Hambourg described him as 'dry as dust'[17] and the great Viennese critic Eduard Hanslick wrote of Diémer's performance of the F major Ballade, 'A more impassioned rendering seems desirable.'[18] However, Bernard Shaw found his execution 'amazing', and his performance in Paris of the E minor Concerto in 1879 was highly acclaimed.* Later in his career, Diémer became very interested in old keyboard instruments and performed early French music on them. As a Chopin pianist, his importance lies principally in the fact that many of his pupils became great Chopin players, among them Cortot, Risler, Victor Gille, Yves Nat, Robert Casadesus, Robert Lortat and Léon Kartun.†

Edouard Risler was born in Baden-Baden of Alsatian parents in 1873, and was a pianist who leaned towards the German school of

* Diémer's pupil Alfredo Casella, the Italian pianist and composer, accused him of being inordinately fond of flattery, regarding his remarks on musical interpretation as 'colourless and banal'. See A. Casella, *Music in My Time*, p. 40.

† Victor Gille, when a young man, came into contact with some of Chopin's surviving pupils; these included Mme Dubois, Laura Duperré, the Baronne d'Ivry, Georges Mathias, F.-H. Péru, Mme de Cournand and Mme Veyret. Yves Nat was a highly respected pianist, rather in the same vein as Risler, and a great interpreter of Beethoven and Schumann. His Chopin, full of intellect, was notable for its all-encompassing programmes; for instance, a typical one included the F minor Fantasy, the C sharp minor Scherzo, the G minor Ballade, three Etudes, the C sharp minor Nocturne, Op. 27 No. 1, two Mazurkas, two Preludes, two Waltzes, the B flat minor Sonata, the *Polonaise-Fantaisie*, and finally the Polonaise in A flat.

playing rather than the French, although his style changed after the First World War and became more dry. When still a child he had lessons (like Cortot) from Chopin's disciple Émile Decombes in the Infants' Class at the Paris Conservatoire. He won a first prize from Diémer's class in 1889, and went to Germany, where he mingled in Cosima Wagner's circle and had lessons from two Liszt pupils, d'Albert and Stavenhagen. Risler was a very large man who played with far greater power and a wider range of dynamics than most other French pianists at that time. He was a player who appreciated the importance of intellect in music, following the tradition established by Bülow in Germany, and he performed cycles of the complete Beethoven Sonatas. Risler applied this approach to Chopin, and was one of those pianists (Brailowsky was another) who would give a series of recitals playing all Chopin's piano works.*

Taking into account his Germanic approach, Risler's Chopin was a good deal more sympathetic than one might expect. His high opinion of the music is summed up in his comment, 'Not to like Chopin! It is as much as saying that one doesn't like music . . . Chopin is both deep and refined.'[19] These last two adjectives well sum up Risler's playing, as demonstrated on his discs of the C sharp minor Waltz, Op. 64 No. 2, and the F sharp Nocturne, Op. 15 No. 2. The playing sounds more natural and spontaneous than that of Pugno's discs, and the use of *rubato* is both tasteful and sophisticated. The quavers of the second section of the Waltz are played in time, and he does not indulge in the habit of holding down the last quaver of each bar so as to produce another melodic line. There are some lovely *pianissimo* touches in the *sostenuto* section, and the final re-entry of the opening bars has an emphasis that points to a very strong and forceful personality: Risler's tone was very full. In the Nocturne in F sharp major it is interesting to note that Risler, who had studied with Decombes, does not opt for a very slow tempo recommended by Pugno in his *Leçons écrites*. Although Risler spreads most of the chords in this Nocturne, his approach is basically that of a modern, rather than a romantic pianist. Like Planté, his approach to Chopin was eclectic, and he represents the French school at its best: emotionally reserved and highly sophisticated, with the full range of dynamics and a communicative tone. Risler died in 1929, having changed his style to that more typical of French pianists – the minimum of pedal and very little expression.

Alfred Cortot, another Decombes pupil, never suffered from any stylistic problems; here was a pianist who, despite memory lapses and unfortunate slips of the finger, possessed extreme virtuosity and one of

---

* Risler may have been the first pianist to perform Chopin's complete piano works; Brailowsky's agents incorrectly claimed this distinction for him.

the greatest musical intellects of all time, who managed to combine the two into a perfect blend, and who had a greater affinity with Chopin's music than any other pianist of our age. His discs (and he made scores of them) are for me and many others the foundation of Chopin playing: subtle, melancholic, heroic, deeply communicative and 'full'. Born in 1877, Cortot had come into contact with more than one of Chopin's pupils when a boy. Aside from being in Decombes's class, he also knew Georges Mathias and Mme Dubois, both pupils of Chopin.[20] However, it was Diémer who was his principal teacher, and from his class Cortot won the first prize at the Conservatoire in 1895. Like Risler, he became a passionate Wagnerian; he worked in Bayreuth as a conductor and later staged the first performance of *Götterdämmerung* in Paris. He made his first appearance in the United Kingdom in 1907, and spent the rest of his long life touring and teaching, and occasionally conducting: the disc of the Brahms Double Concerto with Thibaud and Casals as soloists features Cortot as conductor. It was with these last two musicians that he formed the most celebrated piano trio of all time – the three of them began to play together in 1905, and appeared up to the time of the Second World War. Cortot left as many great pupils as did Diémer and Philipp; the best of these were probably Magda Tagliaferro, Vlado Perlemuter, Yvonne Lefébure, Thierry de Brunhoff, Gina Bachauer and Clara Haskil. His last public performance was at the Prades Festival in 1957.

Cortot's Chopin had an intuitive emotional depth that was lacking in most French pianists who preceded him, and the best of his discs make one believe that his playing is something near to Chopin's own style. Although other pianists had managed to bring out the contrapuntal elements in Chopin, it was in Cortot's playing alone that these were perfectly integrated. Perhaps only Liszt played Chopin with a greater conviction: Anton Rubinstein's Chopin undoubtedly had a degree of wilfulness that was not entirely apt, even though he was especially noted for his practice of bringing out the inner lines and counter-melodies; even in the playing of the young Rosenthal there was a dichotomy between the musical and virtuoso elements, and Koczalski, whose affinity with the music was especially strong, did not possess Cortot's technique. There was no fault in Cortot's Chopin; it was never stylistically inconsistent. Cortot also made use of the best and most responsive pianos of his day, preferring a large Pleyel grand to all others, and the tonal pungency of these instruments added to the powerful effect of his playing. The French writer Henry Prunières wrote of him: 'What one reads about Chopin's touch from his contemporaries might easily be applied to Cortot, but the latter has a tone which the ailing genius lacked.'[21] This view of Chopin's playing may be inaccurate, for Mikuli described his tone in *cantabile* passages as 'immense',[22] but Prunières was convinced that Cortot's Chopin rose to the ideal conception of the works.

Cortot edited Chopin's works, wrote a book on the composer (not of the same quality as his playing, and full of minor errors)[23] and owned a collection of Chopin manuscripts, autographs and letters, now in the Robert Owen Lehman Foundation, Washington. He left a legacy of discs including all the twenty-seven Etudes, twenty-five Preludes, fourteen Waltzes, four Impromptus, four Ballades and many of the Nocturnes and other miscellaneous works. The only one of the Concertos he recorded was the F minor – he disliked the E minor – and there are no published discs of any of the Mazurkas, and only two of the Polonaises (the A flat and the *Grande Polonaise Brillante*, not in this case prefixed by the *Andante Spianato*. He played all Chopin's Polish works, and shortly before his death recorded the complete Mazurkas; it is to be hoped that Pathé Marconi will release a selection of these.[24]

Cortot's released discs date from the years before the First World War until around 1954.* There are also some Duo-Art piano rolls, but these are particularly unconvincing representations of his playing. As he matured, Cortot's identification with Chopin's style grew, and some of the early discs are far more in line with what one visualizes the French school to have been; the 1910 performance of the Berceuse has extremely light and airy textures and is less flexible than the 1929 performance. Cortot was able to play Chopin with a most natural and subtle *rubato*, which was one of the factors that gave his playing its idiomatic distinctiveness. This treatment is especially effective in the Waltzes, which he plays with far more elasticity than his pupil, Dinu Lipatti. Cortot as a rule observed Chopin's markings with a healthy respect, although he did reorchestrate the F minor Concerto (Clara Haskil's released disc uses this version), though without really improving the original scoring. He was fond of supplementing the bass notes with low octaves, and at the end of the development section of the first movement of the F minor Concerto he supplements the final cascade of descending notes which lead into an orchestral tutti. At the end of the first movement of this work, he reintroduces the piano to state the first motif of the opening subject – in the original, the orchestra rounds off the movement alone.

Listening to Cortot, one hardly notices the exquisite pianism, the full tone and the exquisite phrasing; he aims at a deeper Chopin, a Chopin of sentiment but not sentimentality, of structural cohesion but not academic formality. Cortot was one of the first pianists to fully under-

---

* There were some others recorded after this date, but they had a limited circulation and are rarities.

stand that works such as the two Sonatas were not, as Schumann described them, 'four of his wildest children' bound together 'as a caprice, if not a jest',[25] but that the movements are intimately related in a spiritual and dynamic whole. Cortot's two performances of the B minor Sonata on disc were a milestone in the art of Chopin interpretation. His Chopin is multi-faceted; unlike Pachmann, he could rise to the heroic aspect of the music, and his poetry was more subtle than that of a Małcużyński. If one had to single out any of the performances on record as being especially convincing (though he was not a pianist who would play a piece the same way over and over again), the F minor Fantasy, the B minor Sonata, the fourteen Waltzes and twenty-four Preludes are probably the best of the more substantial works, all dating from the 1930s.

Cortot recorded many of Chopin's works several times: the four Ballades twice (in the 1930s), the Berceuse twice, the twenty-four Etudes twice, the E flat Nocturne, Op. 9 No. 2, twice, the twenty-four Preludes three times, the B flat minor 'Funeral March' Sonata three times, the B minor Sonata twice, the Tarantelle four times, the fourteen Waltzes twice, and the Barcarolle twice. His discs of the F minor Fantasy[26] taking up three sides of 78s that are completed with a performance of the Tarantelle, demolishes the view prevalent in this country in the last century that Chopin could not handle large forms. Cortot's secret was to contrast emotions within a basically reflective framework. Not a note in his Chopin playing is without significance, and so the opening chords of the Fantasy are no mere preluding – they take us into a sombre world of dark yet hesitant colours, which gradually evolve into a quest for a higher and higher goal, leading through frenzied passion into tranquillity and, finally, to sublimation in the closing quavers.

The Nocturnes also capture the pianist in one of his most profound moods. He recorded, and in some cases re-recorded, a number of these works after the Second World War: the E flat, Op. 9 No. 2 (Tokyo recording for RCA), the F major, Op. 15 No. 1, the F sharp major, Op. 15 No. 2, the C sharp minor, Op. 27 No. 1, the F minor, Op. 55 No. 1, and the E flat, Op. 55 No. 2. All these performances, despite some hesitations (often in the most crucial places!) display a richness few other pianists have been able to achieve consistently. For example, the C sharp minor Nocturne, Op. 27 No. 1, begins with some mysterious left-hand arpeggios, which are joined by a rising chromatic motif in the right hand. On the second page, when a middle voice is introduced, Cortot seems to have three hands, and the effect of the different voices, each endowed with a life of its own, is astonishing. This playing has a quality that transcends normal music-making – it is as if Cortot is revealing Chopin's soul.

Cortot's approach to Chopin was 'modern' – he was concerned with musical content, rather than using the works as a vehicle for pianistic attainments. This emerges if his performances are compared with those of a well-known Chopin player of a younger generation, Alexander Uninsky, who was a pupil of Cortot's contemporary, Lazare Lévy. In the F sharp major Nocturne, Uninsky employs absolutely minimal changes in tempo between the different parts and uses no *rubato*; there is also little dynamic contrast. But this is not a dull performance, because the Russian relies on variations in keyboard texture and exquisitely finished phrasing for his impact. Cortot's opening tempo in this work is virtually the same as Uninsky's, but he colours the melody with a great deal of *rubato* and employs a wide range of dynamic contrasts; his treatment is free, improvisatory and rhapsodic, and he has the very rare ability to treat a melodic line with simplicity.

When Cortot died in 1962, he had outlived every other French pianist of his generation, with the exception of Marguerite Long, who died in 1966. She was a quite different pianist; possessing an immaculately clear and well-schooled technique, she played with a crispness and intelligence that was generally more outgoing than Cortot's style. She had studied with Antonin Marmontel, the son of the famous Antoine-François, who conducted the Females' Class at the Conservatoire, and for whom she had the highest regard. In 1906 she was put in charge of the preparatory classes there. When Diémer died in the winter of 1919 she took over his class and from then until her death was one of the most sought-after teachers in Europe.

Like most French pianists of her generation, Mme Long played much Chopin, and recorded the F minor Concerto twice – first around 1930, with Philippe Gaubert conducting, and next in the early 1950s with André Cluytens. The first version was very favourably compared with that of Artur Rubinstein, which first appeared around the same time. The later recording, which uses Messager's reorchestration, is a highly successful performance, and reveals Mme Long to have been a very sympathetic Chopin player. Her approach contrasts lyricism with grandeur, and relies on variety of tone achieved by fingerwork, rather than on pedalling. All the right-hand reveries of the second movement are caught with exquisite taste and she concentrates on blending in with the orchestra. The finale is lighthearted, and exploits the dance elements of the piece; there are some horrible *pizzicato* strings here, which have a tendency to reduce the movement into something resembling Saint-Saëns's *Carnival of the Animals*. This scoring becomes abominable towards the end, and although it has the interesting effect of making the piano sound more a *concertante* instrument than was originally intended, this re-orchestration detracts from the role of the soloist, thus changing the nature of the work. Marguerite Long's Chopin had many facets, but that of Léon Kartun, some years younger and a Diémer pupil, was basically simpler. Kartun recorded frequently in the late 1920s and 1930s, and inherited from his teacher a very clean technique. His Chopin was refined and unmannered, and his disc of the G minor Ballade is impressive and well-conceived. His greatest attribute was that he allowed the composer to speak, although there is a relaxed quality in his playing that misses a little of Chopin's essence.

Of much greater interest was Robert Lortat, another Diémer pupil, who died in the 1930s in his early fifties.* Had he lived longer and had his career not been interrupted by the war, he would have come to be regarded as one of the greatest French pianists. We are lucky in having his discs of all twenty-seven Etudes, the twenty-four Preludes, the fourteen Waltzes and the B flat minor Sonata. He appeared in London before the First World War and was much admired for his 'fine spirit and depth of tone'. Like Risler, he performed all the works of Chopin in a series of recitals in London and Paris,[27] and was famed for being the first pianist to play all Fauré's piano works in public; he performed them from memory, and Fauré is extremely difficult to memorize, partly because of his chromaticism. Lortat's Chopin records reveal him as a pianist who had a much larger tone than most of his compatriots, and a fire and masculinity that are not typical of French pianists. Lortat's technique, his pupil Vlado Perlemuter told me, was quite outstanding, and came to him easily.[28] He offered a different Chopin from that of Cortot or Casadesus, one more full-blooded and down-to-earth; Lortat's Chopin was harmonically rich, and touched with a distinctive sense of fantasy. In his discs of the Etudes, there are as many wrong notes as with Cortot, but his fine technique is evident in the C minor Etude, Op. 10 No. 12 (the 'Revolutionary'), which has an exceptionally fine swirling left hand, and in the 'Winter Wind', Op. 25 No. 11, Lortat's virtuoso fingerwork is second to none. He is at his most interesting in the C sharp minor Etude, Op. 25 No. 7, which exploits contrapuntal writing in the form of a miniature tone poem; here his right-hand tone is of fascinating beauty, while the tenor line has a very effective mellowness. In the C sharp minor Etude, Op. 10 No. 4, Lortat demonstrates a technique remarkable even by the standards of today. There is also much to admire in his performance of the Preludes: in the B flat minor, No. 16, one of the most demanding of all, there is real fire and the pianist manages to preserve the harmonic patterns of the right-hand semi-quavers. Lortat's conceptions of Chopin were a careful blend of temperament, good taste and poetry, conveyed through an excellent

* Many early concert notices, from before 1910, refer to him as Robert Lortat-Jacob.

technique, and it is to be hoped that EMI will re-issue some of his recordings.

Fifteen years younger than Lortat, the late Robert Casadesus (1899–1972) achieved an enviable reputation on both sides of the Atlantic. A dedicated Mozart player, he always preserved immense clarity of texture and purity of expression. He had studied with Diémer at the Paris Conservatoire, and won a first prize in 1913. The Prix Diémer followed in 1920, and the following year he began to tour. During the Second World War he taught in the United States, and had the greatest reputation of all French pianists there; he was also a composer of some merit. Like many Diémer pupils he had a stupendous technique, and used to perform all the four Ballades at one recital: his wife Gaby told me he repeated this programme 110 times.[29] Irving Kolodin wrote of his performance of Chopin's B minor Sonata in 1941:

> The recital of Robert Casadesus last night could be honoured with the most telling of compliments . . . Mr Casadesus started from the premise that this was the work of the manly genius of Chopin, rather than of the sick; and he had every resource of tone, technique, imagination and scholarship to make that attitude the inescapable one for the work.[30]

Indeed, Casadesus's Chopin, while containing the most intricate varieties of tone, is playing on the largest scale possible for the composer, achieving almost symphonic proportions. In the four Ballades, recorded from a live concert in Holland in 1960,[31] one gets a good idea of his scope; this is a pianist who sees Chopin as a visionary, probing into a timeless world. His extraordinary technique sometimes has the slightly unhelpful effect of diminishing moments of struggle (both physical and mental) in Chopin – thus the climaxes of the G minor Ballade could slip past almost unnoticed – but he was fascinated by sound, which he used with the finesse of a painter mixing colours. This, combined with his magisterial grasp of the overall structure of Chopin's large-scale works, allowed him to explore paths in this music that others have only occasionally stumbled upon. Mme Casadesus, herself a pupil of Diémer, has also recorded the four Impromptus, and she now teaches at the Maurice Ravel Academy at Ste-Jean-de-Luz. Casadesus's style had many imitators, but none have quite been able to achieve his unusual mastery.

Around the time that Casadesus was making his reputation in the United States, a series of pupils of Isidor Philipp became very well known in France. Philipp was Hungarian-born, and had come to Paris as a young man to study with Chopin's pupil, Georges Mathias. He won first prize at the Conservatoire in 1883, and though he often played in public till around 1900, his main interest throughout his career of over fifty years was teaching. His best pupils were Guiomar Novaës (Brazilian), Ania Dorfmann and Nikita Magaloff (Russian), Rena Kyriakou (Greek), Monique de la Bruchollerie, Jeanne-Marie Darré, Youra Guller, Jean Françaix and Marcelle Herrenschmidt (French) and Phyllis Sellick (English). All these were armed by Philipp with an approach to technique and a standard of virtuosity that never left them.

Nikita Magaloff is very different from other Russian pianists, his playing having little in common with that of Anton Rubinstein's successors; his technique and approach to Chopin are that of the refined and sophisticated Frenchman. Born in St Petersburg in 1912, he was encouraged while still a child by Liszt's pupil Alexander Siloti. Magaloff's family left Russia after the Revolution, and he became a pupil of Philipp in Paris. He gained first prize at the Conservatoire at the age of seventeen, and settled in Switzerland in 1939, later taking Lipatti's class at the Geneva Conservatoire. He is also a composer, and an active concert artist who is among those to have given a series of recitals devoted to Chopin's complete works. Magaloff has made many discs, and has also recently recorded all of Chopin's piano works for Philips. He plays with a scrupulous attention to the markings on the original manuscript, studying autograph copies, and as a rule yields impressive results; his playing reflects many years of study and reflection, and is not especially spontaneous, though in the Mazurkas he reveals a surprising degree of fantasy and he plays these pieces with appropriate caprice. He revels in some of Chopin's less familiar works, and the *Allegro de Concert* emerges as a *tour de force* under his well-schooled hands. He feels the harmonic contrasts in Chopin's music, and guides the listener to the dichotomies in the composer's style. When the music requires geniality and *élan*, as do the Waltzes, Magaloff is a distinguished interpreter, but in the Preludes, where infinite degrees of musical insight are needed, he is relatively uninteresting.

If Magaloff does not play all Chopin's works equally well, he is at his best a very polished and satisfying player. In the three Sonatas (he is one of the very few to have recorded the C minor Sonata) his gradations of tone are inspired and lucid; he does not adopt the practice of exploiting 'inner lines' in the B minor Sonata, as do Cherkassky, Hofmann and Gilels, but underlines the ongoing momentum of the music. Magaloff's weakness in Chopin is that he presents a well-fed composer who has little inner strife. This can be adequate in many works but in others, especially the Polonaises, it does not yield good results: without the sense of struggle, these works sound over-blown and pretentious – they are not as suave as Magaloff portrays them to be.

Many of Philipp's female pupils were highly gifted and made very respectable names for themselves, both as Chopin players and in other repertoire; these include Ania Dorfmann, Jeanne-Marie Darré and Monique de la Bruchollerie. Darré, born in 1905, also had lessons with Marguerite Long and Saint-Saëns, and is one of the last representatives of the traditional French School. She has always played a great deal of Chopin, especially the larger works, and when young was strongly influenced by Horowitz. Her touch is most unusual, having a ringing almost percussive quality. She plays such works as the B minor Scherzo with an aggressively 'spiky' treatment of the quavers, which adds to the movement a buoyancy and litheness that are rare. However, although her Chopin is highly individual and accomplished, I would question her affinity with the music, because her playing, for all its grand gestures, is emotionally and tonally dry. She can play rapid *pianissimo* figurations with the greatest skill (rather like Rosenthal in this respect) and there are certain works of Chopin that respond to this treatment, such as the descending cascades of notes in the C sharp minor Scherzo, and various Etudes and Preludes. I personally find her style better suited to the rather cold and dry compositions of Saint-Saëns, which she executes with stunning bravura.

Ania Dorfmann is a pianist whose discs were very popular in the 1930s and who could play in a very simple and direct manner. Russian-born, she studied with Philipp as a teenager and then, rather surprisingly, sought no other teacher.[32] She began to tour Europe in 1920 and made her American debut in 1936, later being chosen as a soloist by Toscanini, with whom she recorded Beethoven's C major Concerto. She was for many years on the staff of the Juilliard School in New York, and made a number of early long-playing records including Mendelssohn's *Songs Without Words* and the Chopin Waltzes. Miss Dorfmann's playing has a rich and sonorous tone, and a passionate, though well-controlled temperament, ideally suited to works such as the Nocturnes: her disc of the E major Nocturne, Op. 62 No. 2, has some strikingly delicate filigree work and she shows herself to be a communicative artist. Her non-serious treatment of works like the Tarantelle and the three Ecossaises is also refreshing, and she can vary her style convincingly for different works, her prodigious technique allowing her to convey her ideas on the music freely.

A purely virtuoso treatment of Chopin is not usually artistically successful. Whereas Liszt's music thrives on bravura playing, Chopin's music seems to be severely limited by it. However, pianists have often had considerable success with less discerning audiences when mauling the Polish composer in this manner, and a certain thrill can be felt when a pianist performs the B minor Scherzo with the utmost virtuosity – the

brilliant sequences of darting quavers are genuinely exciting. It was in
this area that another Philipp pupil, Monique de la Bruchollerie, scored
her successes. Having also studied with Liszt's pupil Emil von Sauer, she
could play with almost unbelievable power and speed, reaching bravura
climaxes such as perhaps only a Horowitz can achieve. It was her grand
virtuoso manner that led her to win a prize at the 1937 Chopin Competition in Warsaw. Her Chopin was a strange mixture of spontaneity and
detachment; she left a disc of the F minor Ballade which is peculiarly
restrained, but her playing of the E major Scherzo in Poland after the
Second World War received such rapturous applause that she was forced
to play eight encores![33] Sometimes hailed as 'Paganini in skirts' (Novaës
too suffered from nicknames such as the 'Paderewska of the Pampas') de
la Bruchollerie's art seems to have appealed on a very superficial level to
people who thought that speed and passion were the sole attributes of a
great pianist.[34] Her career ended in tragedy – she was involved in a
serious car accident in Rumania and her hands were ruined. Despite
being badly handicapped she bravely continued to teach until her death
in 1973, and Livia Rev, herself no mean technician, told me that
Monique de la Bruchollerie had possessed one of the most perfect
playing mechanisms of any pianist she had ever encountered.

Perhaps the most gifted of Philipp's lady pupils apart from Novaës
(whose playing is described in Chapter Eight) is Youra Guller. Born in
France she now lives in Geneva and has played in public until recently,
though in her eighties and in poor health. She has led a strange and
varied life that has ventured into realms other than music, and particularly in the early stages of her career, was regarded with great esteem
by such diverse musicians as Busoni, Milhaud, Cortot, Ravel and
Casals.[35] There were always wild rumours about her life-style, but she
has remained a very private person, never seeking publicity. Her playing
is in the grand style, and completely unmannered. She treats the piano
as an instrument of boundless tonal possibilities with the range of
texture of the orchestra, and her Chopin playing demonstrates a
probing attention to detail and a grasp of the structure of the music
reminiscent of Busoni and Casadesus. There is a power in her playing
that derives from an almost fanatical dedication to her art, but unfortunately, to my knowledge she has only ever made two discs: one is of
late Beethoven Sonatas, and the other of a mixed recital programme
that includes Chopin's F minor Etude, Op. 25 No. 2. This performance
only heightens the mystery that surrounds her – it is elusive, delicately
pedalled and fleeting.

The greatest Chopin player to emerge in France since the Second
World War is undoubtedly Vlado Perlemuter. Of Polish parentage, he
was born in Lithuania, and came to Paris when young. His first teacher

there was the great Polish-German pianist Moritz Moszkowski, who equipped him with the most complete technical resources, and by the time he went to study with Cortot he had a fully adequate command of the keyboard, although he was still in his early teens. Perlemuter's years with Cortot were illuminating, and brought him into contact with Ravel, whose works he studied with the composer, but his repertoire has always centred around Chopin's music, and he practises a number of the Etudes daily.

Perlemuter's Chopin is in no sense a copy of Cortot's. One reason for this was that Cortot, especially in his celebrated discs of Chopin made in the 1930s, favoured a Pleyel, and this was largely responsible for the very individual sound he produced; Perlemuter has always used a Steinway for his recordings and concert appearances in the United Kingdom, so that his piano sound is less distinctive than that of his master. Although Perlemuter has never been one to employ extremes of dynamics, his tonal range is particularly large, and of the greatest subtlety. When young he was especially impressed by the almost orchestral variety in Rachmaninov's performances, which opened up areas of sound from the piano that Perlemuter had never previously exploited, and it has always been his aim to play with the same vividness.

Although Perlemuter's Chopin is tonally as rich as Cortot's, it does not possess quite the same intellect, though he plays the twenty-four Etudes in a more polished manner than did his master. Unfortunately he is notoriously prone to memory lapses and suffers from very bad nerves; when he recorded the complete solo piano works of Chopin for the BBC he was working under ideal conditions and the results were especially satisfying and memorable. He has also made a number of discs, including the two Sonatas, the fourteen Waltzes, four Ballades and many miscellaneous pieces. It is very difficult to single out which of Chopin's works he plays best, but his style is perhaps less suited to the Scherzos and Polonaises than it is to the Ballades, Etudes, Sonatas and Mazurkas. His playing belongs to the old French school: emotionally reserved, poised and very sophisticated in phrasing and articulation. He does not take the technical demands of the music lightly, and, however much he studies them, Chopin's works do not become stale for him – he has an affection for the music that communicates itself in every note that he plays.

Sir William Glock, the eminent musician, once wrote that Vlado Perlemuter plays Chopin much as Schnabel played Beethoven.[36] However, there is a degree of simplicity and personal sincerity in Perlemuter's character that was absent in both Cortot's and Schnabel's – this is reflected in his Chopin, which is never opinionated, and never totally subjective. Chopin's character may not have been wholly innocent, but Perlemuter's complete musical honesty and humility when playing the music he reveres compels admiration. In 1978 he gave a most profound interpretation of the B minor Sonata at the Queen Elizabeth Hall in London, which created the impression that he had somehow captured the idiom of Chopin's own playing. No pianist I have ever heard has played the twenty-four Etudes as perfectly as Perlemuter. Whether in achieving the whispering effect required in the A minor, Op. 10 No. 2, or the rapt pathos of the C sharp minor, Op. 25 No. 7, Perlemuter masters the music in a way that the younger generation – even Ashkenazy and Pollini – never quite manage.

In the more reflective music of Chopin, the Nocturnes, the Berceuse and the Barcarolle, Perlemuter has few equals and no superiors. An old long-playing record on the Concert Hall label in which he plays the Barcarolle demonstrates his art at its most sublime. In the latter work he immediately takes one into a sound-world that transcends the notes of the piece. It is partly this intense reaction to sounds that makes Perlemuter's playing so riveting, and here there is an extraordinary, magical mixture of Italianate richness and sensuality combined with Gallic intellect and distinction; to my mind this is the most successful version of this work ever recorded.

Apart from Perlemuter, French pianists of today do not play Chopin as successfully as did their predecessors. This is partly because the conditions under which a concert artist now works are not conducive to the specialist; the modern concert pianist is expected to play the concertos of Beethoven, Schumann, Grieg, Brahms, Liszt, Rachmaninov and Bartók, while having several different recital programmes. Furthermore, young French pianists seem to be preoccupied with the music of Debussy, Ravel and Messiaen rather than with Chopin, and because of the great complexity of his musical make-up, Chopin's works need a lifetime of study to play really well. Competition to be acclaimed as a great Chopin player used to be widespread in France, but this is now only kept alive at the Chopin Competitions in Warsaw. Since the late '50s only three French pianists have been widely admired in Chopin: Philippe Entremont, Samson François and Jean-Bernard Pommier.

The characteristic most often associated with French piano-playing is emotional detachment. With much of the music of French composers such as Ravel, Debussy and Saint-Saëns, this approach works, but in Chopin and Fauré, where the music springs from the composer's emotions, however reserved the terms in which he communicates, a sympathy and emotional involvement with the composer on the part of the performer is essential. A pianist such as Philippe Entremont does not always succeed in portraying this. Although he often has a profound insight into the music, as in the A minor Waltz, Op. 34 No. 2, which is perhaps the most elusive of all the Waltzes, this is not characteristic of his Chopin playing, which often sounds uninvolved. He has a tendency to play with ease music which is tormented, and his interpretations are therefore not communicated with much depth of feeling.

There is a perennial problem as to whether an interpreter is justified in making the music of a composer sound more interesting than it was originally intended to be. An interpretative genius such as Alfred Brendel is capable of making an obscure set of variations by Beethoven sound sophisticated and interesting, revealing them as 'little master-pieces', even if they were only written to serve someone else's need. In Chopin, is it right to play an innocently bravura and extrovert work such as the E flat Waltz, Op. 18, with a fussy attention to inner lines and in-teresting turns of phrase? An academic view of the music tends to act against its natural charm. Similarly, a studied *rubato* usually results in mannered playing; unless it is applied naturally, as an integral part of the music, it should be omitted. *Rubato* is the yeast that is the active in-gredient in making the music rise from the level of pure notation; it allows the music to breathe. Unfortunately, a pianist such as Entremont allows it to restrict him, for a vicious circle can develop in which the pianist's attempts to capture the right *rubato* may actually destroy the nature of the music he is playing, and although this is not always the case with Entremont's playing, these points have impressed me at his recitals and on hearing his disc of the fourteen Waltzes.

The late Samson François, like Entremont a pupil of Marguerite Long, was a pianist who allowed his high spirits and musical in-quisitiveness to get the better of him and impede his interpretations. His teacher seems to have failed to communicate to him much of her dis-ciplined approach to Chopin, although she once uttered the extravagant praise 'Samson François? C'est Chopin!'[37] When considering his artistry one must remember that late in his career he became addicted to drugs and alcohol, and in his discs there are passages that no thinking pianist should have allowed to be passed for issue – bars played out of time, extra beats added to bars, inexplicable changes in the composer's markings and so on. François had something of the gypsy in his nature, and many musicians speak very highly of his playing, especially in pieces that required an improvisatory approach. His Chopin was marred by his apparent feeling that he had to make the music sound 'clever' to be effective, whereas the opposite is nearer the truth. He had an excellent technique, and this made matters worse; perhaps he had too much talent for his own safety. Several bars in his discs will be played really brilliantly, but then a 'clever' turn of phrase makes the performance irritating and ultimately absurd.

Many non-musicians (but many musicians too) do not realize that

Chopin needs to be played with as much discipline as Bach and Mozart, his musical models. Just as Mozart's piano music must flow and at the same time by highly expressive, so must that of Chopin. The pianists of previous generations were far more in touch with Chopin's genre than we are today, and this meant that in certain aspects of performing his music they instinctively knew things that we do not. French pianists used to possess a particularly close relationship to Chopin's music, and they took up his pianistic mantle, while a different aspect of his creative genius attracted Polish pianists: the Mazurkas and Polonaises that were specifically relevant to their native music. The postwar generation of French pianists have yet to find their identity where Chopin is concerned; they seem to have lost the sophistication which was the special province of the French school. One pianist of the younger generation who might prove to be an exception is Jean-Bernard Pommier, who plays a masculine and forceful Chopin, contrasted with real lyricism and poetry. His playing is considerably more forthright than that of Perlemuter and it is refreshingly different; he has a real feel for the idiom. Cécile Ousset is another virtuoso French pianist who plays Chopin, but her playing relies too much on a glittering technique and not enough on intellect – in some ways she is another Monique de la Bruchollerie. The French school of pianism is the closest to Chopin in respect of tradition, even more so than the Poles. But there is a danger that this marvellous legacy will be lost unless another great French pianist decides to base his repertoire on Chopin's music, and take up the mantle of his predecessors.

CHAPTER FOUR

The Poles and Chopin

OVER THE LAST two hundred years, the Poles have maintained a musical life of consistent excellence despite the tragic history of their country. Poland was partitioned between Russia, Prussia and the Austrian Empire in the eighteenth century, and King Stanisław II was forced to abdicate in 1795, a year after a revolt against the Russians by the patriot Kościuszko had been crushed. Napoleon I created the Grand Duchy of Warsaw in 1807, but after the Napleonic Wars, Poland was effectively under Russian rule, since the Czar was King of Poland. The autocratic Nicholas I suppressed the nationalist rising of 1831, and it was at this time that many Poles, especially members of the aristocracy, emigrated. Another rising failed in 1846, and Russian administration became increasingly oppressive; a revolt in 1863 was brutally suppressed. A further wave of emigration took place towards the end of the century, when thousands of Polish Jews left to settle in Western Europe and the United States.

The Treaty of Versailles established a Polish Republic, and the first Prime Minister was the Liberal politician and renowned pianist Ignacy Paderewski. During the Second World War, six million Poles – nearly a quarter of the population – perished as victims of Nazi extermination and in the struggle against German occupation; 800,000 of the inhabitants of Warsaw died, many of them in the heroic uprising of 1944. After the Germans withdrew, Poland became a People's Democracy and a signatory of the Warsaw Pact.

Chopin's music has played a significant part in the development of the cultural identity the Poles have managed to preserve against this harsh background. He himself was able to grow up in a period of relative harmony, but political unrest led him to leave his native land in 1830, never to return. Through letters to his family and friends, and through meeting Poles on their visits to Paris, he was able to keep in contact with the mood of his homeland, and some of his fellow-countrymen came to realize that their musical heritage was being kept alive in France by a man who was passionately dedicated to his fatherland. Later in the century, the status of his music increased dramatically, and became very closely associated with the spirit of Polish independence. Chopin was acclaimed as a great patriot, who had been able to express in a most profound way the aspirations and sentiments of the Polish people. He was the symbolic spokesman for the character of the nation, and everything associated with him became revered and idolized in his homeland. The performance of his works was prohibited by the Nazis, but they were played in secret at concerts organized by the Resistance.

At the time of Chopin's birth in 1810, Poland's musical life lacked organization but not talent. Józef Elsner, his teacher in composition, was largely responsible for reorganizing the Warsaw Conservatoire, of which he was Director, introducing musical ideas from other parts of Europe. He was best-known as a composer of religious music and opera – he wrote over thirty works in this medium – and was influenced both by the Germans and the Italians. Poland also had its fair share of able pianists and violinists, many of whom had trained in Russia, such as the tasteful composer and pianist Maria Szymanowska, a friend of John Field in St Petersburg (she denied that she had been his pupil),[1] who lived in Warsaw from 1815 to 1830. She was highly regarded by Schumann as a composer, and as a pianist was favourably compared with Hummel.[2] She died of cholera in 1831, and it is therefore unlikely that she played much of the twenty-year-old Chopin's music, although a Mazurka was discovered in an album of music that belonged to her, probably having been put there by her daughter. In his *Musiciens polonais* Sowiński mentions many Polish pianists of roughly the same generation as Chopin and his pupils, and some of these are known to have played Chopin's music in their native country.

While Chopin was living in Warsaw, some of the greatest virtuosi of the day – Paganini and Hummel among them – played there, and Poland was not cut off from such centres of music as Paris, Vienna and Berlin; Chopin visited the two latter cities before he settled in Paris. After he had left his homeland, Chopin kept up his correspondence with his parents, his sisters, his friends (especially Tytus Woyciechowski) and his old teacher, Elsner. Many of his pupils in Paris were Poles, and some of them returned to Poland in the composer's lifetime and played his music there; Kazimierz Wernik, in the year Chopin died, gave a concert in Warsaw devoted entirely to his music.[3] The Princess Marcelina Czartoryska played in Warsaw and St Petersburg after Chopin's death and other Polish pianists who at an early stage played his music in Poland included Anton de Kontski (a pupil of Field, but a player whose extrovert and shallow style was ill suited to Chopin), Jadwiga Brzowska (who played the E minor Concerto in Warsaw in 1842), Napoléon Orda (another pupil of Chopin), Ignacy Krzyżanowski (who had spent some time in Paris and may have had lessons with Chopin; he settled in Kraków) – and there were many others. Few of these pianists became well known, with the exception of Chopin's pupil Karol Mikuli, who became Director of the Conservatory in Lwów in 1858. Theodor Leschetizky, the great teacher, was slightly younger than Mikuli, and though born in what was then Austrian Poland in 1830, he became a teacher in St Petersburg in 1852, before settling in Vienna. The greatest Polish pianist of the last century, Carl Tausig, also left Poland before becoming deeply associated with its musical life. This tendency for talented musicians to leave Poland for the more attractive musical capitals of Europe prevented any 'school' of piano playing becoming established there until the 1880s, and most of the pianists who then established the tradition of Polish pianism were born in the 1850s, after Chopin's death.

One of these was Xaver Scharwenka, a pianist whose Polish temperament was very evident in his playing. Born in Samter in Prussian Poland in 1850, he graduated from Kullak's academy in Berlin in 1868, and made his debut the following year. (Huneker mentions him among the pupils of Liszt, but if he studied with him it can only have been for a very short time.)[*] Scharwenka was an able composer, and was much admired for his playing of Beethoven. He was also an ideal Chopin player, with a very spirited approach, and the discipline and musicianship necessary for the variety of responses required by the music. In 1874 he began to tour in Europe and the United States, and he was also Berlin correspondent of the English *Monthly Musical Record* in the late '70s. Not a man to subdue his annoyance at having to listen to society pianists, he described one of them as striving to earn the favour of the Berlin public by 'strumming with palsied fingers'. Critics in the 1870s wrote that Scharwenka's playing was 'full of soul and feeling' and that under his hands, 'the instrument seems to be magnetized into life and thought'.[4]

Scharwenka's interpretation of the F minor Fantasy was famous, and he made a Welte-Mignon roll of this work which demonstrates great perception. His performance of the A flat Waltz, Op. 42, also on a Welte roll, is considerably slower than that of many other pianists of the day, and adheres to the precepts of Chopin's pupils. This is a quiet and thoughtful performance, rather than a brilliant one, and demonstrates great refinement in phrasing. Scharwenka's discs, made around 1905 and 1908, include the *Fantaisie-Impromptu*, the A flat Waltz, Op. 34 No. 1, pieces by Weber, Mendelssohn and Liszt, and some of his own works. The *Fantaisie-Impromptu*, in surely one of the most convincing and moving versions of this hackneyed piece ever captured on record, shows him at his best – fluent, alive to the music behind the notes, and infinitely sensitive. The A flat Waltz, played with a truncated introduction, is taken

---

[*] Huneker also includes other names of Liszt pupils that are questionable: Borodin, Rimsky-Korsakov and Leopold Damrosch.

at a leisurely tempo and is rather inaccurate, but displays Scharwenka's natural approach. That he was a conscientious Chopin player is also evident from the accounts of his playing by other musicians, and his success as a teacher can be demonstrated by the fact that da Motta, Fridtjof Backer-Gröndahl (the son of Agathe Backer-Gröndahl) and Selmar Jansen were among his pupils. He was a serious and dedicated interpreter, who inclined towards an intellectual view, but always expressed this with verve, and his discs were among the most popular piano records before the First World War.

Scharwenka spent little of his life in Poland, but his contemporary Aleksander Michałowski (1851–1938) was devoted to his fatherland, and in the last thirty years of his life never played in any other country. Michałowski had lessons with Moscheles and Tausig, and knew Karol Mikuli, Chopin's pupil. He was principally known as a Chopin player – and a great one; and his playing has been described in Chapter Two of this book. The late Zbigniew Drzewiecki, the great Polish piano teacher, said that the influence of the school of Chopin playing founded by Michałowski was still felt in Poland in the 1950s.[5] When he was appointed to the Warsaw Music School in 1898, Michałowski had already had a brilliant career as a virtuoso, and considerable success as a teacher – one of his pupils, Antoinette Szumowska, had already begun an international career.[*] Michałowski taught three generations of Polish pianists, ranging from Henryk Pachulski (b. 1859) and Piotr Maszyński (b. 1855) to Bolesław Kon (b. 1906), Stanisław Urstein (b. 1915) and Edwarda Chojnacka (b. 1918). His best-known pupils outside Poland were the harpsichordist Wanda Landowska and the Russian, Mischa Levitzki. Unfortunately, the careers of many of his students were interrupted by the First World War; had times been different, pianists such as Jerzy Żurawlew, Józef Śmidowicz and Wiktor Chrapowicki would have made wider reputations.

Michałowski's success as a teacher – and nearly a thousand students passed through his hands in over sixty years of teaching – was based on his care in ensuring that his pupils got the best possible technical foundation. His enthusiasm for Chopin's music was unbounded, and he took it on himself to see that Mikuli's ideas about the way in which Chopin should be interpreted, born of so many years' close study and performance, should be passed on to future generations. According to Professor Drzewiecki, he encouraged his pupils to play the fast works with the utmost bravura and speed (he used to have races with them)

---

* She played in Paris in the '90s, and later settled in the US after her marriage to the cellist Józef Adamowski; she made no discs, but left some Ampico piano rolls including a Mazurka and three Preludes.

and this of course is not always conducive to Chopin's music – Planté's remarks on the subject are instructive.* This would be a serious criticism of his teaching had it been part of a systematic approach; so long as it was done in a spirit of fun it was probably harmless. Drzewiecki's views may also be coloured by the fact that in later years he and the older master did not get on well.[6] Drzewiecki also said that Michałowski encouraged his pupils to imitate his own playing, but Michałowski's amanuensis, Jerzy Lefeld, believed that his master was always sufficiently broadminded to let his pupils develop their own interpretations, and would only resort to suggesting they imitate his own playing if they were relatively untalented and needed artistic direction. Wanda Landowska wrote warmly of her lessons with Michałowski, expressing her gratitude for the way in which he would illustrate points at the piano, and she never hinted that he forced his pupils to imitate his style of interpretation.[7]

Michałowski devoted his life to the piano, but two other pupils of Leschetizky, Henryk Melcer and Józef Śliwiński, also made solid reputations as conductors. Melcer was not a typical Leschetizky pupil, and his Chopin playing was very different from the other products of that school. He was an intellectual player, who performed the whole cycle of Beethoven Sonatas. He was fond of monumentally taxing programmes, of the same scope as those of Anton Rubinstein, to whom he yielded little as regards technique. His classical orientation was very evident in his Chopin performances – Professor Drzewiecki described them as 'a little cold' – and Melcer's pupil, the late Margherita Trombini-Kazuro, told me that his Chopin had little spontaneity. But by any standards there was real quality in his playing, and he was especially effective in the Nocturnes, the Scherzos and the Etudes; Roman Jasiński, who was also his pupil, said that Melcer's performance of the Etude in thirds, Op. 25 No. 6, was equal to that of Lhévinne or Friedman.[8]

Melcer was equally well-known as a teacher. He taught many of Leschetizky's pupils theory and composition in Vienna, and then taught in Lwów and Warsaw, where he was the Director of the Conservatory from 1922 until his death in 1928. It was the pianists of his generation who began to treat musical education in a thorough and systematic manner; the days of the eccentric and the amateur were gone, and most Polish pianists from Melcer's time on emerged from the Conservatories with very solid tools with which to express their art. One exception was Juliusz Wertheim, a relative of Tausig and a rather ephemeral figure. He was a sensitive pianist but, according to Professor Drzewiecki, his technique was unreliable and so his musical enthusiasm never bore fruit. However, he encouraged a number of young pianists who later

* See page 183 above.

made a name for themselves: Roman Jasiński, Bolesław Kon and Aleksander Kagan. Like Melcer, who died while giving a lesson, Wertheim expired 'holding the reins' – he was smitten by a heart attack while conducting the *Meistersinger* overture.

Up to the First World War there was considerable cultural interaction between Poland and Russia, while pianists such as von Bülow visited Poland from Germany in the 1880s, and Polish artists ventured great distances in touring. It was at this time that the music of Chopin became popular throughout Europe; it had been neglected in England and Germany because of the classical orientation of such teachers as Reinecke, Moscheles, Kullak and Clara Schumann, all of whom held Chopin in high esteem but did not use his music as a cornerstone in their teaching. By the end of the nineteenth century, Chopin's works were recognized to be far above the piano compositions of Hummel, Weber and Mendelssohn, although it was some time before Polish pianists gained the distinction they now possess as interpreters of his music. Very few discs were made in Poland before 1914, and it was the career of Paderewski (whose playing has been discussed in Chapter Two), the first Polish pianist since Tausig to gain worldwide recognition, that helped to raise the standing of Polish musicians throughout the world.

Two Polish pianists who made their reputation in Europe and then settled in the United States were Leopold Godowsky¹ and Josef Hofmann. Both received their musical training outside their native country: Hofmann was taught by Moszkowski in Berlin and Godowsky by Saint-Saëns in Paris, and their teachers were responsible for some of their technical finesse though neither had much influence in forming them artistically – Godowsky was principally self-taught, and Hofmann came under the tutelage of Anton Rubinstein. The Chopin of these two pianists was highly disciplined, and not typical of the interpretation of Polish pianists, whose approach to Chopin is usually a natural and un-fettered one, with rhythmic elasticity and virtuoso spontaneity.

Godowsky was born in Wilno in 1870, made his first public appearance at the age of nine, and in his early teens went to study in Berlin. His German training gave him a discipline that never left him. He then became a protégé of Saint-Saëns, and when he was twenty he was appointed to the music faculty of the New York College of Music. The following year (1891) he became an American citizen, and apart from the years 1900 to 1914 (when he was based for nine years in Berlin and then moved to Vienna, where he conducted a master class at the Academy of Music) held various teaching appointments in the United States until 1930.

Godowsky always set the very highest standards for himself, and had a complex approach to interpretation. Many musicians testified that his playing in private surroundings was infinitely more satisfying than his public recitals; before a large audience his playing lost its communicativeness, though retaining its extraordinary virtuosity.[9] This latter quality had impressed Bernard Shaw when Godowsky played in London in 1890: Shaw described him as 'an all too rapid executant'.[10]

Early in his career, Godowsky caught the disease of transcribing and adapting the music of other composers, Chopin in particular. A master of contrapuntal writing, he used all his skill to introduce new melodic lines, rewrite parts and 'touch up' original compositions in a manner which, although intricate and fascinating, must of course be challenged on musical grounds. He was fond of the two Chopin concertos, for which he rewrote the orchestral *and* solo parts. In the F minor Concerto, he introduced counter-melodies for the left hand in contrast with the right, thus wrecking Chopin's original intention. He rewrote the twenty-seven Etudes, producing over fifty new creations which include studies for the left hand alone, two Etudes combined together, and many tortuous exercises which take instrumental writing to the heights of complexity.

Today Godowsky's reputation as an arranger and transcriber has virtually eclipsed his fame as a pianist, but (perhaps surprisingly) his recorded performances of Chopin's works in their original form are models of respectable and tasteful interpretation. He left some piano rolls and many discs, and these give a fair idea of his approach to Chopin's music. Amongst the rolls, there is a vast variety of works: the F minor Concerto, the F sharp minor Polonaise, the C sharp minor Scherzo (for Hupfeld); the Berceuse, the A flat Polonaise and four Waltzes (for Ampico); and the G minor Ballade (for the Duo-Art system). The discs include the G flat Etude, Op. 10 No. 5 (the 'Black Key'), the G flat Etude, Op. 25 No. 9 (the 'Butterfly'), the A flat and C sharp minor Impromptus, twelve Nocturnes, the A major Polonaise, the A flat Polonaise (recorded twice), the B flat minor Sonata and some Waltzes. A number of previously unissued discs have now found their way onto long-playing records, including the E major Scherzo, the C sharp minor Polonaise, the Berceuse and two Etudes (an International Piano Library disc, now deleted), and an abridged version of the B flat minor Scherzo (an International Piano Archive disc, still available).

Very few of these performances are entirely successful, though the G minor Ballade has some stunning bravura passages and a grasp of the more brilliant passagework that would eclipse most of today's leading technicians. The B flat minor Sonata, recorded in 1930, although very poetic in places with marvellous tone, lacks drama and overall scope – Godowsky was nearing the end of his career when this recording was made and suffered a stroke shortly afterwards. The disc of the E major

Scherzo (released for the first time on long-playing record by IPL Veritas) and a rare one of the A flat Impromptu are in my opinion far more impressive than Godowsky's better-known recordings. His preoccupation seems to have been creating an atmosphere and achieving aural beauty; his often fragmentary style lacks the formal cohesion of a Cortot's performances. One interesting detail is that in the B flat minor Sonata Godowsky, like his friend and compatriot Josef Hofmann on a piano roll of the same work, observes the repeat of the exposition in the first movement. His recordings of the Nocturnes are masterpieces of balanced and refined playing, but for all their perfection and tonal beauty there is something curiously unsatisfactory about these discs; they lack the warmth and personal conviction which characterized his playing in private.

The career of Josef Hofmann, who was born in 1877, began at the age of five when he played at a charity concert in Warsaw, and continued until he was over seventy. When he was eight years old he played Beethoven's C minor Concerto and the Liszt arrangement of Weber's *Polacca Brillante* with orchestra, joining Michałowski in Schumann's Variations for Two Pianos.[11] Two years later he toured Europe, and then set out on a series of concerts in the United States, making his American debut at the Metropolitan Opera House in New York in November 1887. The young prodigy's tour was halted by the Society for the Prevention of Cruelty to Children, and he returned to Europe for further study. After taking lessons from Moszkowski in Berlin, Hofmann became Anton Rubinstein's only private pupil in 1892. He re-emerged to give a recital in Cheltenham on 20 November 1894, the very day Rubinstein died. From then on he was based in the United States, and became an American citizen in 1926, when he was appointed Director of the Curtis Institute of Music in Philadelphia. In November 1937 he celebrated the Golden Jubilee of his debut with a recital at the Metropolitan Opera, and he went on giving concerts and broadcasting until just after the Second World War.

Hofmann's recording career was of exceptional interest. He was the first pianist of all to be captured on the 'phonograph', having made some experimental cylinders for Edison during his American tour in 1887; unfortunately these were apparently destroyed. His first discs were made in 1903–4 for the Gramophone and Typewriter Company, and from 1912–19 he recorded for Columbia. From 1923–5 he made Brunswick discs, and then strangely refused to allow any of his recordings, including those he made for HMV and RCA Victor in 1935, to be released. It has been suggested that the reason for this was that his interpretation changed so much from one performance to the next that he did not want posterity to remember him by any one rendering of a particular piece of music. However, several of his performances of Chopin's works from this period have found their way onto long-playing records; they include both Concertos (from live performances conducted by Barbirolli in the late 1930s); some unissued RCA experimental discs of the first movement of the B minor Sonata, the D flat Nocturne, Op. 27 No. 2, the A major Polonaise, and the A flat Waltz, Op. 42, from 1935; unissued HMV discs from the same year of the same A flat Waltz, the F sharp major Nocturne and two of the Chopin/Liszt *Chants polonais*; a recital given at the Academy of Music in Philadelphia in 1938, which includes the Berceuse and the *Andante Spianato and Grande Polonaise Brillante*; the whole of Hofmann's Golden Jubilee Concert in 1937, which features the *Andante Spianato*, the Berceuse and the G minor Ballade; and lastly, a recital given at the Casimir Hall at the Curtis Institute in 1938, which includes the F minor Ballade, the E flat minor Polonaise and the B major Nocturne, Op. 9 No. 3. There are also piano rolls made for the Duo-Art and Welte-Mignon systems, including large-scale Chopin works such as the E minor Concerto (arranged for solo piano), the B flat minor Sonata, three Scherzos and other Polonaises.

Hofmann was especially famous for playing Chopin, and over the years his style changed a great deal. In his boyhood, his playing was very serious, with an immense sense of 'rightness' of style, exquisite phrasing, and an overall grasp of structure usually evident only in the playing of a much older man; his style was extremely disciplined, and was considered very modern. With the passage of time, this tendency became more exaggerated; there was no element of risk in his playing, and in his later years, the drama itself was minutely calculated. Hofmann used to say that his secret was to imagine exactly what he wanted to achieve in a performance and impel his fingers to bring this about. During his years with Anton Rubinstein, an extraordinary variety and passion were instilled into Hofmann's playing; these were elements in Rubinstein's nature, but for Hofmann they were 'adopted' as 'components of piano playing'. His own character was far from passionate – it was fussily accurate. A mechanical inventor in his own right, he held several patents to his credit (including that of the windscreen wiper) and all his interpretations were thought out with extraordinary precision, though the playing of his last ten years sounds very extravagant to modern ears because it is too clever and too intricate. If it is not the case that Hofmann actually plotted a graph before playing a work, it is true that if he began a work in a certain way, the next passages would have to balance the former to a specified degree, and so on.

Nevertheless, Hofmann achieved a power and a magnetic attraction that few other pianists have equalled. His Chopin was almost orchestral in the range of sonorities he conjured out of his instrument. Unlike

Anton Rubinstein, he seldom overstepped the boundary of a composition, although one wonders when listening to his discs whether Chopin actually intended all those inner voices and concealed harmonies to be pointed to in quite so explicit a manner. Hofmann's tonal palette was unparalleled, but in the last decades of his career his interpretations were not always musically acceptable, and give the impression that he approached a piece of music like a mechanical experiment – given the right fusion of ingredients, it should work. Certain items from the live performances would raise more than one eyebrow: the bell-like A flat in the accompaniment of the Berceuse is brought out in the last pages in a manner not indicated by the composer, the devastating power of the F minor Ballade has none of the classical reserve that characterized Chopin's own playing, and the composition is therefore taken into a context quite different from what was intended; and the strangely disjointed account of the E minor Concerto is highly unsatisfactory. According to Abram Chasins, the American broadcaster, composer and pianist, Hofmann (with whom he had studied) was past his best when the live performances were recorded in the late 1930s; there are very few examples on disc of his playing at its peak, and none of them feature the large-scale works, save the abridged version of the B minor Scherzo (a Brunswick from 1923). The performances on Hofmann's released discs are well-disciplined and artistically highly successful (the B minor Scherzo portrays exactly the right blend of temperament and virtuosity) but they give the impression that he is always reserving pent-up energy.

His pupil Shura Cherkassky described Hofmann's Chopin to me as above all 'polyphonic', and this characteristic can be observed in nearly all his performances. At the end of the opening phrase of the F minor Ballade, for instance, he brings out the left-hand line, usually treated as merely an accompaniment, to round off the introductory phrase. As the piece proceeds, attention is directed to the left-hand notes as well as the right-hand melody, which creates a more richly harmonic pattern than most pianists have envisaged. The wealth of tone given to these low bass notes and also to the melodic lines of the accompaniment when in the middle register, contributes to an impression of a more solidly written piece than is usually conceived. Hofmann's strength in executing the filigree ornaments in such works as the Polonaise from the *Andante Spianato and Grande Polonaise*, Op. 22, and the Berceuse was unique: some runs are played *legato*, others *leggiero, non legato* and unpedalled. No other pianist has played Chopin quite like Hofmann, and he opened up aspects of the composer's writing that others, save for Anton Rubinstein, had neglected – or left well alone. Hofmann's Chopin playing follows in a direct line from Anton Rubinstein's, showing a complete control over the minutiae that make up an interpretation, and he would reveal aspects of his powers to his audiences in a god-like manner, even his displays of spontaneity being the result of intellectual judgment. Like all geniuses, he defies categorization.

Well-known pianists who had lessons from Hofmann include Nadia Reisenberg, Jeanne Behrend, Ruth Slenczynska, Lucie Stern, Harry Kaufman, Olga Barbini, Ellen Ballon, Angelica Morales von Sauer and Leonard Cassini, but Shura Cherkassky is the only one of his pupils who could be said to have taken up his mantle.

A Polish pianist of great attainments who never became well-known in Western Europe was Zofia Rabcewicz, who, unlike Hofmann, was a very natural player, and never found it necessary to analyse her art. In her teens, she gained a scholarship to study with Anton Rubinstein, this being a very unusual distinction for a non-Russian, and she learned a great deal from him, his instinctive approach to interpretation being very close to her own musical nature.[12] When she graduated from the St Petersburg Conservatory in 1890 with the title of 'liberated artist' she was given a prize of two concert grand pianos. On 10 November in the same year she gave a concert in St Petersburg at which she played Anton Rubinstein's D minor Piano Concerto in his presence; the applause was ecstatic, and she often returned to the city, establishing herself as one of the most popular pianists in the Russian capital. In the late Professor Drzewiecki's words, she was 'very attractive, young and charming,'[13] and was an instant success wherever she played; she never established a European reputation because she ceased to tour after her marriage, although she continued to perform in Poland. She had a big repertoire, and a relaxed approach: even when an old lady she could step into the place of an indisposed artist with only very little preparation, and play a full recital programme with an immaculate finish. She sat on the jury at the early Chopin competitions, and her pupils included Krystyna Kobylańska, the great Chopin scholar. Mme Rabcewicz won tremendous respect for playing underground recitals of Chopin's music during the war, when the Nazis banned the public performance of his works.

It is sad that this immensely gifted artist left only two discs that have come to light; luckily one is of the F major Ballade, with the C major Mazurka, Op. 56 No. 2, completing the second side. The other disc is of the C sharp minor Waltz, Op. 64 No. 2, coupled with the Mazurka in the same key, Op. 63 No. 3. The performance of the Ballade is quite exceptionally distinguished. There is a nobility and poetry in the opening bars, and the fast sections are fiercely powerful, with excellent left-hand technique. Rabcewicz seems to have played with some of Anton Rubinstein's temperament; an oddity in the performance is that just before the final reprise of the opening bars at the end of the work she plays the top A on the piano, rather than the F that is written. The two

Mazurkas she recorded are ideal performances, combining the most sensitive tonal shading with a natural rhythm. The C sharp minor piece receives an edifying reading – to my mind one of the best on disc – and the C major work is equally convincing. Rabcewicz was essentially a modern pianist, who aimed to convey the shape of a work, as much as to execute it with beauty.

The diversity of Polish pianists can be illustrated by considering the playing of a contemporary of Mme Rabcewicz, Józef Turczyński. A thin man with a mass of dark hair and a somewhat frightening face – Professor Drzewiecki described him as having a 'Kościuszko-like profile' – Turczyński was much respected by his many pupils, and had a profound effect on the way that Chopin's music is now played in Poland; his influence was probably greater even than that of Professor Drzewiecki.[14] He studied with Busoni in Vienna and with Essipov in Russia, and his playing showed a formidable intellectual grasp. His repertoire was very wide, but unfortunately he only made two discs before his death in 1953 (he spent his last years in Brazil, but died in Lausanne).

Turczyński began teaching in 1915, when he was appointed to the staff of the Kiev Conservatory. He returned to Poland after the Revolution, and took over the virtuoso class at the Warsaw Conservatory in 1920. His best pupils inherited much of his enthusiasm for Chopin, and include Halina Czerny-Stefańska, Witold Małcużyński, Henryk Sztompka, Stanisław Szpinalski and Ryszard Bakst; all of whom have been inculcated with a real feeling for Chopin's style, devoid of pretension or sentimentality.

The compilation of the edition of the Complete Works of Chopin had just begun when Paderewski himself died in 1941, and Turczyński took over this daunting task with Ludwik Bronarski – the latter had had some lessons with Leschetizky, but was neither a very good pianist nor a good editor, and the bad pedal markings in the Mazurkas are said to have been part of his contribution. It is a tribute to Turczyński's powers both as a musician and as a scholar, that the Paderewski edition is now accepted as one of the most serviceable in existence. It was completed in 1949.

The successor to Paderewski as the Polish pianist of highest international acclaim is an artist of a very different character, Artur Rubinstein, who has become beloved by audiences all over the world and is as celebrated as his Russian namesake. Artur Rubinstein's personality has probably attracted almost as many admirers as his pianism, although the two are indivisible: he communicates with his audience by throwing all his personal charm and intellect into every piece he plays with a unique vigour and commitment. He has been the subject of many books and films, and has been honoured by the governments of many different countries, but whereas Paderewski was also a composer and a politician, Rubinstein is first and foremost a pianist, and one totally dedicated to his art. On a recent visit to Poland I asked the pianists I met which contemporary Chopin player they admired most, and Rubinstein's name was mentioned more often than any other; there can be little doubt that he plays the bulk of Chopin's works with more consistent excellence than any other living pianist.

Rubinstein was born in Poland around 1887 (the year of his birth has variously been given as between 1886 and 1890) and was a child prodigy.[15] He went to Berlin for lessons with Heinrich Barth, who was the teacher of Wilhelm Kempff, Fridtjof Backer-Grøndahl and Aline van Barentzen, and became the protégé of Josef Joachim, the great violinist and friend of Brahms; because of this link he has always felt an affinity with Brahms's music. He started to tour at the beginning of the century, and in 1906 made his first American visit, a very hectic one, giving seventy-five concerts in three months. This led to his partial retirement for nearly three years, but as early as 1924 he was regarded as one of the most celebrated pianists of the time, ranking alongside such super-virtuosi as Sauer, Rosenthal, Backhaus, Friedman and Paderewski.[16] He reacted against the over-sentimental approach taken to Chopin by many of the pianists of his youth, and some critics thought his playing dry and over-objective. In his early days, as he relates in the first volume of his autobiography, *My Young Years*, he relied largely on his inborn musical talent for success, but in his forties he realized that there was more to music-making than creating an effect and taking technical risks that were not always successful (he was shaken by Horowitz's near-infallible technique);[17] he was brave enough to rethink his attitude to the instrument, and so improved his artistic standing.

Rubinstein's playing always displayed a free and natural temperament of the most unusual diversity, and he is therefore ideally suited to Chopin's varied style. Before he went to Berlin he had hoped to study in Warsaw with Aleksander Michałowski, but he was sent to one of the professor's assistants, who took very little interest in the young pianist. Rubinstein's style has often leaned more towards the French school, especially in his elastic and occasionally dry fingerwork. His performances are less studied than those of Michałowski, freer and more spontaneously creative. Like all very great artists, he does not play a work the same way twice – such stylization is anathema to him. He never quite possessed the exceptionally rich tone of Friedman, nor have his interpretations had Cortot's monumental grasp of structure, but the noble and memorable conception he has brought to Chopin has never been surpassed. Up to about the mid-1960s Rubinstein possessed a technqiue of the greatest bravura, especially suited to works such as the Polonaises, the two Piano Concertos, the Scherzos and the Sonatas. Alongside these, there has always been the utmost sympathy for Chopin's more delicate and minutely expressive moods, as displayed in the Mazurkas, Waltzes and Nocturnes.

Rubinstein came to the recording studio relatively late in his career (he made some piano rolls, but no acoustically recorded discs that were released), when already in his forties, but he continued recording until the mid-1970s. When he committed his performances of the two Concertos to disc in the '30s, both conducted by Barbirolli, he gave to posterity playing of the highest bravura, which because of its cavalier daring might raise a few eyebrows today. Rarely has anyone played the development section of the first movement of the F minor Concerto with the same speed, yet rarely have the Nocturnes (from about the same date) been played with such sensitivity and finesse. He can be suave and cosmopolitan in turn, as in the Waltzes, and vibrantly rhythmic in the Polonaises and Mazurkas.

Although he has often featured one or two of the Etudes in his programmes, Rubinstein has never recorded the complete Etudes. He has too much respect for these works, and such a large repertoire, that he has not been able to devote the time needed to perfect them all so as to perform them in a complete set. Anyone buying Rubinstein's set of Chopin's works recorded for RCA in the 1960s will notice that there is no version of the complete twenty-four Preludes; he has in the past recorded these both on 78s and long-playing records, but in his later years did not feel inclined to repeat the complete cycle.

Always one to favour fast tempos, Rubinstein's conceptions of Chopin maintain an inexplicable distinctiveness; nowhere is this more evident than in the Polonaises. The heroic qualities of Chopin's writing are here contrasted with the pathetic; as soon as one hears the C sharp minor and E flat minor works of Op. 26, one receives the impression that this pianist understands the nature of these epic pieces with the same depth that Schnabel understood late Beethoven. Never has anyone brought the Polish Chopin to life in quite the same way as Rubinstein. His extraordinarily comprehensive grasp of Chopin's nature and musical personality is unique; perhaps he tends to treat the music in a rather more masculine way than one imagines Chopin himself would have played – but would Chopin not have wanted to possess Rubinstein's power and élan?

Other Polish pianists of the same generation have not of course achieved Rubinstein's fame, but a number of those born in the 1880s and 1890s were highly distinguished. Most of them were pupils of Michałowski, Turczyński or Paderewski. Wiktor Chrapowicki, Jerzy

Żurawlew, Józef Śmidowicz and Bolesław Woytowicz belonged to almost the last generation of Michałowski's pupils. Chrapowicki, who died of consumption in 1931, may have been the most talented, and was so regarded by Jerzy Lefeld (another Michałowski pupil), but he was the victim of a very nervous and delicate disposition, and was never able to fulfil his artistic promise.[18] Śmidowicz was a serious musician with a classical approach, and his disc of the F major Mazurka, Op: 68 No. 3, is well shaded, with some nice echo effects displaying considerable imagination.

Jerzy Żurawlew became a celebrated pianist and teacher. He founded the Warsaw Chopin Competitions in the 1920s to improve standards of interpretation and broaden ideas on Chopin's music. He was one of Michałowski's favourite pupils, with a particularly well-developed technique and a penchant for big virtuoso works. I met Żurawlew in 1978, when he was in his nineties, and he told me with pride how Michałowski had dedicated his transcription of the 'Minute' Waltz to him, in recognition of his technical accomplishment. He made a number of discs and his Chopin playing was subtle and sophisticated – a little dry in emotional content, but nevertheless dignified and heroic. His recording of the E flat minor Polonaise is for me the most distinguished performance of this work captured on disc. His timing is immaculate and he makes very good contrasts between *staccato* chords and *legato* passagework. There is no element of the sentimental romantic in Żurawlew's performances, and his reading of the G minor Ballade on a long-playing disc released by Muza Records shows that even when he was an old man he retained his grasp of the large-scale works. Bolesław Woytowicz, another Michałowski pupil, a well-known pianist and teacher, also had much to do with the Chopin Competitions. When the complete works of Chopin were recorded for Muza around 1960 to celebrate the 150th anniversary of Chopin's birth, Woytowicz was approached at the last minute to record the twenty-four Etudes; these performances were regrettably ill-prepared, and do not do him justice.

Two other pianists of the same age became well-known Chopin exponents and achieved worldwide fame: Jan Smeterlin, a pupil of Godowsky, and Stefan Askenase, who studied with Emil Sauer. Smeterlin made the quicker reputation, becoming famous not only for his Chopin but also for Brahms. He was a friend of Szymanowski and gave the first performance of some of his piano works.[19] Born in 1892, Smeterlin was a natural pianist who had considerable success in his teens, winning the first state prize at the Vienna Klaviermeisterschule in 1913. In the 1920s he settled down in England and played a great deal in the United States, where he had a considerable following. His Chopin playing was marked by a rare and intense communicativeness, and was direct and unfussy. He had an artistic sincerity that is absent in many Chopin players, and he was always content to follow Chopin's own markings. He played all his great works and was equally successful in pieces such as the A flat Ballade and the F minor Fantasy as he was in the Mazurkas and Waltzes. He recorded very little, his best-known discs being the complete Nocturnes and two mixed Chopin recitals.

Smeterlin was one of the most popular pianists in Britain from the 1930s to the 1950s. An artist who knew all the great musicians of his day, he was never content to give anything other than his best on the concert platform. A recording of a public recital he gave in Holland shortly before his death in 1967 demonstrates him to have been cast in the same mould as Benno Moiseiwitsch, although the approach is simpler. Smeterlin's performance shows that he felt the shape and rhythm of the Mazurka very keenly, and in the F sharp minor Mazurka, Op. 59 No. 3, one can hear all the components of the work displayed with a rare insight and point. His interpretation of this work differs from that of Arthur Loesser, his American contemporary: Loesser's account has a more sophisticated slackening of the rhythm towards the end of each phrase of the opening motif; Smeterlin allows the notes alone to speak, and does not attempt to impose any rhythmic pattern from outside the printed score.

Smeterlin represented the best in Polish Chopin playing of his time, as did Stefan Askenase, who in his mid-eighties is still giving concerts. Born in Lwów in 1896, Askenase studied as a boy with an old lady, a Mme Zacharjasiewicz, who had herself had lessons from Mozart's son, Wolfgang Amadeus II, the conductor at Leschetizky's Viennese debut. Having taken further lessons with a local teacher, the Czech Theodor Pollack, Askenase continued his studies with Sauer in Vienna in 1914-15, and resumed them after the war in 1919; he made his Vienna debut the same year. In 1922 became a professor of piano in Cairo, but settled in Brussels, later moving to Germany. Although he toured a great deal throughout his career, it was not until the 1950s that he consolidated a worldwide reputation, which was greatly enhanced by the gramophone industry.

Askenase, like Smeterlin, takes a direct approach to Chopin. He is an unusual pianist in that he manages to combine the suavity of his Viennese training with a passionate Polish verve. One adjective often used to describe his playing is 'aristocratic' – this is because he generally chooses very unhurried tempos and never plays for purely pianistic effect. If he plays down the bravura of Chopin, he always compensates for this with an intense insight that brings to mind Chopin's admiration for Mozart; the textures have a crystalline clarity and purity. Askenase has recorded much of Chopin's music: the two Piano Concertos, the fourteen Waltzes, the four Impromptus, both Sonatas, the twenty-four Preludes and many other works. He began his recording career very late – when in his fifties – but many of his interpretations have become classics, in particular the E minor Concerto and the complete Waltzes, both discs demonstrating that he has caught the composer's idiom. His playing of the first movement of the E minor Concerto is extremely slow and, as usual, he keeps bravura at a distance. This is Chopin stripped of any varnish and veneer – there are none of the histrionics indulged in by many younger pianists. Like the late Dinu Lipatti, he gives each note its rightful place, whether belonging to the melody or the accompaniment; there is in Askenase's phrasing an authority characteristic of a breed of pianists which has now died out. His Chopin never sounds inconsequential, even though he gives those pieces which are rather light in character, like the F major Waltz, Op. 34 No. 3, very direct readings, resembling those of his teacher, Emil von Sauer. In the Mazurkas he is at one moment rustic, at another pensive, and then rhythmically vibrant. The Op. 41 Mazurkas are played to perfection: nothing is hurried or missed; the C sharp minor retains its marking, *Maestoso*; the E minor is a solemn quest, a desolate search for comfort; the B major, which is rarely played, is revealed in all its humorous and earthy originality, and the final one, the almost impudent A flat, is softly persuasive and intimate. Few pianists have ever achieved the results that Askenase demonstrates in this set of the Op. 41 Mazurkas; this is the inimitable Polish way of playing Chopin: emotionally expressive, disciplined yet possessing an inner fredom, positive and rhythmically assured.

If there have been very few Chopin players who can equal Askenase at his best, there have been even fewer who have rivalled the late Professor Zbigniew Drzewiecki as a teacher of Chopin's works. Of the same generation as Smeterlin and Askenase, he did not study with any famous teacher, but between 1909 and 1914 was a pupil of Leschetizky's assistant Marie Prentner, in Vienna. At the age of twenty-six, in 1916, he was appointed professor of an advanced class for pianists at the Warsaw Conservatory, and from that date until his death in 1971 he had extraordinary success as a teacher. He also gave recitals throughout Poland, and earlier in his career played in Prague, Vienna and Berlin. He left a number of records, and as a pianist he was a little dry and unemotional in style – his playing had an intellectual depth, but was less distinguished than many of his colleagues. His second wife Barbara told me that he liked most of all to perform the Nocturnes and Polonaises, and of the latter he recorded both works from Op. 26 on one of Chopin's own pianos. Professor Drzewiecki was a careful player whose performances were consistent, if slightly dull. He helped to establish the Chopin Competitions, and sat on the jury from 1927 until his death in 1971. An amazingly large number of his pupils have had international careers: Halina Czerny-Stefańska and Adam Harasiewicz (both first-prizewinners of the Chopin Competition), Fou T'song, Felicja Blumental, Roger Woodward, Ryszard Bakst, Regina Smendzianka, Lidia Grychtałówna, Władysław Kędra and Eva Osińska. Many of his students came from foreign countries, including Japan, and he was extremely successful in demonstrating the most important aspects of Chopin's music, especially the rhythmic inner life of the Mazurkas and Polonaises. After the Second World War, and especially after the death of Turczyński in 1953, he was regarded as the greatest Polish piano teacher, with a greater number of talented pupils than his colleague at the Warsaw Conservatory, the near-equally famous Margherita Trombini-Kazuro. She was Italian, a pupil of Sgambati, Landowska and Melcer. Mme Trombini-Kazuro's Chopin was also much praised, notably by the widow of Józef Śliwiński. Barbara Hesse-Bukowska and Miłosz Magin are two of her well-known pupils.

Professor Drzewiecki had one particularly outstanding pupil, Bolesław Kon, who won first prize at a piano competition in Vienna in the early 1930s over the head of Dinu Lipatti, though Alfred Cortot walked out in protest at the decision. Born in 1906, Kon first studied with the great Russian teacher Konstantin Igumnov in Moscow, and then returned to Warsaw and had lessons from Michałowski, Wertheim and Drzewiecki. He won third prize in the second Chopin Competition in 1932, and played in many of the European capitals. Professor Drzewiecki used to say that Kon was the greatest pianistic genius that he had ever heard, and he was proud to pose the question 'Who knows whether or not Kon should have taught Drzewiecki?'[20] Mme Trombini-Kazuro related that Kon's talent had great nobility and extraordinary spontaneity; nothing was preconceived – his music poured out from his soul. According to the Professor, he had 'no inborn finger technique', and Adam Harasowski, who took part in the same Chopin Competition, said that he was often to be found practising extremely slowly (the coda of the F minor Ballade, for instance).*

Kon had a large repertoire of composers other than Chopin, but of the latter's works his best interpretations were of the F minor Fantasy, the A flat Polonaise, the Op. 10 Etudes – especially No. 2 in A minor – and numerous Mazurkas. But there was a fatal flaw in his life – he suffered from a hereditary mental illness and had to go into a sanatorium at regular intervals. Because of the necessity of continuing his career he terminated one of these treatments prematurely, and tragically committed suicide in 1936. It is sad that his outstanding talent was never captured on disc.

* It is interesting that Rachmaninov and Essipov, two of the greatest technicians of all time, used a great deal of slow practice.

In the first Chopin Competition in 1927 three major Polish pianists won prizes: Stanisław Szpinalski, Henryk Sztompka and Róża Etkin; honourable mentions were awarded to Jakub Gimpel, Leopold Muenzer and Bolesław Woytowicz. The three prizewinners had very distinguished careers, but one was cut short – it was tragic that Róża Etkin, a pupil of Michałowski and Drzewiecki, was killed in 1944 when the German army was retreating from Warsaw. A soldier threw a live grenade into a shelter where several people were taking refuge, and Róża Etkin was one of those who died. In the early 1930s she had gone to Berlin to study with Professor Mayer-Mahr and had won very favourable notices there for her performance of the E minor Concerto. She had a very big technique, and her huge repertoire included the late sonatas of Beethoven, Rachmaninov Concertos, the Goldberg Variations, Prokofiev's works and Godowsky's arrangements of Chopin Waltzes. She played much of Chopin's music, and left some discs (some of them available under the label of Tri-Ergon, Berlin) that indicate a very strong musical personality with a remarkable grasp of structure. Her recording of the C sharp minor Mazurka, Op. 50 No. 3, is highly impressive, contrasting the different moods with great originality. Another disc of the F sharp major Nocturne, Op. 15 No. 2, shows her to have had a very deep and subtle tone, with a rich variety of sonorities. Before the Second World War she apparently showed some signs of instability, but since her career was broken off so tragically, one can never know how she would have developed.

This generation began to play Chopin's music with a strict attention to what the composer had actually written. Michałowski would sometimes alter the text of the score, something which Szpinalski, Sztompka and Drzewiecki would never have done. Sztompka, born in 1901, was very much a modern pianist; his teacher, Turczyński, had always been notable for adhering to the composer's markings, and Sztompka played his Chopin in a slightly cold but highly distinguished manner. Both he and Szpinalski had some lessons from Paderewski, although they turned out to be very different pianists. Szpinalski was the more original of the two – his account of the B minor Scherzo, recorded from a live recital, has all the fire Horowitz brought to the piece, and nearly all the technique. Sztompka, who also possessed a very finished technique, was a more objective player, who always allowed the composer to speak but who never really united his own temperament to the music. This reserve, a facet of the composer's own playing, can be successfully applied in the non-virtuoso works, such as the Nocturnes and Mazurkas, which Sztompka played with great refinement. The eminent Polish writer and musician, Dr Czesław Halski, maintains that Sztompka was over-praised in Poland in the 1950s,[21] but his playing had a consistent distinction that is rare.

Szpinalski, on the other hand, as witnessed in a performance from Carnegie Hall that was captured on disc, could excite an audience. He devoted much of his energy to music administration and the performance of modern works, but unfortunately suffered two terrible blows – he was affected by rheumatism in his hands, and then succumbed to leukaemia. Had he lived, there can be little doubt that he would have become another Richter or Gilels. Szpinalski's discs of Chopin show that he favoured fast tempos, but had the technical command to control his fingers. His Chopin playing was extrovert, and he was especially adept with the different rhythmic patterns of the Mazurkas.

Another Paderewski pupil, Stanisław Niedzielski, also had a considerable following between the wars and in the 1950s. Concentrating on Chopin, he had a very clean and articulate keyboard style, but his playing was often marred by eccentricity. He too favoured fast tempos, and some of the Mazurkas which he recorded around 1930 are far too rushed, but his reading of the B flat minor Sonata is highly effective: technique and poetic feeling are here united to perfection. However, another disc that couples the G minor Ballade with Beethoven's 'Waldstein' Sonata and Liszt's Second Hungarian Rhapsody, is more questionable. The Ballade opens in a grand and eloquent manner, but in the climax following the first appearance of the second subject, where the two hands play octave chords, Niedzielski gets hoplessly out of time, and his fundamental musicianship is open to question. His virtuoso approach can be at odds with the spirit of Chopin's music, especially when this aspect becomes an end in itself.

Quite different is Jakub Gimpel, who took part in the first Chopin Competition. A Chopin player of the old school, he plays the large-scale works such as the Barcarolle, the *Polonaise-Fantaisie* and the F minor Fantasy, with a rare unity of purpose. His brother Bronisław Gimpel was a famous violinist, another brother a cellist, and the three used to play as a trio. Never relying solely on his strong technique for effect, there is a nobility in Gimpel's Chopin that combines the best of the romantic school – its spacious phrasing – with the intellectual discipline of the modern approach.

That some pianists attract crowds and others do not is a strange and often unaccountable phenomenon which frequently has little to do with musical talent, and a great deal to do with personality and bearing on the platform. The late Witold Małcużyński had a fierce intensity when at the piano that was in itself striking. One of the last great pianists cast in the romantic mould, his playing was never consistently satisfying, and to some extent this added to the enigmatic aura that surrounded him. Although known principally as a Chopin player, he was considered by many to play the music of other composers equally well, if not better, and his accounts of the Liszt Sonata and *Vallée d'Obermann* were deeply impressive. Perhaps the best-known pupil of Paderewski, Małcużyński was born in 1914 and studied as a boy with Jerzy Lefeld (Michałowski's pupil) and later with Turczyński. He was awarded the third prize at the 1937 Chopin Competition, and was launched into an international career when he gave a recital in Paris in 1940. His American debut took place at the Carnegie Hall in 1942, and until his death in 1977 he played all over the world, returning to Poland in 1958 after a twenty-year absence.

Małcużyński was a very prolific recording artist, committing some of his Chopin interpretations to disc many times over. It is very difficult to survey his art without concluding that his playing, although it could be stunningly inspired and beautiful, was often marked by a prosaic quality that was odd in an artist of his calibre. However, I can remember moments in one of his recitals that took one into a world inhabited solely by hypnotic sounds. His style was masculine and large-toned, although he could also play with exquisite poetry. His particularly strong interpretations were of the F minor Concerto, the F minor Fantasy, the two Op. 26 Polonaises, the B flat minor Sonata and the C sharp minor Scherzo. At his best he could convey the unity of purpose behind the large-scale works as well as any other pianist, and could also perform such small pieces as the Waltzes and Mazurkas with a disarming directness. Some of Małcużyński's performances recorded in Warsaw in 1975 and released by Muza Records, with an introduction by the pianist and a reminiscence of him by his brother, a well-known diplomat, are especially convincing representations of his art. In the F minor Fantasy we have a Chopin both majestic and fearless; this is playing rich in noble gestures, in deep bass sonorities (unobtainable of course on the pianos of Chopin's day), revealing Małcużyński as a tough man sweeping aside the conventional view of the music. In the F major Nocturne, Op. 15 No. 1, there is little of the mysterious sound-world that Pachmann created; the refinement of a Perlemuter is lacking too. The middle section of this work is almost too violent, but then Małcużyński visualizes Chopin as a violent man, full of constrained anxiety and passion.

Małcużyński's conceptions at their best contained the right combination of close study and musical inspiration. Turczyński taught him to have a deep reverence for what Chopin actually wrote, and his detailed playing of the Mazurkas was entirely apt. A collection of these, released on the Classics for Pleasure label in the UK, is probably the most satisfying and successful disc he ever made. It is blessed with very good piano sound, and one can admire his exquisite rhythms and natural phrasing – the more common Mazurkas, such as the B flat from Op. 7 and the B minor from Op. 33, are communicated as spontaneously as is possible.

The Waltzes are equally good, and although perhaps a little less monumental than Rubinstein's versions, preserve a unity of style and a simplicity of vision that are both valuable and enjoyable.

For all his attention to Chopin's spirit, Małcużyński belonged to the era of Paderewski. Founded in the sonorities of the modern grand piano, his Chopin had little of the delicate pastel nuances of the French school, although his connections with that country were strong, and he married a Frenchwoman. The consistency of his interpretations enabled him to organize his musical expression within a solid framework. Vigorous as his Chopin was, it never went against the spirit of the music; if Chopin himself was not able to play like this, he would have admired those who could, as he admired his pupil Gutmann. Since Małcużyński there have only been two Polish pianists who have achieved equally consistent results: Halina Czerny-Stefańska and Adam Harasiewicz, both winners of the first prize at different Chopin Competitions in Warsaw.

Jan Ekier, the well-known teacher, Chopin scholar and pianist, presents a cool and rather detached view of the composer; lacking in warmth, he does not possess the finesse to be really successful. He sees the large-scale works as the best-suited to his style, and he has recorded impressive versions of the two Sonatas, and still better ones of the four Ballades. Another pianist of the same generation was Władysław Kędra, a highly skilled technician, although intellectually rather shallow; such works as the 'Là ci darem la mano' Variations (which he recorded) exemplify his entertaining bravura. Unfortunately he died of leukaemia in the late 1960s. Natalia Karp, who settled in England after the Second World War after suffering at the hands of the Nazis in the concentration camp of Auschwitz, plays a very simple and deeply felt Chopin. She refuses to succumb to the brilliant side of the composer, never pandering to mere display, and her disc of the *Andante Spianato and Grande Polonaise Brillante* is highly interesting and original. A pupil of Schnabel and Drzewiecki, she has a very warm tone and suffers from none of the old-fashioned mannerisms of the players of the beginning of the century. She was favourably compared with Róża Etkin when she played the E minor Concerto in Berlin in the 1930s, and her playing has won deserved critical acclaim.

Halina Czerny-Stefańska is now the most famous pianist of the older generation resident in her native country. Her father Stanisław Czerny, a piano teacher, was descended from the famous pedagogue Carl Czerny, and she was sent to Paris as a girl for six months to study with Cortot.[22] The years 1935–9 were spent with Turczyński, and after the war she had lessons from Professor Drzewiecki. In 1949 she won first prize at the Chopin Competition in Warsaw jointly with the Russian Bella Davidovitch, and has since played all over the world.

Mme Czerny-Stefańska has a tendency to restrict her Chopin repertoire to a few chosen works, although she does play the majority of Chopin's *oeuvre*; those which feature especially often in her programmes are the E minor Concerto, the C minor and D minor Polonaises, the Nocturnes in C sharp minor and C minor, Opp. 27 and 48, and various Mazurkas. These works she plays quite outstandingly well, with a depth of concentration that few can manage. Her Chopin is full of pathos and possesses rare maturity. Her identification with his music is such that one can almost imagine Chopin himself playing the piano; she finds inner lines and undercurrents in the C minor Polonaise that not even Rubinstein touches upon. She has a very large technique, ideally suited to such works as the *Andante Spianato and Grande Polonaise*. Her playing does not always achieve a consistent degree of excellence, but when she played in London in the early 1970s she gave a very fine performance of the F sharp minor Polonaise that was full of fire. She plays compositions by other composers, but always centres her repertoire around Chopin, and is an instinctive player whose conceptions have altered very little over the thirty years since she won the award.

When I heard Mme Czerny-Stefańska play in Warsaw in 1978, I detected an element of pedantry in the way she executes trills in the Mazurkas. The trill plays a very prominent role in the Mazurka in A minor, Op. 68 No. 2, and I was sorry that this pianist leaned towards point-making when performing this work. She has recently recorded the complete Mazurkas, and as she follows in the tradition of her teacher Turczyński, one might expect that these interpretations will be faithful representations of Chopin's text.

There seems to be a dichotomy in the way that the modern Polish pianists play Chopin: either they err on the side of over-exuberance, or they go in the other direction and are too objective and detached. A balance between these extremes can be very hard to achieve, and those that accomplish this do not always attract attention, because their approach is neither novel nor sensational. The pianists Barbara Hesse-Bukowska, Lidia Grychtałówna, Regina Smendzianka, Ryszard Bakst, André Tchaikowsky and Miłosz Magin have all achieved some fame in their own country, and have been well-received abroad; both Bakst and Tchaikowsky live in Britain. All belong to the modern school, which attempts to combine intellect with emotion. All are serious players whose approach reflects the precepts of their respective teachers: Hesse-Bukowska and Magin studied with Mme Trombini-Kazuro; Bakst, Smendzianka and Grychtałówna with Drzewiecki; Tchaikowsky with Szpinalski. All have won prizes at the various Chopin Competitions.

Strangely enough, it was not until the fourth Chopin Competition in 1949 that a Pole won the first prize; in the three previous Competitions a

Russian had been the winner.* The second Chopin Competition after the last war in 1955 was a very special one, a vintage year for Chopin players, and the first prize went to Adam Harasiewicz. Other participants that year were Vladimir Ashkenazy, Fou T'song, Bernard Ringeissen, Lidia Grychtałówna, André Tchaikowsky, Peter Frankl, Tamás Vásáry, Miłosz Magin, György Bánhalmi and Naum Shtarkman, all of whom have had international careers and won other prestigious prizes, many of whom have achieved more fame than the recipient of the first prize. Born in 1932, Harasiewicz studied for six years with Professor Drzewiecki, and went on to win many other awards. A pianist with an exceptionally well-developed technique, he can play the big virtuoso works with the grasp of a Richter. His playing has all the ingredients for pianistic success: a lovely tone, and a lively virtuoso approach. Commentators at the time of the Competition said that Harasiewicz was 'one of the last of the Polish romantic pianists', since his playing possessed a characteristic temperament.[23] But for all its tonal beauty, there is something a little unsatisfactory about his playing of the big works – they lack an overall sense of purpose.

Harasiewicz has recorded all of Chopin's works, which show that aside from his virtuosity, his greatest strength is in his lyrical imagination. Of the performances recorded at the time of the 1955 Competition, the most beautiful are the C sharp minor Prelude, Op. 45, the B major Nocturne, Op. 62 No. 1, and the G flat Impromptu, Op. 51; there is a calm and sad air about these readings. But his playing, always highly finished, lacks the character of Rubinstein, the sophistication of Perlemuter, and the volatile imagination of Argerich. There is little sense of struggle in the more taxing works, since his technical capacity is never fully stretched; he nearly always chooses fast tempos in the virtuoso works, but these lose their thrill because he is too efficient. He seems to have little trouble in interpreting Chopin's music, and this may easily be the flaw in his artistry. Temperamental response seems to be calculated with him, and any of the risks that he takes with fast tempos seem to be carefully judged. Occasionally Martha Argerich plays beyond her technique, but she excites the emotions more.

In a work such as the F minor Fantasy one appreciates Harasiewicz's solidity and musical assurance. He keeps up the momentum of the piece, but it has none of the monumental quality of Cortot's conception, nor Nelson Freire's inner tension. But on the other hand, the *lento sostenuto* section achieves a remarkable degree of poignancy, and one is grateful for the lack of pomposity. Viewing Harasiewicz's playing in some sort of stylistic perspective, it would be easy to state that he blends

---

* See Appendix 2 for a list of prizewinners at the Chopin Competitions.

a romantic approach with classical discipline. Yet this is unsatisfactory because it seems that it is his technical mastery that plays a very important role in his interpretations. He has the means to do whatever he thinks appropriate with the music, but this is itself centred around the creation of aural beauty and structural proportion. Everything is bound together with musical feeling, but he seems to envisage no development of his playing other than making it more polished, and consequently more suave.

After Harasiewicz won the contest he left Poland and spent some years in Belgium; he now lives in Austria. Since the time that he made his reputation, few Polish pianists save Krystian Zimerman and Emanuel Ax have become well-known as Chopin players. This is partly due to problems of style. Even Zimerman, who won the 1975 Chopin Competition in Warsaw, has changed his Chopin a good deal since that date. Emanuel Ax, born in Lwów in 1949, left Poland for Canada before the age of ten, although when at the Juilliard School of Music he studied with a well-known Polish pianist, Mieczysław Münz, a pupil of Busoni. Ax was the winner of the first prize at the first Artur Rubinstein International Piano Competition at Tel Aviv in 1974. His Chopin, like Harasiewicz's, is polished and refined, but is emotionally very reserved. His latest disc of Chopin – the F minor Piano Concerto – demonstrates that to an even greater extent than Harasiewicz he sees the music from a highly disciplined classical perspective. He achieves his effect by the use of exceptionally beautiful pianistics, and a lucidity of thought that can make the music that he interprets sound fresh and unfettered by tradition. His magically poetic sonorities are entirely apt for the quieter and more intimate moments in Chopin, and the powerful passages have a solidity and richness of texture that makes his playing distinctive. Ax's Chopin has a strongly intellectual base and has greater weight of thought behind it than does Harasiewicz's, and he demonstrates that the B minor Sonata is worthy of comparison with the great classical works in this form. He does not repeat the exposition of the first movement here, but this is acceptable because of his expansive phrasing. The finale has none of the humour that other pianists have brought to it. Ax plays it with a mature weight – this is not a neurotic Chopin, but one who knows precisely what he wants to achieve in musical terms. The recording of the F minor Concerto has a shallower piano tone than the Sonata, and the pianist does not produce such rich basses as in the solo work. He has adapted his style in the Concerto to suit the more youthful Chopin, an approach which occurs to very few pianists. There are certain similarities in Ax's playing of this work with that of the most recent recording of Artur Rubinstein – an earnestness of intention and a classical poise that was a characteristic of the composer's own performances. Ax is also noteworthy for always choosing the most natural-sounding tempos, and this adds to the rightness of his conceptions.

Aside from Krystian Zimerman, there are two other young Polish pianists, slightly older than he, who have made a name for themselves in Chopin: these are Janusz Olejniczak and Piotr Paleczny. Both took part in the 1970 Chopin Competition, Olejniczak winning the sixth prize and Paleczny the third. They are both highly sensitive players, if perhaps lacking the final distinction that separates the very talented from the truly original artist.

Zimerman, on the other hand, shot to worldwide fame in an almost meteoric fashion. His Chopin playing at the time that he won the 1975 Competition was a good deal more flamboyant than it is now. A comparison of the winning performance of the E minor Concerto with the studio recording with Carlo-Maria Giulini conducting reveals that within a space of three years his style has matured considerably. Born in December 1956, Zimerman began piano lessons with his father when he was five. Two years later he went to a little-known teacher and pianist Andrzej Jasiński, his only other instructor. He gained experience as a performer at an early age, winning many major competitions and awards. However, at the time of the Competition he was only eighteen and was virtually unknown, even inside Poland. It was his extraordinarily finished bravura technique that helped him on his way at the Competition, together with a delightfully youthful *élan*. The recording of the E minor Concerto from the contest reveals the astonishment of the audience when he played the coda of the first movement with unparalleled speed and force. However, the score of this work shows that this coda section is meant to begin *piano*, not *fortissimo*!

From the time of the Chopin Competition Zimerman's playing became less tense and frenetic. He seems to have realized that the attributes required to win a competition are not necessarily those needed to establish a worldwide reputation. The Competition itself places very great strains on the winner; he or she is expected to maintain a standard which they have worked years to achieve. In some ways it is probably more advantageous to win such a contest *before* one's education has been completed and one's artistic nature formed, and Zimerman appears to have learned much since his success. The studio recording of the E minor Concerto well demonstrates this; there is a greater discretion in the use of bravura, and a tighter control on the emotions.

Zimerman's sonorities in Chopin are light and graceful; there is very little depth to his bass. His style, surprisingly, is rather French in that it has an emotional reserve, combined with these light and transparent textures. The sustaining pedal is used sparingly, and this heightens the brilliance and fragility of the conceptions. All Zimerman's Chopin has a 'bloom' to it; alongside the great bravura there is a well-judged and mature artistic insight. Anyone who has heard him perform the B minor Sonata or the fourteen Waltzes in the concert hall will agree that he plays Chopin with a rare authority.

The freedom with which the Poles used to play Chopin has all but disappeared, largely because of the more scholastic approach of such teachers as Ekier, Drzewiecki and Turczyński. Zimerman may play the Mazurkas with a simple and unaffected poetry, but without the buoyancy of artists such as Małcużyński and Friedman. It is to be hoped that this slightly 'disembodied' approach will not be a lasting one. Many lesser-known pianists in Poland, who never get enough exposure to merit criticism, play the Mazurkas in a more convincing manner than some of those who achieve fame through their pianistic perfection.

The reader may have gleaned that I believe there to be no definable Polish school of Chopin playing. Even Michałowski allowed his best pupils to grow in an individual manner, and he was the teacher who was most advantageously placed to form a 'school'. The Poles do not share a common temperament, and their intellectual priorities prevent any uniformity in their playing. They have of course a greater innate feeling for the Mazurka and Polonaise rhythms than any other nation, but their way of performing these has never resulted in routine. Friedman, Hofmann, Godowsky, Paderewski, Śliwiński, Michałowski, Tausig, Józef Wieniawski, Scharwenka, Sztompka, Małcużyński and the rest, were all individuals who used melody and rhythm in their own distinctive way.

CHAPTER FIVE

Russian Schools of Chopin Playing

IT APPEARS THAT the Russians have a special affinity with Chopin's works, and there have been as many great Chopin players from Russia as from Poland or France. Anton Rubinstein had as great an influence on the way that Chopin's music is now played as did the composer himself, or Liszt. On a visit to Paris in 1841 Rubinstein played to Chopin, who performed a few of his Mazurkas for him, and this event left a strong impression on the boy; Chopin remained the composer closest to his heart.[1] Together with his brother Nikolay, who was almost his equal as a pianist, Rubinstein studied with only one master, Alexander Villoing, who described teaching the brothers in his excellent book *L'école practique du piano*. Villoing must have been a very thorough pedagogue, since both his pupils displayed an extraordinary technical facility and the most refined musical intelligence.

Aside from his career as a virtuoso, which began when he was a child, Anton Rubinstein found time to teach and to compose. He was Director of the St Petersburg Conservatory, and those who came under his tutelage included Zofia Rabcewicz, Józef Śliwiński, Teresa Carreño, Vera Timanov, Felix Blumenfeld, Ossip Gabrilowitsch, Arthur Friedheim, Alberto Jonas and Carlos Sobrino, though his most celebrated protégé – said to be his only private pupil – was the Polish-American pianist Josef Hofmann. All Rubinstein's pupils had one very remarkable attribute in common – a penetrating and beautiful tone, which was one of the strengths of their master's playing. But the power of Rubinstein's artistic imagination was such that he could be in turn explosive and gentle, proud and innocent, these contrasts deriving from his own personality; his playing was so supremely impressive because he felt everything he played very deeply, and he was often so moved by his own playing that he could not speak after a recital and would hide away.[2] His performances showed the re-creative artist at his most original. He did not always follow the text of Chopin's music very closely (although he did not encourage his pupils to follow his example in this respect) and some of Chopin's pupils complained that he distorted the original;[3] the evidence suggests that Chopin himself would not have adopted this somewhat old-maidish attitude. Rubinstein was more explosive than Liszt, more a pianist of extremes, and Hofmann (though there is no certainty that he heard the latter play) compared them thus:

Rubinstein excelled by his sincerity, by his heaven-storming power of great impassionedness; a quality which, with Liszt, had passed through the sieve of a superior education and gentlemanly elegance. Liszt was, in the higher sense of the word, a man of the world; Rubinstein was a world-stormer, with a sovereign disregard for conventionality and Mrs Grundy.[4]

Although these words now sound quaint, they well contrast the difference between the two pianists. Rubinstein was one of the greatest 'naturals' of all time, a man who followed his musical instinct and was never inhibited by pedantry. He never played a composition the same way twice, and for this reason would not demonstrate during lessons. During his last years, when his health was failing, his playing deteriorated badly and was marred by fistfuls of wrong notes and memory lapses, but at the height of his career his powers were astonishing.[5] He would often attack the instrument with terrible ferocity, and when he played at Windsor, Queen Victoria found it necessary to back her chair away from the piano when he was not looking.[6]

The monumental scale of Rubinstein's programme would daunt even the most ambitious pianist today. One of his Chopin recitals might include the F minor Fantasy, six Preludes from Op. 28, four Mazurkas, all four Ballades, two Impromptus, three Nocturnes, the Barcarolle, three Waltzes, two Scherzos, the Berceuse and three Polonaises![7] He was a man of very powerful build, and referred to his large hands as 'my paws'. He appeared very relaxed when at the piano, and was given to throwing his hands above his head in flamboyant gestures.[8] He was the first pianist since Chopin himself to pay much attention to the pedal, and this helped to give his playing an originality his contemporaries lacked. The young Rachmaninov wrote:

The pedal has been called the soul of the piano. I never realized what this meant until I heard Anton Rubinstein, whose playing seemed so marvellous to me that it beggars description. His mastery of the pedal was nothing short of phenomenal. In the last movement of the B flat minor Sonata of Chopin he produced pedal effects that can never be described; for anyone who remembers them they will always be treasured as one of the greatest of musical joys.[9]

Chopin's biographer Frederick Niecks attributes to Sir Charles Hallé the comment that Rubinstein's playing was 'clever, but not Chopinesque'.[10] But Rubinstein, like Liszt, widened the field of Chopin interpretation far beyond the confines of the Paris salon. At a time when few

Polish pianists championed Chopin's music, he demonstrated the almost infinite variety of interpretations which could be brought to Chopin's works. Whether it was in his almost explosive playing of the Polonaises, the concentrated and refined emotion of the Nocturnes, or the wildness of the Mazurkas, Rubinstein opened up Chopin as no other pianist had previously done.

Although Rubinstein was not admired among Chopin's circle in Paris, another Russian pianist, Vladimir de Pachmann, born in 1848, played with many of the characteristics that marked the composer's own playing, and was by general consent a near ideal interpreter. Coming from Odessa, a town which has produced many world-famous musicians, he claimed to be largely self-taught. He was born into a very musical family, and in 1866 had lessons from the well-known pedagogue Dachs, who taught at the Vienna Conservatory (Emil Liebling, Laura Kahrer-Rappoldi, Isabelle Vengerova and Juliusz Zarębski were among his other pupils). Pachmann used to relate with pride the story of how, when asked to learn a couple of the Chopin Etudes, he told Dachs at his next lesson to name any one of the twenty-four; he had learned them all! During his long career he retired from the public for lengthy periods,[11] but by the 1880s he had consolidated a great European reputation. In the early years of his career, Pachmann's repertoire included large-scale works by Beethoven, Schumann and Mendelssohn, but he had a particular affection for Chopin, and it is as a Chopin player that he is especially remembered.

Pachmann has received a bad press. During the last twenty years of his life (he died in 1933), he developed a habit of talking to the audience and carrying on antics which gave rise to doubts about his mental stability. His playing at that time became a subsidiary element in his 'performances', and this was popular with undiscriminating audiences, but he could never be relied on to play any music sensibly. But despite his antics, Pachmann was no charlatan. His habit of speaking to the audience went back to his early years, and until the late period he managed to keep it at bay. (It has been suggested that he caught this habit from Planté, and both pianists also retired for long periods.) However, the discs he made before the First World War, and a few later discs, demonstrate that he was an artist of the highest calibre. He developed an astounding *pianissimo* technique that restored to Chopin's music the sonorities of the early pianos, and he mastered the delicate intonation of the instrument so thoroughly that in his last years his sound rarely rose above a *piano*. His prowess was appreciated by other musicians, and Wilhelm Backhaus, who played with Pachmann in a two-piano recital at the Albert Hall in the late 1920s, had the highest respect for his technique and wrote:

The ultra-modern teacher who is inclined to think scales old-fashioned should go to hear de Pachmann, who practises every day. De Pachmann, who has been a virtuoso for a great many years, still finds daily practice necessary, and, in addition to scales, he plays a great deal of Bach. Today his technique is more powerful and more comprehensive than ever, and he attributes it in a large measure to the simplest of means.[12]

These words were written before 1914 by a pianist who himself had one of the most complete techniques in the history of the instrument.

Pachmann's Chopin repertoire narrowed a good deal when he was old (his love of Chopin was not exclusive and he stated in 1914 that he thought Schumann a more original composer)[13] but in his early years and maturity he played a wide range of Chopin's works, including the Concertos, the Polonaises, the Sonatas, the Scherzos and the Impromptus. Niecks wrote that no other pianist he had heard managed to make the *Allegro de Concert* sound great music, and Pachmann claimed that Liszt had told him that he played Chopin's music better than the composer. However dubious that claim may be, some of Pachmann's early discs have an uncanny similarity to the accounts of Chopin's playing.

Pachmann's discs of Chopin's works include performances of the Barcarolle, the second half of the A flat Ballade, six Etudes, two Impromptus, several Mazurkas, seven Nocturnes, five Preludes, movements from both Sonatas, and a few Waltzes. Some works were recorded more than once. The most impressive perhaps are his performances of the Nocturnes, and of those other pieces that require elegant sensitivity above every other attribute. The International Piano Archives recently released a disc with a performance by Pachmann of the F minor Nocturne, Op. 55 No. 1, which had never been issued commercially. Unfortunately it demonstrates Pachmann's playing at something near its worst – the phrasing is mannered and there are no dynamic variations – although this was recorded as early as 1911. There are other recordings which show the artist at almost his best, including the E flat Nocturne, Op. 9 No. 2 and the F major, Op. 15 No. 1. These present the most imaginative phrasing, and an elasticity deriving from the nature of the music. Pachmann developed the habit of lengthening the first beat of each bar to a very pronounced degree, but in these recordings this does not sound mannered. The rare disc of the Barcarolle also has many very attractive insights, and Pachmann's performances provide a glimpse of a tradition of music-making that had its roots in Chopin's own playing.

His last electric discs, those of the E minor Nocturne, Op. Posth., and the A flat Mazurka, Op. 50 No. 2, are especially successful, though the former has some textual alterations. The Mazurka has an other-worldly richness, in which the earthy beat of the dance is captured with great vividness. Pachmann also made a number of piano rolls, some of them being performances of pieces he did not record on disc: the roll of the C sharp minor Nocturne, Op. 27 No. 1, and the F sharp major, Op. 15 No. 2, reveals his art when his playing was still very impressive. Pachmann's variants in ornaments and phrasing almost always sound spontaneous, and as if they reflect a performing tradition, rather than being mere eccentricities.

Although he did coach some pianists, Pachmann never became well-known as a teacher, and his specialized style of *pianissimo* playing had few imitators. His importance in interpreting Chopin's works lay in his closeness to the composer's era and his ability to capture the 'right' atmosphere for a work; for this last attribute, he was fêted throughout Europe as an authoritative interpreter. People used to talk of his 'feline grace', and greatly admired his attention to the left-hand part of such works as the Waltzes, which gave these compositions a new dignity and interest.[14] The disadvantages in his mechanism were his inability to rise to the heroic aspect of Chopin's music: under his hands, the more stormy Preludes, the Scherzos and the Polonaises were robbed of much of their power. However, in the Nocturnes and similar works, Pachmann was supreme in his day, and the only artist who has equalled him since in this respect has been Cortot.

Of the same generation as Pachmann, the Russian pianist Constantin von Sternberg was born in 1852, and studied with Liszt, Moscheles, Kullak and Dorn. A sensible artist who did not achieve a lasting reputation on the concert platform, he later became a well-known teacher in the United States. A pianist of greater standing was Vassily Sapelnikov, who achieved considerable success as a virtuoso. He was born in 1868, and studied with Brassin and Sophie Menter, both of whom were noted for their powerful technique. Bernard Shaw heard Sapelnikov play several times in the 1880s, and remarked on his highly developed left hand; Mark Hambourg described him as 'a robust and matter-of-fact artist',[15] more concerned with manual dexterity than with poetic sentiment. He was at his best in the big virtuoso pieces, such as the A flat Polonaise: Shaw wrote that the middle section 'comes from his puissant hands like an avalanche'.[16] Unfortunately, the few discs of his playing Chopin are very rare.

It was during the last quarter of the nineteenth century that the Russians began to produce an apparently unending stream of first-rate pianists whose repertoire centred around Chopin. Vassily Safonov and Felix Blumenfeld were noteworthy pianists of this generation who turned to conducting and teaching; Safonov taught Josef and Rosina Lhévinne, Cécile de Horvath, Nikolay Medtner, Leonid Nikolayev and

Wiktor Łabuński, all of whom were important teachers and soloists, and of Blumenfeld's pupils, Simon Barer, Vladimir Horowitz and Maria Grinberg became well-known pianists.

Pachmann and Anton Rubinstein felt that they possessed a special closeness to Chopin because they belonged to a generation near to the composer's. However, the Russian pianists who were born in the 1870s and later, played Chopin because they felt an instinctive sympathy with his music, and they were responsible for a flowering in its interpretation. The greatest figures of this era were Josef Lhévinne, Sergei Rachmaninov and (among the pupils of Leschetizky whose playing has already been discussed) Ossip Gabrilowitsch, Mark Hambourg and Benno Moiseiwitsch.

It is rare to find a composer equally distinguished in the performance of another composer's work as in his own. The great conductor-composers such as Richard Strauss, Gustav Mahler and Louis Spohr, and the pianists Nikolay Medtner, Ernö Dohnányi and Franz Liszt were among those who were outstanding interpreters of the great classics, and to this distinguished category belongs the composer and pianist Sergei Rachmaninov, who turned to playing the piano as a career relatively late in life because of financial need. Rachmaninov was stupendously gifted, with very large hands that could stretch enormous lengths on the keyboard. He had a naturally flexible technique and a very large and sonorous tone. Towards the end of his life he suffered considerably from neuralgia in his hands and, through illness, had some loss of feeling in the tips of his fingers, which affected the quality of his late recordings. If his musical nature was rather melancholic, this was ideally suited to playing much of Chopin's output. Rachmaninov felt a natural affinity with Chopin, and visualized his music in an almost symphonic context, bound together with limitless ranges of colour. Anton Rubinstein's pianism had a profound effect on his playing and, not being exposed to the mainstream European schools, he developed a highly original approach to Chopin. When composers of merit attempt to play the music of other great composers, a re-creative process is usually put into action, rather than a simple 're-reading'. Such was Rachmaninov's view of Chopin; his playing contained an extraordinary spontaneity that few others have achieved. It was quite unlike the closely-studied interpretation of a Cortot, something that had matured over the years like old wine; Rachmaninov played a piece of Chopin's music as if it was one of his own compositions – with the result that some passages of his Chopin sounded a little too like Rachmaninov for comfort!

Though Rachmaninov's success as a pianist was as much due to his playing his own works and some by other composers (his performance of Schumann's *Carnaval* was especially memorable), he performed and recorded much Chopin. As would be expected, his genius is most evident in his interpretations of the large-scale works – in the Mazurkas and Waltzes his style can be a little mannered. For example, in the 'Minute' Waltz he hesitates slightly on the top B flat of the rising scale in the first bars (Chopin, according to his pupil Mathias, also used to pause at these points), and in the trio section makes the grace notes which occur at the repetition of the second melody sound as if they were another melodic line. The result is an alteration in the shape of the composition, making it sound infinitely more complicated than the composer may have intended. Rachmaninov's Chopin has the widest variety of emotions: he brings humour to the F major Waltz, Op. 34 No. 3, and simplicity to the B minor Waltz, Op. 69 No. 2; none of his interpretations was ever boring or lacking in imagination. He was never averse to introducing small changes into the text: in the G flat Waltz, Op. 70 No. 1, there is a variation at the end of the trio section which is charming but rather sentimental, and now sounds dated.

Particularly famous among Rachmaninov's interpretations was that of the B flat minor 'Funeral March' Sonata, which was fortunately captured on disc at a time when standards of recording had greatly improved. This performance shows the pianist at his most compelling. From the jaunty right-hand motif of the first section of the opening movement to the ghost-like finale one is spellbound by his extraordinarily vivid conception of the work. There are some moments in the first movement where the phrasing sounds a little drawn-out and mannered, but the portrayal of the composer as a virile and strongminded man is exceptionaly compelling. The fierce treatment of the Scherzo introduces an element of technical risk that contributes to make the performance all the more exciting. This very full-toned view is far more explosive and 'unclassical' than was Chopin's own – there is none of the reserve that was often said to characterize his performances. Like Cortot, Rachmaninov was able to view the work as a whole, and the Funeral March emerges as the central and most important movement. This begins with an air of distance and mystery, and the tension and proximity of the cortège gradually become more apparent, only to be broken by an unearthly trio section. The pathos achieved in this last part is deeply moving, and the eventual re-entry of the opening march has a devastating force that little by little fades away and finally disappears. The finale is a mass of pedalled half-tones, and the general effect is more one of Rachmaninov than of Chopin.

Rachmaninov's performances of two other large-scale works – the A flat Ballade and C sharp minor Scherzo – were recorded in the early 1920s, but were not released for many years. They enable one to hear the pianist with all the immediacy of a live concert. The Ballade begins in an improvisatory mood and has unusually elastic phrasing. There are no noticeable changes in tempo as the first subject progresses, and the basic pulse is maintained until the end of the first section, though most pianists increase the speed here. The biggest climaxes of the second subject are rather curiously phrased and the pianist sounds distracted. The opening of the Scherzo in C sharp minor is excessively mannered – the dramatic octaves have inconsistent emphasis. The high point of the performance is the infinitely coloured and shaded treatment of the cascades of liquid quavers. Rachmaninov supplements the descending octaves which lead into the coda, and plays this last section with the highest bravura.

Rachmaninov used Chopin's music to express as wide a range of musical ideas as one finds in his own compositions. Vlado Perlemuter told me that to hear Rachmaninov play was to hear an orchestra,[17] a remark which conveys the variety of responses of a pianist of genius. However much one might disagree with Rachmaninov's conceptions of Chopin, it is undeniable that his view of the composer, transmitted with such inner conviction and spontaneity, was valid and will remain so for all time.

Josef Lhévinne was also a Chopin player whose name will always be remembered. Born a year after Rachmaninov, he received much the same musical education, and made his debut at the age of fifteen in the 'Emperor' Concerto, with Anton Rubinstein conducting. He lived in Germany for about twelve years around the time of the First World War, and then settled in the United States, where he joined the staff of the Juilliard School. He married Rosina Bessie in 1898. Like him, she had been a pupil of Safonov, and in 1906 they made their debut as duo-pianists, a venture which had been suggested to them by the composer Cui in 1899.[18] They celebrated their fortieth anniversary of playing together in 1939, at a concert in which Rosina played Chopin's E minor Concerto, Josef Tchaikovsky's B flat minor Concerto, and they played the Mozart Double Concerto in E flat together.

Josef Lhévinne is remembered for his infallible and astounding technique, but he was always able to use this to produce beautifully poetic performances. There was very little exhibitionism in his artistry, and his touch had a bell-like clarity that was quite different from Rachmaninov's. As a rule, his playing was more disciplined and contained than that of Friedman or Rachmaninov, yet he yielded to neither as a technician. It was in Chopin's music that he excelled, and from his discs it is immediately clear that Lhévinne, unlike Josef Hofmann, never indulged in bringing out quirky inner lines; he played the music just as it was written, using a fair degree of *rubato*, but always with perfect taste.

Lhévinne was recorded playing the F minor Concerto, but this set of

discs was never released and has apparently been lost.[19] His Chopin performances on disc are limited to a handful of Etudes and Preludes, the A
flat Polonaise, and a number of piano rolls. The Ampico roll of the B
major Nocturne, Op. 9 No. 3, a work that is played much less than other
Nocturnes, demonstrates a wide variety of tempos for the opening
melody, but Lhévinne moulds the whole into a highly poetic rendering.
If one compares this reading with that of Arthur Loesser, the American
pianist born in the 1890s, Lhévinne is revealed as very much a pianist of
an earlier epoch; his approach is so elastic that it would now be labelled
over-romantic. On the other hand, his disc of the A flat Polonaise shows
that he could play in quite another style; the passagework is dry, exceptionally clear and even brutal, each entry having a bite that can only be
achieved under the hands of a stupendous technician. Even though the
explosive quality Hofmann brought to such works is absent, the general
impression of Lhévinne's performance is highly aggressive, the contrasts
achieved in some delightfully sensitive, lyrical moments.

Lhévinne's discs of the Etudes and the two Preludes present the
Russian as a precision tool of unparalleled accuracy, but with a natural
manner and perfect discretion. His disc of the G sharp minor Etude in
thirds, Op. 25 No. 6, silences any criticism. The opening tempo is extremely fast, and all the right-hand entries have an icy precision. It is
said that Henryk Melcer and Ignaz Friedman played this Etude with
equal speed and accuracy, but Lhévinne's bell-like clarity has never been
surpassed on disc. The A minor Etude, Op. 25 No. 11, the so-called
'Winter Wind', on the reverse side of the same disc (they were recorded
on the same day in June 1935) has the same bravura; Lhévinne comes
across as a highly dynamic keyboard personality, more musically conscious than that other Russian super-technician, Simon Barer. His tonal
shading is always extremely subtle, and this quality is especially evident
in the performance of the E flat Etude, Op. 10 No. 11, on the same disc.
Lhévinne's tone here is even more ethereal than that of Michałowski,
who also recorded this work. Another of his greatest triumphs is the performance of the B flat minor Prelude, Op. 28 No. 16, where the tempo is
incredibly fast and fierce, and the spread left-hand extended chords
create an impression of unsurpassed passion and wildness.

Lhévinne and his wife shared much the same musical views, and like
him, she excelled in lyrical passages, but she was a more feminine player
whose keyboard style did not generate quite the same electricity. After
her marriage she played very little as a soloist, apart from appearances in
Vienna, St Petersburg and Berlin between 1910 and 1912, and when the
Lhévinnes came to the United States, Rosina soon began to concentrate
on teaching, although she did play in public as late as the mid-1960s.

In a recording of a live performance of the E minor Concerto from the 1960s, with Leonard Bernstein conducting,[20] there are many technical slips and split notes, but from the first piano entry in the opening movement one is aware that the reading is going to be an 'interpretation' and not just an exercise in pianistic display. The pedal is used very carefully, and the mood varies a good deal. The coda of the first movement is exceptionally well-played – the left-hand octaves and trills have a marvellous rhythm and vitality astonishing in view of the fact that the pianist was eighty-three years of age. The slow movement has a very slow and meditative opening with plenty of momentum and combines well with the orchestra: like Horszowski and Perahia, Rosina Lhévinne's general approach was very much that of the ensemble player. Towards the end of this movement the piano's reveries achieve an almost impressionistic effect, broken by the advent of the lively third movement. The pianist wisely decided upon a relaxed tempo here, but plays with plenty of lilt. She never allows her technical shortcomings to interrupt her concentration, and manages to bring out many details missed by other pianists of greater fame. The performance ends with a competent and very delicate treatment of the final unison triplets. It is a pity that Rosina Lhévinne did not make more recordings of the solo works of Chopin, for this performance is so interesting from an interpretative angle. Perhaps her temperament was a little more dreamy and feminine than her husband's, but they shared the idea that poetry was one of the most important priorities in piano-playing.

Josef Lhévinne died during the Second World War, but his wife lived until 1976, and both of them were good teachers who trained many able pianists. Josef's pupils include a number of well-established performers – Sascha Gorodnitzki, Stell Andersen, Celius Docherty, Adèle Marcus, Jan Chiapusso among them – while Rosina taught Van Cliburn, John Browning, Garrick Ohlsson and Mischa Dichter among hundreds of students. Mme Lhévinne was able to discriminate between the good and bad elements of the romantic approach, and combined this fastidiousness with a modern outlook, in which communicating the music is the chief priority.

Josef Lhévinne, Alexander Scriabin and Sergei Rachmaninov are often grouped together because they were born within two years of one another and received the same musical training as pupils of Zverev. But another pianist and teacher may in the long term have had an even greater influence on the playing of Chopin's music – Konstantin Igumnov, professor at the Moscow Conservatory for nearly fifty years, from 1899 to 1948. Born in 1873, the same year as Rachmaninov, he too studied with Zverev, and with Siloti and Pabst. His life was dedicated to teaching, and he was respected by all who knew him, though he appears to have had a somewhat remote character, and was described by his fellow-student Mikhail Bukinik as 'looking like a sexton'.[21] Igumnov was a very accomplished pianist, who championed new works throughout his extraordinarily long career. He made some piano rolls, and one or two discs of Chopin's music.* However, his special sympathy with Chopin must be inferred from the quality of his pupils, among whom were many outstanding Chopin players – Bolesław Kon (discussed in Chapter Four), Lev Oborin (who won first prize at the inaugural Chopin Competition in Warsaw), Bella Davidovitch (joint winner of the first prize at the fourth Chopin Competition), Naum Shtarkman, Elena Beckman-Scherbina, Jakov Flier, and the conductor Issay Dobrowen. All these pianists were noted for their direct and unfussy playing of Chopin's music and, together with the pupils of Harry Neuhaus and Alexander Goldenweiser, they represent the modern school of Russian pianism.

The 1880s and 1890s witnessed the birth of many Russian pianists who made enviable careers as virtuoso performers and teachers. The most notable Chopin players among them were Leonid Kreutzer, Leff Pouishnoff and Simon Barer (pupils of Essipov), Tina Lerner (who studied with Pabst and Godowsky), Harry Neuhaus (a pupil of Godowsky and Michałowski) and Mischa Levitzki (taught by Michałowski, Dohnányi and Stojowski). Annette Essipov had been one of the greatest pupils of Leschetizky, and his second wife, and all the pianists who studied with her came indirectly under the influence of the great pedagogue. Leonid Kreutzer was himself a very able teacher, who edited Chopin's works and made a number of discs of the highest quality. He was a spontaneous pianist, whose interpretations were well-conceived and full-toned, both these strengths being characteristic of Essipov's performances. Kreutzer was able to feel the rhythm of the Waltzes and Polonaises with a refreshing natural ease, and his disc of the C sharp minor Mazurka, Op. 41 No. 1, is especially successful. In the 1930s he emigrated to Japan, where he remained until his death in 1953.

Tina Lerner's name is unfamiliar in Britain, although she was a major artist of international acclaim. Born around 1890, she made her debut in Moscow in 1904 playing the 'Emperor' Concerto. In 1915 she married the violinist and conductor Vladimir Shavitch in San Francisco, and she joined the piano faculty of the College of Fine Arts at Syracuse University in 1926; at the end of her life she moved to Florence to live with her daughter. Tina Lerner had a reputation for being a difficult artist, though a brilliant pianist. When she played at the Queen's Hall in

---

* A four-record set of Igumnov's discs was issued by Melodya on 33C 10–05519–26, including a previously unissued 78 recording from 1935 of the Mazurka in B major, Op. 56 No. 1.

London in 1911, a critic remarked on her 'wonderful interpretation of Chopin's F minor Concerto. . . . Seldom has this beautiful work been rendered with such perfect sympathy and comprehension, and the brilliant Russian received a well-merited ovation at the close.' However, the critic of the *Monthly Musical Record* thought she took liberties with the tempo of the music – presumably excessive *rubato*. Hans Richter, who had conducted this concert, described her playing as 'magnificent', and it is regrettable that she made no recordings that have come to light, other than some piano rolls which include a wholly misconceived performance of the C sharp minor Etude, Op. 10 No. 4, which has been transcribed onto long-playing record from an Ampico roll.

Many Russian pianists have had a rather perplexing approach to the keyboard; there seems sometimes to be a dichotomy between their musical and pianistic personalities, the first inclining towards the poetic expression of their innermost feelings, the second inclining towards extrovert virtuoso display and dazzling aural effects. The case of Mischa Levitzki well exemplifies this paradox. His name is now only familiar to collectors of old piano discs, for he died tragically when only forty-three, but had he lived to resolve some problems of stylistic integration, he might well have become one of the greatest pianists of the century. He was born in Krementchug in Russia in 1898 when his parents, who were naturalized Americans, were on a visit to their fatherland. At the age of seven, Levitzki was sent to Warsaw to study with Aleksander Michałowski, and he also attended the Institute of Musical Art in New York (later incorporated into the Juilliard School of Music), under the supervision of Sigismund Stojowski, finishing his training with Dohnányi in Berlin. Levitzki's playing suggests that his approach to Chopin owed much to Michałowski.

Levitzki's performances compel one to question the artistic basis of his playing. In his later discs particularly, there seems to be an emphasis on pianistic perfection which excludes emotional involvement, and though everything is played with a sumptuously warm tone, this detracts from the scope of the music. Another factor which complicates his artistic personality is that he often chose to record salon music which, although much of it is well-written (such as his own compositions and those by Moszkowski and Tchaikovsky), is not the sort of music that most serious pianists would want to leave for posterity. Most of his serious records are of Liszt and Chopin, and his only recorded performance of a concerto was the Liszt E flat. Of the large-scale works of Chopin, there are the A flat Ballade, the C sharp minor Scherzo, the C minor Nocturne, Op. 48 No. 1, and the A flat Polonaise. There are also Ampico rolls of the A flat Ballade, the F minor Fantasy, the F minor Nocturne, Op. 55 No. 1, and several other smaller works.

The chief attributes of Levitzki's playing were an extraordinarily beautiful tone, great clarity of texture, and a royal technique; it is only in the area of emotional commitment that one questions the stature of his performances. The sham melodrama that occasionally marred some of Hofmann's late readings was quite foreign to him, and he was incapable of playing in a manner that distorted the music. One of his best records is an early (1923) disc of the A flat Etude, Op. 25 No. 1, which he plays with immeasurable good taste and attention to detail. Instead of treating the inner melodic lines in a carefree manner, Levitzki plays them with as much careful shaping as the top treble line. The C sharp minor Scherzo was another of his most successful Chopin discs: the descending quaver sweeps are richly sonorous and colourful, and the coda is as exciting as the opening bars. The A flat Polonaise however is disappointing; the pianist sounds rather bored with the music, and the general effect is pedestrian. His performances of the C minor Nocturne (not originally issued) and the A flat Ballade are not wholly satisfactory – the cohesion of each piece is diminished by the pianist's basic lack of involvement. However, Levitzki understood the capabilities of the piano as did few others – perhaps only Hofmann, Godowsky, Barer, Rachmaninov, Busoni and Lhévinne – and he was able to explore and master the most intimate nuances of the instrument. His approach to the piano was one of quiet confidence and calm that was unusual in those days of exhibitionism,[22] and he seems to have bridged the gap between the nineteenth and twentieth century schools of playing.

The Revolution of 1917 had a traumatic effect on music-making in Russia. Many artists disagreed with the policies of the new regime in regard to music, and many felt a wider lack of sympathy which led them to leave their homeland. It is perhaps only in the present generation that artists in the USSR have become fully integrated into the Communist ideological system. Those mature musicians who stayed in Russia after 1917 were forced to restrict their repertoire to conform with the requirements of narrow-minded bureaucrats, and to endure severe restrictions on their freedom of movement. But those who left Russia lost much of their artistic stability, and many musicians who moved to the New World found that American audiences applauded a more brash style of performing than they had cultivated in Russia. Such pianists as Horowitz and Brailowsky relied on their fabulous technique for much of their early acclaim in the United States.

This tendency is relevant to the career of Leff Pouishnoff, a near contemporary of Levitzki, and whose performances contain even more paradoxes. Born in Kiev in 1891, he was a child prodigy, and studied with Essipov and with the composers Liadov and Glazounov. After the

Revolution he came to live in England, which remained his base, although he made many successful tours to the United States. Pouishnoff used sometimes to have himself billed as 'The Greatest Chopin Player in the World', which of course led to his being ridiculed by many members of his profession. However, it is questionable whether Pouishnoff actually believed this claim, and his behaviour is more understandable if his self-publicizing is viewed as part of the quest for recognition of an alien artist. A musician friend of mine, who heard Pouishnoff many times, remarked that she noticed during his recitals that the easier the music was, the worse he played it! But another acquaintance has told me she considered Pouishnoff's Chopin the best she had ever heard, and she was taking many famous artists into account. The two views are reconcilable if, as is suggested from other evidence, Pouishnoff's playing varied a good deal in quality. Apparently he sometimes allowed his immense technique to cloud his musical judgment in order to increase his popularity with the musically less-aware members of his audience.

If there was little emotional stability in Pouishnoff's playing, the beauty of his tone is undeniable. Most of his Chopin discs are convincing: the *Polonaise-Fantaisie* is especially imaginative, and his very crisp fingerwork is ideally suited to the E flat Rondo, Op. 16, both of which he recorded on LP in his later years. His earlier 78s of Chopin are all distinguished and tasteful, with careful attention to style and detail, though there are later performances, such as the Barcarolle, in which he overdoes his displays of passion, and a nearly first-rate interpretation becomes mannered and exaggerated. Pouishnoff was a natural musician who lacked that final ounce of artistic consistency that raises a very good pianist into an immortal one.

Another Russian pianist whose name must be mentioned at this point, although he was not primarily a Chopin player, was Simon Barer, who studied with Essipov and Felix Blumenfeld, Horowitz's teacher. His greatest attribute was his technique, which well merits the overused adjective 'legendary'. He was a sensitive musician, whose tone and general control over the resources of the keyboard were only equalled by Godowsky, Lhévinne and Hofmann. Nevertheless, his playing lacks musical interest, even though he was capable of arousing extraordinary excitement – his performance on disc of the coda of the C sharp minor Scherzo has rarely been equalled in drama. Barer's playing can be compared with a present-day pianist who follows rather the same path, the Cuban-American Jorge Bolet. Both seem to be sensitive musicians who are nevertheless satisfied with portraying Chopin as a composer who aimed primarily to draw dramatic contrasts and express these through the medium of beautiful sounds. However, the genius of

Chopin contains something more profound than this; he was able to convey, through the sounds of the piano, emotions and sentiments inexpressible in the human vocabulary, and the listener can find his aspirations and thoughts mirrored in Chopin's music in a unique way. The performer has to act as an intermediary in this process, and if he only manages to please the ear and arouse excitement, he has failed. The greater the pianist's technique, the more difficult he finds it to achieve artistically satisfying results – he can easily do too much. However, if Horowitz and Hofmann had been able to use their technique to reproduce the music in its simplest and most direct form, their careers would probably have been less spectacular. A pianist such as Barer, whose principal aim was to play with the greatest beauty of sound, often failed to communicate the essence of the music – his approach became over-sophisticated and dehumanized. His performances of the A flat Waltz, Op. 42, and the C sharp minor Scherzo have the finish of a master-craftsman, but they lack perspective.

Another pianist of the same generation, Harry Neuhaus, was one of the best-known teachers of the present century. A cousin of Karol Szymanowski, he had lessons from Aleksander Michałowski, and so received the training of a great Chopin tradition; he was also a champion of Scriabin. Neuhaus taught at the Moscow Conservatory from 1922 until his death in 1964, and was also an accomplished performer, though towards the end of his life he seldom played in public as he suffered acutely from bad nerves.[23] Among his best pupils were the established Chopin players Sviatoslav Richter, Emil Gilels, his son Stanislav Neuhaus, Jakov Zak (winner of the third Chopin Competition), Alexander Slobodyanik, Vladimir Kraiynev, Yevgeny Malinin, Ryszard Bakst, Tatiana Goldfarb and Tamara Gusyeva.

Neuhaus recorded the E minor Concerto (his favourite among all concertos), the B minor Sonata, the F minor Fantasy, the E flat Rondo Op. 16, the Berceuse and the *Polonaise-Fantaisie*. As he relates in his book, *The Art of Piano Playing*, he had very small hands and encountered considerable problems because of this. In the second subject of the first movement of the E minor Concerto there are several bars that require the pianist to play the melody with right-hand *legato* octaves: Neuhaus would have found this difficult, as his recording of the work, from the late 1950s, demonstrates. The melodic lines are communicated on a deep level, but when the writing becomes more taxing the pianist obviously has to struggle. The second movement is thus more successful, and the general approach is dreamy and lyrical; the finale has plenty of caprice. This recording may well not show Neuhaus at his best, but from all accounts his Chopin was poetic and sensitive, if slightly feminine. Neuhaus's approach to Chopin's music, as to Scriabin's, was that the listener should be raised to a higher plane of vision, and that the heroic aspects of the music should never be allowed to obscure the lyricism; this view is surely not inconsistent with Chopin's own thoughts.

A greater pianist, who shares these musical sympathies and managed to put much of Neuhaus's thinking into practice, was the late Vladimir Sofronitsky. Born in 1902 (some sources say 1901), his family moved to Warsaw when he was very young, and he studied there with Anna Gecewicz and Michałowski. Returning to St Petersburg, he became a pupil of Leonid Nikolayev (who taught Shostakovitch) and studied composition with Glazounov. Sofronitsky was widely regarded as the finest exponent of Scriabin, and was a pianist with an almost mystical imagination, allied to a brilliant virtuoso technique; he was almost a cult figure when he died in 1961.

A number of Sofronitsky's live performances were captured on tape and transferred to record, and demonstrate his compelling artistry. Chopin was his special interest after Scriabin, and he was very successful in the larger works. Not particularly concerned with the composer's exact markings, Sofronitsky's aim was always to present the music as a spontaneous re-creation; his involvement with the music he played was almost obsessive. A performance of the D flat Prelude, Op. 28 No. 15, the so-called 'Raindrop', has a startling vividness: the lovely right-hand tone in the opening melody is counteracted by the remorseless repetition of the A flats in the left hand, which convey an almost insane compulsion. The composer is revealed as full of bitterness, and never attaining fulfilment. Despite the ambitious nature of Sofronitsky's aims, there was no element of pretension in his playing. The first few pages of his reading of the F minor Fantasy set a meditative mood, and he takes the listener through an odyssean journey of artistic discovery. The freedom of his phrasing typifies the natural, Polish approach to Chopin's music, and the tremendous excitement generated in the climaxes has seldom been equalled. Sofronitsky obviously had a very strong personality, and the heroic aspect of his nature is well demonstrated in a very compelling performance of the F sharp minor Polonaise, Op. 44, in which there is some amazing bravura. The performances recorded in the last years of his life are a little uneven, but a version of the C sharp minor Etude, Op. 10 No. 4, from this period is one of the best readings of this dynamic work ever to be captured on disc. This is playing in the best tradition of Anton Rubinstein.

In comparison with Sofronitsky, many Russian pianists of his period sound prosaic, but not of course the outstanding artists Alexander Uninsky, Jakov Flier, Lev Oborin, Vladimir Horowitz and Shura Cherkassky. There were also a number of lesser pianists, such as Yuri Bryushkov, Vera Razoumovskaya, Grigory Ginzburg, Abram Lufer and

Pavel Serebryakov, and all of these pianists participated in the Warsaw Chopin Competitions.

Lev Oborin, born in 1907, was a pupil of Igumnov, and won the first Chopin Competition in 1927. From 1935 until his death nearly forty years later he devoted much of his life to teaching, although he used to perform with the violinist David Oistrakh. He was essentially a modern pianist, who played the music exactly as it was written. But he was also a real poet, and the style that won him many admirers at the Competition changed little over the years. His recordings of the E flat minor Etude, Op. 10 No. 6, and the F minor, F major and E minor Etudes, numbers 2, 3 and 5 from Op. 25, show him to have had a full tone and a rich imagination, the ideal equipment for a Chopin player. His pupils Vladimir Ashkenazy, Mikhail Voskresenski,[24] Tamara Gusyeva and Irena Smolena are all highly regarded in Chopin, and share a basically direct approach.

Alexander Uninsky was a pianist more in the French tradition than in the Russian. Born in 1910, he studied at the Kiev Conservatory with Sergei Tarnowsky,* a pupil of Essipov, and also at the Paris Conservatoire with Lazare Lévy. At the second Chopin Competition in 1932, Uninsky and the blind Hungarian Imre Ungar both won the same number of points, and the winner was decided by tossing a coin; Uninsky won. Ungar was a more dynamic player, and the more original in Chopin, but Uninsky's quality as a pianist of the first rank was never doubted.

Uninsky joined the French army during the Second World War, and after the war settled in Toronto, where he performed and taught until his death in 1973. He had a very large technique, and could always be relied upon to play big virtuoso works, such as the Brahms B flat Piano Concerto, with great finish and aplomb. His style was more suave and more contained than that of most Russians; everything was well-ordered, a little detached, and in perfect taste. His playing of Chopin employed minimal *rubato*, and he favoured fast and brilliant tempos. His disc of the twenty-four Etudes is a fitting memorial to his immaculate approach; the inner lines are brought out with exemplary clarity, and all the textures are entirely apt. His natural-sounding readings display a combination of study and innate flair.

The late Jakov Flier, very well-known as a teacher in the USSR, was another good Chopin player who never attracted much attention in Western Europe, though some of his discs, especially that of the B flat minor Sonata, have been much admired. His phrasing suggests that he was a romantic rather than a modern pianist, but although they are im-

---

* Tarnowsky also gave some lessons to Vladimir Horowitz, and later settled in the United States; in the 1970s he made an unusual record of Russian salon music.

aginative, his recordings show a lack of artistic consistency. The most impressive are the Barcarolle and the E flat minor Polonaise, Op. 26 No. 2, the former distinguished by large-scaled, relaxed phrasing, and the latter by great vividness.

The best characteristics of the Russian school are apparent in the playing of Ginzburg, Bryushkov and Serebryakov, all of whom played with a full tone, had large techniques, and took a broad view of Chopin's music. They were trained before the Revolution, and belong to a tradition that is fast disappearing.

The most celebrated Russian pianist born in these years before the First World War is Vladimir Horowitz, whose reputation as a great Chopin player was established in the 1920s. Although he now plays as much of the music of Liszt and Schumann, Chopin's music still has the highest place in his repertoire. Horowitz was born in Kiev in 1904, and studied with Sergei Tarnowsky and Felix Blumenfeld. He was trained in the romantic tradition, and his approach to Chopin's music is quite different from that of Lev Oborin or Alexander Uninsky. His family left Russia after the Revolution, and after making a reputation in Europe, Horowitz settled in the United States. His phenomenal technique has seldom been equalled, and never surpassed. It allows him to do whatever he wishes with Chopin's music, and it is a tribute to his musical judgment that he very rarely distorts the composer's works by pyrotechnic display. Horowitz's technique, especially in more recent years, has always taken a second place to his artistry, and he resembles Chopin himself in his intensely nervous and energetic character.

When the late Neville Cardus wrote that Vladimir Horowitz was surely the greatest living pianist, the greatest who had ever lived, and the greatest who could ever live, he was perhaps carried away by the euphoria of hearing Horowitz play at a concert.[25] The magnetism this pianist generates seems not to depend on the quality of music he plays, but to arise from the way he plays it. Horowitz's versatility is immense. He plays the music of Scarlatti, for example, with great simplicity and purity of texture, yet he also enjoys works that demand massive, almost orchestral, effects. Josef Lhévinne probably excelled in particular areas of technique (Chopin's Etude in thirds, for example), but Horowitz demonstrates a complete command of Chopin's most taxing works. He took up the mantle of the great Russian pianists of the past, and plays with a refinement that belongs to a bygone age. He has that acute sense of rhythm that seems ideal for every aspect of Chopin's writing, and plays the Mazurkas with an absolute mastery over their musical variety and insight.

It is revealing that many of Horowitz's favourite works of Chopin were those that the composer himself liked most: the G minor Ballade and the A minor Waltz, Op. 34 No. 2, in particular. His performance of the former, whether from live recitals or the recording studio, illustrates many aspects of his view of Chopin's music. Horowitz favours a shallow-toned Steinway with a brittle attack, and this colours the character of many of his interpretations in a highly individual manner. These taut-sounding pianos have a range of sound very different from those of Chopin's day, and Horowitz's tone has a knife-edge definition that was unobtainable on the older pianos, with their more muffled tones. The variety of his playing can be witnessed in the G minor Ballade, where his phrasing has the greatest freedom, and he moves from the gently intimate to the explosive, from great ease to enormous tension. The opening rising motif has an unshakeable firmness of purpose that immediately shows Horowitz's view of Chopin as a strong and determined personality; the phrasing of the second subject is beautifully moulded, and the ensuing climaxes show that the instrument he prefers imposes no limitation on his objectives; the final coda, played *piano* rather than *fortissimo* as written, is of unparalleled excitement, and his famous octave-playing rounds off this work with magnificent power. Horowitz always visualizes the longer compositions as a whole, and never gets lost in detail.

Unfortunately, he has not recorded the Concertos, the B minor Sonata or the Berceuse, and he is not a pianist to record complete sets of works – there are no discs of his playing the twenty-four Preludes or fourteen Waltzes. It is difficult to single out his best performances, but in my opinion his most notable successes include the disc of the B flat minor Sonata, the *Polonaise-Fantaisie*, the F sharp major Nocturne, Op. 15 No. 2, and some of the Mazurkas, Etudes and Waltzes. Of his virtuoso readings, the more recent discs of the B minor Scherzo are better than the older ones, and the *Andante Spianato and Grande Polonaise Brillante* shows wonderfully crisp and vital playing.

Horowitz does not always opt for fast tempos; what sounds very fast is often actually slower than the performances of other artists. For example, he takes the 'Black Key' Etude more slowly than many other pianists – Backhaus, Cortot, Novaës, Levitzki and Hambourg all play the work more quickly. In the Nocturnes he generally takes a very relaxed pace, and concentrates above all on shaping the melodic lines. Horowitz's Chopin is generally less weighty, if less spontaneous, than that of Rachmaninov, and his textures are more sharply defined. Despite playing the mature works with a serious insight, he can also unwind to play the early ones with plenty of youthful zest, illustrating a complete grasp of Chopin's idiom.

Horowitz has consistently championed works of Chopin which used seldom to feature on recital programmes. In the happy and youthful E flat Rondo, Op. 16, the E major Scherzo and little-played Nocturnes and Mazurkas, he has shown that all of Chopin's works are the products of a creative genius. The *Polonaise-Fantaisie* was until recently seldom played in public, and Paderewski considered it inferior to the other Polonaises, but Horowitz reveals it as a work representing Chopin at his pinnacle as a composer.

There have been times when he has produced a Horowitzian, rather than a Chopinesque, approach, the worst example of this being the performance of the B minor Scherzo from a recital at Carnegie Hall in 1953,* but he has in recent years shown a real concern only to transmit the essence of Chopin's music and let virtuoso display take second place. His Chopin has a regular style, and is free from any idiosyncratic delving into inner lines; everything is in proportion. This is one of the factors that makes him the genius that he is – he has a definite way of doing things that is clearly recognizable, whereas some pianists present a hotch-potch of styles. The public can therefore 'get to know' Horowitz's Chopin, and the way that he plays certain works. But he is too great an artist to play all the pieces in the same way, and he finds in the music a variety which constantly fires his imagination.

Some seven years younger than Vladimir Horowitz, the Russian pianist Shura Cherkassky is another Chopin player who commands the greatest attention. An extraordinary child prodigy, he conducted a symphony orchestra and wrote a five-act opera while still in his teens.[26] Cherkassky was born in Odessa in 1911, and studied with his mother, Lydia Cherkassky, herself a pupil of Annette Essipov. He went to the United States after the Revolution, and became a pupil of Josef Hofmann and David Saperton. Cherkassky was Hofmann's greatest pupil, but his playing is not a blueprint of his master's, and Hofmann is said to have acknowledged this himself. Cherkassky's playing of Chopin has nearly all the strengths that Hofmann brought to the works, and virtually none of the weaknesses. A staggering technician, with very small hands (like his master), Cherkassky does not shirk any of Chopin's music, however difficult; Hofmann avoided works which he did not think showed him in the very best light.

Cherkassky's art relies more on spontaneous whim than that of any pianist now active before the public, and this approach can lead to problems, especially when he is not in the right mood. His singing tone in melodic lines is as rich as Hofmann's, and his attention to inner lines is equally great, although Cherkassky somehow manages to integrate more naturally than his master. When playing at his best, Cherkassky

---

* This concert was arranged to celebrate the twenty-fifth anniversary of his American debut; soon afterwards, Horowitz retired from public performance for more than a decade.

can give totally convincing performances of certain works; amongst the most successful I have heard in live recital are the E flat Nocturne, Op. 55 No. 2, the B flat minor Sonata, the Barcarolle, the B flat minor Scherzo, the F minor Ballade, and the F sharp minor Polonaise, Op. 44. It would be almost impossible to give an accurate description of how he plays a particular work, for his performances change from one recital to the next. He has an extraordinarily wide repertoire, and so cannot really be termed a Chopin specialist, although at his best he is certainly one of the greatest living Chopin players. He makes relatively few discs, although he has over the years recorded a fairly large proportion of Chopin's works. The characteristics of his Chopin include a luscious tone, attention to the polyphonic side of the music, marvellously detailed phrasing, and a grasp of the overall shape of a work. It would be impossible to say that he favours fast tempos, because he never follows any rules. He is like a magician at the keyboard, conjuring up near-miraculous sounds that the most assiduous listener may hear only once in a lifetime from another pianist. His artistry is often taken far too much for granted, and some have scoffed at his playing of classical composers, such as Beethoven, Schubert and Brahms. But he holds a unique place amongst the pianists of today because he upholds the old values of beautiful sounds and nuances.

Cherkassky's attention to tone is one of the most necessary attributes for a great Chopin player, as is real familiarity with the idiom. Deriving from the tradition of Anton Rubinstein, whose 'grand-pupil' he is through Hofmann, Cherkassky never allows his music-making to become stale. His nature has more genuine spontaneity than that of Hofmann, and so his priorities are better combined. Many have remarked that he takes liberties with Chopin, but it is often his departures from routine interpretation that bring the music to life. He is one of the few pianists who play Chopin's early C minor Sonata, and other little-played works, such as the 'Là ci darem la mano' Variations, the Tarantelle, the Bolero and the *Allegro de Concert*.

Sviatoslav Richter, Emil Gilels and Jakov Zak were all born within five years of Cherkassky, but from a superficial level they appear to approach their instrument in a very different way. Richter and Gilels have achieved their fame in the West playing music by composers other than Chopin: both have recorded concertos by Brahms, and works by Bach, Schumann, Schubert, Liszt and Prokofiev, but very little by Chopin. However, every Russian pianist of standing in this century has played a great deal of Chopin. His music features as strongly in the teaching material of the Russian academies as it does in France, and the Russians approach Chopin as a composer with whom they can identify particularly closely. Although a number of Russian composers in the last century, including Liadov, Liapunov, Tchaikovsky, Arensky and Balakirev, wrote keyboard music of a high quality, none of them are comparable with Chopin. His music provides Russian artists with a ready vehicle for self-expression immediately suited to their temperament, and has always been popular with them, and Richter, although his repertoire includes a great deal of Bach, Schubert, Beethoven, Debussy and Prokofiev, plays nearly as much Chopin.

Born in Zhitomir in 1914, Richter came from a musical family, and was spurred on by his father, a competent pianist. He gave his first concert in Odessa at the comparatively late age of twenty, and three years later went to Moscow to study with the great teacher Harry Neuhaus, graduating in 1947. He was awarded the Stalin Prize in 1949, but on account of the Cold War did not play in the United States until 1960, when he gave a series of recitals in Chicago and New York. Since then, his reception in the West has always been rapturous, and his concerts in London are sold out soon after they are announced. Richter possesses a techique as powerful as Horowitz or Michelangeli, but it is not this feature of his playing that attracts acclaim; it is his stirring and deep musicianship, which derives from an almost limitless musical imagination. Richter's eminence is unquestionable, but it is perhaps unfortunate that his popularity has to some extent rested on political factors, and the result has been that his concerts have sometimes received ecstatic applause which has not always been merited by his performances, which are sometimes very detached.

I particularly associate Richter with the *Polonaise-Fantaisie*, the Barcarolle, the Op. 34 Waltzes, the C sharp minor Polonaise, Op. 26 No. 1, and some of the Etudes. His degree of involvement in the music seems to vary from one recital to the next, as does his use of tone and his general stylistic approach. Halina Czerny-Stefańska, herself one of the greatest Chopin players, recalled to me a performance of the F minor Concerto in which Richter held down the *una corda* pedal throughout the performance![27] In recent years, he has seldom used the full range of dynamics, and seems to deliberately scale down the sonorities he uses in Chopin so as not to overstep those the composer intended. However, Richter can also play like an undisciplined savage, with little regard to the limits of taste, as is witnessed by two different versions of the G minor Ballade captured on disc from live performances several years ago. Here the pianist plays the *presto con fuoco* coda with a total disregard for propriety and balance, and forces his fingers to play at an almost impossible speed.

But these peculiarities are unimportant compared with the factors that make Richter a great performer of Chopin's music. In the first place, it is clear that he has rethought his Chopin over the years, and developed the more rarefied and luminous textures of the music. There is little overt emotionalism in his Chopin today, whereas an early performance of the F major Ballade on a Melodya disc demonstrates a furious anger, which only attains relief in the working out of passion in the coda; the final entry of the opening quiet bars is just like the last words of the narrator in Schubert's 'Erlkönig' – 'das Kind . . . war tot.' Richter now represents the composer as being more remote and detached from earthly matters.

The avid collector can find Richter's performances of all four Ballades, the four Scherzos, about ten Etudes and several smaller pieces on disc, nearly all from live recitals (many of them pirated). There is also a very interesting version of the *Andante Spianato and Grand Polonaise Brillante* with orchestra, from a live concert; the opening movement has a lovely calm, and the ensuing dance is played with minimal *rubato*. Richter takes a stately view of the Polonaise, and every embellishment is executed with minute accuracy; there is no trace of the irritating histrionics Hofmann brought to this work. The imaginative use of colour Richter displays here is also demonstrated in his different recordings of the *Polonaise-Fantaisie*: an aura of mystery is created, and the dance elements are treated in an impressionistic manner. Nevertheless the climaxes are passionate enough, and the pianist uses the work to show Chopin as a revolutionary composer – his roots were in the classical tradition, but there are elements in his compositions that point to the music of the twentieth century.

Richter is one of the supreme Bach players of our time; his grasp over the intricacies of contrapuntal style is absolute, and so he is admirably equipped to exploit this aspect of Chopin's writing. Thus his playing of the C sharp minor Etude, Op. 25 No. 7, is highly successful – the pianist does not treat this as a cold study, but brings out the various lines with a compelling warmth of tone. In gentle pieces such as this, Richter's emphasis is always on delicacy of sound and light textures, best exemplified in his playing of the little Waltz in A minor, Op. 34 No. 2 (Chopin's favourite), and the middle section of the E minor Etude, Op. 25 No. 5, where he brings out left-hand lines that most other pianists ignore. Something very special happens when Richter, at his best, plays Chopin – or the music of any other composer.

Of the same generation and standing, Emil Gilels is generally a more even performer, and some regard him as Richter's equal. Born in Odessa in 1916, he studied with Berthe Ringold, who was his most influential teacher, and later with Harry Neuhaus at the Moscow Conservatory.[28] He made his debut at the age of thirteen in his native city, and won first prize at the Queen Elisabeth Competition in Brussels in 1938. (It is surprising that when he entered an All-Ukrainian Piano Competition in 1931 he failed to win a prize, and yet the discs he made within three years of that event are very impressive.)

Gilels's style has changed greatly over the years. His recordings show that his early priorities were high bravura and daring pianism, and that he had an almost improvisatory approach to any music that was rhapsodic in form; this was ideally suited to Liszt. A recording of Chopin's G minor Ballade from before the Second World War begins with great pathos, and progresses to climaxes of tremendous force and grandeur, comparable with Horowitz's performances of the same work. In those days Gilels's playing was much more elastic than it is today, especially in phrasing. One recording from the period when his style was evolving into that which is more familiar to today's record enthusiasts is that of the 1951 performance of the *Andante Spianato and Grande Polonaise Brillante* with orchestra. Gilels plays this with a more full-blooded tone than Richter; he uses the virtuoso writing, rather than the dance elements, to make his impact. These readings have a largesse of character in depicting the exuberance of an uninhibited composer – this is a relatively young Gilels playing a young Chopin.

These can be compared with Gilels's interpretations of the E minor Concerto, two of which have been captured on disc: a live performance with Kondrashin conducting (from the 1950s) and a studio recording with Ormandy (1964). The live performance is the more spontaneous – this is a warm-hearted Chopin: the second is in the modern tradition, which eschews pianistic display for its own sake. There is a sense of deep involvement by the pianist in the meaning of every note of the solo part, and the general impression is one of seriousness. The coda of the first movement, which often sounds like a meaningless toccata-like display of rapid figurations, becomes under Gilels's hands a passionate plea following on from what has already transpired. The heroic drama of the movement reaches a culmination here, as if Chopin has reached a breaking-point. Gilels's refined pianism allows him to concentrate a wealth of emotion into each note of the Larghetto, and the Finale comes as a light-hearted respite.

In the mature works, such as the B flat minor 'Funeral March' Sonata, Gilels portrays a far more profound Chopin, and underlines the philosophic weight of the music; his Chopin is as powerful as Beethoven. Surprisingly, he does not observe the first movement repeat, with the result that the whole range of fervent emotions is conveyed in a very concise span, the only calm being the reappearance of the second subject in the development section. The poetry, emphasized by Kempff for example, gives way to a dynamic and forceful interpretation, and Gilels also employs extremely fast tempos. Since he plays with a much fuller sound, Gilels is able to communicate where Richter sounds remote. Directness of statement also distinguishes his reading of the Funeral March from that of Cortot or Rachmaninov, and he plays the Finale *prestissimo*, giving a whirlwind kaleidoscope of Chopin's musical personality.

Gilels's reading of Chopin is both original and consistent. In 1979, he played the B minor Sonata at the Royal Festival Hall, and gave a delicately shaded performance of the first movement reminiscent of Josef Hofmann. On that occasion he showed the emotional reserve absent in his early recordings, and donned the garb of 'Chopin the dreamer' to cast a spell of magical sounds. Gilels's artistry is unique, and on account of his large repertoire he brings to the music a wider perspective than most Chopin specialists.

The pianist Jakov Zak lacked the artistry of Richter or Gilels, but had a wide following in Eastern Europe. He won the 1937 Chopin Competition over such entrants as Witold Małcużyński, Agi Jámbor, Monique de la Bruchollerie, Jan Ekier and Robert Goldsand, by virtue of the maturity and tonal colour of his playing, and he also won the special prize for the best performance of the Mazurkas. His disc of the Mazurkas in C sharp minor, Op. 63 No. 3, and C minor, Op. 30 No. 1, show him as a fluent and natural player, and his grasp of the smaller works is also illustrated by his recordings of the Waltzes in F major, Op. 34 No. 3, and B minor, Op. 69 No. 2. He has recorded the Brahms and Prokofiev Concertos and is not primarily a Chopin specialist.

The pianists now being described show the results of the 'modern approach' adopted by great teachers such as Neuhaus, Igumnov, Flier, Goldenweiser and even Essipov, who managed to instil into their pupils the priorities of discipline and attention to the spirit of the music. If the idea that Chopin was merely a salon composer belongs to the more distant past, these teachers have also rejected the view that he is a composer whose music could be interpreted merely in pianistic terms. All of them, like the great Polish teachers Żurawlew, Drzewiecki and Trombini-Kazuro, were passionately devoted to Chopin's music, and firmly convinced that it was sufficiently distinguished to be classed with the sonatas of Beethoven and Brahms. Like Anton Rubinstein, these Russian teachers have discovered the richness of Chopin's works, and have been able to communicate this to their pupils. Richter and Gilels belong to the first generation of pianists who have entirely cast aside the traditional idea of the Chopin player as a melodramatic figure, making grand and overblown gestures, though there are still some performers today who follow this outdated tradition.

There are other Russian pianists of somewhat lesser genius who have followed the same lines of development as Richter and Gilels. Some are little known outside the Soviet Union; others have made their career almost entirely in the West, such as Nina Milkina (b. 1919), who left Russia as a child and studied in London with the late Harold Craxton and Tobias Matthay, and in Paris with a Professor Conus, who had formerly been a teacher at the Moscow Conservatory. Milkina is not really a Chopin specialist, but she has recorded the complete Mazurkas, and these show a loving attention to every detail of the score. The career of Rosa Tamarkina (1920–50) was cut short by her tragically early death, at the age of only thirty; she had a brilliant talent. A pupil of Goldenweiser, she came second in the third Chopin Competition, over the head of Małcużyński, when she was only seventeen. Unfortunately, none of her discs have been circulated outside the Soviet Union, although she made a recording of the C sharp minor Scherzo and other works. Tatiana Goldfarb (1914–64) was a pupil of Neuhaus, and made a reputation as a Chopin player before devoting herself to teaching. A more interesting pianist is Oleg Bochnyakovitch, who has recorded a strikingly original performance of the B minor Sonata. His playing in this reading is very idiomatic, beautifully judged, and executed with exemplary technical mastery. A pupil of Igumnov and Neuhaus, his approach is a good deal more old-fashioned than that of Gilels or Richter. Vera Gornostayeva is another pianist and teacher who plays Chopin with spontaneity and taste; very direct in the Mazurkas, she has a feminine and refreshingly unpretentious musical personality.

Tatiana Nikolayeva (b. 1924) is another artist not much known in the West, except as an adjudicator on the jury of piano competitions. She won the first prize at the inaugural International Bach Competition in Leipzig in 1950. She is a composer of note,* and as a pianist has a technique equal to that of Richter or Gilels. Although not pre-eminently a Chopin player, she has recorded the F sharp minor Polonaise, Op. 44, the Bolero, and the seldom-played *Variations Brillantes*, Op. 12, which display her ability to adapt her style to whatever music she plays; she has no qualms in varying the tempo considerably in the introduction to the variations. However, Bach's *Art of Fugue* is more her line. Victor Merzhanov (b. 1919) has perhaps a less dazzling talent, but he has made some extremely impressive discs of Chopin's music, notably the twenty-four Preludes. A highly imaginative artist, he won the first prize at the All-Union Competition for Interpretative Musicians competing against Richter in 1945, and his Chopin has sensitivity as well as virtuoso dash.

A Chopin player of quite another category was the late Stanislav Neuhaus (1927–1980), the son of the famous teacher, who began giving concerts in 1949, and toured in Poland, Hungary, France and Italy.

* Her Piano Concerto No. 1 has been recorded with the composer as soloist and Kondrashin conducting the USSR State Symphony, on USSR D 0264 (from the early 1950s).

Towards the end of his life he suffered from acute mental problems, and these regrettably restricted his concert activity. He followed in the tradition of the great romantic pianists – Horowitz and Rachmaninov – and like Horowitz gave performances scattered with wrong notes that never marred the general effect. A very powerful technician, his Chopin had the greatest dynamism and momentum. He had the gadfly sensitivity of an Argerich, and was ideal in the more rhapsodic works, such as the Barcarolle and the F minor Ballade. A romantic figure at the keyboard, Neuhaus had few qualms in altering Chopin's dynamic markings and varying the tempos, but he nevertheless managed to make his readings appear to be allied with the intentions of the composer. His art has been described as a development of that of his father, but Harry Neuhaus was drawn to Chopin's lighter, optimistic works while the dramatic and heroic aspects of the music were more attractive to his son.[29] In the F minor Ballade, Stanislav Neuhaus had the technique to achieve climaxes in a manner equalled only by pianists such as Horowitz, Bolet or Hofmann, and his emotional commitment to the music was such that his effects never seemed mere outbursts of temperament, but almost to represent the way Chopin might have played, had he had the resources to do so.

Emotional identification with Chopin's music is also an important component in the playing of Bella Davidovitch (b. 1928). One of the last pupils of Igumnov, she also had lessons with his successor, Jakov Flier, and in 1949 was joint winner of the Chopin Competition with Halina Czerny-Stefańska. Her spiritual identification with the composer is extraordinary, and I shall never forget listening to a tape of her performance of the Barcarolle, in an attic of the Chopin Institute in Warsaw very early one morning in 1978; the sincerity of the reading made this a remarkable experience, and her performance was distinguished by an unusual direction of purpose, as if she aimed to take hold of the listener's imagination and lead it through the vicissitudes of human experience, each phrase having a yearning inexpressible in words.

Bella Davidovitch has recorded the four Impromptus, both Concertos, the fourteen Waltzes, and some mixed recitals, and though these discs are of varying quality that of the Waltzes is one of the most pleasing interpretations of these pieces available. The bright, early compositions such as the F major, Op. 34 No. 3, have plenty of virtuoso *brio*, and this is well-contrasted with those later works that require more pathos and depth of expression. In the first movement of the E minor Concerto, the pianist opts for sedate tempos which allow her to underline the meaning of every note, and under her hands the four Impromptus are as convincing as those of Schubert. Bella Davidovitch has a feminine acuteness of sympathy which is often lacking in Soviet lady pianists: her Chopin has more heart than Richter's, and is more directly communicative than that of Gilels. She has now emigrated to the United States, and has recently recorded the twenty-four Preludes for Philips.

The fifth prize at the Chopin Competition 1955 went to another Russian, Naum Shtarkman, who was a year older than Davidovitch, and had also studied with Igumnov. He also won first prize at the 1954 da Motta Piano Competition in Lisbon, and made a considerable reputation. He has not become well-known in Western Europe, though his playing contains many of the traditional strengths of the Russian school: a very rich tone, vivid poetic passagework, and dreamy, almost reminiscent, imagination. His Chopin is not so successful when the writing is formal, such as in the A minor Etude, Op. 10 No. 2; it is when the music is quieter and more relaxed, for instance in the E flat minor Etude, Op. 10 No. 6, and in the gentler Mazurkas such as the A minor, Op. 17 No. 4, that he comes into his own.

The transformation in the approach to Chopin which has come about through the modern interpretation taught by Igumnov, Oborin and their colleagues, is exemplified in the career of Lazar Berman, who has travelled nearly full circle in his treatment of Chopin's works. Born in 1930 and a child prodigy, he seemed when young to marvel at how fast he could play the virtuoso passages, and tended to ignore musical considerations. After many years of study with Alexander Goldenweiser, he changed his approach, and now plays a very simple and extremely disciplined Chopin, in an emotionally reserved but somewhat uninspired style. The explosive wizardry exemplified by Bolet or Hofmann is alien to Berman's present style, and that he does not apply this restraint only to Chopin and has outgrown mere showmanship, was demonstrated in his recent recording of Tchaikovsky's first Piano Concerto with von Karajan conducting. Berman first made a great reputation in the West in the 1970s as a performer of Liszt, though he had given a recital in London in the late 1950s. His stylistic restrictions may make his playing of Chopin somewhat calculated, but there is much to be said for his simple and direct approach.

His contemporary Dmitri Bashkirov (b. 1931), however, follows in the train of the romantic pianists, revelling in virtuosity. Very fine in Chopin's Polish works, and with a wide repertoire of many composers, he uses great tonal resources and his style has the freedom of phrasing usually associated with Horowitz. His dynamic temperament in the F sharp minor Polonaise, Op. 44, recorded from a live performance, is close to Horowitz's reading; there is the same aggressive, biting tone, contrasted with the delicacy of the quiet central Mazurka. Bashkirov's playing can sound mannered, for anyone who takes an overtly romantic approach today is open to charges of exaggeration. If he lacks something of Stanislav Neuhaus's imagination, his Chopin is no less brave and passionate.

Other artists of the same generation – Vladimir Ashkenazy, Mikhail Voskresenski, Igor Zhukov, Elisso Virsaladze and Irina Zaritskaya – have all followed a consistent, disciplined path, and all have a natural affinity with Chopin. Zhukov (b. 1936) specializes in Russian music and sees his Chopin on a very large canvas – his disc of the B minor Sonata is of almost symphonic conception, and has a variety of colour absent from the more classical reading of an artist like Voskresenski. Zhukov feels the contrapuntal forces in the music, and always plays with an unremitting forward thrust. A pupil of Neuhaus and Marguerite Long, he is an intense player who feels at home in the mystery of Scriabin's writing; some might consider his approach 'un-Chopinesque', for he does not stay long enough to savour the melodies. He uses varieties in texture to far greater effect than do most pianists of his generation, and in the B minor Sonata one hears almost Brahmsian textures from him. Compared with Zhukov, the Chopin playing of Mikhail Voskresenski may sound a little prosaic, for though his Chopin is perfectly proportioned (similar to that of his teacher, Lev Oborin), poetic and ordered, it lacks individuality. His deep tone is used to add weight to the more serious side of Chopin's writing, and his playing is always intelligent.

Vladimir Ashkenazy, who won second prize at the 1955 Chopin Competition when only eighteen and was joint first prizewinner of the 1962 Tchaikovsky Competition in Moscow with John Ogdon, has had a career of continuous success, and since he came to live in the West he has established a high reputation as a pianist and conductor. He was a pupil of Oborin, whose unaffected approach to Chopin is evident in Ashkenazy's performances. In 1955 he played a more mature Chopin than the winner of the Competition, Adam Harasiewicz, with more substance to his music-making. The disc of the F minor Concerto, recorded at the Chopin Competition with Zdzisław Gorzyński conducting, is a serious and intellectually weighty reading, distinguished by its classical poise, and remarkable in view of the pianist's youth. There is a total identification with Chopin's musical language, and the intensity of feeling brought to the first two movements is well contrasted with the third, where Ashkenazy takes a sprightly tempo and stresses the light and capricious aspect of the music.

Ashkenazy differs from most contemporary Russian pianists in adopting a literal attitude to Chopin's works, eschewing histrionics and personal idiosyncrasies while missing none of the passion or emotional content of the writing. He has the rare attribute of a technique sufficiently reliable and comprehensive to enable him to perform all Chopin's works with ease and demonstrate every facet of the composer's genius. He is in no way bound by stylistic limitations; when he plays a simple piece such as one of the early Waltzes, he never sounds contrived – as so many great artists can – while in the Scherzos and Ballades his virtuosity is fully integrated into a formal conception of the work as a whole. Other pianists may play individual works better than he, but few equal his comprehensive grasp of Chopin. His early recording of the twenty-four Etudes, on the Saga label, demonstrates a propensity for fast tempos (though Wilhelm Backhaus, in his pre-war recording, played them even faster), which makes some of the pieces sound too much like 'hurdles to be overcome', but as a keyboard virtuoso Ashkenazy is infallible.

He is now engaged in recording all Chopin's important piano works for Decca, and his basic view of the composer remains the same as it was in 1955. His playing has gained musical insight, but his recent recordings do not necessarily supersede the earlier performances because he is not an artist constantly attempting to explore new ways of playing familiar works, nor one with a predisposition to stress inner lines so as to sound 'interesting'. He is an instinctive and highly dynamic musician, who in Chopin combines spontaneous poetry with a dramatic drive and intellectual sturdiness. He has said that his principal aim is to play Chopin in a direct and unfettered manner, and he nearly always succeeds in achieving this.

Elisso Virsaladze, a pianist of the same age as Ashkenazy, is a player whose Chopin relies heavily on her rather forceful technique, and Irina Zaritskaya (runner-up in the 1960 Chopin Competition, which was won by Pollini) bears a closer resemblance to Ashkenazy, although she has less imagination. A pupil of Jakov Flier, her approach to Chopin is essentially optimistic: her discs from the Competition show her playing at that time to have been distinguished by extremely clear textures if small-scale phrasing, and her reading of the *Polonaise-Fantaisie* is almost jaunty in gait, which is an unusual and pleasing approach to this work. More attuned to the Polish works than Pollini, she won the special prizes for the best performances of Mazurkas and Polonaises at the 1960 Competition, and she has been well received on her subsequent appearances in Western Europe.

Among the Russian artists born during the Second World War or later those who have achieved standing as Chopin players include Nikolay Petrov, Vladimir Kraiynev and Irena Smolena, as well as younger pianists such as Andrei Gavrilov and Pavel Yegorov, whose playing is still in a formative stage. Among the former group, Vladimir Kraiynev leans towards a romantic interpretation, and is in my opinion a more successful Chopin player than his equally well-known contemporary

Nikolay Petrov. A pupil of both Harry and Stanislav Neuhaus, Kraiynev has won second prize at the 1962 Leeds Piano Competition and first prize at both the da Motta and Tchaikovsky Competitions in 1964. His playing has fire and emotional commitment, and his disc of the 'Funeral March' Sonata is exceptionally powerful; he portrays a decidedly masculine Chopin of strong feelings. He has the necessary control to be able to organize his response to the music in the most effective fashion. His reading of the Barcarolle is quite different from the Sonata, and is gentle and soothing in character, but the final climaxes have an assured power that leaves one in little doubt as to the mature Chopin's emotional security. Stanislav Neuhaus creates the opposite impression in this work, but it is one which contains material that can be played quite differently, according to the performer's mood. I believe that Chopin himself did not aim to convey only one type of emotional expression in his music, and Stanislav Neuhaus and Vladimir Kraiynev present the diversity of the composer's character, bringing out both the active and passive, masculine and feminine elements in his musical personality.

The long line of talented Russian Chopin players reflects not only the size of that country but the racial composition of its people: the population of Byelorussia (the Soviet Republic bordering on Poland) is ethnically similar to that of Poland, and it must also be noted that the majority of great Russian pianists have been Jews, whose racial origins may play an important role in their musical sympathies – Jewish pianists, like Slavs, appear able to feel the rhythmic pulse of the Mazurkas and Polonaises with instinctive keenness. It is also interesting that the folk music of Poland, Byelorussia and the Ukraine has many shared characteristics.

Anton Rubinstein's influence was the most profound force in shaping the progress of Russian Chopin playing; he was a powerful musician who played the piano in a totally masculine way and composed music in a nationalistic idiom, and he was thus a patriot whose approach was to be emulated by successive generations. Rachmaninov, Lhévinne, Horowitz, Cherkassky, Richter and Gilels have all embodied something of this tradition in their playing. Rachmaninov and Lhévinne maintained the staggering keyboard virtuosity of Rubinstein, and this heritage was passed on to Horowitz. The great teacher Konstantin Igumnov, a boyhood friend of Lhévinne, Rachmaninov, Scriabin and Blumenfeld, was for nearly fifty years professor at the Moscow Conservatory (he died in 1948), and he acted as a guardian, a link between the old school and the new. He stressed the genuinely musical aspects of the romantic style, but under his influence Russian pianists became more disciplined, better organized artistically, and more attentive to the wishes of the composer. Goldenweiser and Harry Neuhaus also maintained the highest musical values in their teaching, so that the playing of the younger generations of Russian pianists has been stripped of excess emotionalism, and they are presented as finished and sincere musical personalities.

CHAPTER SIX

German, Austrian and British Pianists

German Pianists

At the time of Chopin's death in 1849, German audiences were accustomed to the music of the Viennese school, and favoured the dazzling if superficial brilliance of the compositions of Moscheles (whose first concert tour in Germany was in 1816), Thalberg (who first toured there in 1830) and Mendelssohn, who founded the Leipzig Conservatory in 1843. Not all of Beethoven's works were popular, and Moscheles was puzzled by the late sonatas. Chopin's music was not at first appreciated, but was promoted by Liszt at Weimar, and then taken up by Clara Schumann in her concerts and – to a lesser extent – in her teaching.

The standards of technical accomplishment in the German conservatories in the middle of the nineteenth century were high. The foundations of keyboard technique laid by J. S. Bach had been developed by such teachers as Czerny and Reinecke, and the materials used for basic teaching were the studies of Czerny, Cramer and Moscheles, together with the keyboard works of Bach; the virtuoso playing of Hummel, Moscheles and Mendelssohn was taken as a yardstick for instrumental accomplishment. The other great German pedagogues followed Clara Schumann in using Chopin's works for teaching purposes, and his works were thus employed by Plaidy (actively teaching from 1842 to 1865), Moscheles (who taught at Leipzig from 1846 until 1870), Carl Reinecke (professor at Cologne from 1851 until 1860, and then at Leipzig), and Bülow (who taught at the Stern Conservatory in Berlin from 1854, and after 1866 in Munich). The greatest number of outstanding Chopin players emerging from the German conservatories at this period were the pupils of Kullak, who taught in Berlin from 1850 and whose pupils include Agathe Backer-Grøndahl, Xaver Scharwenka, Moritz Moszkowski, Alfred Grünfeld, Hans von Bronsart, Georg Liebling and Martha Remmert, though many of them also had lessons from Liszt. Kullak and Reinecke also brought out editions of Chopin's works.

Although Ignaz Moscheles rarely performed Chopin's works in later life, he had met the composer and played his compositions in public as early as 1838. Teaching at the Leipzig Conservatory from 1846 to 1870, Moscheles was important in establishing Chopin's fame in Germany. Although finding some of the Etudes nearly impossible to play himself, Moscheles was sufficiently forward-looking to use Chopin's works in his classes, and noted as Chopin players among his pupils were Aleksander Michałowski, Marie Pleyel and Marie Blahetka, Edward Dannreuther, Franklin Taylor and Rafael Joseffy. Moscheles was primarily interested in the pianistic aspect of Chopin's writing, and all his important pupils, like the other graduates of the Leipzig system, played their instrument with the right combination of musical discipline, pianistic refinement, and a concern for Chopin's idiom.

The fact that Chopin owed so much to Bach, and that his compositions show the meticulous craftsmanship of Mozart, helped to attract German pianists to his works which, even when they appear most free and rhapsodic, have an inherent discipline in both harmony and form. In the middle of the nineteenth century, German musicians were very interested in the integration of the rhapsodic treatment of melody in classical forms, and Chopin's music, with that of Robert Schumann, is of course most important in this context. Enthusiasm for Chopin grew with the liberating effect which the promotion of Schumann's music by his wife and the teaching of Liszt had on piano playing in Germany. However, their training and, perhaps, their artistic instincts, have always drawn German pianists towards Chopin's more classically-oriented compositions. In the area of innate rhythm, they have been at a disadvantage because they have had to work to acquire the rhythmic sense which in Slav artists seems to allow the music to breathe. In Leschetizky's view, even the best German pianists never quite mastered 'the nuance for Chopin',[1] and they are apt to sound contrived when they impose what they believe to be a Chopin *rubato*, because lack of instinctive judgment here can spoil the most careful conception.

Chopin never reciprocated Schumann's admiration – but then he had little respect for the compositions of his contemporaries, with the exception of Bellini.[2] Clara Schumann shared her husband's reverence for Chopin's music, and anything she lacked in innate response to his rhythms was compensated by her virtuosity, tone colour and sensitive phrasing. Anyone who could play the then revolutionary works of her husband – which in some ways are even more original than Chopin's – with such success was capable of approaching Chopin's music with skill and understanding, as the accounts of her playing quoted in Chapter One of this book show.

The most notable advocate of Chopin's music in Germany next to Clara Schumann was Hans Guido von Bülow. His reputation was that of a great intellectual, and by playing much of Chopin he saved the composer from denigration as a salon writer; Bülow demonstrated that Chopin's music was worthy of inclusion in a programme alongside that of Mozart, Bach and Beethoven. Severely academic, remote, peppery and sardonic,[3] he was perhaps the first of the modern 'giants' of the pianoforte. Born in 1830 (eleven years after Clara Wieck), he was not perhaps the type of pianist one would immediately associate with Chopin's music, but he had the intellectual breadth of a Busoni or a Schnabel. He began playing Chopin when still in his teens,[4] and by 1855, shortly after the composer's death, was already playing a representative proportion of his works in public.

Bülow was totally uninterested in Chopin's music as a vehicle for pianistic display. There was an element of pedantry in his readings that led Moritz Moszkowski to remark, 'Rubinstein plays the piano as if it was his wife, Grünfeld as if it was his fiancée, but Bülow as if it was his old grandmother!'* Very modest about his attainments, he despised personal adulation and, after a highly successful recital, when his rapturous audience recalled him time after time, he threatened to play the complete Bach Preludes and Fugues if they did not cease their applause.† He was obviously proud of his Chopin playing, writing after a visit to Warsaw in February 1872, 'I have established myself as a Chopin player *par excellence*.' However, others were less enthusiastic about his interpretations; one contemporary wrote that his style was 'fine, of a class that is: it was academic, correct and dry.'[5] This was not an isolated opinion, for Alfred Cortot, in his preface to Opieński's biography of Paderewski, wrote: 'The rational approach of Bülow only half measured up to our young idealism; empty of feeling, we found that the music came to life in far less dogmatic hands.'[6]

A Chopin recital Bülow gave in St James's Hall in London in 1875 indicates the scale of his programmes: it included the B minor Sonata, the *Variations Brillantes*, Op. 12, the G major Nocturne, Op. 37 No. 2, the G minor Ballade, a Prelude, the F sharp major Impromptu, the E major Scherzo, the three Waltzes, Op. 34, the *Allegro de Concert*, the three Mazurkas, Op. 59, the Tarantelle, the Berceuse, and the A flat Polonaise. But despite his importance, Bülow is not remembered as a great Chopin player, probably because he had to consciously interpret the music. It is known that he recorded a Chopin Mazurka[7] on a cylinder, but to my knowledge it has never come to light, and his edition of Chopin's works has been criticized for its misplaced scholastic intentions, and tendency towards over-editing.

Another product of the German school, like Bülow a pupil of Liszt, was Moritz Moszkowski (1854–1925), of Polish descent and born in

---

* Moszkowski was famous for his witty remarks, the most celebrated of which also concerns Bülow. The latter had just given his signature to a manifesto which stated 'Bach, Beethoven, Brahms! Tous le autres sont crétins.' Moszkowski, when adding his name, wrote 'Mendelssohn, Meyerbeer, Moszkowski. Tous les autres sont chrétiens!'

† This might not have been quite as excessive as it appears, since he frequently played Beethoven's *Waldstein* Sonata as an encore. Anton Rubinstein did the same.

Breslau. He also studied with Kullak, and settled in France, where he became a successful teacher. He possessed a technique of extraordinary brilliance, and also made a reputation as a composer of the most exclusive type of salon music, which was played by most virtuoso performers until very recently, especially as encores. His writing is entertaining and graceful, and pieces such as *La Jongleuse, Caprice Espagnole, Etincelles* and his Spanish Dances once had a great vogue. Although their content is shallow, they are extremely cleverly put together, and achieve a brilliant effect with minimal physical effort. Despite composing music in this genre, Moszkowski was a Chopin player of no mean standing, and was highly respected as a pianist from the time of his debut in 1873. He played Chopin's B flat minor Sonata in Berlin in 1879, and Xaver Scharwenka, the eminent Chopin player who had also studied with Kullak, wrote that Moszkowski had 'placed himself, at once, in the front rank of our younger pianists'. In the same recital he played the celebrated Etude in G sharp minor, Op. 25 No. 6, the one in thirds, which had apparently not been played by a major artist since Tausig's death eight years before.

Moszkowski's style was at the opposite extreme from Bülow's. He managed to use his technique to express the deeper side of his musical nature, and even hostile critics of his compositions, such as Bernard Shaw, agreed that he was one of the great pianists of his time. Some of his pupils became famous for their Chopin playing, among them Henryk Melcer, Wanda Landowska, Ernest Schelling and Vlado Perlemuter.

The presence of Liszt at Weimar from 1847 had a very important influence on the development of German pianism. The Leipzig training attracted many able pianists, but those who were looking for something extra, many of them having really original talents, were drawn to Liszt's circle. Before the 1850s there was no established method in Germany for training 'romantic' pianists; Clara Schumann was herself the product of the classical training she had received from her father Friedrich Wieck. Liszt did for the piano what Paganini had done for the violin, and showed that the instrument was capable of a range of virtuoso writing that had not been dreamed of by the classical keyboard composers. Many of the younger Germans were greatly attracted by Liszt's more liberal ideas on piano-playing, and came to him after they had been 'processed' by Leipzig and the other conservatories; Liszt helped them break away from slavish adherence to classicism. The master's teaching of his own approach to the piano affected the attitude of most German pianists to their instrument.

Chopin's music is dependent for its effect on rhythmic subtleties which, if they do not come naturally to the performer, have to be learned or instilled. This is not an easy matter, especially if the teacher is a great pianist who will vary the rhythms he applies in any piece, and when Liszt's pupils – most of whom possessed only a fraction of his talent – tried to mimic his playing, the results were seldom satisfactory. Perhaps his German pupils came off worst of all, because they lacked an instinctive rhythmic sense for Chopin's music. Some of Liszt's best pupils – Ansorge, Bülow, Arthur Friedheim, Sophie Menter, Josef Weiss and Emil Sauer – were, on the evidence of discs and accounts of their performances, very vivid performers of Liszt's works. But with the exception of Sauer, their Chopin playing was controversial, and even Sauer played the E major Etude, Op. 10 No. 3, in an incongruous style, with an extremely pedantic rhythm, as can be heard on his recording of this work. Weiss's playing of the A flat Waltz on disc is unrhythmical and tends to get out of time; Friedheim's Funeral March from the B flat minor Sonata is very erratic with changes of tempo, and Ansorge's playing of the *Chant polonais* 'Moja Pieszczotka' is a little stiff; Menter exploited the brilliant side of Chopin's writing to the detriment of the poetic. Despite all the possibilities which his inspiration opened out, Liszt's influence on German pianists attempting to achieve a balanced interpretation of Chopin may have been detrimental. The pianists who were trained in the classes of Kullak and Moscheles were generally much better disciplined in Chopin and produced more satisfactory performances.

Leschetizky had no German pupils who became even moderately well-known as Chopin players; perhaps the excellence of their own conservatories discouraged German pianists from studying with him. But later in the century an increasing number of virtuosi visited Germany from farflung countries, and the many students who came from abroad to study in the German academies helped to broaden the approach of pianists there, who often furthered their studies with a foreign teacher: Egon Petri studied with Busoni, Backhaus had lessons with Siloti in St Petersburg, Sauer was a pupil of Nikolay Rubinstein, and Alfred Hoehn studied with Lazzaro Uzielli.

Egon Petri was born in Hanover in 1881, the son of a famous Dutch violinist, Henri Petri. He achieved considerable proficiency on the violin, and played in his father's quartet. (Petri was not the only talented pianist to be a string-player – Sembrich, Bauer, Korngold, Kreisler, Casals and Rostropcvitch mastered both instruments; Petri could also play the French horn and the organ.) Joachim and Brahms, who were both friends of the family, advised him on his career, the great virtuoso suggesting that he concentrate on the voilin, but Brahms that he should try to obtain a good general education before he embarked on any particular course, and this he did. Petri's teachers for piano were Teresa Carreño and Ferruccio Busoni, who was a friend of the family and remained Petri's mentor for the rest of his life. It was Carreño who encouraged him to develop his technique to a level that set him aside from most other artists of his generation, although he denied that she had much influence on him; she used to tell him that a pianist should be able to support a glass of water on the back of his hand while playing!* Petri's high intelligence, discernment, and industry led to his acquiring one of the most powerful virtuoso techniques. He performed both as a solo pianist, and in duets and two-piano works with Busoni, and was a highly successful teacher. He lived in Berlin from 1921 until 1926, for some time at Zakopane in Poland (the home of Szymanowski), and then moved to the United States, where he remained until his death in 1962. Among his many pupils the best-known include John Ogdon, Earl Wild, Vitya Vronsky, Gunnat Johansen, Jan Hoffman, Franz-Joseph Hirt and Karol Szreter.

Petri had a very large repertoire that centred around the works of Bach, Liszt and Busoni; his Chopin performances captured on disc are of the complete Preludes, the A flat Polonaise, the A flat Waltz, Op. 42, and the D flat Nocturne, Op. 27 No. 2 (the last coming from a live performance). Many have assumed that his style was very similar to that of Busoni, but Petri's pupil, the well-known teacher Gordon Green, thought that the resemblance should not be exaggerated and described Petri as the more 'human' player whereas Busoni's playing was more 'ethereal'. Petri's performances reflect his intellect and his discs of the Preludes are model interpretations – balanced, broad-toned, imaginative virtuoso readings, which are very serious and more idiomatic than many might expect. In the B flat minor Prelude, Op. 28 No. 16, one of the most technically demanding, the right-hand semi-quavers are treated with the utmost virtuosity and fire; the tempo is extremely fast, and the pianist has to struggle a little to keep up the pace. Petri's Chopin had plenty of grandeur and nobility, but was also beautifully detailed. His pedal effects were extraordinarily vivid, and his performance of the A flat Prelude, Op. 28 No. 17, is a whirlwind of richly colourful sounds blending together with great originality. There was no hint of sentimentality in his Chopin: he played in a masculine and forceful way, far removed from the salon style. However, his disc of the A flat Polonaise is a little disappointing, and sounds as if he was not in complete sympathy with the *rubato* required for the piece. Many said that Petri's master played 'Chopin-Busoni', but Petri himself always adhered to Chopin's own notes and markings, and saw himself as an 'interpreter', whereas Busoni virtually 're-composed' works.

Born in Leipzig in 1884, and three years younger than Petri, Wilhelm Backhaus taught at the Royal Northern College of Music in Manchester

---

* The pianist Moscheles often used to demonstrate that he could play the most taxing piano music with a coin balanced on the top of his hand.

before the First World War, but soon gave up teaching to concentrate on concert-giving. His chief teacher had been Alois Reckendorf, a Moravian professor at the Leipzig Conservatory, with whom he studied for seven years from 1891; he also had a few unprofitable lessons from d'Albert, and three from Siloti.[8] Backhaus's grasp of the keyboard was as leonine as that of Petri, and even when he was in his eighties he could play the most difficult Chopin Etudes. He played a great deal of Chopin's music, chiefly in his early years, and though he is principally remembered for his Beethoven and Brahms, his Chopin should not be underestimated, since at its best it was deeply impressive. Like Petri, Backhaus was not especially convincing in the Polonaises, but in the works that required more conventional musical attainments – the Sonatas, Etudes and Ballades – he could rise to heights that would remind the listener that when young he was ranked with Hofmann, Godowsky and Josef Lhévinne. His discs of the twenty-four Etudes, which date from the late 1920s, are among the most technically accomplished ever recorded, and display a firm preference for fast tempos. The most difficult among them, like the A minor, Op. 10 No. 2 (which requires the right-hand third, fourth and fifth fingers to play *legato* chromatic scales), the infamous G sharp minor, Op. 25 No. 6 in thirds, and the B minor, Op. 25 No. 10 in double octaves, receive staggering performances. When a quieter and more musical approach is demanded, as in the C sharp minor, Op. 25 No. 7, Backhaus shows the enormous variety of his resources and invests the different voices with a life of their own to create a very moving effect.

The sheer comprehensiveness of Backhaus's ability sets him apart from most pianists of his time. He had the capacity to make such difficult works as the A flat Polonaise sound like child's play, and an early disc of the A flat Waltz, Op. 42, is executed with the utmost bravura, if with less than sufficient attention to the musical side of the work. He did not vary his dynamics a great deal in Chopin, and his playing is always well-ordered. Some of the recordings he made after 1945 indicate the imaginative abilities he could bring to the works: his disc of the B flat minor Sonata from this period shows an impressive command of its structure, and the coupling of the G minor Ballade with a selection of Mazurkas is a compelling performance; when in the right mood (not all these Mazurkas are equally good), Backhaus played these short pieces with the rhythmic sensitivity of Pachmann or Friedman. The recordings Backhaus made in the 1960s, when in his eighties, well illustrate the playing of the old school. In slow sustained works like the E flat minor Etude, Op. 10 No. 6, his old-fashioned mannerisms include spread chords and playing the left hand before the right. In a few places he also supplements Chopin's notation – for example, doubling up the first note of the left hand in the Berceuse.

Few German pianists of Backhaus's generation played quite as much Chopin as he did. Among them was Alfred Hoehn (1887–1945), another pianist whose abilities were always highly regarded although his name is now little known. He studied in Frankfurt-on-Main with Lazzaro Uzielli, a pupil of Clara Schumann, and in 1910 won the Anton Rubinstein Piano Competition in St Petersburg when the other contestants included Artur Rubinstein, Julius Isserlis, Leff Pouishnoff, Emil Frey and Edwin Fischer. Backhaus had won the 1906 Rubinstein Prize competition held in Paris, and there were some similarities in their playing. Hoehn was also a composer, and became professor at the Academy of Music in Frankfurt (Erik Then-Bergh was one of his pupils). He was one of the judges of the third Chopin Competition in Warsaw in 1937, and, although he made few discs, it was as a Chopin player that he chose to be remembered for posterity: he recorded two Etudes and the Barcarolle around 1928. Frank Merrick, who also competed in the Rubinstein Competition in 1910, commented on the disc of Hoehn playing the C minor Etude, Op. 10 No. 12, when I played it to him in 1978, with one word – 'Execrable!' The piece receives a terrrible battering from the German, who plays the final cascade of semi-quavers in interlocking octaves – a considerable pyrotechnic feat, but wholly inappropriate. Hoehn's reading of the Barcarolle is artistically far more convincing, and in this performance one can gain a glimpse of Clara Schumann's school at its best – he plays with great imagination and sensitivity, and the rushed ending which mars the reading is probably due to the limited space on the disc. This disc shows that Hoehn was a deeply dedicated musician, tending towards a visionary interpretation of Chopin.

If many German pianists seem to be concerned above all with transmitting the form and harmonic content of Chopin's music, an exception is Walter Gieseking. His Chopin was much more relaxed than that of Backhaus and Hoehn, whose approach was intense and concentrated; Gieseking was more concerned with tone, texture and mood. He was born in 1895; there were few other German pianists of his generation who concentrated on Chopin, and when they played his works the results were seldom impressive. Joseph Pembaur (a pupil of Reisenauer), Walter Rummel (a pupil of Godowsky) and Georg Bertram, (who was taught by Jedliczka) played some Chopin, with varying success. Bertram was a sensitive and delicate pianist, who made an impressive recording on disc of the A flat Ballade; Rummel was a member of Debussy's circle and a good Bach player, but he never seems to have mastered Chopin's *rubato*. Although Bertram (like Hoehn) could be rhapsodic when the music required this, the general approach of these pianists was detached and objective.

Gieseking's road was different: he treated Chopin's music as a series of mood pictures, an approach resulting from his deep attachment to the music of the French Impressionists. Although he did not play much Chopin in his later years, Gieseking often included works by Chopin in his programmes during the early stages of his career, and made some recordings of his music. In the mid-1920s he made some discs under the Homocord label, which feature the B major Nocturne, Op. 9 No. 3, and two Etudes from Op. 25. The Nocturne demonstrates his aims in Chopin: eschewing the formal approach of many German pianists, he plays this work with a delightful intimacy and point that Chopin himself would surely have admired. Instead of being a nebulous string of reveries, the performance is full of wit and character, with a free use of *rubato* and most imaginative pedalling. Gieseking's reading of the Etudes brings to mind his prowess in French Impressionist music: the A flat (Op. 25 No. 1) is dreamy and ethereal, and the F minor (Op. 25 No. 2) fragile and elusive. His easy mastery of technique always allowed him to play in a most natural style; he was one of those exceptional pianists who never need to practise, and he had a near-photographic memory and a brilliant ability for sightreading. Unfortunately he left no recordings of his Chopin playing apart from the Homocord discs and a few pieces recorded in the 1930s.

If very few people today think of Gieseking as a Chopin player, there would also be few who consider Wilhelm Kempff in the same light. But, whereas Gieseking played Chopin primarily from a pianistic angle, Kempff is attracted solely by his musical stature. He shared the same teacher as Artur Rubinstein – Heinrich Barth – but it should not be assumed that Barth formed the approach of either of these pianists to Chopin's music; Kempff has always been quite a different type of pianist to Rubinstein, and has also been an organist and a composer of some note. Although endowed with a natural and adequately comprehensive keyboard facility, Kempff has always been a musician who has tended towards stressing spontaneous poetry above all else. In Chopin's most taxing works one is aware that there are places in which his technique is only barely adequate for the task in hand, but the compensations usually outweigh the disadvantages, for Kempff has marvellous reserves of lyricism, and a very profound grasp of formal structure: like Cortot, he demonstrates how wrong Robert Schumann was to criticize the relationship between the four movements of the B flat minor Sonata, and has a masterly understanding of the musical content of this work. Kempff's limited technical resources often force him to take rather slow tempos in the most taxing works, such as the *Andante Spianato and Grande Polonaise Brillante* and the finale of the B flat minor Sonata. However, he does sometimes take risks: his disc of the B flat minor Sonata has one of the fastest first movement expositions on record. In the 1950s he played the F minor Concerto regularly, and he has recorded the B minor

Sonata and the F minor Fantasy, as well as many other shorter works. A reviewer once wrote that Kempff's Chopin was surely much the same as Clara Schumann's must have been – everything he touches sounds both individual and distinguished, and stems from a tradition that puts music above pianistic considerations. His Chopin is both romantic and intimate and he offers a personal response with constant emotional involvement.

Few pianists from Germany since the Second World War have had Kempff's success in playing the large-scale works of Chopin. Christoph Eschenbach is perhaps an exception, but his performances, for all their intelligence and luminosity, lack sympathy with the composer's idiom. Eschenbach is a performer who seems always to manage to reveal aspects of the music that have hitherto remained hidden; his recording of the twenty-four Preludes is of great interest. The German pianists of the present time are drawn to the Viennese classics above all other music of the past, but it may be that in the future the ever-increasing internationalization of the concert platform will lead them to venture into Chopin.

The Austrian School

During the years Chopin was composing in Paris, Viennese pianists and their audiences preferred the shallow and easily accessible works of Hummel, Moscheles, Mendelssohn and Czerny to the great classics. Mozart's music was little played, because it was quite mistakenly considered to be technically undemanding, Schubert's went undiscovered, and Beethoven's late works were deemed incomprehensible. Viennese pianists liked to play music that was quick to learn, impressive on first hearing, and stressed the virtuoso capacities of the piano. Carl Czerny, the greatest piano pedagogue of the first half of the nineteenth century, lived in Vienna, and his preoccupation was with attaining the highest degree of technical facility. It is true that certain aspects of the Viennese approach were ideal for the performance of Chopin, especially the insistence on textural clarity and delicate finger-*legato*, but these were insufficient for the adequate interpretation of his works.

Twenty years after Czerny's death, Leschetizky settled in Vienna, and under his influence Viennese pianists began to widen their repertoire to encompass Chopin's works. They found in them much that fulfilled their highest musical ideals and this, combined with a growing awareness of the greatness of Mozart, Beethoven and Schubert, allowed them to play Chopin with a stylistic consistency emanating from a great tradition of piano music. But the awakening to the Viennese classical masters also had the contrary effect of diverting many pianists from Chopin, and it was mostly pianists from other countries living in Vienna who felt able to tackle this relatively new music; among them was the great Viennese pianist Alfred Grünfeld, who was of Czech and Jewish origin: he played a great deal of Chopin and made a very interesting piano roll of the C minor Nocturne, Op. 48 No. 1, which is both personal and forceful.

Rudolf Serkin, although he has never committed any Chopin interpretations to disc, used to play Chopin in recitals, and his playing was received favourably. Another pianist, also of the older generation, is Robert Goldsand, who has made something of a speciality of his Chopin playing. Born in 1911, and an extraordinary child prodigy, he had lessons from Moriz Rosenthal, and this great Chopin expert seems to have left his mark on Goldsand's approach to the composer. Goldsand failed to win any prizes at the two early Chopin Competitions in which he took part, but on the hundredth anniversary of Chopin's death he gave recitals presenting all the works for solo piano. He has a big technique, and is one of the few pianists who have managed to maintain a very personal and idiomatic style in Chopin, without ever sounding mannered. His discs of the complete Etudes, from the early 1950s, are full of interesting effects. His readings are eclectic – they take some of the best points of various schools. There is complete clarity, a variety of texture, and a skilful use of *rubato*; the hand of Moriz Rosenthal is never far away.

Many of the younger generation of Viennese pianists, such as Badura-Skoda and Brendel, were strongly influenced by Edwin Fischer. Fischer himself played some Chopin in public, but received a number of unfavourable notices; some have said that he played Chopin's music well in private, notably the *Trois Nouvelles Etudes*. Accounts indicate that he did not feel at home with Chopin's *rubato*, and it is perhaps this deficiency above all others that can be levelled at the younger Viennese school. It is as if Serkin, Goldsand and Fischer felt it necessary to instil emotional content into the music from outside. Serkin and Fischer never played much Chopin because their priorities lay elsewhere; it is difficult to integrate the personal commitment required by his music into a tradition founded on the works of Mozart, Beethoven and Schubert. Most Viennese pianists have played Chopin from a classical rather than a romantic standpoint, and contemporary pianists such as Alfred Brendel, Ingrid Haebler, Friedrich Gulda, Jörg Demus, Paul Badura-Skoda, Walter Klien and Ludwig Hoffmann all play a Chopin that sounds as if it carries on naturally from Mozart.

None of these very gifted pianists regards Chopin as the lynchpin of his repertoire, but Paul Badura-Skoda has made several Chopin discs and edited his piano works, and Haebler has recorded the complete Nocturnes and Waltzes. This group of pianists usually steers clear of the more idiomatic works, although Brendel's only Chopin disc presents a selection of the Polonaises.

One of the chief characteristics of the Viennese school is an immaculate technical training, although it is always subsidiary to their music-making. This enables them to approach any work from a very strong initial position: they can do almost whatever they want with the music, their only limitation in Chopin being that their imagination is often not equal to their intellect. For instance, Gulda's account of the E minor Concerto is full of mannered phrasing, unconvincing emotionalism and overblown grandeur, and is worthy of note only for using Balakirev's re-orchestration, thus providing a tantalizing combination of an Austrian pianist and an English conductor (Sir Adrian Boult) playing a work by a Polish composer re-orchestrated by a Russian! Gulda's performance of the *Andante Spianato and Grande Polonaise Brillante* has also found its way onto disc; this, by contrast, is a beautifully poised reading of considerable charm, relaxed and intelligently phrased, and he has also made other Chopin discs. Brendel has a fuller tone and plays Chopin with greater character. His disc of Polonaises contains a very impressive version of the C minor work, in which he binds together Chopin's contrapuntal writing with great skill; his playing has greater rhythmic freedom than most of the other Austrians'.

The musical priorities of Ludwig Hoffmann are very different from Brendel's. He possesses a large and extrovert artistic personality, and can play virtually any piano music, however difficult, with the greatest ease; the Op. 25 Etudes sound simple under his fingers, and he has a cultivated sense of style which prevents works such as the B flat minor Scherzo from sounding vulgar. That sense of struggle, both mental and physical, which, some might argue, is a necessary component in the performance of Chopin (as it is in the two Brahms Piano Concertos) is entirely absent from Hoffmann's performances; everything glitters, with the result that Chopin is revealed as a suave cosmopolitan. (Sauer's Chopin was rather in the same vein, but more intellectually and emotionally impressive.) However, in works such as the Berceuse, Ludwig Hoffmann's approach is ideal; he has none of the gadfly imagination of Josef Hofmann, with whom he is occasionally confused. Even if one cannot admire Ludwig Hoffmann's power in a work like the B flat minor Scherzo, his enterprise in playing the way he does commands admiration. He can play with great spontaneity, and in the 'Minute' Waltz, for instance, has tremendous style. The problem with Hoffmann's playing, on the evidence of discs from the 1960s, is that however ingratiating and stylistically acceptable his Chopin may be, he fails to move one on more than a superficial level.

This is not the case with Paul Badura-Skoda, who in some works can play Chopin like a master. Born in Vienna in 1927, Badura-Skoda studied mathematics and engineering as well as music. The winner of many awards, he began his career in earnest after the Second World War, making his American debut in 1953. His record of the twenty-four Etudes is among the most technically immaculate ever made, but he never allows this side of the music to obtrude. He is a considerable Chopin scholar, as is evident from his expert editing of the Etudes[9] and also in his record of the E flat Nocturne, Op. 9 No. 2, in which he introduces some variants originating from a manuscript annotated by Chopin for his pupil Karol Mikuli. (This version with its full variants has been recorded by Raoul Koczalski, Mikuli's pupil, and also by the young English pianist, Angela Lear; Badura-Skoda does not play all the variants to the original text, but those that he does include are stylishly and spontaneously played.) We know that Chopin himself often took many years to arrive at a definitive version of a work that he was happy to send to his publisher, and did not adhere rigorously to all the details of his printed music when performing it himself. The printed versions should not therefore be treated as the composer's last word on the subject, and Badura-Skoda is the only major living pianist willing to follow this idea to its conclusion and perform works in this manner; other pianists make minor changes such as playing single notes as octaves, but these belong to a different category.

Like Kempff, Badura-Skoda is unfettered by constraining tradition, and this enables him to reveal the B minor Sonata with an almost symphonic scope. It is clear from the opening bars that this is no purely pianistic view of the work, but a large-scale representation of the composer's multi-faceted personality; this is achieved by varying the mood and the texture of the writing so as to reveal a new and luminous conception which surprises the listener. Badura-Skoda convinces one that Chopin had no need to write orchestral music because his piano-writing, when played by a master, has all the variety of expression attainable from the instruments of the orchestra. He has also recorded the two Piano Concertos, which are spoiled by having the accompaniments truncated so as to fit one work on each side of a disc, but the solo playing is extremely expressive and successful.

Jörg Demus also takes a richly-textured approach, but he has less sympathy with the composer's idiom than Badura-Skoda. His Chopin, especially in the large-scale works, is almost offhand, and his lack of a communicative tone is a handicap. As a rule, he cares little for pianism, but a notable exception is his reading of the Berceuse, which he plays with sensitive colouring. Walter Klien and Ingrid Haebler are musicians too intelligent and committed to play with anything but good taste; however in the final analysis, this is not enough, and their results in Chopin's music are no more than satisfactory. Klien is the more imaginative of the two – Miss Haebler's approach is more suited to the small-scale works, the Nocturnes and Waltzes.

The Viennese school appear to lack the basic temperament for Chopin. Although their intentions are always laudable, Chopin without tears, without drama, and without heroism is bereft of his character. He cannot successfully be viewed as an updated Mozart, and this is what many of these pianists seem to do; Chopin used Mozart's music to refine and inspire his own style, and his works are distorted if the classical tradition is used to suppress the beautiful melodies, the vibrant rhythms and the outburst of emotional expression.

British Pianists

The British have never evolved a recognizable style of piano-playing, as did the French in the last century. The British pianist has always been eclectic, and most of the virtuosi held in highest esteem in this country in the nineteenth century were Germans. The piano only came into its own in the late eighteenth century, and two of its early proponents, Cramer and Clementi, made their home in England. A few years later, the impact of Felix Mendelssohn on British music reached its apogee with his reception by the Queen and Prince Consort, and one effect of this was that British pianists of talent were to an increasing extent sent to do their formative training in Leipzig. Mendelssohn himself founded the Conservatory in that city, and after his death his classical approach was continued through the teaching of Moscheles and Reinecke. The influence of the Leipzig tradition helped to deter British pianists from attempting music outside the classical repertoire.

Chopin himself gave some concerts in England and Scotland the year before his death, but his music first reached a wider public through the concert tours of Clara Schumann and Charles Hallé – both classical pianists who achieved results primarily through finger-work – and then those of Bülow and Anton Rubinstein, whose styles were at opposite ends of the interpretative spectrum. Hallé was the first pianist to play Chopin's E minor Concerto in Britain at a Philharmonic Society Concert in 1859, though the F minor Concerto had been performed as early as 1843 by Mme Louise Dulcken, sister of the great violinist Ferdinand David. Hallé was an excellent pianist, although his style was very reserved; his technique was so comprehensive that he could play virtually anything, and he gave the first performance in this country of Tchaikovsky's fiendishly difficult Second Piano Concerto in 1886 (this was before it had been revised by Siloti).

Among British-born pianists of the mid-nineteenth century, Mrs

Anderson (Lucy Philpot) was widely admired. She won great prestige because she gave lessons to the young Queen Victoria, and although not a very strong technician she was renowned for her very musical playing. She performed some works of Chopin, but she was more at home in the music of Hummel and Beethoven, much of which she introduced into this country. Her greatest pupil (in terms of musical rather than sovereign worth!) was Arabella Goddard, who can probably be regarded as the outstanding British pianist of the last century. Born in 1836, she played Beethoven's 'Hammerklavier' Sonata in London when she was seventeen, and during her long career she played the other late sonatas regularly; she died in 1922.

Shaw wrote that Arabella Goddard could play any music, but had little original to say about it; she included Chopin in her programmes, but her style was probably too classical for his works. But she had a total command of the keyboard, and her style was praised by Alice Diehl-Mangold, herself a good Chopin player, who wrote that 'Arabella Goddard was the most faithful and reverent classical player it was possible to hear.'[10] Mark Hambourg recounts a very amusing tale about her in his autobiography: when Leschetizky visited London in the 1870s, it was arranged that he should play a duet with Miss Goddard. As soon as they sat down at the piano to rehearse, Arabella put her foot down firmly on the sustaining pedal and would not allow Leschetizky to use it. At the performance, she started off by doing the same thing, and so Leschetizky gave her foot a sharp kick and did the rest of the pedalling himself![11] She married J. W. Davison, the eminent music critic of *The Times* who also coached her as a pianist, and though she played some of Chopin's music (in programmes which often included works of dubious quality) she did not make any original contribution to Chopin playing in this country.

By the 1870s, Chopin's music had declined in popularity in Britain.[12] Most of the pianists engaged to play with the most prestigious orchestras and in the best concert halls were products of the Leipzig school or pupils of Clara Schumann, and were more interested in the music of Mozart, Beethoven and Mendelssohn than that of Chopin. The four pianists who were most influential in British music-making during the late Victorian period were Oscar Beringer, Edward Dannreuther, Ernst Pauer and Franklin Taylor; only Taylor was British and, apart from Pauer, all had been pupils of Moscheles and Plaidy at Leipzig; the three German musicians settled in London in the early 1850s. Dannreuther pioneered the concertos of Tchaikovsky, Grieg, Brahms and Scharwenka in Britain, and gave lecture-recitals on Chopin's music with great musicianship and finish. He numbered many competent Chopin players among his pupils. Notable too was Agnes Zimmerman, who was taught by Pauer, and whose Chopin was highly respected if a little dull.

None of Chopin's British pupils achieved much in their later careers. Jane Stirling died in the 1850s, and Lindsay Sloper and Brinley Richards became well-known as teachers and composers of salon music: Richards wrote 'God Bless the Prince of Wales', and Sloper entitled his Opus 1, a collection of three Mazurkas, 'Czartoryska'. The British seemed to have formed the conclusion that foreigners were the best interpreters of Chopin's works. Nor did any of Clara Schumann's British pupils – Adelina de Lara, Fanny Davies, Leonard Borwick, Amina Goodwin and Mathilde Verne – become especially interested in Chopin, though Borwick and Fanny Davies played his works quite frequently and gave straightforward and reliable readings. Bernard Shaw was probably being hypercritical when he said that Borwick had 'all the faults of an amateur',[13] a judgment which cannot be taken seriously of a pianist who could play Liszt's 'Don Juan' Fantasy. Hambourg was more generous, and acclaimed Borwick as the best pianist of his generation. Borwick was an effective interpreter of the larger works of Chopin, and his playing of the F minor Fantasy was applauded by the critics. A keen advocate of Debussy, he arranged the *Prélude à l'après midi d'un faune* for solo piano, and this was recorded by Hambourg. Unfortunately Borwick died in 1925, at the age of fifty-seven, and left no discs.

Adela Verne was another British-born pianist whose career attracted great attention. She was the sister of the pianists Marie Wurm (who kept their original surname), Mathilde Verne and Alice Verne-Bredt. Adela Verne had lessons from her sisters, and from Marie Schumann, the daughter of Robert and Clara Schumann. She also received some instruction from Paderewski, who made her his protégée and when she was fourteen she made her debut at the Crystal Palace, with Manns conducting. Adela Verne gave the first London performance of the Brahms B flat Concerto, and this large-scale music was better suited to her style than the more delicate works of Chopin. She made a disc of the A flat Polonaise, which is spoiled by overblown virtuosity – Chopin may indeed not have been her *métier*. Her son, the pianist John Vallier, studied the piano with his aunt Mathilde Verne, who also taught Moura Lympany, Herbert Menges and Solomon. Vallier has recently played a great deal of Chopin in London; he has a popularist approach, and favours the heroic side of the composer's nature.

Many British-born pianists of the last century made their homes abroad, including Richard Hoffman, Sebastian Bach Mills, Helen Hopekirk, Eugen d'Albert and Ethel Leginska. Hoffman played the E minor Concerto in New York in 1854,[14] and Sebastian Bach Mills performed the F minor Fantasy and the F minor Concerto there in 1860 and 1861 on the newly developed Steinway piano.[15] But there were also pianists from foreign countries, often fleeing from political upheaval, who made their homes in Britain, and these include Julius Benedict, Wilhelm Kuhe, Wilhelm Ganz, Max Mayer, Ilona Eibenschütz, Mark Hambourg, Benno Moiseiwitsch, Leff Pouishnoff and Jan Smeterlin. The Eastern European background of these pianists was believed to give them a natural sympathy with Chopin's music, and this idea tended to deter British pianists further from attempting his works. The first British-born pianists to make international reputations were born towards the end of the last century. Harold Bauer was not a very notable Chopin player, as his playing, though very musical, was not sufficiently idiomatic. Herbert Fryer, who had lessons from Busoni, Beringer and Franklin Taylor, was an admirable pianist who left one disc of Chopin, demonstrating his cultured and imaginative playing; he was a pianist of considerable accomplishments and catholic taste.

But from about the turn of the century there was a renaissance in British piano-playing which coincided with the emergence of composers of talent such as Cyril Scott, John Ireland, Frank Bridge, Joseph Holbrooke, Granville Bantock and others. Among the products of this renaissance are such pianists as Irene Scharrer, John Hunt, York Bowen, Edward Isaacs, Moura Lympany, Lance Dossor, Myra Hess, Adela Verne, Solomon, Peter Katin and Paul Crossley, all of whom have made a valuable contribution to the art of Chopin playing. Most of this generation of pianists studied abroad, but only Frederic Lamond, Katharine Goodson and Frank Merrick went to Liszt or Leschetizky.

York Bowen was a talented and now much underrated composer, and a Chopin player whose discs demonstrate a real affinity with the music. He studied with Tobias Matthay in London for two years, and had great virtuosity and a marvellous tone which earned him the title 'the English Rachmaninoff'. He recorded the A flat Ballade, the E minor Etude, Op. 25 No. 5, the C sharp minor Polonaise, three Preludes from Op. 28, the B flat minor Scherzo and the A flat Waltz, Op. 34 No. 1. This choice shows that he attempted works that contain the essence of Chopin's style. The well-known English pianist and Matthay assistant, the late Vivian Langrish, told me that Bowen's performance of the B minor Sonata at his farewell recital, when he was in his late seventies, was especially impressive; the depth of his tone was unusual.

Bowen's recordings display an original and refined mind. There is a freedom in his phrasing that is very unusual in English pianists – he was one of the first to show that the Leipzig influence was becoming defunct. His C sharp minor Polonaise is full of heroic fervour and dash, as is the disc of the B flat minor Scherzo. The colouring is always imaginative and spontaneous, the tempos are on the fast side and the shape of the music is the primary consideration. The poetic moments of the Polonaise and particularly the Prelude, Op. 28 No. 23, are especially convincing; this is a personal and highly effective Chopin. Bowen devoted most of his later years to teaching and composing, and many of his attributes as an interpreter were consequently overlooked.

A pianist of the same generation, and another pupil of Matthay, was Irene Scharrer, a real virtuoso who could play any of the Chopin Etudes with technical perfection. A cousin of Myra Hess, she was the only one of the famous triumvirate of female pupils of Matthay (Hess and Harriet Cohen were the other two) who achieved real fame as a Chopin player. In April 1935 the critic of the *Musical Times* perspicaciously summed up her playing: 'Few pianists deliver Chopin's splendid virile truths better than Irene Scharrer – with meaning and without mauling.'[16] Her playing was well-developed in tone and stylistically unmannered. Like Bowen, she had a tendency towards fast tempos, but being an admirable exponent of the Matthay school she could play at great speed with relaxed musicianship. Although her contribution to the understanding of Chopin may not have been as great as that of other pianists, she was important in demonstrating that a British-born pianist had no impediment in playing his music. Miss Scharrer retired after the war, and died in 1971.

Among her recordings, an early HMV Black Label disc of the E minor Waltz, Op. Posth., demonstrates a keen appreciation of the youthful high spirits of this work. The textures are bright and luminous, and there is no tinge of melancholy even though the piece is in a minor key. Her performance of the G sharp minor Etude in thirds would be the envy of most pianists today – even the most difficult passages are handled with natural ease and musicality. The B flat minor Scherzo is brilliant and shapely; the first theme is played with such distinction and commitment that, at her best, Irene Scharrer can be ranked with Moiseiwitsch. She manages to contrast passion with relaxation in this piece, and brings out the melodic content of the passagework which so many pianists neglect.

Neither Harriet Cohen nor Dame Myra Hess was ever especially admired for her Chopin, although both played his works and made a few records of them. Harriet Cohen's disc of the C sharp minor Etude, Op. 25 No. 7, shows her affinity with the contrapuntal writing (many critics thought she was at her best in playing Bach); the different voices are brought out with exemplary clarity, although the right-hand line is sometimes disturbed so as to achieve sounds distinct from the left. Her disc of two of the *Trois Nouvelles Etudes* is slightly marred by over-pedalling. The only record of Chopin's music by Myra Hess was made in about 1931, and is of the F sharp major Nocturne, Op. 15 No. 2, coupled with a Nocturne by John Field. But she performed many of the large-scale works at her celebrated National Gallery concerts during the Second World War, and in these she featured the F minor Fantasy, the C sharp minor Scherzo, the G minor Ballade and the Waltz in E flat, Op. 18.[17] However, her musical sympathies lay more in the music of Scarlatti, Mozart, Beethoven, Schumann and Brahms.

The greatest Chopin player produced in Britain is unquestionably Solomon. Born in 1902, he was a phenomenal child prodigy who blossomed into one of the greatest pianists of the century. His career was tragically curtailed by a stroke in the mid-1950s; he is still living as this book is written.

Solomon's playing showed that he always put the music before pianism. This is not to imply that his pianistic attainments were less than perfect, but that his musicianship was overwhelming. He made many discs, and his near-perfect virtuoso technique can be heard in works such as Liszt's *Hungarian Fantasy*. Many regarded him as primarily a great exponent of Beethoven and Brahms, and perhaps less outstanding in Chopin, but his recordings of the D flat Nocturne, Op. 27, the F minor Fantasy and the Berceuse show his mastery of this composer's works. Solomon approached Chopin with a classical purity of expression and the most exquisite poetic feeling. His phrasing was unconstrained, and – like his *rubato* – entirely natural. He played Chopin with great spontaneity, as if he had re-thought the works, and the extraordinary intensity of his musical vision, conveyed through a virile manner and full tone, makes his Chopin discs quite unlike those of any other pianist.

Solomon's grasp of Chopin's musical stature was not dissimilar to that of Cortot. It is easy to contrast Solomon's sobriety in Chopin with a pianist such as Josef Hofmann, but when he is considered beside Cortot, one can detect many of the same priorities. Solomon's use of *rubato* was more sparing than Cortot's, and his tone was more dynamic; the sheer beauty of sound he produced from his instrument had a firmer and more forthright quality than that of the Frenchman. Solomon's Chopin was technically more polished and secure than Cortot's, and he always attended to the composer's markings – he did have some lessons in Paris with the great French pedagogue Lazare Lévy, and always retained that objective and controlled attitude to interpretation that was one of the hallmarks of the French school. However, unlike many French Chopin players, with the exception of Cortot, Solomon played his Chopin with the deepest personal emotional involvement, which was always channelled into interpreting the music, not into imposing his own personality. He revealed Chopin as a great composer whose music had no need to rely on the personal impact of the performer.

Solomon's determination to play Chopin 'without frills' arose from an inner conviction, and is brilliantly illustrated in his 1934 recording of the A flat Polonaise. This disc, one of the most successful readings of the work, has a grand poise and dramatic sweep entirely in keeping with the music. Both the freshness of the conception and the absolute refusal to distort the music are most unusual; Lhévinne was one of the few pianists of the older generation to follow this path, and Solomon's style was prophetic – many pianists now turn to this natural and direct response to the notes of the music. Perhaps Solomon's affinity with Chopin was not as great as that of Cortot, who somehow gave the impression of being in the possession of Chopin's soul, but Solomon still ranks with the greatest interpreters; artistic sincerity counts for much in evaluating the lasting worth of a performance.

Because Chopin is no longer thought of as the sentimental romantic of the salons, a purely pianistic approach to his music is now outmoded. However, there are certain works that thrive on lush textures and exotic beauty, such as the E flat Nocturne, Op. 55 No. 2, the Berceuse, the *Andante Spianato and Grande Polonaise* and the A flat Impromptu. This is the realm in which a pianist such as Moura Lympany comes into her own. A master of the luminous and light textures, she revels in atmospheric nuance and is a convincing Chopin player, without paying much attention to the structure of the music. Everything that she plays has a pianistic finish which is founded on the strengths of the Matthay system. Aside from these attributes of tonal purity, she also has a commanding technique that enables her to play works like the Rachmaninov Second Sonata. Her immaculate phrasing and sheer beauty of sound were the salient features of her performance when she played the B minor Sonata of Chopin at her fiftieth anniversary concert at the Royal Festival Hall in London in 1979. Shura Cherkassky, in quite another way, achieves his effects from the same source, and this approach should not be devalued; if the performer has enough musical awareness and sensitivity, the form of the music will reveal itself.

If the structural and pianistic methods are two ways of interpreting the music of Chopin, there is a third way – the scholastic approach, usually associated with music of the Baroque period and the early Viennese classics. Recently, two pianists of note have applied to Chopin's music the search for stylistic accuracy. They are Ronald Smith and Paul Badura-Skoda, who applied this method to Viennese music before trying to adapt it to his Chopin playing.

Ronald Smith was born in 1922 and concentrated much time in his early career on composing. In more recent years he has achieved justified fame in championing the works of lesser-known piano composers, such as Balakirev, Alkan and Busoni, and devotes much of his time to playing music that he believes in. It has been to their credit that well-known recording companies have supported some of his enter-prises, so bringing some of his original ideas to a wider public. He has played many of Chopin's works in recitals, and has recorded the complete Mazurkas and a disc of the lesser-known works. His style in Chopin is eclectic; he has understood the different dance-rhythms included in the generic title 'mazurka', and this awareness of the idiom contributes to make his performances stylistically convincing. However, his phrasing can lack distinction and personality, and he has a tendency to interpret consciously, from his head rather than from his heart, in a manner similar to Józef Turczyński. Smith plays all Chopin's works with zest and enterprise, and obviously enjoys rediscovering the more obscure pieces, and although he may not be an outstanding Chopin player, there is always a place for scholarly performances of great music; occasionally when he tries to play in a more instinctive manner he can lapse into excess, particularly in his interpretations of Liszt.

If the British lack the spontaneity and rhythmic sense of the Slavs in Chopin, they possess other attributes that other nationalities tend to lack – the most notable of these is a consistency of musicianship, grounded in the musical training of the last century. The well-known British pianist Peter Katin is a good example of an excellent and tasteful artist who is incapable of playing Chopin's music with any harshness. Blessed with extreme sensitivity of response, his Chopin can be very dis-tinguished and he has become something of a specialist in this field. He has the necessary technique to play everything that Chopin wrote and he is very much a thinking musician, interested in the performing styles of the great pianists of the past. The high standards of such pianists as Peter Katin and Moura Lympany have been taken too much for granted in this country. Perhaps we are attracted to those soloists who are temperamentally opposite to our own – the Russians and Poles have a certain glamour attached to them that acts strongly in their favour.

Of the younger generation of British pianists, both Howard Shelley, a very meticulous and gifted pianist, and Paul Crossley, whose style is in-novatory, have played Chopin with success. They are not alone in this field, although neither can be considered to have an especially convinc-ing identity with the composer at the moment. I believe that as the century draws to a close, British pianists will to an increasing extent find they have a natural sympathy with Chopin's music; they should take courage from the fact that pianists from as far afield as Australia, China and South America have won international recognition as Chopin players. The greater interaction of musical ideas and national characteristics that has come with the jet age will have a profound effect on the standing of various composers, and the ability of pianists of all nationalities to identify with them.

CHAPTER SEVEN

Eastern Europe, the Iberian Peninsula and Italy

Hungary, Czechoslovakia and Rumania

The countries which until the end of the First World War were part of the Austro-Hungarian Empire have produced a great many pianists of outstanding quality, who seem to have a natural affinity with Chopin's music. A strong tradition of piano playing was established in Prague at the beginning of the nineteenth century under the inspiration of Johann Wenzel Tomašek (1774–1850); his pupil Wilhelm Kuhe (1823–1912) used proudly to relate that he had been taught by a man who had played the fiddle at the first performance of *Don Giovanni*.[1] All the pianists who came from Tomašek's school were notable for their solid grounding in general musicianship, and most of them were composers as well as performers. Alexander Dreyschock and Julius Schulhoff established European reputations, and the latter strongly influenced Leschetizky in his approach to the piano. Born in Bohemia in 1818, Dreyschock was a virtuoso who played some of Chopin's music, but his approach cannot have been conducive to a satisfying interpretation of the composer's works – renowned as a staggering technician, he arranged the 'Revolutionary' Etude with left-hand octaves to replace the single semiquavers![2] Wilhelm Kuhe studied with Thalberg as well as Tomašek, and came to live in London around the middle of the century; although he played some Chopin, his main contribution to the musical life of this country was as a teacher and organizer of concerts. Another Bohemian pianist who achieved fame was Wilhelmine Clauss-Szárvady (1834–1907) whom Planté described as one of the 'ladies in mittens' (the other was Clara Schumann);[3] she concentrated on the classical repertoire, although some of her Chopin playing was much admired.

Franz Liszt was born in Raiding, near Oedenburg (Sopron) in 1811, but from childhood he studied abroad, first in Vienna with Salieri and Czerny, and then in Paris with Reicha and Paër. He spent some of his later life in Pesth (now Budapest) and, like Chopin, came to be considered as a patriotic composer. A number of Hungarians came to study with him, the most notable being Rafael Joseffy (1853–1915), one of the most distinguished interpreters of Chopin and a pianist whose influence on Chopin playing in the United States has been particularly strong. The son of a rabbi, Joseffy began his studies in Budapest with Brauer, who had been the teacher of Stephen Heller. When he was fourteen he entered the Leipzig Conservatory, where he had lessons with Reinecke and Moscheles, followed by two years of study with Tausig in Berlin. He was a pupil of Liszt in the summers of 1870 and 1871, but the greatest influence on his playing was that of Tausig, who had been Liszt's favourite pupil.[4] (Joseffy later edited the complete works of Chopin for Schirmer, and an interesting detail in this edition is that he shows how Tausig played the final rising scale on the last page of the G minor Ballade – in double thirds.)

When Joseffy made his Berlin debut in 1872, his brilliant technique and fluent passagework won immediate acclaim. But there were critics of his playing, and Xaver Scharwenka wrote in 1878:

> His extraordinary manipulation he still retains, and he is able to perform his little tricks as deftly as ever – but who nowadays can find any pleasure in such things? Thank goodness, the days of emaciated 'virtuosity' and musical trifling are gone; we don't want fiddling acrobats or feats of tumbling on the pianoforte, tricks which can only tickle an ignorant public, and help to hide the performer's empty brains and want of thought. . . . Herr Joseffy is upon a wrong road.[5]

Joseffy himself was not satisfied with his early success, and after a tour of the United States in 1879 he withdrew from the concert platform for five years to study. On resuming his performing career, he played a great deal of Chopin's and Liszt's music, and also pioneered the piano works of Brahms in America. He retired from concert-giving once more in 1888, when he became professor at the National Conservatory in New York, where he taught until 1906. Among his pupils were Moriz Rosenthal, Edwin Hughes, Clarence Adler, Ellen Ballon and James Huneker, who became his assistant and wrote biographies of Chopin and Liszt.

Although Joseffy did make occasional public appearances, he was an exceptionally shy man, who cared very little for the applause of an audience. Once his playing had reached maturity, it was beyond criticism. Albert Parsons, an American who had studied with Tausig at the same time, contrasted Joseffy's playing with that of their teacher as being 'like the multi-coloured mist that encircles a mighty mountain; but beautiful'.[6] James Huneker, who was his assistant for ten years, said that Joseffy achieved his *legato* playing by using the pedal, rather than by fingerwork alone (as he says was the case with Pachmann, Thalberg and Paderewski),[7] and he believed that Joseffy's playing had greater intellect and greater brilliance than that of Anton Rubinstein.[8]

It is greatly to be regretted that Joseffy left neither discs nor piano rolls. His interpretations probably had a basically classical orientation, since several critics thought him best suited to the music of Bach and Mozart, but he also possessed great reserves of poetry and an artistic imagination; it was the monumental quality of Tausig's playing that he lacked. He was a man of charm and humour who became something of a cult among his admirers. Huneker relates an anecdote describing a private meeting between Joseffy and Pachmann during which the two became locked in argument and Pachmann became unpleasant and so abusive that Huneker intervened by flinging a glass of beer in Pachmann's face. Joseffy afterwards scolded him for his rudeness but ended by commenting 'And you, of all men, wasted such a lot of good beer!'[9]

Both Dohnányi and Bartók influenced the playing of Hungarian pianists. Dohnányi was a very great pianist, and although he is principally remembered as an interpreter of Mozart and Beethoven, he played a fair amount of Chopin's music early in his career, and even made some piano rolls of his works. He was never a specialist in Chopin, but his style of playing influenced his pupils Géza Anda, Edward Kilenyi, Julian von Károlyi and Balint Vázsonyi, who have all played and recorded a great deal of Chopin. Dohnányi put particular emphasis on clarity of thought, spontaneity of expression and beauty of sound, and always put musicianship above pianism. The best qualities of Dohnányi's pupils are exhibited in the playing of the Hungarian pianists Annie Fischer and Livia Rev (who has lived in France for some years) and the late Imre Ungar.

Similar attributes characterized the playing of Clara Haskil, the Rumanian pianist who died tragically in Brussels in 1960 after sustaining a fall. One of the most exceptional figures in twentieth century music, Clara Haskil was born in Bucharest and was a child prodigy. After lessons with Dohnányi, she studied at the Paris Conservatoire under Cortot and (for composition) Fauré, later attending masterclasses by Busoni. She was also a talented violinist, and became a finished artist of great profundity, whose piano playing exemplified sublime musicianship. Although she played relatively few of his works in public, Miss Haskil was something of a Chopin specialist. She had unusually large hands for a woman, and could span wide chords with ease. Even from an early age, she could move her audiences through the depth of her interpretations. She included the Berceuse, the Nocturne Op. 62 No. 2, and the G minor Ballade in her early recitals, and towards the end of her life she often performed the F minor Concerto, which she recorded with Cortot's reorchestration, conducted by Igor Markevitch, another of his pupils. Arthur Hedley, the leading English Chopin scholar wrote of this performance, 'Chopin must have played this concerto that way . . . I've heard almost every Chopin player perform the F minor Concerto, but never like that,'[10] though there were some critics who thought Miss Haskil's approach too mature and too 'wise' for this relatively youthful work. Her pupil Peter Feuchtwanger, himself a well-known teacher, believes that Clara Haskil shared Chopin's 'mental disposition';[11] there may be some truth in this statement, though Feuchtwanger's assertion that she shared the composer's physical disposition is misleading – Clara Haskil's life was beset by physical trials and her experience of bodily suffering may have added to the depth of her interpretations, but Chopin himself enjoyed adequate health until his condition deteriorated sharply in the last years of his life and his later illness cannot be grafted onto his earlier works.

The fourth Ballade in F minor was the only large-scale work Clara Haskil played consistently throughout her career[12] – she performed it from 1920 to 1954 – but the F minor Concerto was a work she made particularly her own, and her interpretations of it can usefully be compared with that of her teacher, Alfred Cortot. Haskil's reading of the solo part has the seriousness of intent of a Schnabel; each note has an intensity not normally associated with the performance of romantic keyboard music. What Miss Haskil managed to convey was a stream of intention, running through the music from beginning to end. She is one of the few pianists capable of convincing us completely that Chopin's genius was equally effective in works of large form. Like Bella Davidovitch, she reflects Chopin's inner striving, and seemingly his very soul. Whereas Cortot's performance is limited in its effect by dated *rubato* and mannerisms of phrasing, Clara Haskil's playing, unfettered by any schooling (some of her trills are even idiosyncratic), remains untouched by time.

Another Rumanian pianist who possessed something of genius in his playing was the late Dinu Lipatti, who was a friend of Miss Haskil. His was also one of the most tragic lives in the history of music, but he was especially famous as a Chopin interpreter, and his discs of the fourteen Waltzes, made nearly thirty years ago, are regarded by many as the most successful versions ever recorded. Lipatti had one of the shortest careers of any great musician – he died when he was only thirty-three – but he built up a reputation as one of the greatest pianists of all time. The extraordinary nature of his talent was evident from his teens, and when he was seventeen he won second prize in a piano contest in Vienna; Cortot, with whom he began lessons in Paris soon afterwards, was a member of the jury and walked out in disgust when the first prize was awarded to the Pole, Bolesław Kon. Lipatti was also a talented composer, who studied with Paul Dukas and Nadia Boulanger. In 1943 he was appointed professor of the virtuoso class at the Geneva Conservatoire, and he resumed his international career when the war ended. It was at this time that he made most of his discs. However, his career was soon tragically interrupted by the disease which was to kill him – an incurable cancer of the lymph glands – and he died in 1950.

Although Lipatti's discs are very few, several of them are of Chopin's music, of which he was a supreme interpreter. The major recordings of Chopin that we have are of the B minor Sonata (1947), the E minor Concerto (1948, with an unnamed, though very distinguished, orchestra), the fourteen Waltzes (1949), the Barcarolle (1948), and the Waltzes again (thirteen this time, from the Besançon Festival of 1950, recorded when the artist had only a few months to live). The E minor Concerto and the thirteen Waltzes come from public concerts. Most of the discs represent his playing with great fidelity, since he was a pianist who always gave of his best.

Lipatti's Chopin had a unique quality; there was no hint of affectation in anything he did, no mannered *rubato* and no stylistic inhibitions. The playing was first and foremost classical, with a clarity of texture that was Mozartian in its purity and a technique that stressed directness of communication rather than hazy pastel colours. Whether or not Lipatti's playing of Chopin was similar to that of the composer himself can, of course, only be conjectured, but I believe that he was able to reveal the essence of Chopin's intentions with greater fidelity than most other pianists and 'Chopin specialists'. His musical sympathies were very close to those of the composer (he played Bach and Mozart with unerring poise), and he was as reserved in his use of emotion as, by all accounts, was Chopin. He achieved his effects by allowing the notes to speak in their own harmony and melody; he believed that the performer was only a channel through which the composer could express himself, and that the more the performer allowed his personality to obtrude, the less faithful or successful the interpretation would be. (This view of the role of the performer is of course different from seeing his role as 're-creating' the music afresh, an alternative approach which can be identified in the playing of other artists described in this book.)

Lipatti's interpretations were startlingly convincing. In the E minor Concerto, one is aware from the first piano entry of being in the presence of a persuasive force – Lipatti's sound-world has a magical quality, full of thought and dedication, which entirely captivates the listener. He resembled Cortot in his grasp of the composer's idiom, but he did not possess his teacher's very distinctive *rubato*, nor quite the same monumental stature. Lipatti was able to play Chopin's best-known works and make them sound as if he was performing them for the first time, whereas Cortot's playing conveys the sense that he had absorbed the music into his blood and played from a wealth of experience. Lipatti's playing had the clarity and precision of the French school, combined with a greater imagination and greater inner freedom than most French pianists possess. His mood in this concerto is in general one of gentle persuasion, though the variety of his approach is shown by the coda of the first movement, which has an alarming menace, the desperate wildness also heard on Rosenthal's version.

The strength of Lipatti's character and his determination to fulfil his musical aims are very evident in the disc of the Barcarolle, where he gives one a vision of the beauty of a higher world. The same is true of the B minor Sonata which, even if it was the only disc he had ever made, would qualify his inclusion in a list of interpretative geniuses. Lipatti's version of this last work has nearly all the sense of structure Cortot brings to it, and is characterized by a seriousness akin to Schnabel's playing of Beethoven. Lipatti reveals the composer as a man full of fears – inhibited, but possessing great beauty of soul. The Scherzo of this work has a fleet elusiveness that reminds one of the lightness and colours of the butterfly, but there is great profundity in the Largo.

Lipatti's tempos in Chopin were always exactly apt (the only one that I would dare to question is in the recording of the E flat Waltz, Op. 18, from 1949, which is perhaps too fast) and his choice in this respect always seems to derive from inner commitment rather than preconceived ideas. The full and rounded tone of his playing in the 1949 Columbia recordings of the Waltzes is well represented on the discs; these have been criticized for a certain coldness of delivery, but I do not find them to be lacking in warmth. The pianist uses very little of the *rubato* one finds in Cortot's playing, but Lipatti's perspectives were different. He saw these works as containing many passages of deep thought – in the A flat, Op. 42, the A flat, Op. 69 No. 1, and the A flat, Op. 64 No. 3, one can glimpse his artistry at its height, and the left-hand motifs achieve a significance that is especially moving. Lipatti's Chopin represented all the different human emotions – perhaps some of the discs of the last period have little humour (but who could expect a dying man to incorporate this emotion in his artistic expression?), although the performance of the third movement of the E minor Concerto is dance-like and light. The pathos of the Waltz in F minor, Op. 70 No. 2, is very touching, and encapsulates all the pianist's most persuasive qualities. Lipatti's discs will always be admired, and it is sad that he never recorded the F minor Concerto, which he was preparing for performance together with the B flat minor Sonata, when he died.

Another career which was cut short in its prime was that of the Hungarian pianist Géza Anda, who died from cancer at the age of fifty-five, and at the peak of his fame, in 1976. He was an artist whose musical intentions were as high as Lipatti's, and although not well-known as a Chopin player, his discs are sufficiently interesting to merit attention.

Anda's importance as a Chopin player lay not in his having an especially distinctive idiom that others tried to emulate – indeed this is far from the case. His stylistic affinity with the composer, particularly in his early years, was not always convincing, but Anda was able to take a totally fresh approach to Chopin's music, and the results are comparable with some of the best-established performers of his works. Few pianists can achieve this successfully. Anda cannot be classified as a pianist who played Chopin in a manner which could be summed up as 'instinctive', 'stylistically schooled,' 'academic' or the like; his approach was his own. A disc he made in 1943 is devoted to Chopin, with the Etude in E minor, Op. 25 No. 5, on one side, and two Mazurkas (Op. 67 No 4 and Op. 68 No. 2) on the other. There is a beautiful singing tone throughout, but the Etude nearly grinds to a halt because the pianist adopts an unconvincing and unsuitably ponderous approach, and fails to achieve the intended sense of breadth and depth. The two Mazurkas suffer from the same fault: the dance-like phrases are beautifully shaped, but the passages that join them together – and the rests – are so drawn out that the phrases are nullified; this is over-thoughtful playing. However, in the twenty-four Preludes Anda emerges as a mature pianist who has been able to develop his instinctive gifts and has abandoned his earlier affectation. His spontaneity in these works defies analysis – he has re-thought the music and its inner lines, giving the enviable impression that he is presenting a new work. In the D major Prelude, Op. 28 No. 5, he finds voices others neglect to seek, but he does not invent effects the composer never intended, for in the Prelude in E major, Op. 28 No. 9, he is one of the very few pianists who use Chopin's staccato marks for the notes concluding the trill at the end of the fourth bar. In observing such details, Anda is allying his own creativity to that of the composer.

Anda was a pupil of Dohnányi, and this may help to explain his ability to make everything he played sound spontaneous. This quality is rare among Chopin specialists – the fresh poetry Anda conveys in the Prelude No. 17 in A flat is seldom to be found in the performances of Magaloff, Brailowsky or even Cortot. When Anda wishes to strike terror into the listener, he does so not by increasing dynamics and speed, but by phrasing of the utmost sensitivity, as in the F minor Prelude, No. 18. He also brings out the struggle in the final Prelude in D minor, in which the composer seems to be shouting out in fear for his soul. Anda's technique was capable of fulfilling everything he undertook, but he was a pianist who realized that musical honesty is the surest road to consistent success, and that mechanical histrionics have little to do with musicianship.

A fine example of Anda's ability to play Chopin with originality and success is his disc of the A flat Polonaise, Op. 53. He uses less pedal than virtually any other pianist (Lazar Berman, Karl Müller and da Motta are the others who also use a minimal amount of pedal in this work); he purposely plays down the heroic aspect of the piece, and returns us to the rightful nature of the Polonaise, which is a dance. On the pianos of Chopin's day, it was impossible to achieve the thundering octaves that we too readily associate with the work (in Rubinstein's performance for example), and Anda's firm and rhythmical reading must therefore be closer to what was intended by the composer. Very few pianists have the technique to play this Polonaise in this way, and the difficulties of recording a completely clean reading are unfortunately accentuated on this disc by an especially clumsy tape-joint, which obliterates the end of a phrase! Nevertheless, the performance is outstanding, and in contrast with this basically 'straight' reading of the opening, Anda plays the lyrical parts with an extra warmth of tone. It is only in the last pages, when the opening subject returns, that he allows the heroic aspect of the work to take shape. It is a pity that more pianists do not try to emulate Anda's aims in playing Chopin.

Four living pianists, all of them older than Anda or Lipatti, deserve some attention as Chopin players, although two of them – Andor Foldes and Annie Fischer – are not usually considered in Chopin, and Louis Kentner is equally famous as a Liszt player, as is Julian von Károlyi.

Although he is now less famous than the others, there was a time when Károlyi was very well-known as a Chopin player. He was born in 1914, and was a child prodigy who trained in Budapest under Dohnányi together with the late Imre Ungar, the brilliant blind pianist who lost the 1932 Chopin Competition on a toss after securing the same number of points as Uninsky, who was declared the winner. Károlyi also studied with Margrit Varro, a celebrated Hungarian teacher who recently died in her nineties, with Josef Pembaur, and with Cortot. His later career has been overshadowed by the fact that he played in Germany during the Second World War. Károlyi made a number of discs of Chopin during the war years, and they present him as an accomplished technician and an altogether stylish performer. Of the large-scale works, he recorded the G minor Ballade (1944), the F minor Fantasy and the B flat minor Nocturne, Op. 9 No. 1, and he also made long-playing records of the four Impromptus and both Concertos.

Károlyi's Chopin has certain qualities in common with that of Brailowsky, although he always played with an extreme refinement that sometimes eluded the Russian. His appeal seems to be directed towards the less-discerning public which might be blinded by displays of technique. He is most successful in the early works of Chopin, where brilliance and speed count for much; it is not that he cannot play a slow work, such as the B flat minor Nocturne, Op. 9 No. 1, very well indeed, but this piece requires little musical planning – the principal need is for delicate tonal shading. In terms of pure sound Karólyi is very satisfying, and his finished technique is a valuable asset. The right-hand ornaments of the Nocturne have a lovely liquidity, a slightly feminine style of execution, and a communicative singing tone. However, in a work such as the G minor Ballade, his playing, despite his command of the music, is unimpressive considered beside the interpretations of Horowitz, Pollini or Ashkenazy. When Deutsche Grammophon Gesellschaft selected a mixture of Chopin pieces for an album entitled *Chopin in Brilliant Interpretations*, Karólyi's disc of the Bolero was chosen – an appropriate choice, since he plays it with great finish, variety and panache. But his reading of a mature work, such as the F minor Fantasy, shows that he relies solely for effect on producing exciting or beautiful sounds – he entirely fails to convey the profundity of the music, as can be measured by comparing his performance with that of Solomon, Cortot, Fou T'song or Rubinstein. This is one of the reasons why Karólyi, who is so successful in works such as the *Andante Spianato and Grande Polonaise* and the two Concertos, has never consolidated a reputation as a Chopin player of the first rank, and many think that he is better-suited to Liszt.

Andor Foldes (b. 1913) is almost an exact contemporary of Karólyi, and he also studied with Dohnányi. Although the knowledgeable German critic Joachim Kaiser dismisses Foldes as merely 'technically well-versed', he is a pianist whose aims are not dissimilar to those of Géza Anda, though he does not quite possess the latter's imagination. The C sharp minor Mazurka, Op. 63 No. 3 (a favourite with many pianists) is played with the greatest taste and an admirable sense of style. Foldes is a pianist who never allows anything to escape from his fingers in a disorderly way; his playing is admirably proportioned and the changing moods are spontaneously expressed.

Another well-known Hungarian Chopin player is Louis (Lajos) Kentner, who was born in 1906 and has lived in London since 1935. He studied in Budapest and began his virtuoso career when only fifteen. He won only fifth prize in the 1932 Chopin Competition, but the placing is deceptive because in this remarkable contest those ahead of him were Uninsky and Ungar, Bolesław Kon and Abram Lufer. Kentner's placing was higher than that of Karólyi, Maryla Jonas (a favourite Polish pianist), Pavel Serebryakov, Carlo Vidusso (Pollini's teacher), Niedzielski and Eduardo del Pueyo, all of whom have had international careers.

Kentner is a musician of impeccable taste and wide culture, who plays music ranging from Bach to that of contemporary composers, and though he is above all a great Liszt player, he is particularly well-loved and respected in Britain for his playing of Chopin. He recorded many of Chopin's works for Columbia on 78s, having made his first disc as early as 1928 – this was recorded in Hungary and bought by Edison Bell, and is a performance of the A flat Impromptu, Op. 29, and the C sharp minor *Fantaisie-Impromptu*, Op. 66. These are beautifully shaped readings, which according to some critics the pianist has never matched. Kentner has a deep tone, phrasing of real distinction, and an apparently easy mastery of his instrument which can lead to distortion: in a work such as the G minor Ballade, where Chopin's youthful high spirits are expressed in passages of great brilliance, Kentner's response sounds almost facile because it is too relaxed; he seems to be able to play the music so easily that the inherent sense of urgency is lost. There are undoubtedly many pianists who often read too much into the music they play. This is especially true in Chopin, and there are performers who try to make an early Mazurka sound as if it was a profound and philosophically potent work. But in Kentner's playing the sense of struggle is sometimes missing. It is not that he is cool – on the contrary, his tone is rich and penetrating – but more that he does not seem to associate readily with the passionate side of Chopin's nature. His command of the technical problems of the final pages of the G minor Ballade is very impressive, and he plays the two passages of rising scales at the very end with the unusual practice of re-depressing the keys of the lowest notes of the scale passages after the run has been concluded. Simon Barer does the same on his Remington disc of the same work. With Kentner the effect is not entirely convincing.

Like his younger compatriot Tamás Vásáry, Kentner's response to the melodic content of the music is highly impressive. He is musically convincing in a work such as the *Fantaisie-Impromptu*, which many treat in a rather cavalier manner, in both his early and later recordings, and makes one question Chopin's decision not to publish a work of such exceptional qualities. Kentner is at his best when the music is rhapsodic in nature – the Barcarolle suits his style very well – and this quality is one of the factors that makes him such a magnificent Liszt player. He is of a generation whose phrasing can tend to sound mannered, but even if this is sometimes apparent in his playing, he is too creative a performer ever to allow his readings to become routine.

Annie Fischer was also born in Budapest, and is renowned as an interpreter of Mozart and Beethoven. Nevertheless, she has played a certain amount of Chopin throughout her career, and at a recital at the Queen Elizabeth Hall in London in 1973, for example, she performed the G minor Ballade, the C sharp minor Nocture, Op. 27 No. 1, and the A flat Waltz, Op. 42. She has recorded little Chopin, but her disc of the *Fantaisie-Impromptu* illustrates the strengths of her playing – clarity, musical intelligence, spontaneity, and a concern for the ongoing flow of the music. Miss Fischer is an erratic performer who can disappoint, and who suffers from very bad nerves. But when she plays at her best, she is a musical force to be reckoned with, and the way in which she points to details in the *Fantaisie-Impromptu* suggests that if she turned to his music she could be a leading Chopin player. There are many pianists who play Chopin well, but who do not choose to do so in public – and, conversely, many who play Chopin and would be better advised to keep to their regular repertoire; Gieseking used to say that he preferred to leave the performance of Chopin to those pianists who really wanted to play it, and as a rule, he did not![13]

It is immediately apparent on hearing György Cziffra play that he is a musical phenomenon. Cziffra's career has been hazardous – he fought in the Hungarian Army during the Second World War, served a considerable time doing forced labour as a road-builder, and afterwards survived by working in cabaret acts and playing in cafés. He left Hungary at the time of the 1956 uprising, and made his home in Paris. His fame has recently suffered something of an eclipse, largely due to his musical indiscretions; he is not the only pianist whose reputation has suffered because of his repertoire and method of presentation – Leff Pouishnoff, José Iturbi and Karol Szreter have also been affected by their association with light and fanciful music and by distorting the original in bad transcriptions.

There is a strong element of the gypsy in Cziffra's playing, very noticeable in his interpretations of Liszt, particularly the Hungarian Rhapsodies. He plays Chopin with great panache, and it is important to bear in mind that Chopin himself welcomed a certain degree of abandon and even recklessness in the performance of his works; he admired Gutmann's playing, and may have envied Liszt the freedom which he himself, with his more reserved style, was unable to bring to his own compositions. A performer who is at times guilty of excess is as much a serious musician as those whose control is always immaculate, like Pollini and Brendel. Cziffra's startling records of Liszt's music might suggest that he would play Chopin in a bizarre and exaggerated way, but he is a serious musician who can adjust his approach to suit the music he plays. The twenty-four Etudes display any pianist's art in a kaleidoscopic form, demonstrating his ability to cope with every facet of Chopin's idiom, but in Cziffra's performance there is a haphazard element that can either infuriate or cause intense pleasure. The beautiful line and continuity of his playing of the E flat minor Etude, Op. 10 No. 6, is ingratiating and persuasive, but on the other hand, his caricature of the left-hand part of the G flat Etude, Op. 10 No. 5, the 'Black Key', is grotesque. He adopts extreme tempos in the brilliant Etudes, yet it is in the slower ones that he shows his best-planned playing; the C sharp Minor, Op. 25, No. 7, is particularly thoughtful and pleasant. Toscanini once said that he hated piano recitals because pianists tended to pull the tempos about to suit themselves – this tendency is too often apparent in Cziffra's playing, as in the Etude in A minor, Op. 25 No. 11, the 'Winter Wind'. Judgments about whether a particular interpreter transgresses the bounds of musical taste are always particularly subjective, and perhaps this is so in Chopin's music to an even greater extent than other composers', because repeated listening to his works always seems to reveal something new.

Another Hungarian pianist who has recorded a great number of the composer's works and established a reputation as a Chopin specialist is Tamás Vásáry. He made his first public appearance at the age of eight in a Mozart piano concerto, and Dohnányi was impressed by his talent. Vásáry studied in Budapest with József Gát and Lajos Hernádi, and in 1955 took part in the Chopin Competition in Warsaw. The standard that year was particularly high (among the prizewinners were Adam Harasiewicz, Ashkenazy, Fou T'song, Ringeissen, Shtarkman and André Tchaikowsky, and Vásáry was awarded an honourable mention. He went on to take part in the Queen Elisabeth of Belgium Competition the following year, and, together with his compatriots Peter Frankl and György Bánhalmi, was awarded a prize. (Bánhalmi, who was then about thirty, later settled in Chicago as a teacher, and has made a very good disc of Chopin rarities including the E flat Rondo, Op. 16, the *Variations Brillantes*, Op. 12, and the Variations on a German Air, Op. Posth.; he is an excellent technician and a sound musician).

After the 1956 uprising, Vásáry left Hungary and having spent some time in Switzerland settled in London. He brings to Chopin a deep understanding of the roots of the composer's musical style, an understanding strengthened by his study of other composers, particularly the Viennese masters and Liszt. He had the greatest admiration for the playing of Horowitz, Lipatti, Clara Haskil (with whom he tried unsuccessfully to study) and Annie Fischer during his formative years.[14] At an early age he was made aware of the highest technical standards after hearing such pianists as Karólyi, Dohnányi, Gilels and Richter. When still a boy he built up an enviable technique, practising so much that he nearly damaged his hands.

Vásáry has told me that the pianists who he especially admires in Chopin include Fou T'song for his exceptional playing of the Mazurkas, Haskil in the C minor Nocturne, Op. 48 No. 1, Arrau in the *Trois Nouvelles Etudes* and Backhaus, from a technical standpoint, in the twenty-four Etudes – his 78s of these works were a milestone in forming Vásáry's conception of Chopin. These preferences reveal something of his own attitude in interpreting the composer, and spontaneity of rhythm, clarity of thought, musical control and technical finesse are high on his list of priorities. His response to Chopin is both personal and enlightened. He can neither be classified as a miniaturist nor a player who especially succeeds in visualizing the music as painted on a large canvas; his art is born of a natural response, and he is equally successful in both large and small-scale works. The distinctive attribute of his playing is above all lyricism, but he has that ability always to rise to the requirements of the music, which is the mark of a great pianist. The level of his professionalism can be measured by the fact that in the late '70s he replaced Claudio Arrau (who had strained his arm when closing a hotel window) in the Chopin E minor Concerto at the Royal Festival Hall at very short notice, and gave a performance with the fervour and virtuosity of a great master although he had not played this work in public for a considerable time. It is unfortunate that the discs of Chopin he made between 1960 and 1965 have been so frequently re-issued, because Vásáry's Chopin has matured significantly over the intervening years. His playing contains many of the best features of Annie Fischer's art – directness of intent and textual clarity – combined with more reliable technical equipment and a romantic temperament. He manages to endow the F minor Concerto with the aristocratic simplicity of a Rubinstein, and uses the sophisticated passagework to contribute to the general impression he wishes to convey. The key to his success is the directness and purity of his intentions, his fervour, and his ability to express his emotions because he is also able to organize them.

Vásáry always produces a finely finished product, but this very factor can act against him – he can play with such care that there is no margin left for spontaneous expression, but this criticism can only occasionally be made of his performances. His slight and slender build, his cordiality and reserve, are reminiscent of descriptions of Chopin himself, and he has the same strength of purpose under an unassertive exterior; he possesses the determination to follow his convictions characteristic of great artists.

Other Hungarians of this same generation have played Chopin with success. Bálint Vázsonyi, who is a little younger than Vásáry, has recorded a few of the works, and takes a very different approach. In 1958 he went to Florida to become one of Dohnányi's last pupils (he later wrote a biography of his master, who had settled in the United States after the Second World War), and he is a pianist who usually specializes in large-scale works. His extraordinary attempt to play all thirty-two sonatas of Beethoven continuously in two days may reflect something slightly foolhardy in his character, but nevertheless, when he has prepared himself well, he is a pianist to be considered seriously. In an interesting sleeve-note on his disc of the B flat minor Sonata, the F minor

Fantasy, and the Barcarolle, he discusses the works of Chopin that are in large forms, and comments: 'The secret of any master is the ability to compose music in which the form grows out organically of the substance, and not the other way round.'[15] This admirably expresses an important factor in performance: that the pianist who fully understands the nature of a work will convey its unity in his performance. But Vázsonyi himself, in his Chopin disc, offers an approach that neglects much of the substance of the phrasing; this Chopin playing is slightly callous, though always musical. Vázsonyi never waits long enough to savour a phrase, as would Vásáry, because he has made continuity his first priority.

Peter Frankl, of the same generation as Vásáry and Vázsonyi, is another respected pianist who plays Chopin in a poetic and sensitive way. He has recorded the complete Polonaises (including the juvenile ones), the Ballades and the F minor Fantasy. Like Vásáry, he studied with Lajos Hernádi, and also with Marguerite Long and Ilona Kabos (who was married to Louis Kentner for many years). A searching player, whose art is more associated with the music of Schumann than with that of Chopin, he has all the best traits of the school that I have been describing. His tone is fuller and more emotionally warm than that of Vásáry, but he does not perhaps quite possess the same degree of virtuosity.

All these artists are now in their forties, and their successors among the young generation of Hungarian pianists are equally impressive. I am most familiar with the Chopin playing of Sándor Falvai, Dezsö Ranki and András Schiff from among this group, all of whom are beginning to realize the greatest potential, as is Zoltán Kocsis, whom I have not had the opportunity of hearing in Chopin. Falvai is the oldest, and was born in 1949, and is less well-known in Western Europe than the others. His disc of Chopin's E minor Concerto is of considerable interest. All the great Hungarians have developed their technique to an unusually high standard, which may be partly due to the figure of Franz Liszt, the arch-virtuoso, looming over their past. Falvai's superb ensemble playing in the first movement of the Concerto is exemplary, and he gives a highly satisfying account of the work, with the right blend of virtuosity and youthful vigour. The Mozartian clarity of his phrasing is reminiscent of Haskil and Lipatti. Perhaps a little lacking in personality, he concentrates on the music rather than on a personal imprint, and the end result has the beauty of a highly polished gem. There is little use of *rubato* here and it seems that this is a facet of Chopin playing that has been moderated if not largely abandoned by the post-war generation. Falvai plays the first movement coda with a notable absence of accents in the left-hand octaves, which are interspersed by those trills that can strike terror into the listener, as in the playing of Rosenthal and Lipatti. Falvai treats this section as a strictly classical 'rounding off', and its characteristic menace is missed. He has none of the warmth of a Novaës in a work such as the C major Mazurka, Op. 24 No. 2 – he is determined to stress the folk origins of the dance (showing the influence of Bartók) and manages to make the piece sound almost modern. In the C sharp minor Nocturne (*Lento con gran espressione*) he chooses the harmonically less regular version of the text.

Dezsö Ranki gives a very brilliant and totally shallow account of Chopin. Though the Etudes have staggering accuracy and speed, his playing is superficial in emotional commitment – he seems to be too preoccupied with the mechanical aspect of the music to convey any great originality. However, his Etudes have a young man's dash, with fresh rhythms, and show a musical intelligence of a high order. He presents much the same picture in his recording of the four Scherzos.

András Schiff, the youngest pianist of these three, and perhaps the most interesting pianist of his generation, has not played much Chopin in this country, although I have heard a lovely performance of the A flat Waltz, Op. 42, from him that made me see this much-played work in a new light. He reduced the atmosphere of rhythmical complexity that normally surrounds this Waltz, and revealed it as a piece with a Mozartian directness of communication. Schiff's ability to play with complete spontaneity could make him into one of the great pianists of the century; his interest in Bach and Mozart should help to give him all the necessary musical insight to become a first-rate Chopin player.

The Czechs have for many years been more concerned with their own music than any other, and in the works of Dvořák, Suk and Janáček there is a freshness of conception emanating from their unique cultural heritage and incorporating both the melodies and rhythm of folk dances. There was no piano department at the Prague Conservatory until 1881, but since that date many fine pianists have been among its graduates, among them František Rauch, Josef Páleníček and Rudolf Firkušný, all of whom were born around 1914 and became Chopin players of some fame. (The other well-known Czech pianist of the same generation, Pavel Štěpán, has not to my knowledge ever specialized in Chopin.) They were also composers: Páleníček, Rauch and Firkušný wrote piano concertinos (their interest in this form no doubt deriving from Janáček); Páleníček also composed a concerto for piano and a concerto for saxophone, and Rauch a suite entitled *Jaro* (Spring). They established a standard of piano-playing to which the present generation of Czech keyboard artists owe much of the solid reputation they enjoy.

Páleníček has recorded a number of Chopin's works, and is very much a re-creative musician, whose performances are marked by an imaginative re-thinking and a solid musicality that yields to none. He is undoubtedly most effective in the music of his native country – his mantle has fallen upon Radoslav Kvapil, who was born in 1934 – and his playing of Chopin, despite his imaginativeness, is unidiomatic. This could never be said of František Rauch's performances, and when playing at his best he is one of the most satisfying of all Chopin's interpreters. He now spends most of his time teaching, and his ability is demonstrated by the quality of the pupils that emerge from his class. Some years ago Rauch made a recording of the F minor Concerto with that sterling Czech conductor, Václav Smetáček, and the results were very moving and artistically successful. Rauch, like many Czech and Hungarian pianists, is one of those artists who refuses to be dominated by Western European ways; they re-create their Chopin, and though their playing is not divorced from that which we have come to accept, they play from an inner conviction and with a genuinely personal response. Rauch's style contains some mannerisms from an earlier era, such as the way in which he plays spread chords, but his conception of the Concerto is dynamic and stimulating. In the first movement one recognizes a freedom of spirit that allows him to express every aspect of the music's emotional substance – he is not afraid to take time to savour and communicate a particular phrase. His very individual playing presents Chopin the composer, the man who works out his convictions in his art, the prophet of the purely personalized means of expression. The development section of the first movement is taken very slowly; it is pensive and lightly-coloured. Rauch's technique, even by today's standards, is highly finished, and there is never any unnecessary sense of struggling. He lifts the music from the humdrum concerns of the pianist obsessed with displaying his prowess, to that of the poet and the visionary. The extraordinary delicacy of the filigree passages of the second movement shows that Rauch is quite prepared to take risks to secure musical effects – it is extremely difficult to play this degree of *pianissimo*. The third movement, in complete contrast, is played like a witty dance. Rauch's keyboard character is less extrovert than that of Artur Rubinstein; like Arrau, he is the thinking man's Chopin player, achieving his effects from the mind, rather than from the fingers alone.

In a later work, such as the 'Funeral March' Sonata, he adopts a different style; here his vision of the music is serious and almost orchestral. In the Scherzo and the March itself he is both responsive and self-assured. The March is seen as a funeral cortège approaching from the distance, coming nearer and nearer, until death itself is visible, and then the Trio brings the sublimation of death in the after-life. The Finale, in which the composer gives one so concentrated a view of his personality, is played by Rauch with virtually no sustaining pedal, and the results are rich beyond belief (Robert Casadesus's treatment is similar). This is a great pianist playing with absolute control and strength of purpose; his performance of the B minor Sonata is equally impressive.

Firkušný's playing of Chopin is somewhat more conventional. He has recorded the B minor Sonata, and possesses a brilliant virtuoso technique and a richly varied mind. He is quite capable of rising to the bravura of the B flat minor Scherzo and executing it with marvellous sparkle, just after playing an exquisite Nocturne.

In more recent years there have been fewer Chopin players of note in Czechoslovakia; Stanislas Knorr, who took part in the 1955 Chopin Competition, has a brilliant style of great dynamism, but the great Chopin interpreter of the same generation is Ivan Moravec, a pianist widely admired in this country. He was a pupil of Ilona Kurz (the daughter of the great Czech piano pedagogue Vilem Kurz, whose wife Ružena later married the pianist, Vaclav Štěpán) and then studied with Arturo Benedetti Michelangeli. It is only since the late 1960s that Moravec has established a reputation in Western Europe, and he is now regarded by some as one of the greatest living pianists. Unfortunately his appearances in the West have been very rare, but there are several discs of his playing Chopin's music, some of them available on a Connoisseur Society label.

A great technician must not only have the ability to play fast, but the equipment to fulfil his artistic creativity, and there are several pianists of the younger generation who while having a well-developed technique do not have the capacity to play a sustained *legato* line *pianissimo*, to maintain clarity of texture, and to play with absolute adherence to rhythmic detail. Moravec is by any standards a prince among pianists. He can play Chopin's very taxing B minor Scherzo with the virtuosity of a Horowitz or Szpinalski, combined with the sensitivity of a Moiseiwitsch. He is generally at his best, however, in slow lyrical passages, in which he reveals a rare sensitivity. In a work such as the Barcarolle he cultivates a beautifully cultured sound-world in which there are infinite degrees of poetry. There are many pianists who, by playing quietly, create a hushed atmosphere when they perform certain phrases, but there are few who can play like this with a full range of expressive nuance. To play *piano* for a great length of time requires tremendous control; in his recording of the C sharp minor Etude, Op. 25 No. 7, Moravec shows that he can do this, and the results are magical. He fully appreciates that a developed sense of Chopin's contrapuntal style is a necessary component for a good performance of many works, and therefore plays a work such as the C sharp minor Mazurka, Op. 50 No. 3 (surely the most interesting of all the Mazurkas), with rare insight and colour. His reading does not quite possess the imperious confidence of Małcużyński's Columbia 78, nor the dynamism of Horowitz's older version, but he underlines the modernity and the inventiveness of Chopin's pen in this piece. That Moravec plays Beethoven with equal distinction shows that his sympathies are as wide-ranging, and he responds to all the minutiae of the music he plays. He has Michelangeli's ability to evoke atmosphere, a great asset few possess, even if he sometimes shares the Italian master-pianist's tendency to play in a rather detached and prosaic manner.

The Iberian Peninsula

Few Spanish or Portuguese pianists have ever specialized in Chopin. The earliest recording of a Spanish pianist playing Chopin is a privately-recorded cylinder of 1903 with Joaquin Malats in the C sharp minor Waltz, Op. 64 No. 2. The playing is exceptionally spontaneous and very impressive, and this pianist must have been an extremely convincing Chopin interpreter. The quality of improvisation which is evident both in this performance and in Malats's cylinder of Liszt's thirteenth Hungarian Rhapsody is something that has never been developed in the established schools of music in the rest of Europe. Liszt's Portuguese pupil, José Vianna da Motta, whose playing has been described in Chapter Two of this book, recorded the A flat Polonaise, and one of da Motta's pupils, Sequeira Costa plays much Chopin today, and has an extraordinarily powerful technique, if little originality of style.

José Iturbi had lessons with Malats when a boy, and was an able pianist (though some said that his sister Amparo was even more talented than he) who spoiled his reputation as a serious artist by appearing in Hollywood films. In the 1950s and 1960s his playing became more and more exaggerated and sensational, but when young he was a very good pianist with a fluent style and admirable in Mozart. His natural musicianship is displayed in a recital on a Baldwin piano for the Turia Record Company. His version of the A flat Polonaise has the minimal use of the sustaining pedal, and demonstrates his very good technique; the playing is unaffected and charming.

Alicia de Larrocha derives from the same school, and studied with Granados's pupil, Frank Marshall. Miss de Larrocha's style is, however, much more sophisticated, and her reputation is justifiably high. Her captivating personality is always apparent in her music-making. She has recorded little Chopin, but her earliest disc, made at the age of nine, is a performance of the A minor Waltz, Op. 34 No. 2, and the B major Nocturne, Op. 32 No. 1, and these show her naturalness and innate ability. Her version of the twenty-four Preludes is disappointing, but her disc of the F minor Concerto is a good example of her warm and richly imaginative art.

Of the younger generation of Spanish pianists, Rafael Orozco has played a fair amount of Chopin, but he seems to have a tendency to allow his temperament and technique to take precedence; although he is highly gifted, his playing lacks dependability. In recent years, there has been an increasing demand for Spanish piano music, and understandably many artists have chosen to specialize in their native music, and appear to avoid Chopin.

The Italians

In the nineteenth century, before the advent of Ferruccio Busoni (1866–1924), the Italians were more involved in the art of the voice than in any individual instrument, although there were always capable musicians emerging from that country. Busoni himself was very much influenced by Liszt, who gave him encouragement and advice although no formal lessons, and if he cannot be labelled as a pupil of Liszt, he was his disciple and played a great deal of his music. His other loves were Bach, Mozart, Beethoven and, in varying degrees, Chopin.

Busoni was born in 1866 into a musical family – his father was a virtuoso clarinetist and his mother an accomplished pianist. He was immersed in music from the earliest age, and played in a concert in Vienna when he was nine. By the age of fifteen he was touring all over Italy, and in his late twenties began his career as a teacher when he was appointed professor of piano at the Helsingfors Conservatory in Finland. He won the composition prize at the Anton Rubinstein Competition in St Petersburg in 1890 with his *Konzertstück* for piano and orchestra, and his compositions are in many ways prophetic, although they often gave rise to the complaint that they were so inventive that they gave no pleasure to the listener, and during his lifetime Busoni's fame was as a pianist rather than as a composer. A pacifist who during the First World War refused to play in any of the belligerent countries, he spent much of his life in Switzerland.

According to Hugo Leichtentritt, Busoni's piano playing was always 'subservient to a most powerful intellect'.[16] He was the first really 'modern' pianist, who experimented exhaustively with the tonal resources of the instrument, and as a contrapuntalist was without peer. A passionate Mozartian, his love for this composer, and for Bach, helped form him into an interesting Chopin player, who broke many of the 'rules' that had already been established in performing his works. The four pianists I have met who heard Busoni – two of them received advice from him – have all agreed that there was something 'odd' about his Chopin. Vlado Perlemuter said that he played 'Chopin-Busoni' rather than pure Chopin, and Frank Merrick told me that he would never forget the strange way in which Busoni played the opening page of the G minor Ballade, using an unpedalled *staccato*, which Merrick found unacceptable, for the repeated chords in the middle range.[17] Busoni's biographer Edward J. Dent says of his Chopin:

> His playing of Chopin was always difficult to accept. The smaller works of Chopin he never cared to play at all, except for the Preludes, which remained in his repertoire up to the end; he said that they were the most 'prophetic' things which Chopin ever wrote, those which looked furthest into the future. . . . He preferred the Etudes and Ballades [to the Mazurkas]. His conception of Chopin was always terrifyingly grandiose; passages which most pianists play dreamily and tenderly, he would bring out with a solidity and dignity which seemed ruthlessly severe.[18]

In the years immediately preceding the First World War Busoni went through something of an artistic crisis from which he never fully emerged. He began to find practising extremely tedious, and contemplated giving up piano playing altogether.[19] It is in this light that one must view his records. Sacheverell Sitwell wrote that he 'outsized Chopin' and could degrade the music by underlining the more 'pretty' aspects of the pieces,[20] but this seems to contradict the conception most had of him as being severely classical. *Grove's Dictionary* says that Busoni played even the twenty-four Preludes 'in a monumental manner'.[21] It has been suggested that as a pianist Busoni took up Liszt's mantle, but it is hard to see the basis for this suggestion, since Busoni had none of the Hungarian gypsy quality which made Liszt's performances of all dance works so impressive. There was in Busoni a spiritual force at work – he was obsessed with the piano as an instrument on which the player could work out his Faustian nature. As a young man he had regarded Anton Rubinstein as a model, and his programmes were of equal scope: in 1883, when he was seventeen, Busoni gave a recital in which he played, in the following order, Beethoven's Sonata Op. 111, Bach's Italian Concerto, Schumann's *Etudes Symphoniques*, Chopin's *Andante Spianato and Grande Polonaise Brillante*, and Liszt's transcription of the music from Mendelssohn's *Midsummer Night's Dream*.[22]

Busoni made a few recordings of Chopin, and all of them are interesting. He recorded the G flat Etude, Op. 10 No. 5 (the 'Black Key') twice, the E minor Etude, Op. 25 No. 5, the F sharp Nocturne, Op. 15 No. 2, and the Prelude in A, Op. 28 No. 7, on disc, and also made a number of piano rolls for Welte Mignon and Duo-Art, which include such big works as the A flat Polonaise and the G minor Ballade. Most would agree that he was best suited to performing large-scale works, and it is therefore a pity that the limited recording devices of the early days were only able to capture him in miniatures; his discs were all made in

1922, and the rolls do not seem to capture his greatness. Busoni's attention to every detail of the piano's mechanism and its effect was especially notable. His pupil Edward Weiss has attested to the great originality with which he used the pedals, but he always sustained the final chords of a work by the hands as well. Unfortunately, when Busoni came to record at the end of his life, much of the enthusiasm with which he had approached the piano in his youth had evaporated, and he conveyed the impression of a disappointed man.[23] Nevertheless, his discs show his imaginative pedal effects, and the technique in both recordings of the 'Black Key' Etude is amazing. The Duo-Art piano rolls are perhaps the most characteristic demonstration of his Chopin playing, and the final Prelude from Op. 28, in D minor, is given a demonic treatment making it clear that the idea of Chopin as a spineless romantic is a complete misconception.

That Busoni was a very great teacher can be gleaned from the names of his pupils; among those who played Chopin were Brailowsky, von Zadora, Petri, Haskil, Grainger, Sirota, Münz, Turczyński, Zecchi, Fryer, Agosti, Carreras and Ganz – and there were many others. Busoni was the first great Italian pianist to play Chopin, but Liszt's pupil Giovanni Sgambati, born in 1846, must also be mentioned in this context. He was a very influential figure who, according to his pupil the late Margherita Trombini-Kazuro, was always at pains to stress the contrapuntal elements in Chopin's piano writing. Sgambati was an influential teacher, very much interested in German music, especially Wagner, for which he was roundly criticized by Alfred Casella, who accused him of 'Germanizing' Italian music.[24] One of his best pupils was Maria Carreras, who also had lessons from Busoni. She was born around 1872, and was a prodigy who as a child was awarded a prize by Liszt. She was from all acounts a master-pianist, and had many admirers. In 1914 she was chosen to participate with Paderewski, Rosenthal and Busoni in gala concerts with the Warsaw Philharmonic, and in the same year was invited to Kiev by the Czar to play in concerts commemorating the tenth anniversary of the death of Anton Rubinstein. She made her American debut in New York in 1923, and the critic W. J. Henderson described her as 'a strong powerful personality.... Her playing was virile, commanding and brilliant.'[25] She later settled in the United States, and put much of Sgambati's teaching into practice. Her varied style enabled her to play almost anything that Chopin wrote, and the *Allegro de Concert* often featured in her recitals. She made some piano rolls but not, to my knowledge, any discs, although she died as recently as 1966.

Another great Italian pianist, also an eminent teacher and conductor, is Carlo Zecchi. A pupil of Busoni, he became interested in early Italian keyboard music, but has very far-reaching tastes. A man who can play a

Scarlatti sonata with extreme purity, who can conduct a very impressive performance of Berlioz's *Symphonie Fantastique*, and who sits on the jury of almost every prestigious music competition in the world, is no ordinary musician. Zecchi's Chopin, although rather unidiomatic, is magical because of his ravishing tonal palette, which alone would make his playing irresistible. He plays the B minor Mazurka, Op. 33 No. 4, too slowly for some tastes, but the dreamy sounds he draws from the piano are unique.

In the last century, there were a few Italian pianists who played Chopin well – Alfonso Rendano was one of them – but with the advent of Michelangeli and Pollini Italian pianists become especially associated with his music. Arturo Benedetti Michelangeli was born in 1920, and has always been something of an unknown quantity. A student at the Milan Conservatory (where Galli-Curci received a first prize for piano in 1903!), he won first prize at the International Piano Competition in Geneva in 1939, and in the same year was appointed to the teaching staff of his old academy. He is a man who is intrigued by mechanical equipment (his accomplishments include being a pilot and a racing driver) but he is one of the most spiritual of today's performers. He refuses to give public performances unless conditions are perfect – he will only play if he regards the arrangements as ideal, if he is in the right frame of mind, and on a piano shipped if necessary from Italy, and he is notorious for cancelling and delaying his public performances. However, when playing at his best he can unquestionably lay claim to be ranked as one of the great pianists of the present century. His conceptions are less austere than were those of Busoni, and unlike him, Michelangeli is sometimes willing to use the piano solely to entice the ear with beautiful sounds. Since the very beginning of his career, certain works have remained in his repertoire, including the Bach/Busoni Chaconne, the Brahms 'Paganini' Variations and the Schumann Concerto, and he has always played a good deal of Chopin. He made a disc of the Berceuse as long ago as 1943, which is one of the finest interpretations of this work ever captured on record. His use of *rubato* here is charming, and the whole performance is characterized by refined emotion, though his style is very relaxed. He is too good a pianist to try to instil into the music a philosophical weight it does not possess.

Michelangeli's discs are hard to find, and a number of them have been taken from public recitals or radio broadcasts and have surreptitiously found their way onto the record market; in many cases the sound quality is far from adequate, but Michelangeli's exceptional qualities emerge none the less. His style as a Chopin player cannot easily be categorized – he does not stress the organic structural unit, so carefully shaped by Cortot; he does not play with the prime concern of pianistic beauty, like

Godowsky; nor, like Sofronitsky, can he be said to have a total absorption in re-creating the music. His Chopin, at its best, is an amalgam of all these styles. The works most frequently associated with him are the second Scherzo (in B flat minor), the G minor Ballade, the B minor Mazurka, Op. 33 No. 4, the Berceuse, the A flat Waltz, Op. 69 No. 1, and the A minor Mazurka, Op. 68 No. 2; he has recorded most of these both on 78s and on long-playing records.

Harold Schonberg wrote in *The Great Pianists* that Michelangeli was a super-virtuoso of the order of Horowitz,[26] but the Italian uses these gifts to serve the music, not for display. He possesses a unique charisma on the platform; a journalist once compared his presence with that of St Francis of Assisi (an analogy which may have been prompted by the fact that Michelangeli has been attracted to the monastic life) and his playing is immensely profound. He has it within his power to demonstrate a full range of emotions, ranging from the demonic to the deeply spiritual, from the reminiscent to the bright and open, and when he is at his best the total effect of his playing conveys the art of a very great man who is not limited by the personal failings or the lack of spiritual values that beset most other artists.

Michelangeli's respect for Chopin is evident in every note he plays. There are none of Busoni's distortions of the composer's intentions – his approach is similar to that of Zecchi, with whom he shares the ability to create a tonal world that establishes an immediate rapport with the listener. In the B minor Mazurka, Op. 33 No. 4, both Michelangeli and Zecchi (who recorded this work twice on 78, once for Ultraphone and once for Cetra) take the opening theme at a relatively slow tempo; in the central chordal passages, Michelangeli portrays the majesty of the music rather than its drama (this belongs to a Friedman), and his reading is distinguished by the delicacy and poise with which he conveys the composer's imaginative ideas. Michelangeli can transform the usually shallow-sounding B flat minor Scherzo into a work of great dignity in which (like Irene Scharrer) he maintains the melodic content of the virtuoso passages, the notes having perfect evenness and an almost miraculous clarity; the work retains its shape and there are no bombastic bass octaves. He also eschews the bravura approach in the *Andante Spianato and Grande Polonaise Brillante*, in which he shows no want of dexterity but succeeds in bringing out the polonaise rhythm with greater originality and wit than any other pianist. The delicacy of the filigree decorations have all the virtuosity of Hofmann, but none of his excessive changes of tempo. In this work, the Italian omits the interlocking passage between the *Andante Spianato* and the *Grande Polonaise* (Hofmann made much of this section) and heralds the Polonaise with dotted rhythm solo octaves – this passage is played by the orchestra in the other version. Unlike so many great technicians, Michelangeli is a musician of moderate tempos, and when his right hand plays a particularly taxing passage, it is a joy to find that he shapes the left-hand part with the same care as the right – many pianists are so preoccupied with technical problems that they do not have the control to vary the accompanying part as well. Thus, in the final *presto con fuoco* coda of the G minor Ballade, where Richter, in two discs of public recitals, tries to play impossibly fast, and where Horowitz changes the dynamic markings from *fortissimo* to *piano*, Michelangeli maintains a fast and steady tempo, from which he does not stray. The lack of a sense of 'risk' might disappoint those who are addicted to pianistic fireworks, but Michelangeli's pianism is always put at the service of the music he performs. Even in Richter's and Horowitz's accounts of this work the shape of the music suffers, because of their wilfulness.

Michelangeli is a Chopin player of extreme perfection and depth of thought. Many people prefer a more impassioned and fiery pianist, and he will not appeal to them. Contrary to the popular stereotype, most Italian pianists are in fact very controlled. There are those who play with extreme virtuosity, such as Sergio Fiorentino, but the best members of Italy's pianistic elite are 'thinking' rather than 'performing' artists. Orazio Frugoni is another Chopin player of great subtlety and poetry, whose account of the F minor Concerto is one of the most deeply-felt and searching performances on record. He presents the work as full of hope, the musings of an idealistic dreamer. His playing is similar to that of Novaës – it is distinguished by spontaneity and a generosity of emotion, and Michael Gielen is, as always, a most sensitive conductor. Frugoni is well known in the recording studio, especially for unearthing little-played works, and his recordings of the Mazurkas have also been highly praised.

Maurizio Pollini is the greatest pianist, and the greatest Chopin player, to have emerged from Italy since the Second World War. He was born in 1942, the son of a well-known architect, and studied with Carlo Vidusso (another Italian Chopin player with a very big technique) and Carlo Lonati in Milan. At the age of eighteen he won the 1960 Chopin Competition in Warsaw. Małcużyński, who sat on the jury, acclaimed his 'sensational pure talent', and the eminent Polish critic Józef Kanski described him thus: 'His classicism is entirely modern, illuminating Chopin's music with strong floodlight, rather than with mellow sunshine. The predominant attitude was one of moderate lyricism, not synonymous with romanticism, but rather with mildness of sentiment.'[27]

Despite this startling success, the beginning of Pollini's career was not easy, and within a short time of the Competition he retired to study, emerging several years later as a mature artist. There was more fire and more emotion in his playing in 1960 than there is in his Chopin today; he has shed some of the youthful passion that makes his early recording of the E minor Concerto so compelling, and there are those who find his mature style in Chopin a little clinical, and believe that he is at his best in Schubert. He is basically a classical player, who maintains a certain poise and inner reserve in all his music-making, but this is of course suited to Chopin, and Pollini's full and rounded tone ensures the beauty of his interpretation of the music. Like Michelangeli, he is a sovereign technician, and his playing has an extraordinary finish and verve. He plays some works Michelangeli does not care to perform – the older man is too much of a perfectionist to have recorded 'complete' Polonaises, Preludes or Etudes – and perhaps Pollini is less experimental than Michelangeli in terms of tonal variety, but he is none the less a master of piano sound.

Pollini has recorded the Etudes in their entirety (save for the *Trois Nouvelles Etudes*), and he plays them with the greatest precision and virtuosity, though not quite that of Lhévinne, Friedman, Godowsky or Saperton. In many ways, Pollini's execution differs from that of the older generation of great pianists: he would never commit the 'sin' of playing the left hand before the right in chordal passages (even Michelangeli uses split chords in the middle section of the *Andante Spianato*), and he seems totally without personal mannerisms. This immense control has its drawbacks as well as its advantages; Chopin's music thrives on the personal touch, and the composer himself never played a composition the same way twice – it is hard to imagine this being the case with Pollini. Nevertheless, in my opinion Pollini plays the D minor Prelude, Op. 28 No. 24, better than any other pianist in history (only Busoni's Duo-Art piano roll matches his performance), and his performance clearly shows that he can rise to the passionate content of the music when he feels that such treatment is necessary. His playing of the F sharp minor Polonaise, recorded by Muza from the winning performance at the 1960 Chopin Competition, is a testament to his early mastery, and over the years his playing has grown in stature if it may for some have become less interesting.

If any distinguishing characteristics are to be ascribed to Italian pianists, their clarity (similar to that of the Hungarians, but expressed in a fuller and rounder tone), their exploitation of the contrapuntal side of Chopin's writing, and their imaginative use of the pedal (distinguishing them from most French pianists) come to mind. They lack the inherent sense of rhythm necessary for Chopin's Polish works, but in these the Italian pianists tend to stress the elements in which their own strength lies – counterpoint and tone. When Leschetizky said of Italian pianists,

'They could not, as a rule, play the pianoforte in the very least,'[28] he was, as was his wont, making an overstatement which is wholly refuted by the emergence of the great Italian pianists of this century. Pollini and Michelangeli play with few of the half-shades that were characteristic of Chopin's own playing, but (unlike the French) their playing is especially well-attuned to the capabilities of the modern concert grand, and their interpretations have an architectural grandeur of conception which sets them aside from other artists.

CHAPTER EIGHT

The United States, South America and other countries

The United States

Pianos were manufactured in the United States from the late eighteenth century but imported instruments were always preferred by the Americans as, until the late nineteenth century, was a European musical training. Once the Leipzig 'system' acquired its reputation as the most reliable source of a sound musical education, an increasing number of American pianists were sent to study in Germany. One of Chopin's disciples, a Captain Johns, came from the United States,[1] but it was some time before an American pianist made a wide reputation, and the first one to do so was Louis Moreau Gottschalk (1829–69). His father was an Englishman of German descent and his mother the daughter of a French count, and he was born in New Orleans. Gottschalk was brought up in cultured circles, and studied in Paris with Charles Hallé, Chopin's friend, and also with Stamaty. He became widely known for his performances of flashy and extrovert salon music, much of it his own – he was able to present elements of the music of the black slaves in the form of pianistic showpieces, and his compositions became immensely popular. *Le Bananier* and the *Grande Fantaisie Triomphale sur l'Hymne National Brésilien* were particular favourites, the latter often being played by Guiomar Novaës. There was speculation that Gottschalk had studied with Chopin, but this was denied by Georges Mathias, one of the composer's best-known pupils, who had lived in Paris during the years 1840–6 when Gottschalk was studying there.[2] There is no doubt that the American was influenced by Chopin, but he always concentrated on performing his own compositions rather than those of established masters, and he had little influence on piano playing in his homeland.

From the middle of the nineteenth century, musicians from many parts of Europe came to settle in the United States, often – though by no means invariably – as the result of political insecurity in their homeland, and always to take advantage of the opportunities opening up in the New World. Richard Hoffman and Sebastian Bach Mills came from England in 1847 and 1859, von Sternberg from Germany in 1877, Joseffy from Hungary in 1879, and de Kontski from Poland in 1885. This generation founded the music schools which became centres of teaching of such distinction that an increasing number of American musicians studied at home rather than going to Europe. Towards the end of the last century there was a growing number of immigrants from Russia and Poland to the United States, and the pianists who made their home there included Horowitz, Hofmann, Godowsky, Lhévinne, Rachmaninov, Friedheim and Siloti. By the 1930s there were as many famous musicians in the United States as in the whole of Europe and styles of piano-playing there were therefore very eclectic; the strengths of all national schools were brought together in a melting pot. (Those pianists who were already mature musicians when they emigrated have been considered under their country of origin, and the American-born pianist Ernest Schelling among those who studied with Chopin's pupils.)

Among the leading teachers who influenced the development of pianism in the United States was Carl Friedberg, a pupil of Clara Schumann, who settled there permanently in the 1920s. His pupils included Elly Ney and Percy Grainger (in Europe) and Bruce Hungerford and Malcolm Frager in the United States. Friedberg was a straightforward and highly sensitive Chopin player, but his sympathies were closer to the music of Schumann and Brahms. His Chopin was marked by a very strict adherence to the score, but according to one of his pupils was remarkable for its delicacy and warmth.[3]

The Swiss-born pianist, cellist and teacher Rudolph Ganz trained in Europe with Busoni, Robert Freund (a pupil of Liszt), Fritz Blumer (a pupil of Moscheles) and (for cello) Julius Hegar. Ganz was not only an exemplary pianist, but played an important part in America's musical life as a teacher and organizer. He was not a startlingly original Chopin player, but he was one of the first pianists to make discs before the First World War, and his performance of the E minor Waltz, Op. Posth., dating from this period is thoughtful and unmannered, while that of the E flat Nocturne, Op. 9 No. 2, from the early 1920s, is similarly unaffected, and shows a commitment to the music beyond the search for pianistic effects; however, in the A flat Waltz, Op. 34 No. 1, he does take excessive licence with the tempo. Ganz's sterling qualities as a musician were evident in his teaching, and his pupils included Edward Ballantine and Charles Haubiel.

Another pianist of the same generation, equally influential in a different way, was Olga Samaroff. She was born in America, and studied for a year in Paris with Antonin Marmontel, son of the famous professor of piano, before applying to enter the Conservatoire. She was auditioned by Élie Miriam Delaborde, illegitimate son of the composer and pianist Alkan, who greeted her with the remark, 'Americans are not meant to be musicians.'[4] However, she became the first American woman to be admitted to the Conservatoire, and later had lessons with

Ernest Hutcheson and Jedliczka. She made her debut with the New York Symphony Orchestra under Walter Damrosch in 1905, and was a successful concert performer for some years before she turned to teaching and music criticism. She joined the faculty of the Juilliard School in the mid-1920s, and later that of the Philadelphia Conservatory. She had a large and extremely accurate technique, and her disc of the finale of Chopin's B minor Sonata shows her to have been a compelling pianist, who committed all her concentration to every note. This performance shows a deep awareness of the structure of the music, which helps to explain her success as a teacher – everything she played was carefully planned and executed with tremendous determination. She was a musical thinker first and a performer second, and her combination of scholarship and pianistic ability contributed much to the success of her pupils, among them Alexis Weissenberg, Raymond Lewenthal, Eugene List, Rosalyn Tureck and Claudette Sorel.

The most masterly technician among this group of American pianists was David Saperton, who was also the least-known – he lived a secluded life, seldom appeared in public, and taught only a few selected pupils.[5] Saperton's principal teacher was a man called Spanuth, but he also had lessons with Joseffy, and went to Europe to attend Busoni's master classes. He made his New York debut at the age of fifteen in 1904 playing the Chopin E minor Concerto; and ten years later he came to know Leopold Godowsky, and this association altered the course of his life. He married Godowsky's daughter Vanita, and became totally dedicated to perfecting the performance of Godowsky's compositions and transcriptions. At his zenith, Saperton's command of these works was almost as great as the composer's, and his discs are very remarkable. He made a special study of Godowsky's rewriting of the Chopin Etudes, and his pupil Jorge Bolet also plays these transcriptions. Saperton also recorded the complete Etudes in their original form, including the *Trois Nouvelles Etudes*, and his style bridges the gap between the romantic approach of Godowsky, Josef Lhévinne and Hofmann, and the 'modern' interpretation of Busoni, Samaroff and Rosina Lhévinne.

Saperton's life was devoted to living Godowsky's principles and putting into practice his master's dictum that the technical range of the pianist should be extended in all directions. His performance of the twenty-seven Etudes is one of the most technically adept on record. The emphasis in all his recordings, some of which have recently been reissued, is on the pianistic aspect of the music. He seldom tries to bring out the powerful nature of the more stormy Etudes, and aims at clarity rather than passion. In works such as the 'Revolutionary' Etude, Op. 10 No. 12, and the mighty 'Winter Wind', Op. 25 No. 11, Saperton offers a light treatment of the passagework – such as the left-hand part of the former and the right-hand part of the latter – which so many other pianists play with the greatest force. It is very difficult to gauge whether Saperton was emulating Godowsky's playing of these works, since the latter recorded very few of the Etudes; close listening suggests that Saperton's performances bear some imprint of Busoni's teaching: his playing of the G flat Etude, Op. 10 No. 5, is similar to Busoni's, and like him Saperton slightly delays the tempo of the descending torrents of semi-quavers.

There is undoubtedly a great deal of poetry in Saperton's readings. In places, his use of tone is slightly extravagant, and he tends to stress aural beauty rather than musical form, with the result that the middle section of the E major Etude, Op. 10, for example, is almost trivialized. But his technical mastery, as displayed in the notorious Etude in thirds, is so complete as to vie with Lhévinne's. In one of the chromatic descents in thirds, Saperton manages to accentuate the *lower* notes of the right-hand part, thus producing an effect I have never heard attempted by any other pianist. As one would expect, his tempos are on the fast side. His recording of the Etudes is affected by the quality of the reproduction, which lacks the 'ringing' sound that distinguishes clear tone in Lhévinne's famous disc of three of the Etudes (the E flat, Op. 10 No. 11, the G sharp minor and the A minor, Op. 25 Nos. 6 and 11). In Saperton's version, there are no thundering basses, and one misses a certain amount of characterization in the left-hand parts, especially in the G flat, Op. 10 No. 5, and the C major, Op. 10 No. 7, so well brought out by Planté. Saperton's primarily pianistic approach stems from the era of Hofmann and Godowsky, and was influential in shaping the outlook of his pupils, especially that of Cherkassky, Jorge Bolet, Abbey Simon and Jacques Abram.

Far more satisfying, and far more musical than Saperton's performances, is the Chopin playing of the late Arthur Loesser, a pianist little known outside the United States, and in my opinion one of the really great Chopin interpreters. A child prodigy, he was a pupil of Paderewski's protégé Sigismund Stojowski, who had received advice from Chopin's favourite pupil, Princess Marcelina Czartoryska. Loesser was a man of wide culture and many interests; although he was a technician of the highest order, he did not pursue a career as a soloist but spent much of his time accompanying singers and instrumentalists and in duo-piano work; he was also a teacher of repute and author of the well-known book *Men, Women and Pianos*, an informal social history of the piano.[6]

Loesser's strengths in Chopin were very much those one identifies from the accounts of the composer's playing: infinite variety of nuance, the most delicate *piano* and *pianissimo* playing, and an overall control of the emotional content of the music. He played the B major Nocturne, Op. 9 No. 3, for example, with a melancholy and exquisite pathos that makes his performance of this work one of the handful of entirely successful recordings of Chopin's Nocturnes. (Loesser played this version at a recital which was recorded and later released by the International Piano Archives; in his own programme note, he described the work as being in the lightest mood – a description far removed from his own interpretation!) Loesser had extraordinary control over the exact placing of notes, and in conjuring up and sustaining a mood. But his playing was not confined to this type of 'Pachmannesque' performance, and his textures always had much greater clarity than those of the Russian. In the F sharp minor Mazurka, Op. 59 No. 3, Loesser opens with a jaunty rhythm, which slackens as the thematic line progresses, and then returns with all its tautness. Few pianists seem to have the necessary imagination to achieve this subtle variation in Chopin's music. Loesser's effects are always highly idiomatic and perfectly judged, and it is lamentable that he did not record more Chopin, since he was a very great performer.

The artistry of Jorge Bolet, the Cuban-American pianist who has performed a great deal of Chopin throughout his career, has always been of considerable interest. Born in 1914, he studied at the Curtis Institute with David Saperton, and learned to share his fascination for Godowsky's art, and that of the other pianistic giants of that era – Hofmann, Lhévinne and Rachmaninov. Instead of reacting against their sometimes excessive style, Bolet – like Cherkassky, who was also a pupil of Hofmann and Saperton – revels in their art, and reveals his attachment to the romantic period not only in his choice of repertoire but in his general approach to his instrument. Like Michael Ponti, he favours a Bechstein piano, and his brilliant technique amazes all critics. His Chopin playing, whether of the original works or Godowsky's transcriptions, reflects the attitude of a highly individual musician, and hearing him play the four Scherzos or the four Ballades at a recital is an unforgettable experience. Bolet's style derives from the Russian school, and he was influenced by Hofmann (who had been the pupil of Anton Rubinstein), Lhévinne and Rachmaninov. It is not a style which is close to the playing of the composer, and in some ways relies on a tradition established by pianists whose approach was very different from Chopin's, but Bolet seems to be trying to capture some of Rubinstein's 'storm and passion' in his Chopin playing.[7]

Though some of his musical ideas are open to question, Bolet's pianism has an immaculate pedigree. He usually manages to steer a successful course between purely virtuoso excitement and what is musically acceptable, a tribute to his control and aesthetic judgment.

One of the functions of music is surely to entice the ear with beautiful sounds, and Bolet combines this approach with real poetic feeling; he is generally an interesting interpreter, and though he lacks the profundity of thought of Cortot, the emotional range of Rubinstein, and the wistful melancholy of Koczalski, he realizes his own priorities with complete success.

American Chopin playing today is largely the product of the teaching and pianistic style of musicians from Central and Eastern Europe, among them Josef and Rosina Lhévinne, Godowsky, Hofmann, Loesser, Stojowski, Horszowski, Rosenthal, Vengerova, Joseffy, Rachmaninov and Levitzki. Other well-known and competent pianists who have settled in the United States or were the children of immigrants include Oscar Levant, Nadia Reisenberg, Ania Dorfmann, Clarence Adler, Sascha Gorodnitzki, Jeanne Behrend, Abram Chasins, Ruth Slenczynska and Tina Lerner, many of whom played a great deal of Chopin. (Tina Lerner's playing has been discussed together with other Russian pianists, and Ania Dorfmann is mentioned in Chapter Three, as she was a pupil of Philipp.) Oscar Levant's discs demonstrate an affectionate view of the composer, but not a very original one; he was far more successful in works such as Rubinstein's D minor Piano Concerto and Gershwin's *Rhapsody in Blue*. Reisenberg and Gorodnitzki played Chopin with greater control and creative thought, while Chasins turned to music criticism and broadcasting, and made some Chopin discs with a spoken commentary.

The pianists who enjoyed a high reputation in the United States in the late 1930s and 1940s included Earl Wild, Edward Kilenyi and the Viennese-born Robert Goldsand. All of them had techniques capable of encompassing the complete Etudes, but from a stylistic point of view their approach is not very satisfying. Wild's account of the E minor Concerto, with Sir Malcolm Sargent conducting, lacks conviction, and Kilenyi's recording of the same work is only noteworthy for the sensitivity with which he plays the slow movement. Kilenyi was one of Dohnányi's favourite pupils; he made a number of other good recordings of Chopin in the early 1940s, and was also a successful teacher.

It was not until the advent of the generation of pianists born in the 1920s that a distinctive American approach to Chopin emerged, exemplified in the playing of a number of leading artists who have always included many works by Chopin in their repertoire, such as Ivan Davis, John Browning, Gary Graffman, Byron Janis, Abbey Simon, Bruce Hungerford and Van Cliburn. All of them have very big techniques (on which perhaps they sometimes rely too much) and their Chopin is closely associated with the sonorities and dynamic capacity of the modern Steinway Grand. This does not necessarily mean that American pianists always emphasize the brilliant and forceful side of musical expression rather than the delicate and subtle shades associated with Chopin's own playing, because in recent years there has been a reaction against the former approach, and Murray Perahia, who comes from the next generation, exploits the subtle colours of the instrument, and does not rely for his effect on heavy and dramatic basses. Graffman, Davis, Janis and their contemporaries became more closely associated with the big works of the romantic repertoire than with any other music, and made numerous discs of the concertos of Liszt, Tchaikovsky, Rachmaninov and Prokofiev. The influence of Josef Hofmann and Vladimir Horowitz, who were their models of technical achievement, is strongly evident in their playing, which is in consequence both intelligent and beautifully polished. Browning and Cliburn both came from Rosina Lhévinne's class; Davis was taught by Zecchi; Janis (at Josef Lhévinne's suggestion) studied with Adèle Marcus, and Graffman had lessons from Isabelle Vengerova, a pupil of Leschetizky who also taught Ignace Hilsberg, Anna Berman (Lazar Berman's mother), Leonard Bernstein, Leonard Pennario, Abba Bogin and Jacob Lateiner. Graffman, Davis and Janis also had lessons with Vladimir Horowitz.

One attribute all these pianists possess is imagination; their Chopin is broadly eclectic, as would be expected from artists of such a varied cultural background. Janis and Davis have a mercurial quality ideally suited to Chopin, especially when they play in a spontaneous mood. Cliburn is a bravura pianist, and this creates some difficulties in Chopin; a disc from a live recital of the C sharp minor Scherzo has an immaculate technical finish which is riveting, but he plays the descending cascades of quavers in the middle section out of time with the preceding chords. The emphasis that Cliburn has put on the 'impressive' side of pianism has made him rather unsuitable for Chopin.

The late Bruce Hungerford, like Saperton and Loesser, was a pianist whose career never attracted the attention that was due to it. He created a very special sound-world of great dynamic range. Very much a musician who followed in the line of Friedman and Lhévinne, he had that largesse of phrasing that especially characterized the playing of the pianists of previous generations. He was fully appreciative of all of the details of Chopin's scores, and his disc containing the F minor Etude, Op. 25 No. 2, is extremely successful and beautifully moulded. Eugene Istomin, aside from playing a great deal of chamber music, has also performed and recorded Chopin, but his vision of the composer is not especially imaginative, especially when compared to Hungerford's. Charles Rosen, an expert and scholarly musician, who has written extensively about the interpretation of the classics and also plays modern music, is a pianist who has performed and recorded Chopin with success. He studied with Rosenthal and with his wife, Hedwig Kanner-Rosenthal, and is a serious pianist with a big technique; his disc of the F minor Piano Concerto is refined and musical.

However, it is Abbey Simon – a pianist whose reputation as a Chopin player is based on his recordings – who is, I believe, one of the most impressive interpreters of this composer among his generation. Comparing his disc of the F minor Concerto with that of Rosen, it is readily apparent that Simon feels the music more naturally; this is one of the best versions in existence. His music-making is ardently involved, and contains a greater wealth of pianistic nuance than that of most of his contemporaries, with the possible exception of the late Bruce Hungerford. Simon lived in Europe for a number of years, and this seems to have had a broadening effect on his musical outlook. A pupil of David Saperton, his technique is slightly suave, but the sounds that he produces are of the greatest beauty. In the Etudes of Chopin, which he is at present recording, he demonstrates a perfect blend of technical prowess and emotional warmth. His natural affinity with Chopin is everywhere evident in his playing, and his venture to record the complete piano works of Chopin will, when completed, be of enormous worth. Simon plays the big works of Chopin with a full understanding of their structure. Having been educated at the Curtis Institute in the days when Josef Hofmann was the Director and guiding force, he had plenty of opportunity to come into contact with the great pianists of the older generation. Along with Bolet, Cherkassky and Hungerford, he has taken up the mantle of Godowsky, Hofmann and Lhévinne.

It was a great pity that the young American pianist William Kapell died in an accident in 1953 at the age of thirty-one, before his art had achieved fruition. He was a highly sensitive, though dynamic, pianist and an extraordinarily finished craftsman who would have risen to become a major figure.[8] A few of his Chopin performances were captured on disc, among them seventeen of the Mazurkas, the B minor Sonata and the B flat minor Sonata (the last from a public performance). The disc of the B minor Sonata is as impressive as any on record: there is a perfect blend of musical inspiration and virtuosity. One is reminded that Kapell came under the tutelage of Josef Lhévinne and Olga Samaroff; the values of the 'Golden Age' of Godowsky, Hofmann and Rachmaninov are everywhere evident. The tempos are fast throughout, though both the second subject of the first movement and the slow movement are played with great poetic feeling. This disc gives one a startling glimpse of a young artist of enormous maturity and real genius.

The Bulgarian-born Alexis Weissenberg, who has lived in America since he was a child, is highly respected, although his artistry is rather controversial. He studied at the Juilliard School with Olga Samaroff until 1946, when he was seventeen, and the next year won a Leventritt award. Even by this early age he had played frequently in public, and he went on to make a worldwide reputation. A very highly finished performer with a powerful technique, it is my impression that his primary aim in playing is to demonstrate that he is capable of thinking for himself, something which is admirable when put at the service of the music, but too often leads to waywardness. His discs of the B minor Sonata, two Scherzos and the complete Nocturnes well demonstrate that he has a real affinity with Chopin, but there are some passages where he verges on sentimentality. He revels in purely pianistic effects, and his rather brittle brilliance is ideally suited to works such as the 'Là ci darem la mano' Variations and the *Andante Spianato and Grande Polonaise Brillante*. He is capable of raising an audience to a pitch of great excitement, and even if his contrived effects sometimes detract from his success, he displays a consistently original approach.

Garrick Ohlsson, ten years younger than Weissenberg, won the 1970 Chopin Competition, the first American pianist to do so. He had played in public from the age of twelve, and had already won both the Bolzano and Montreal Piano Competitions when he came to compete in Warsaw; surprisingly, his winning performance of the E minor Concerto was nearly spoiled by nervousness, but his musical poise won through. He displays excellent schooling in everything that he does and is a basically serious player, whose Chopin has an aristocratic grandeur of conception. He chooses to follow Horowitz's practice of supplementing the final run at the end of the B minor Scherzo, showing that he sees himself as the inheritor of a great tradition. At an International Piano Library Gala Concert in London some years ago he chose to perform Balakirev's transcription for solo piano of the slow movement of Chopin's E minor Piano Concerto; this setting is seldom revived, and once again demonstrated Ohlsson's respect for the playing of a bygone age. Little in his artistry is left to chance, but he never sounds calculated; he has the ability to allow the music to inspire him. All his Chopin discs are impressive; these include the Scherzos, the sixteen Polonaises, the F minor Fantasy and the concertos.

Of all the pianists of the younger generation in America, the most promising talent to have emerged in recent years is Murray Perahia, who was born in 1947. His approach to the instrument marks a departure from the style of Janis, Davis, Browning and Graffman, for in concerted works he views the pianist not as an autocrat, but more as an ensemble player or, in solo compositions, as the presenter of a multi-faceted instrument that has its roots in the orchestra. He eschews the dynamism of the resonant bass, and opts for something more subtle, something cleaner and purer, while maintaining both an iron discipline and tonal variety. His Chopin playing is exquisite and direct: Halina Czerny-Stefańska, the eminent Polish pianist, told me that when Perahia played a Chopin Sonata at the Leeds Competition, members of the jury had tears in their eyes at the close of the performance.

Perahia is a near-perfect Chopin player. Following in the footsteps of his mentor, the great Polish pianist Mieczysław Horszowski, he has a strong inclination towards chamber music and accompanying. His consequent understanding of and sympathy with other instruments, and the voice, is rare in a virtuoso pianist, and it adds to the richness of his musical vision. His grasp of the vital place of counterpoint in Chopin's style also helps to give his playing a depth of understanding that many others lack. He has a keen ear for absolutely faithful and untarnished sonorities, and requires from himself a very high degree of technical command to effect these. With his amazing virtuoso technique, he can render Chopin's B flat minor Prelude, Op. 28 No. 16, with as much bravura as any famous pianist of the past, but with greater sensitivity and vitality than many. His pure and luminous textures (which also make his Mozart playing so successful) add an unusual freshness to his Chopin.

Perahia cannot be said to adhere to any particular style of Chopin playing; he reads the music anew in the way that comes most naturally to him. In consequence, he can play the B flat minor Sonata in a way which shows that a modern pianist can still adopt a subjective approach without the excesses of the romantic style. Through the way in which his phrases complement each other, he conveys how Chopin's creative process was at work in the elucidation of the thematic material. An artist born 150 years after Chopin's works were written can thus be more successful in making his audience hear the master's music with 'new ears' than were those pianists who had studied with Liszt and Leschetizky, or who had direct links with the composer. Perahia's exquisitely poignant treatment of melody makes his Chopin emotionally appealing, and it is above all through the communicativeness of his musical ideas that he conveys the impression that this is the way Chopin *should* be played and, possibly, the way the composer would have played himself.

The South Americans

A number of great pianists have been born in South America and their playing has often been particularly interesting, reflecting a cultural background which for much of the nineteenth century was isolated from the mainstream of Western Europe. There were no great South American composers in the last century, and although visiting musicians from Europe were enthusiastically received, their tours were few and far between. South American musicians were influenced by native folk songs and the Spanish dance, and Latin pianists were attracted by the passionate and sensuous qualities in Chopin's music; they also brought to it a rigorous dedication to technical perfection. Most South American pianists have furthered their careers by living abroad, contributing relatively little to the musical life of their native countries (although Claudio Arrau has founded a teaching institution in Chile). However, there were from the end of the nineteenth century a number of excellent teachers of the piano in the South American capitals – they were usually recent immigrants from Western Europe – who helped to further the musical life of these countries, despite having to work in difficult circumstances.

A striking number of the leading South American pianists have been women – Teresa Carreño, Rosita Renard, Guiomar Novaës, Martha Argerich and Ilana Vered – all of whom have had a commanding technique and an exciting musical temperament. Teresa Carreño came from a very distinguished family (she was descended from Simon Bolivar) and was born in Caracas in 1853. She was first taught by her father, and gave her first important recital in the Irving Hall in New York when she was only eight; the family left Venezuela and settled in that city soon afterwards. Carreño studied with Louis Moreau Gottschalk, and then went to Europe, where she became a pupil of Georges Mathias, and had some lessons with Anton Rubinstein, though she was already a finished artist when she went to him. Regarded as one of the finest pianists in the world, she was also an accomplished opera singer,[9] and she was married four times – to the brothers Giovanni and Arturo Tagliapietra, to the pianist Eugen d'Albert, and to the eminent violinist Émile Sauret.

Described as 'the Valkyrie of the piano', her playing was described as having an almost superhuman force even when she was a child. She never regarded herself as being limited by the need to adhere to the composer's marks, and when she was young, her personality usually overwhelmed whatever music she played, whether it was Bach, Beethoven or Chopin. Her growing maturity as an artist was linked with her marriage with d'Albert in 1892,[10] and in her later years she was compared as an equal with such pianists as Sauer, Rosenthal, Hofmann and Rachmaninov. A critic in Leipzig wrote of her performance of the Liszt *Hungarian Fantasy* and Chopin's E minor Concerto in the 1890s:

> Through constant purification she has abandoned the amazonlike fury with which she used to pounce upon the greatest tasks of virtuosity as if upon an iron-fast cohort of enemies, and that without loss of glowing fullness of expression and freshness of temperament.[11]

It seems that d'Albert taught her that the composer, not the performer, was the most important force in musical interpretation, and her total command over the keyboard, her control of both its mechanics and its sonorities, enabled her to adapt her playing to a more mature approach.

Carreño's repertoire was large, and she was devoted to Chopin's music. Unfortunately she made no discs, but she recorded some Chopin piano works for the Welte-Mignon piano roll company, including the G minor and A flat major Ballades, and the C minor Nocturne, Op. 48 No. 1. These demonstrate her technical ability, but she used mannerisms such as spread chords which can be irritating to the modern listener. Her touch is very varied, and there is in her playing evidence of a concentrated musical thought that is always compelling. She could execute many of the most taxing passages of the A flat Ballade with an extraordinary deftness that is at times almost eerie. As a Chopin player, Carreño was in the tradition of Anton Rubinstein; her effects were the product of a spontaneous response to the music, executed with a bravura exploiting all the resources of the instrument. Carreño enjoyed adulation, and played in public until 1917, the year of her death. No other woman pianist has equalled her as a virtuoso, and her playing was far more exciting than that of Clara Schumann. She was also an enthusiastic teacher, whose best pupils were Egon Petri, George Copeland and Carl Lamson.

It may have been the lack of Carreño's family connections and privileged status that from the outset made the career of Rosita Renard so difficult. She was born in Chile in 1894, and died in 1949 at the height of her powers. At the age of sixteen she was awarded a scholarship by the Chilean Government to study at the Stern Conservatory in Berlin, where she became a pupil of Martin Krause, who was also the teacher of Claudio Arrau, Vera Benenson and Edwin Fischer. Krause had studied with Liszt, and was a gifted musician who transmitted to his pupils Liszt's ideas about the art of interpretation. At the outbreak of war in 1914, Rosita Renard left Europe and made her American debut in 1917 with two recitals at the Aeolian Hall in New York, one of them an all-Liszt programme including the 'Don Juan' Fantasy, Liszt's B minor Sonata, and some of the *Transcendental Studies*. Her playing was said to bear an uncanny resemblance to that of Teresa Carreño, who had recently died; Renard undoubtedly had much of Carreño's inborn temperament and equal technical expertise, but she did not have the same exuberant approach to concert-giving and her modest and retiring character prevented her from consolidating her early success.[12] In 1921 she returned to Germany, and her fears about performing in public became acute – she could not bear the sound of the audience's applause, and her platform career virtually came to an end.[13] In 1930 she returned to Chile, and devoted her life to teaching, rarely giving concerts, though she did appear at the Carnegie Hall in January 1949 and gave a memorable concert which was fortunately recorded. She succumbed to a rare tropical disease a few months later, and died at the age of fifty-five. It was only in her last recitals, after the Second World War, that she began to receive her due recognition as a remarkable pianist.

Rosita Renard's playing can only be assessed from the two discs of the Carnegie Hall recital and a curiously unimpressive performance of the Schulz-Evler transcription of Johann Strauss's *Blue Danube*, recorded on the Brunswick label. The 1949 recital shows that she must have been one of the most naturally gifted technicians of all time. She specialized in the performance of Chopin's Etudes and Mazurkas, and favoured extremely fast tempos. Few pianists have ever played the treacherous chromatic study, the Etude in A minor, Op. 10 No. 2, with the same perfectly regular whispering scales, or the C sharp minor, Op. 10 No. 4, with as much virtuosity, musicality and panache. It is true that there are times when the artist's virtuosity almost goes out of control; her choice of extremely rapid tempos gives her playing a frenetic quality, but there is also a rhythmic vibrancy in the Mazurkas that is extremely attractive.

Two women pianists from Brazil, Magda Tagliaferro and Guiomar Novaës, both of whom had most of their pianistic training in France, became Chopin players of the very highest calibre. Tagliaferro, born in 1891, had lessons from Jan Chiapusso, Olga Samaroff (in America), and Cortot. A highly original artist, full of life and originality, she is a great musician. A highly successful concert artist since the 1920s, she has recently returned to the concert platform, and has received an ecstatic reception at the Carnegie Hall. The possessor of a very big tone and a marvellous range of pianistic sounds, she can play Chopin's B minor Sonata with the utmost originality; her playing is very much that of Cortot's school, but more capricious, and has always demonstrated high spirits and enormous energy. Her role as a teacher has also been of considerable importance. When in her late eighties she recorded the Chopin F minor Ballade for a Brazilian company, and this performance is notable for the way in which she preserves the line of the music; no listener would guess her age from the recording.

Guiomar Novaës, four years younger than Tagliaferro, was also born in Brazil, and had lessons there with a well-known teacher, Luigi Chiafarelli, until 1909, when she went to Europe on a grant from the Brazilian Government, and entered the competition for a scholarship to the Paris Conservatoire. She was only fifteen, and there were two hundred other entrants, all of them older than she was. Fauré, Moszkowski, and Debussy were among the judges, and Novaës was awarded the first prize and the scholarship. Having entered Philipp's class, she seems to have perplexed her professor by following her musical instincts even when they were against his instructions, but he had great respect for her,[14] and after only two years of study with him she won first prize at the Conservatoire. She made her American debut in the New York City Hall in 1915, and the eminent critic of the ˙*Sun*, W. J. Henderson, wrote: 'In the range of tonal beauties and immense virility, only Paderewski or Hofmann could have equalled her.'[15] Her natural and charming manner, which was carried into her playing, won many admirers, and her style never had any detractors. She played much Mozart, Beethoven, Schumann and Debussy, but from an early date she specialized in Chopin. When she played at the Aeolian Hall in December 1925 the critic of the *Musical Times* wrote, 'Taking her at her best, which was surely in Chopin's "Funeral March" Sonata, she struck us as quite the most remarkable woman pianist who has appeared in London for many years.' Novaës was inevitably compared with Carreño, but any similarities in their style were superficial, Novaës being more in-gratiating, more feminine and more poetic. Unlike Martha Argerich, she always warmed to the intimate side of Chopin's writing; her playing was always entirely approachable and she never set out to stun by bravura display.

Novaës's recording career, which lasted for about forty years, was strangely unsatisfactory. She made several discs in the 1920s (some acoustic) and a great many in the early '50s. In 1951 she changed from Columbia to Vox, and she also made discs for Vanguard in the late '60s. She recorded more Chopin than any other composer, and left discs of both Concertos, the twenty-four Preludes, the twenty-four Etudes, fifteen Waltzes, both Sonatas and the complete Nocturnes. It is often said that her art is best represented by the discs from the early years of her career. Although many of those made in the 1950s are undoubtedly very fine, only a few show her at her best. Like all Philipp's pupils, she had a very big technique; she was prone to finger-slips, but in the last analysis these were inconsequential. Her French training is evident both in her careful phrasing and in her rigorously disciplined keyboard manner; she left little to chance and never presented any music that had not been meticulously prepared.

There are many indications in her recordings of Novaës's originality and importance as a Chopin player. Her performance of the Waltzes shows real spontaneity and freedom. In the A minor Waltz, Op. 34 No. 2, which was Chopin's own favourite, the equally famous Brailowsky opens with a slightly unsteady tempo, and understates the melancholy aspect of the first theme, using little dynamic contrast; the wistful nature of the piece is lost and its charm played down. Novaës's opening of the same work is considerably faster, and the whole metre is more assured. The first theme is given a puckish lilt with which no other pianist, to my knowledge, endows it. She reveals the waltz-like nature of the piece, and seems to be telling the listener that it is usually played too slowly: she always displayed a penchant for quick tempos, but never sounded rushed or flustered as a result – this is another characteristic of the French school.

Novaës's disc of the complete Etudes shows her to have had a technique equal to that of other great pianists of her day. There are a few places where she gets into a little trouble; in the C major Etude, Op. 10 No. 1, a study in extended right-hand arpeggios, but this shows ineptitude in only a very small area of technique. She can 'trot off' such difficult works as the C sharp minor Etude, Op. 10 No. 4, with real aplomb, and the so-called 'Black Key' Etude, in which there are no slips, receives one of the fastest readings ever captured on disc (Mark Hambourg's early acoustic 78 is even faster). It is interesting to compare Novaës's version of the C sharp minor Etude, Op. 25 No. 7, with that of Mikuli's pupil, Raoul Koczalski, recorded in 1936. Koczalski plays this work virtually without pedal, thus submitting himself to great exposure, and treats the contrapuntal writing as if it were an exercise in classical style – each new entry of the different voices comes in with renewed emphasis. The left-hand chromatic runs are dry and so lose their surging expansive effect. Novaës, whose opening tempo is marginally faster, pedals throughout the piece and manages the different lines with care. The left-hand runs have the spaciousness and dramatic quality that are necessary; the only criticism that can be levelled is that some of her entries lack a little character. Koczalski and Novaës are poles apart in this piece, the Pole being cold and rather academic, treating the piece as a study in the narrow sense of the word, and the Brazilian seeing the work as being a study in touch and tone, rather than merely in counterpoint.

A disc on the American Vanguard label, made when Novaës was in her seventies, has excellent sound quality, and is the only recording from which one can judge her tone with assurance. The gem of this recital is the A flat Ballade, which she played in the competition for her scholarship at the Paris Conservatoire. The reading shows spontaneously shaped inner lines, delicate and feminine phrasing, relaxed tempos and a rare control over the structure, as well as a clear grasp of the contrapuntal nature of the work when a right-hand line is taken over by the left. None of the details of the accompaniment miss this treatment – Bach's pen is never far away.

When turning to Chopin's Mazurkas, surely the most elusive of all his compositions, one encounters another Novaës – delicate, intimate and a perfect miniaturist. Her playing of these works, so personal and subtle, can be ranked with those other masters, Rubinstein, Małcużyński and Friedman. In the famous B minor Mazurka, Op. 33 No. 4, she uses more *rubato* than do most other pianists, and in bar 49, where most pianists increase the tempo, she strictly maintains it; her overall conception of the piece is sprightly, and totally devoid of the over-dynamic power with which Horowitz or Friedman endowed it. Her disregard for Chopin's dynamic markings might lead one to believe that her approach is a little undisciplined, but her *pianissimo* playing of the closing passages of this piece reveals that all her effects are carefully planned. If Novaës's playing does not really fit comfortably into the category of the French school, it cannot be thought of as entirely typical of any other: her ordered approach, always bounded by requirements of taste and style, was self-reliant and emerged from her spontaneous musicality.

Claudio Arrau may not seem to be the most obvious candidate for consideration in Chopin's music, though he is one of the most towering figures among twentieth-century pianists, and as an interpreter of Beethoven, Schumann, Liszt and Brahms has few rivals. Arrau has always played a good deal of Chopin, though with varying success, because of his difficulty in dealing with the problem of Chopin's *rubato*. But he is unquestionably a great Chopin player and his recent disc of the complete Nocturnes bears testimony to both his musical genius and his interpretative supremacy. Since the retirement of Cortot, no pianist other than Rubinstein has played these works with greater depth and insight.

Arrau blends a strictly disciplined German training with a Latin warmth and generosity. His career, which stretches to before the First World War, has been one of unqualified success. He has a virtuoso technique which enabled him at seventy-four to record the Liszt *Transcendental Studies* with a finish that is equal to that of the Russian super-technician Lazar Berman; he can do anything he wants with the music, but unlike so many virtuosi, he always chooses a purely artistic course with the greatest personal integrity.

Arrau was born in Chillan in 1903, and first played in public at the age of five. In 1910 he was sent by the Chilean Government to Berlin, where he entered Martin Krause's class in 1913. He gave his first Berlin recital in 1914 and played in Germany and Scandinavia shortly afterwards. In 1918, the year that Krause died (Arrau was then only fifteen and never sought another teacher), he undertook his first European tour, and in 1921 returned to South America. In both 1919 and 1920 he won the Liszt Prize, which had then not been awarded for forty-five years. His American debut in 1923 had a curiously unenthusiastic reception, and from 1924 to 1940 he lived and taught in Berlin. Since 1941 he has lived in the United States, where he soon consolidated a phenomenal reputation.

Arrau has a repertoire that is extraordinarily large by any standards, and he has given recitals featuring the complete Bach *Klavierwerke*, the complete Mozart works for solo keyboard, and the complete Beethoven sonatas. His playing has the individuality which is the mark of the very greatest artists. He made his first discs in around 1927, and in the 1930s he first recorded some Chopin pieces; these include the F major Waltz, Op. 34 No. 3, the A flat and F minor Etudes, Op. 25 Nos. 1 and 2, the F major Prelude, Op. 28 No. 23, the Tarantelle and the C sharp minor Etude, Op. 10 No. 4. The only large-scale work he recorded at this time was the C sharp minor Scherzo, in a fascinating reading full of subtle shading and rich textures. He sees the Tarantelle in quite a different light from that of the more familiar versions by Cortot: Arrau plays this piece with a greater feeling for its dance aspects, with a greater range of dynamics, and with more *rubato*. The Etudes are model interpretations; Arrau divests them of any routine drudgery, and colours the passagework with the imagination of one of the Impressionists – there is a far greater use of the pedal in these early recordings than is evident in his 1950s version of the same works, which emerge as curiously dry. Among the Waltzes, the F major, which many have considered to be the most shallow of the fourteen, sparkles with charm and variety of mood; this is a memorable reading of the greatest subtlety, ranking with the performances on disc of the same piece by Janina Familier (an outstanding pupil of Michałowski, and who was killed during the war) and Emil Sauer.

In the mid-1950s Brunswick undertook a venture to record the complete piano works of Chopin with Arrau as pianist. This was not completed, but the first volume of these records, which appeared as a set of two discs, presented the public with Chopin playing of the most unusual power and virtuosity. Both the F minor Ballade and the B minor Scherzo are played here with the sort of finish that is rarely captured on disc. The conceptions are those of a musician whose every thought is profound; the seriousness of intent is equal to that of Cortot, but Arrau, being a great individual musician, sounds entirely himself. There is never any pandering to those whose admiration for Chopin is founded on the purely pianistic aspects of the composer's art; Arrau uses the greatest virtuosity, but always to reveal the music to its fullest extent. He even manages to make the slighter works, such as the *Fantaisie-Impromptu*, sound convincing.

In the concertos, Arrau's set from the early 1970s fails to capture his interpretations at their most compelling. The *rubato* seldom sounds entirely natural. However, a disc recorded from a live performance of the E minor Concerto in the early 1950s, with Klemperer conducting, and also a concert in which Arrau played the F minor Concerto, remain imprinted on my mind as very exceptional performances. Perhaps because a concert is more transitory than a studio recording, Arrau can at his public performances rely on spontaneity rather than planned interpretation, and the disc of the E minor Concerto with Klemperer gives us a reading that cannot be ignored. Arrau's solo part seems to reflect all the vicissitudes of life as experienced by the composer, and his interpretation seems to me to represent the way Chopin might have played this early work in his maturity, with an iron will and heroic thrust. Like Cortot, Arrau demonstrates that Chopin's rightful place as a piano composer is alongside Mozart, Beethoven, Schubert, Schumann and Brahms.

Arrau plays the Weber *Konzertstück* with more point and pathos than any other pianist, and his success in this apparently rambling work helps to explain how he can transform the least-known Nocturnes of Chopin into highly impressive works. He also plays the *Allegro de Concert* with a force and overall unity that has escaped most other pianists, though Magaloff has recently made an exceptionally good recording of this work. Arrau has grasped the style of the nineteenth-century keyboard composition with a degree of sympathy that has often eluded pianists who have specialized in 'apt' or 'authentic' interpretations. Much of his greatness arises from the fact that his performing style has its origins in the playing of Liszt, which was conveyed to him in an 'apostolic succession' from his teacher Krause; Arrau began his training only twenty-five years after Liszt's death, when there were in Berlin a great many of the master's pupils and disciples.

That Arrau is a highly intellectual player is very evident in his Chopin. He plays the C sharp minor Nocturne, Op. 27 No. 1, with a depth of understanding only equalled by Cortot. He has the ability so few possess of being able to allow the phrases to breathe; in a slow tempo he usually plays slower than most, creating a hush which totally captures the audience. Even the sparkle of his fingerwork seems to have a philosophical depth – the arabesques and reveries of the right-hand part in the D flat Nocturne, Op. 27 No. 2, are played by Rubinstein with a near-sensual, amorous appeal, but in Arrau's disc of this work the word 'depth' comes again to mind, and it is this quality of deep understanding which always distinguishes his performance. He never uses stylized *rubato*, and offers a Chopin of his own, but a Chopin who is also universally relevant.

Other South American pianists who have played Chopin include Arnaldo Estrella (1908–80), a Brazilian pupil of Cortot whose recordings, made in the late 1940s, show some of his master's appreciation of Chopin's form; however, Estrella's most distinctive attribute was his rhythmic flair, which especially fitted him for performing the music of his native country. Antonio Barbosa, a pupil of Estrella, is an extremely impressive Chopin player, who achieves a depth of poetic feeling that eludes many better-known pianists. His playing fully conveys the structure of the large-scale works, and there is something of Cortot's approach in his artistry. He has recorded both the Sonatas and the fourteen Waltzes, and everything he plays is executed with admirable polish.

The winner of the first prize at the 1965 Chopin Competition in Warsaw was Martha Argerich (b. 1941), who has established a secure reputation as an outstanding Chopin player. She is an enigmatic figure, both beautiful and stormy. Following in the tradition of Carreño, Renard and Novaës, she has a formidable technique that permits no barriers to stand in its way. Like Carreño too, she has a wide imagination, and her repertoire includes Beethoven, Liszt, Schumann and Prokofiev as well as Chopin. Argerich studied in Buenos Aires with Vincenzo Scaramuzza, and went to Europe for lessons from Friedrich Gulda, Nikita Magaloff and Michelangeli. She had made her orchestral debut before the age of ten in a Mozart piano concerto, and won both the Busoni and Geneva Piano Competitions in 1957. In the 1965 Chopin Competition, she was not only winner of the first prize, but was also awarded the special prize for the best interpretation of the Mazurkas, in which she had received coaching from Fou T'song, winner of the same prize in the 1955 contest. Jerzy Żurawlew, the pupil of Michałowski and founder of the Chopin Competitions, told me that of all winners of the first prize, he found Argerich's artistry the most impressive and best-equipped to fulfil her musical aspirations[16] – though his judgment would necessarily have been influenced by the fact that being himself a renowned technician he was particularly awed by Argerich's mastery in this sphere. However, one of the most telling features of Argerich's performances is that she always manages to preserve her musical taste and judgment even when playing fiendishly difficult music. I have never heard the C major Etude, Op. 10 No. 1, for extended arpeggios in the right hand, played with the same speed and temperament: the right-hand semi-quavers have a steely assurance remarkable by any standards. Yet Argerich is in no sense a mechanical musician – her temperament always makes her playing exciting but above that, her insight and extreme subtlety and sensitivity make her genius unique.

The E minor Concerto was chosen by Martha Argerich for performance at the Warsaw Competition, and it is a work in which she displays all her bravura and high spirits. It is interesting to compare the disc made on this occasion with the recorded performances of other first prizewinners of the Chopin Competitions: Halina Czerny-Stefańska (1949), Bella Davidovitch (1949), Adam Harasiewicz (1955), Maurizio Pollini (1960) and Krystian Zimerman (1975). The performances show considerable variations in tempo, and this is a work in which the tempo set by the conductor for the opening orchestral exposition does not necessarily dictate that taken by the solo entry – many pianists seem to ignore what has gone before and set out on an apparently new piece of music once they begin playing! Although the actual time taken for a performance can be measured in minutes and seconds, the results can be deceptive: a player who infuses the music with a sense of struggle will often sound faster than a pianist who actually takes a faster tempo but plays in a more relaxed style. Thus of these six versions of the E minor Concerto, the Argerich/Abbado and Zimerman/Giulini discs (the latter from a studio performance) have the slowest orchestral exposition in the first movement – they both take 4.08 minutes – but Argerich and Zimerman give the impression of the greatest speed, for the reasons explained above. However, from the beginning of the second subject until the end of the coda, Argerich is almost always quicker than the other pianists, and a close analysis of the time taken for the different sections of this movement by these pianists bears out the view that Argerich's approach to the Concerto is more hectic than tranquil; her critics have described this performance as neurotic. Of course this is arguably a justifiable interpretation of Chopin's personality, and in my own experience of hearing Argerich both in the concert hall and on disc, she has never played with anything but the greatest artistic imagination. Her discs of both Chopin's sonatas are quite exceptional, as is that of the twenty-four Preludes, and her high-pitched tension is always controlled by her artistry and musical intelligence.

Another South American pianist whose playing in Chopin is of a very high order, and who has perhaps never become quite as well known as his playing deserves, is Nelson Freire. His playing has that overall sense of order and consistency of style that are among the most important assets of any successful player. His interpretations are marvellously finished pieces of craftsmanship, expressed with a perfect measure of virtuosity. Freire was born in Brazil in 1944, began to play the piano when he was only three, and was soon performing in public. He had lessons in Vienna with the great teacher Bruno Seidlhofer. He tends to take fast tempos, but has the technique to play at speeds at which other pianists would risk sacrificing clarity, rhythm, and the right notes. His tone is wonderfully limpid, and his artistic constitution well-attuned to Chopin. His impeccable musicianship was very well revealed in a recital in the Queen Elizabeth Hall in London in 1979, when his performance of the B minor Sonata and the F minor Fantasy vied with the greatest interpretations ever captured on disc. Freire never allows his virtuosity to get the upper hand, and if on this particular occasion some of the textures in the first movement of the Sonata were slightly blurred, this work as a whole and the Fantasy showed the confidence and musicianship of an artist of the highest calibre.

Ilana Vered is a talented Argentinian pianist who takes a more direct route to Chopin's music than many, stating everything with poetry but never veiling her intentions in obscurity. This approach is in itself pleasing and attractive, and even though she may not have much that is original to relate about Chopin's genius she possesses a truly artistic sensibility that counts for much and deserves success. Miss Vered's keyboard sound is full-toned and self-assured, although she is also effective in the smaller, more tranquil pieces such as the A minor Waltz, Op. 34 No. 2. The technical side of the music seems to come to her so easily that she occasionally employs little 'tricks' which act as a diversion for the listener, such as the highlighting of inner harmonies and secondary themes, but fortunately she has enough artistic discipline not to allow these to distract her from the structure of the whole composition.

The warmth of tone and generosity of spirit with which South American pianists generally respond to Chopin makes them immediately attractive. Their playing generally possesses far more passion than that of the French, and derives from an inner response to the music, not from intellect alone. They do not rely on preconceived notions of how Chopin should be played, and one can only admire the independence of the artistry of Novaës and Argerich. However unlike Chopin's own playing their performances might be, their interpretations might well have appealed to him because of their freshness and individuality.

Pianists from other countries

Because the pianists of today have in this book been considered in terms of their country of origin, it is inevitable that there should be a number of outstanding individuals from countries which have produced relatively few Chopin players: Fou T'song is the only Chinese pianist to have achieved real fame as a performer of Chopin's works, and there are a number of outstanding Israeli and Australian exponents of Chopin, if not enough to constitute a 'school'. A number of Japanese pianists have won prizes at the prestigious competitions, but their approach seems to be more imitative than a natural response, and they are therefore unable to offer a distinctive approach to Chopin.

The Australian Percy Grainger was, both on the evidence of his discs and from the accounts of those who heard him, one of the most original and enlightened interpreters of Chopin, and his recordings of both the Sonatas are remarkable. He was an eccentric personality, whose bound-less energy and freedom from convention spurred him on to re-think the classics of the piano with startling success. His was a fresh approach, entirely unbounded by the limitations of any performing tradition. Born in Melbourne in 1882, he studied in Europe with James Kwast and Busoni, and had some lessons with Carl Friedberg. He made a highly successful debut in New York in 1915, and spent most of his life in the United States, where he died in 1961.

Grainger was a composer as well as a concert pianist whose public performances were acclaimed throughout his career. His Chopin discs are unfortunately few in number – the Sonatas, an abridged version of the A flat Polonaise, the B minor Etude, Op. 25 No. 10, the C minor Etude, Op. 25 No. 12, the A flat Prelude, Op. 28 No. 17, and the A flat Waltz, Op. 42. The Sonatas have tremendous vitality, bold tone colours and a rhythmic athleticism which distinguishes them from any other pianist. The phrasing is so convincing that Grainger makes one wonder how the works could be performed in any other way. Few other pianists have matched the grandeur with which he plays the opening movement of both Sonatas; his tone is richer than even that of Cherkassky and Gilels. In the B minor Sonata, Grainger's absolute refusal to gloss over any of the material, whether it is melodic or harmonically subsidiary, leads to a completely integrated interpretation; he draws out many of the phrase endings in a way that would sound excessively mannered under the hands of a lesser musician.

Grainger had a very fine virtuoso technique, and although in his later years he often complained about his execution of octaves, a perform-ance of the Grieg Piano Concerto captured on disc shortly before his death (he was a supreme Grieg player all his life) shows that his tech-nique remained unimpaired even though he was at the time suffering from cancer. His disc of the A flat Polonaise, which dates back to the 1920s, demonstrates his capabilities with great fidelity, and the heroic and lyrical aspects of the work are perfectly counterbalanced. All Grainger's recordings transmit the zest and vitality of his personality – they are musically forceful and his spontaneity and artistry are little short of miraculous.

Another Australian, William Murdoch, was a less dynamic per-sonality, but a capable pianist who also wrote a competent biography of Chopin. He settled in the United Kingdom when a young man, achieved a sound reputation, touring as a soloist and also playing chamber music. His disc of the A flat Ballade is noteworthy for its seriousness and sense of proportion – perhaps it is too forceful in places, but the overall effect is rhapsodic. A younger and promising Australian is Roger Woodward

(b. 1943), who studied for six years in Warsaw with Professor Drzewiecki. Woodward had for many years had a special interest in the performance of *avant garde* piano writing. Some years ago he made a Chopin disc which includes the *Allegro de Concert*, a work that only a handful of pianists have recorded. He plays some Mazurkas and other short pieces on the same record, and in all of them displays originality and a secure grasp of the idiom of the music, the Mazurkas showing his understanding of the priorities necessary in playing Chopin. His style is an unusual mixture of the assertively masculine and delicately feminine aspects which were present in Chopin's own musical personality, resulting in a paradox which only the most able interpreters can convey.

Among Israeli pianists, the most famous is Daniel Barenboim, who was born in Argentina in 1942 and had his first lessons from his parents. The family settled in Israel when he was a child, and he had lessons from Edwin Fischer in Salzburg. His career has advanced in many directions, and as a pianist, he is above all a player of enlightened intelligence, with the capacity to bring his amazingly versatile mind to bear on any musical interpretation. His Chopin is both serious and forceful; the Sonatas benefit from this approach, but the lack of poetry in his playing can in the small-scale works rob the music of some of its nature. Less of an interpretative musician, but a pianist of the greatest perfection, is Daniel Adni, who was born in Israel in 1952. His readings of Chopin have an immaculate polish, though they do not exploit the darker and more tantalizing side of the composer's musical nature; however Adni is young and will surely develop as an artist.

Some of the most skilled pianists have preferred chamber music to solo performances, and among them is Menahem Pressler. He played in public from an early age, and some years ago recorded a number of Chopin's works, including the E minor Concerto, the *Andante Spianato and Grande Polonaise Brillante*, and various Mazurkas and Polonaises. Most famous as the pianist of the Beaux Arts Trio, his Chopin playing cannot be ignored; it is small-scale, intimate and extremely sympathetic. He has few rivals as a Mazurka player – he understands the sentiment and emotional range of these works. His playing is superbly finished, and he is a master of *pianissimo* playing and delicate shading. Pressler's reading of the E minor Concerto may lack the heroic drama other pianists bring to this work, but he reveals Chopin in a reminiscent and quietly attractive mood, impressing the listener by subtlety rather than force. Even the E flat minor Polonaise, Op. 26 No. 2, is portrayed by Pressler in a manner that is lyrical and mysterious rather than bombastic. His approach may not display some of the more positive sides of Chopin's nature, but it well reveals its beauty and poetry.

The Chinese pianist Fou T'song has specialized in Chopin ever since he entered the 1955 Warsaw Competition, where he was awarded third prize and the award for the best performance of the Mazurkas. His skills are those of the great romantic pianists, and when he is at his best he has few equals, for example in his recent discs of the complete Nocturnes and the Sonatas. In his personal commitment to Chopin he has some of the dedication of Cortot, whose playing Fou greatly admires. Fou's interpretations of the Mazurkas resemble those of Friedman, and like him, he sometimes uses what many regard as excessive *rubato*, but Zbigniew Drzewiecki, who was his teacher in Poland, rated his playing of the Mazurkas very highly – he brings to them an emotional and pianistic variety neglected by many performers of his generation. Fou aims not at studied charm but at spontaneity, a difficult goal to achieve because it so much reflects the artist's mood on a particular occasion.

Fou T'song has a phenomenal technique, and has on occasion attempted over-ambitious programmes, such as the complete Preludes and the complete Etudes in one programme, which he gave at the Royal Festival Hall in the mid-1970s. Essipov and Berthe Marx-Goldschmidt also performed this programme, but very few pianists can maintain the peak of technical and musical concentration necessary for this test of endurance. In less ambitious programmes, his Chopin performances are of the highest quality. His recent disc of the F minor Fantasy is capable of being compared with that of Cortot, which in many ways it resembles – he has the necessary sense of overall structure and the right degree of *rubato* – and when Fou plays works such as the F minor Fantasy, the F minor Ballade and the B flat minor Sonata on his best form, he joins the ranks of the most distinguished pianists of our time.

Fou has cultivated a much greater range of dynamics than most pianists of today; he can play a sustained *pianissimo* line with extraordinary effectiveness, as in his masterly renderings of the trio section of the Funeral March from the B flat minor Sonata. That he traces his musical sympathies to the pianistic tradition of the past is obvious from his style, which as a result is sometimes criticized for excess and mannerism. He even uses a slightly tilted piano stool, like Josef Hofmann, to assist him in the most advantageous disposition of the weight of his arm. But when he is at his best he fully justifies the course he has adopted, and plays a magnificent Chopin. It is striking that a Chopin pianist from a 'new' country should so strongly embody the great European tradition of the past.

CONCLUSION

ALTHOUGH IT IS often suggested that there are 'traditions' of Chopin playing deriving from a particular pianist or teacher or linked with a particular nationality, it remains true that only the relatively superficial characteristics of any individual's playing can be transmitted to another; the copyable aspects of a performance are musically the least important ones. Those pianists trained in Paris towards the end of the last century were favourably placed for transmitting a deep and genuine understanding of the essence of his music, but the fact that so many different pianists with such very different styles have played Chopin's music with great success demonstrates that it is almost uniquely malleable. 'Authenticity', as I have hoped to show in this study, is a concept which has a very limited application to performing Chopin, and even Anton Rubinstein, when he altered dynamic markings at will, was following the composer's practice; Chopin's pupils objected to the Russian's performances not because of this practice, but because his temperament was entirely different to that of the composer, and so much more extreme and violent in its expression.

It has been said that from the time of the super-virtuosi Hofmann, Godowsky, Rachmaninov and Lhévinne, Chopin's music has been played too quickly, and that pianists have in the past tended to treat the Etudes on the premise that they should be played as fast as was compatible with accuracy. The extraordinary heights reached by Friedman and Hofmann now sound excessively sensational, but it must be remembered that these pianists were also able to respond to the lyric side of Chopin's writing. Conversely, pianists of today have a tendency to stress the form of Chopin's music without fully warming to its emotional and poetic life. The older pianists possessed a more communicative singing touch than do most today, and this characteristic is one of the most important components of a successful reading of Chopin.

It is impossible of course to know how Chopin playing will develop. However, I believe that pianists will in the future be encouraged to play with greater spontaneity, and a greater respect for the overall character of a piece of music, than do many leading performers today. At the moment we are in the grip of an academic approach to music, but there are many young pianists who tend towards more emotionally involved music-making. I have often thought that Chopin's music may have been taken to its limits as far as the variety of interpretations is concerned, but a new and original performance has always presented itself and dispelled this fear!

APPENDIX I

The Pupils of Chopin

IN ATTEMPTING TO enumerate all the pupils of Chopin, I have gathered altogether around 130 names, but most of these are of little importance in attempting to gain greater knowledge of his playing and teaching because the majority of them were amateurs, members of the European aristocracy or the *nouveau riche* who never became noteworthy pianists. The list printed here includes only those of Chopin's pupils who were of importance as pianists, teachers or critics, and most of them are mentioned in the text. There is some doubt as to whether some of them should be described as pupils of Chopin, or as his 'disciples'; d'Ábrányi, Decombes, Krzyżanowski, Lenz, Orda, Péru, Richards and Sloper are included here because they lived in Paris while Chopin was teaching there and probably had lessons with him.

Kornél d'Ábrányi (1822–1903)
Princess Marcelina Czartoryska (1817–94)
Émile Decombes (1829–1912)
Laura Duperré
Countess Elise de Eustaphiew (Mme Peruzzi)
Carl Filtsch (1830–45)
Adolf Gutmann (1819–82)
Caroline Hartmann (1808–34)
Vera de Kologrivoff (Mme Rubio) (1816–80)
Mlle R. de Könneritz (Mme von Heygendorf)
Ignacy Krzyżanowski (1826–1905)
Wilhelm von Lenz (1809–83)
Ignace X. J. Leyback (1817–91)
Georges Mathias (1826–1910)
Mme Antoinette Mauté de Fleurville (d. 1893)

Karol Mikuli (1821–97)
Friedericke Müller (Mme Streicher) (1816–95)
Camilla O'Meara (Mme Dubois) (1830–1907)
Napoléon Orda (1807–83)
F.-Henri Péru (1829–1922)
Anton Rée (1820–86)
Brinley Richards (1817–85)
Mme Marie Roubaud de Cournand (1822–1916)
Zofia Rosengardt (Mme Zaleska) (1814–68)
Marie de Rozières (1805–65)
Lindsay Sloper (1826–87)
Princess Catherine de Souzzo
Jane Stirling (1804–59)
Thomas Tellefsen (1823–74)
Emilie von Timm (Mme von Brülow, later Mme von Gretsch) (1821–77)

APPENDIX II

Prizewinners of the Frédéric Chopin International Piano Competitions

First Competition 1927
1. Lev Oborin (USSR)
2. Stanisław Szpinalski (Poland)
3. Róża Etkin-Moszkowska (Poland)
4. Grigory Ginzburg (USSR)
5. Henryk Sztompka (Poland)

Second Competition 1932
1. Alexander Uninsky (USSR, though not living there at time)
2. Imre Ungar (Hungary; same amount of points as Uninsky – result based on toss of a coin)
3. Bolesław Kon (Poland)
4. Abram Lufer (USSR)
5. Louis Kentner (Hungary)
6. Leonid Sagalov (USSR)
7. Leon Boruński (Poland)
8. Teodor Gutmann (USSR)
9. Julian von Károlyi (Hungary)
10. Kurt Engel (Austria)
11. Emanuel Grossman (USSR)
12. Joseph Wagner (Germany)
13. Maryla Jonas (Poland)
14. Lily Herz (Hungary)
15. Suzanne de Mayère (Belgium)

Third Competition 1937
1. Jakov Zak (USSR)
2. Rosa Tamarkina (USSR)
3. Witold Małcużyński (Poland)
4. Lance Dossor (UK)
5. Agi Jámbor (Hungary)
6. Edith Axenfeld (Germany)
7. Monique de la Bruchollerie (France)
8. Jan Ekier (Poland)
9. Tatiana Goldfarb (USSR)
10. Olga Iliwicka (Poland)
11. Pierre Maillard-Verger (France)
12. Lelia Gousseau (France)
13. Halina Kalmanowicz (Poland)

Fourth Competition 1949
1. Halina Czerny-Stefańska (Poland)
1. Bella Davidovitch (USSR)
3. Barbara Hesse-Bukowska (Poland)
4. Waldemar Maciszewski (Poland)
5. Georgy Muravlov (USSR)
6. Wladysław Kędra (Poland)
7. Ryszard Bakst (Poland)
8. Yevgeny Malinin (USSR)
9. Zbigniew Szymonowicz (Poland)
10. Tamara Gusyeva (USSR)
11. Victor Merzhanov (USSR)
12. Regina Smendzianka (Poland)
13. Tadeusz Żmudziński (Poland)

Fifth Competition 1955
1. Adam Harasiewicz (Poland)
2. Vladimir Ashkenazy (USSR)
3. Fou T'song (Chinese People's Republic)
4. Bernard Ringeissen (France)
5. Naum Shtarkman (USSR)
6. Dmitri Papierno (USSR)
7. Lidia Grychtałówna (Poland)
8. André Tchaikowsky (Poland)
9. Dmitri Sacharov (USSR)
10. Kiyoko Tanaka (Japan)

Sixth Competition 1960
1. Maurizio Pollini (Italy)
2. Irina Zaritskaya (USSR)
3. Tania Achot-Haroutounian (Iran)
4. Li Min-Chan (China)
5. Zinayda Ignatyeva (USSR)
6. Valery Kastelski (USSR)

Seventh Competition 1965
1. Martha Argerich (Argentina)
2. Arthur Moreira-Lima (Brazil)
3. Marta Sosińska (Poland)
4. Hiroko Nakamura (Japan)

5. Edward Auer (USA)
6. Elżbieta Głabówna (Poland)

Eighth Competition 1970
1. Garrick Ohlsson (USA)
2. Mitsuko Uchida (Japan)
3. Piotr Paleczny (Poland)
4. Eugene Indjic (USA)
5. Natalia Gawriłowa (USSR)
6. Janusz Olejniczak (Poland)

Ninth Competition 1975
1. Krystian Zimerman (Poland)
2. Dina Joffie (USSR)

3. Tatiana Fiedkina (USSR)
4. Pavel Gililov (USSR)
5. Dean Kramer (USA)
6. Diana Kacso (Brazil)

Tenth Competition 1980
1. Thai Son Dang (Vietnam)
2. Tatiana Szebanova (USSR)
3. Arutiun Papazyan (USSR)
4. (not awarded)
5. Ewa Pobłocka (Poland) and Akiko Ebi (Japan)
6. Erik Berchot (France) and Irina Pietrova (USSR)

NOTES

Full titles of books referred to will be found in the Bibliography on p. 270.

Introduction

1. Quoted in F. Niecks, *Frederick Chopin*, Vol. 2, p. 103.

Chapter I   The Playing of Chopin and his Contemporaries

1. Quoted in O. Bie, *History of the Pianoforte and Pianoforte Players*, p. 257.
2. W. von Lenz, *Great Piano Virtuosos*, p. 28.
3. C. Hallé, *Autobiography*, p. 34.
4. C. Moscheles, *Aus Moscheles' Leben*, Vol. 2, p. 39.
5. A. Michałowski, 'Yak grał Fryderyk Szopen?', *Muzyka*, Vol. IX, pp. 74–5, and J. Kleczyński, *F. Chopin: de l'interprétation de ses oeuvres*, p. 75.
6. Niecks, op. cit., Vol. 2, p. 101.
7. K. Mikuli, Preface to his edition of Chopin's works, p. 2.
8. Niecks, op. cit., Vol. 1, p. 274.
9. Ibid., Vol. 2, p. 98.
10. Ibid., pp. 181–2.
11. G. Mathias, Preface to I. Philipp's *Exercices quotidiens*.
12. Lenz, op. cit., p. 44.
13. H. Schonberg, *The Great Pianists*, p. 147.
14. Lenz, op. cit., p. 15.
15. Letter from Liszt, Chopin and Franchomme to Hiller, 20 June 1833; see A. Hedley, *Selected Correspondence of Fryderyk Chopin*, p. 117.
16. S. Sitwell, *Liszt*, p. 170.
17. Lenz, op. cit., p. 35.
18. A. Siloti, *My Memories of Liszt*, p. 19.
19. Ibid., p. 24.
20. R. Smith, *Alkan*, p. 98.
21. Ibid., p. 63.
22. Niecks, op. cit., Vol. 2, p. 336.
23. Letter from Schumann to Dorn, 14 September 1836, in Hedley, op. cit., p. 137.
24. Niecks, op. cit., Vol. 2, p. 337.
25. Ibid., Vol. 1, p. 140.
26. Letter from Chopin to Tytus Woyciechowski, 5 June 1830, in Hedley, op. cit., p. 48.
27. A-F. Marmontel, *Les Pianistes célèbres*, p. 77.
28. J. F. Porte, *Chopin*, p. 87.
29. Ibid., p. 164.
30. An excellent account of Henselt, the man and his teaching, is given in B. Walker, *My Musical Experiences*, pp. 153–224.
31. Quoted in the entry on the pianist in *Grove's Dictionary of Music* (5th ed.), Vol. 4, p. 244.
32. Lenz, op. cit., p. 84.
33. Ibid.
34. Ibid., p. 33.
35. J. W. Davison, *Frederic Chopin*, p. 13 (footnote).
36. Lenz, op. cit., p. 33.
37. Niecks, op. cit., Vol. 2, pp. 179–80.
38. Ibid., p. 176.

39. A. Diehl-Mangold, *Musical Memories*, p. 28.
40. Entry on Chopin in A. Sowiński, *Les Musiciens polonais*, and Niecks, op. cit., Vol. 2, pp. 176–7.
41. Mathias, op. cit.
42. A. Benoist, *The Accompanist*, pp. 20–1, and B. Gavoty, *Alfred Cortot*, various pp.
43. Michałowski, op. cit., p. 76.
44. A. Hedley, 'Some observations on the autograph sources of Chopin's works', pp. 474–7.
45. A. Ehrlich, *Celebrated Pianists*, pp. 200–1.
46. J.-J. Eigeldinger, *Chopin vu par ses élèves*, p. 215, n. 180.
47. M. Long, *At the Piano With Debussy*, pp. 19, 51.
48. E. Ganche, *Dans le souvenir de Frédéric Chopin*, p. 81 and footnote.
49. L. Ostrzyńska, *Wspomnienia o F. Chopinie i uczniu jego F.-H. Péru*.
50. A. Rubinstein, *My Young Years*, p. 131.

Chapter II   The Pupils of Liszt, of Leschetizky and of Chopin's Pupils

1. Liszt's comments on 'authentic performances' of Chopin are recorded in H. R. Haweis, *My Musical Life*, p. 662.
2. Ehrlich, op. cit., p. 332.
3. Lenz., op. cit., pp. 52 and 56.
4. A. Fay, *Music Study in Germany*, p. 276.
5. Lenz, op. cit., p. 50.
6. Schonberg, op. cit., p. 242.
7. Lenz, op. cit., p. 53.
8. Fay, op. cit., p. 40.
9. This was related to me by Michałowski's pupil, Stefania Allinówna.
10. G. B. Shaw, *London Music in 1888–89*, p. 151.
11. Shaw was writing for *The Star* under the pseudonym 'Corno di Bassetto'.
12. Shaw, op. cit., p. 151.
13. Ibid., pp. 169–70.
14. Marmontel, op. cit., p. 4.
15. I. Schwerké, 'Francis Planté', *Recorded Sound*, No. 35, p. 474.
16. F. Berger, *Reminiscences, Impressions and Anecdotes*, p. 91.
17. *Monthly Musical Record*, 1 November 1875, p. 159.
18. Fay, op. cit., p. 39.
19. Schonberg, op. cit., p. 292.
20. *Dictionary of Modern Music and Musicians* (ed. A. Eaglefield-Hull), entry on d'Albert by A. Einstein, p. 10.
21. Schonberg, op. cit., p. 295.
22. *Dictionary of Modern Music and Musicians*, entry on Sauer by A. Einstein, p. 437.
23. See extract from Sauer's autobiography quoted on sleeve-note of IPL disc Veritas VM 114.
24. Shaw, *Music in London, 1890–94*, Vol. 1, p. 33.
25. Shaw, *London Music*, p. 338.
26. Shaw, *Music in London*, Vol. 1, p. 114.
27. Schonberg, op. cit., p. 299.
28. V. Cernikoff, 'Pianists: Some Memories and Reflections', *Monthly Musical Record*, Vol. LXIII, p. 28.
29. This was related to me by the English pianist and teacher, Gordon Green.
30. Extract from review in *Neuen Musik Zeitung* by Otto Lessmann, quoted in E. Ehrlich, *Celebrated Pianists*.
31. G. Saleski, *Famous Musicians of Jewish Origin*, p. 543.
32. A. Hedley, *Chopin*, p. 147.

33. G. Woodhouse, 'How Leschetizky Taught', *Music and Letters*, Vol. XXXV, p. 220.
34. A. Potocka, *Theodore Leschetizky*, p. 43.
35. Ibid., p. 51.
36. *Monthly Musical Record*, 1 November 1871, p. 147.
37. W. Ganz, *Memories of a Musician*, p. 128.
38. Schonberg, op. cit., p. 332.
39. Ganz, op. cit., p. 128.
40. The veteran Polish pianist, Jerzy Lefeld, related this to me.
41. Schonberg, op. cit., p. 287.
42. Ibid., p. 282.
43. Ibid., p. 289.
44. This was related to me by his pupil and friend, Marcella Barzetti.
45. Shaw, *London Music*, p. 375.
46. See article by the late Zbigniew Drzewiecki accompanying *The Golden Pages of Polish Pianistic Art*, Muza Records, XL 0157–60.
47. Related to me by the late Mme Trombini-Kazuro in Warsaw, 1978.
48. Quoted in Saleski, op. cit., p. 468, originally appearing in the *New York World*.
49. H. Neuhaus, *The Art of Piano Playing*, p. 154.
50. Saleski, op. cit., p. 467.
51. Schonberg, op. cit., p. 308.
52. M. Hambourg, *From Piano to Forte*, p. 219.
53. D. Ewen, *Living Musicians*, p. 59.
54. Saleski, op. cit., p. 453, states that Brailowsky played this cycle 16 times in 24 years in these cities, but I have not had the opportunity of verifying this.
55. A. Chasins, *Speaking of Pianists*, p. 150.
56. *Current Biography 1956*, p. 75.
57. See F. Planté and others, 'Lettres sur Chopin', *Courrier musical*, 1910, p̓p. 36–8.
58. See S. Allinówna, *Zeszyty naukowe,* No. 10, pp. 21, 24. This information was also related to me by the author.
59. This was related to me by two of Michałowski's pupils, Stefania Allinówna and Jerzy Lefeld.
60. This was related to me by Mme Allinówna.
61. Drzewiecki, op. cit.
62. See entry on Koczalski in *Baker's Biographical Dictionary of Musicians* (5th ed.).
63. Drzewiecki, op. cit.
64. See obituary of Schelling in *Current Biography 1940*, p. 718.
65. Ibid., p. 719.
66. V. Cernikoff, op. cit., p. 28.
67. R. Pugno, *Les leçons écrites de R. Pugno*, p. 66.

Chapter III   French Pianists and Chopin

1. A. Harasowski, *The Skein of Legends around Chopin*, p. 120.
2. A. Dandelot, *Francis Planté,* caption for picture appearing between pp. 56–7.
3. Diehl-Mangold, op. cit., p. 15.
4. Planté and others, op. cit., pp. 36–8.
5. See entry on Planté in *Cyclopaedic Dictionary of Musicians* (ed. R. Dunstan), 1925.
6. Dandelot, op. cit., various pp.
7. D. Milhaud, *Notes Without Music*, pp. 223–34, and Schwerké, op. cit., p. 485.
8. Schwerké, op. cit., p. 483.
9. Letter from Mme Gaby Casadesus to the author, 29 February 1978.
10. Schwerké, op. cit., p. 474.
11. Ibid., p. 484.
12. Ibid., p. 483.

13. See Discography for piano rolls of this work.
14. K. Kobylańska, *Manuscripts of Chopin's Works: A Catalogue*, Vol. 1, p. 246.
15. Published by Durand, Paris.
16. Rubinstein, op. cit., p. 131.
17. Hambourg, op. cit., p. 162.
18. Extract quoted from Ehrlich, op. cit., p. 80.
19. Planté and others, op. cit. The other pianists of note who contributed to this article were E. Risler, A. Cortot and Auguste de Radwan. The last-named was a pupil of Philipp and Leschetizky, and was a highly respected 'society' pianist, who excelled in Chopin's small-scale works.
20. B. Gavoty, *Alfred Cortot*, p. 37.
21. See entry on Cortot in *A Dictionary of Modern Music and Musicians*, op. cit., p. 102.
22. Mikuli, op. cit., p. 2.
23. Harasowski, op. cit., p. 190.
24. This information was given to me by Cortot's pupil, the Scottish pianist, Guthrie Luke.
25. See G. Ashton Jonson, *Handbook to Chopin's Works*, pp. 198–9 for a convincing explanation of this often-quoted description.
26. There is also an LP version of this work on Japanese Victor JAS 273, but this is a rarity.
27. See entry on Lortat in *International Cyclopedia of Music and Musicians*, ed. O. Thompson (9th ed.) pp. 1232–3.
28. See the author's interview with Vlado Perlemuter in *Records and Recording*, April 1979.
29. This information was given to me by Mme Casadesus in a letter from Paris, February 1978.
30. *Current Biography 1945*, p. 93.
31. Casadesus's recital was broadcast by Radio Hilversum. It was given in the concert hall of the *Concertgebouw* in Amsterdam, March 1960.
32. Saleski, op. cit., p. 464.
33. See obituary of de la Bruchollerie in *Ruch Muzyczny*, Vol. XVII, No. 3, February 1973, p. 3.
34. J. Kaiser, *Great Pianists of Our Time*, p. 190.
35. See sleeve-note on disc *The Art of Youra Guller*, Nimbus 2106.
36. See sleeve-note on Perlemuter disc, BBC REB 153.
37. See *Peuples Amis*, 1960, p. 31.

Chapter IV   *The Poles and Chopin*

1. See entry on Szymanowska in supplementary volume of *Grove's Dictionary of Music and Musicians* (5th ed.) Vol. 10, p. 431.
2. Schonberg, op. cit., p. 91.
3. See entry on Chopin in Sowiński, op. cit.
4. *Monthly Musical Record*, 1878, 1879.
5. Drzewiecki, op. cit.
6. This antagonism was related to me by Michałowski's pupil, Stefania Allinówna.
7. W. Landowska, *Landowska on Music*, p. 6.
8. Roman Jasiński contributes a retrospective column for the Polish music magazine, *Ruch Muzyczny*.
9. Chasins, op. cit., p. 36.
10. Shaw, *Music in London*, Vol. 1, p. 19.
11. E. Pauer, *The Pianist's Dictionary*, p. 50.
12. K. Kobylańska, 'Zofia z Poznańskich Rabcewiczowa', *Ruch Muzyczny*, Vol. XVII, p. 3.
13. Drzewiecki, op. cit.

14. This opinion about Turczyński and Drzewiecki was related to me by Roman Jasiński, the Polish pianist.
15. Kaiser, op. cit., states the date 1889 as being authoritative for Rubinstein's birth, but I am unconvinced.
16. Entry on the pianist *A Dictionary of Modern Music and Musicians*, p. 425, written by the distinguished Polish scholar, Z. Jachimecki.
17. A. Rubinstein, op. cit., pp. 134–5.
18. Drzewiecki, op. cit.
19. See B. Maciejewski, *Karol Szymanowski and Jan Smeterlin*. Towards the end of this work, there are some notes by Smeterlin for a projected work on the interpretation of Chopin.
20. This was related to me during an interview with Mme Drzewiecka in Warsaw, 1978.
21. See entry on pianist in *Grove's Dictionary of Music and Musicians* (5th ed.) Vol. 8, p. 271.
22. This information was related to me by Mme Czerny-Stefańska during an interview in Warsaw in 1978.
23. See sleeve-note by Dr Jan Weber in 2-record set of first prizewinners of Chopin Competitions (1927–65), Muza XL 0654–5.

Chapter V   Russian Schools of Chopin Playing

1. A. McArthur, *Anton Rubinstein*, p. 12.
2. C. D. Bowen, *Free Artist*, p. 287.
3. See Mathias's view as recounted in J. Huneker, *Steeplejack*, Vol. 1, p. 143.
4. J. Hofmann, *Piano Playing with Piano Questions Answered*, p. 159.
5. Bowen, op. cit., pp. 322–3.
6. Ibid., pp. 261–2.
7. For programmes of Rubinstein's 'Historical Concerts' of 1885, see Bowen, op. cit., between pp. 186–7.
8. Ibid., p. 358.
9. J. F. Cooke, *Great Pianists on Piano-Playing*, p. 214.
10. Niecks, op. cit., Vol. 2, p. 103.
11. Saleski, op. cit., p. 353.
12. Cooke, op. cit., p. 54.
13. Ibid., p. 185.
14. Porte, op. cit., p. 87.
15. Hambourg, op. cit., p. 162.
16. Shaw, *Music in London*, Vol. 1, p. 20.
17. See the author's interview with Vlado Perlemuter in *Records and Recording*, April 1979.
18. D. Ewen op. cit., p. 219.
19. See H. R. Anderson, 'Josef Lhévinne Discography', *Recorded Sound*, No. 44, October 1971, p. 793.
20. Ibid., 'Rosina Lhévinne Discography', p. 797.
21. See extract in S. Bertensson, *Sergei Rachmaninoff*, p. 28, from M. Bukinik, 'The Young Rachmaninoff', *Local*, 802, 1943. A set of 4 long-playing records of Igumnov's discs was issued by Melodya on 33C 10–05519–26, which included an unissued 78 from 1935 of Chopin's Mazurka in B major, Op. 56 No. 1.
22. See sleeve-note by E. Blickstein for Levitzki disc on IPA 114.
23. Related by Neuhaus, op. cit., p. 209, where the author attempts to rationalize his nervous state.
24. This pupil, Voskresenski, wrote an interesting article in tribute to his teacher, Oborin, which is printed as a sleeve-note on disc of Oborin playing two piano concertos, Melodya 33M 10–36095/6.
25. Article by Cardus reprinted as sleeve-note accompanying disc CBS BRG 72067.

26. Saleski, op. cit., p. 459.
27. Mme Czerny-Stefańska related this to me during an interview in Warsaw, 1978.
28. Ewen, op. cit., Supplement 1, p. 62.
29. This description appears on an anonymous sleeve-note on Neuhaus's Chopin recital on Melodya S 04513/4.

Chapter VI   German, Austrian and British Pianists

1. G. Woodhouse, 'How Leschetizky Taught', *Music and Letters*, Vol. XXXV, p. 225.
2. Niecks, op. cit., Vol. 2, p. 113.
3. Berger, op. cit., pp. 80–1.
4. Letters from Bülow to his mother, 23 May 1841, and 24 June 1848, in *The Early Correspondence of von Bülow*, pp. 10, 29.
5. Berger, op. cit., p. 81.
6. H. Opieński, *I. J. Paderewski*, p. xvi.
7. J. Bescomby-Chambers, *Archives of Sound*, p. 49.
8. Ewen, op. cit., p. 24.
9. P. Badura-Skoda, *Chopin Etudes*, Wiener Urtext.
10. Diehl-Mangold, op. cit., p. 107.
11. Hambourg, op. cit., p. 65.
12. See various issues of *Monthly Musical Record* in the 1870s.
13. Shaw, *Music in London*, p. 34.
14. H. E. Johnson, *First Performances in America to 1900*, p. 112.
15. A. Loesser, *Men, Women and Pianos*, p. 511.
16. *Musical Times*, Vol. LXXVI, April 1935, p. 330.
17. D. Lassimonne and H. Ferguson (eds), *Myra Hess by Her Friends*, p. 109.

Chapter VII   Eastern Europe, the Iberian Peninsula and Italy

1. Tomašek wrote a book of memoirs, extracts from which were published in *Music Quarterly*, Vol. XXXII, 1946, pp. 244 et seq.
2. Schonberg, op. cit., pp. 195–6.
3. Long, op. cit., p. 31.
4. There is a good biographical sketch of this pianist in *The Dictionary of American Biography* (ed. D. Malone) Vol. X, pp. 217–18.
5. *Monthly Musical Record*, for which Scharwenka wrote as Berlin correspondent.
6. Huneker, op. cit., Vol. 2, p. 207.
7. Letter from Huneker to Pitts Sanborn, 27 March 1917, in *Letters of J. G. Huneker*, p. 228.
8. J. Huneker, *Steeplejack*, Vol. 2, p. 42.
9. Ibid.
10. P. Feuchtwanger, 'Clara Haskil', *Recorded Sound*, Nos. 63–4, p. 550.
11. Ibid.
12. Ibid., see lists of concert programmes, pp. 559–608.
13. Related to the author by Gieseking's friend and pupil, Marcella Barzetti.
14. Related to the author during an interview, 1976.
15. See sleeve-note on Pye Virtuoso, TPLS 13053.
16. *A Dictionary of Modern Music and Musicians*, op. cit., entry on Busoni by Hugo Leichtentritt, p. 72.
17. Mr Merrick demonstrated this to the author on the piano.
18. E. J. Dent, *F. Busoni*, p. 108.
19. See sleeve-note by his pupil E. Weiss on disc IPA 104, and also various letters to his wife, F. Busoni, *Letters*, tr. R. Ley.
20. Sitwell, op. cit., p. 294.

21. See entry on Busoni in *Grove's Dictionary of Music and Musicians* (5th ed.) Vol. 1, p. 1042, written by his biographer, E. J. Dent.
22. Dent, op. cit., p. 46.
23. See E. Weiss, sleeve-notes on disc referred to in note 19 above.
24. Casella, *Music in My Time*, p. 224.
25. Ewen, op. cit., p. 72.
26. Schonberg, op. cit., p. 424.
27. J. Prosnak, *The Frederic Chopin International Piano Competitions*, p. 105.
28. Quoted in *Grove's Dictionary of Music and Musicians* (5th ed.) Vol. 5, p. 145, from A. Hullah's biography of the teacher.

Chapter VIII   The United States, South America and other countries

1. M. J. E. Brown, *Chopin: an Index of His Works*, p. 62.
2. J. Huneker, *Steeplejack*, Vol. 1, p. 40.
3. See J. Smith, *Master Pianist: the Career and Teaching of Carl Friedberg*, p. 138.
4. O. Samaroff-Stokowski, *An American Musician's Story*, p. 20.
5. See sleeve-note by Saperton's pupil, Sydney Foster, on IPA 118–19.
6. See sleeve-note by A. Petrak on Loesser disc, IPA 102.
7. Ehrlich, op. cit., p. 291.
8. Chasins, op. cit., p. 238.
9. See *A Dictionary of Modern Music and Musicians*, op. cit., p. 80, entry on Carreño written by the editor.
10. Schonberg, op. cit., p. 221.
11. Quoted in M. Milinowski, *Teresa Carreño*, p. 250.
12. See sleeve-note by E. Blickstein for discs of Renard, on IPA 120–21.
13. Ibid.
14. Chasins, op. cit., p. 119.
15. Ibid., pp. 118–25, giving a sympathetic tribute to Novaës's artistry.
16. The author had an interview with the then ninety-two-year-old pianist in Warsaw in 1978.

DISCOGRAPHY

The discography covers all the recordings described in this book, and also many others mentioned in passing where these are of importance. Unless otherwise stated, all the discs are long-playing records. The discography is intended only so that the reader can identify discs mentioned in the text, and has therefore been reduced to essentials. When a 78 or an LP has been reissued, I have given the number of the reissue *first*, and the original number in the right-hand column. I have not attempted to list reissues of piano-roll material, as these are often insubstantially documented. The dates of recordings are approximate.

The following abbreviations have been used:

PR	piano roll
p.p.	recorded from a public performance
n.d.	date of recording not known
n.n.	record number not known
e	early
m	mid
l	late
ac.	acoustic 78
BIRS	British Institute of Recorded Sound
CFP	Classics for Pleasure
CIW	Chopin Institute, Warsaw
DG	Deutsche Grammophon, Polydor Records
G & T	Gramophone and Typewriter Company
Gram. Co.	Gramophone Company
IPA	International Piano Archives
IPL	International Piano Library (later IPA)
USSR	early Russian 78s and LPs, before Melodya
FMRA	Merrick Record Association

Allegro de Concert in A major, Op. 46

C. Arrau	Columbia	33CX 1443	*m* 1950s
N. Magaloff (see Miscellaneous Collections)			
R. Woodward	HMV	HQS 1303	1973

Andante Spianato and Grande Polonaise Brillante, Op. 22 – solo piano version

M. Argerich	DG	2530 721	1975
A. Cortot	Victor Japan	JAS 269	*e* 1950s (Polonaise only)
F. Gulda	Mace	MCS 9060	p.p., n.d.
J. Hofmann (1)	RCA	VIC 1550	p.p., 1938
(2)	IPA	5001–2	p.p., 1937

V. Horowitz	RCA	VH 008	1945, from 78s, Vic. 11–9043–4
N. Karp	Saga	5457	1977
W. Kempff	Decca	Eclipse ECS 769	1958, reissue
A. B. Michelangeli	Discocorp	IGI 350	n.d., from radio?
F. Planté	Hupfeld	13612 & 13629	PR, pre-1912

Andante Spianato and Grande Polonaise Brillante, Op. 22 – version with orchestra

C. Arrau/Inbal	Philips	6500 422	1972
E. Gilels/Eliasberg	Ariola Eurodisc	25 810 XAK	p.p., 1951, reissue
M. Pressler/Auberson	Concert Hall	SMSA 2408	1966
S. Richter/Kondrashin	Rococo	2093	p.p., n.d.
A. Weissenberg/ Skrowaczewski	HMV	ASD 2377	1968

Four Ballades (Collections)

C. Arrau	Brunswick	AXTL 1043	1954
V. Ashkenazy	Decca	SXL 6143	1965
R. Casadesus	CBS	AC 3	p.p., 1960
A. Cortot (1)	HMV	DB 1343	78s, 1930
(2)	HMV	DB 2023–26	78s, 1934
J. Ekier	Muza	SX 0061	Poland, 1960
P. Frankl	Decca Turnabout	TV 34271	1964
R. Koczalski	Polydor Germany	67528–31	78s, 1938
V. Perlemuter	Nimbus	2110	*m* 1970s

Ballade No. 1 in G minor, Op. 23

W. Backhaus	Decca	LX 3044	1953, 8″ LP
F. Busoni (1)	Hupfeld	12355	PR
(2)	Ampico	50047H	PR
T. Carreño	Welte	367	PR
E. Gilels	Ariola/Melodya	XAK 85312	*l* 1930s, from 78s USSR 016271/2
L. Godowsky	Duo-Art	5793	PR
J. Hofmann	IPA	5001–2	p.p., 1937
V. Horowitz (1)	RCA	VH 011	1948, from 78 HMV DB 6688
(2)	CBS	S 72376–77	p.p., 1965
(3)	CBS	72720	p.p., 1968
J. Károlyi	Polydor	68089	78, 1944
L. Kartun	Parlophone	E 10960	78, 1929
L. Kentner	Columbia	DX 1391	78, 1947
A. B. Michelangeli (1)	Discocorp	IGI 350	n.d., from radio
(2)	DG	2530 236	1972
S. Niedzielski	Edici	003111	n.d.
M. Pollini	HMV	ASD 2577	1970
R. Pugno	Hupfeld	13731	PR, pre-1912
S. Richter (1)	Melodya	8935/6	p.p., n.d.
(2)	Decca Turnabout	TV 34359S	p.p., n.d.
J. Zurawlew	Muza	XL 0373	*e* 1950s

Ballade No. 2 in F major, Op. 38

F. Merrick	FMRA	No. 3	1961
Z. Rabcewicz	Muza	XL 0157–60	*e* 1930s, from 78
			Syrena 217129
S. Richter	Melodya	8935/6	p.p., n.d

Ballade No. 3 in A flat, Op. 47

G. Bertram	Parlophone	E 10572	78, 1927
Y. Bowen	Vocalion	X 9666	78 ac., 1925
T. Carreño	Welte	369	PR, 1905
I. Friedman	Columbia	DX 466	78, 1933
M. Levitzki (1)	Ampico	59273H	PR
(2)	IPA	114	1928, from 78
			Electrola EW 64
W. Murdoch	Columbia	9367	78, 1927
E. Ney	Colosseum	COL M 2003	Germany, *e* 1960s
G. Novaës	Vanguard	VCS 10059	*l* 1960s
V. de Pachmann	Pearl	GEM 103	1911, from 78 ac.,
			HMV D 262
			(excerpt)
S. Rachmaninov	Melodya	033755–60	1925, 78 ac.,
			originally unissued
S. Richter	DG	2548 223	p.p., n.d.

Ballade No. 4 in F minor, Op. 52

J. Bolet	Opus	81	p.p., 1972
M. de la Bruchollerie	HMV	DB 6731	78, 1949
J. Hofmann	IPA	5007–8	p.p., 1938
S. Neuhaus	Melodya	S 04513/4	p.p., 1972
S. Richter	DG	135013	p.p., n.d.
Solomon	HMV	SLS 701	1946, from 78
			HMV C 3403
M. Tagliaferro	Copacabana	COLP 12463	p.p., 1979

Barcarolle in F sharp major, Op. 60

S. Cherkassky	Tudor	73018	Switzerland, 1977
A. Cortot (1)	HMV	DB 2030	78, 1934
(2)	Electrola	C 047–01 400	1951, from LP
B. Davidovitch	CIW	Tape 268	p.p., *l* 1950s
J. Flier	Melodya	33SM 03265/6	n.d.
A. Hoehn	Parlophone	E 10850	78, 1929
L. Kentner	Saga	5233	*e* 1960s
V. Kraiynev	Melodya/	78518	*m* 1970s
	Chant du monde		
D. Lipatti	HMV	HQM 1163	1948, from 78
			Columbia LX 1437
I. Moravec	Connoisseur	CS–2019	1969
	Society		
S. Neuhaus	Melodya	S 04513/4	p.p., 1972
V. de Pachmann	IPL Veritas	VM 115	1907, from 78 ac.,
			G & T 05502
V. Perlemuter	Concert Hall	2223	1962

L. Pouishnoff	Saga	XID 5013	*l* 1950s
B. Vázsonyi	Pye Virtuoso	TPLS 13053	1972

Berceuse in D flat, Op. 57

W. Backhaus	HMV	DB 1131	78, 1928
A. Cortot (1)	HMV	DB 167	78 ac., 1910
(2)	HMV	DB 1145	78, 1929
L. Godowsky (1)	Pearl	GEMM 167	1913, from 78 ac. Columbia L 1171
(2)	IPL Veritas	VM 103	n.d., from 78 ac., previously unissued
(3)	Ampico	50214H	PR
L. Hoffmann	Europa Klassik	114 0175	*e* 1960s, reissue
J. Hofmann (1)	IPA	5001–2	p.p., 1937
(2)	RCA	VIC 1550	p.p., 1938
R. Koczalski (1)	Polydor	65787	78 ac., 1925
(2)	Polydor	95202	78, 1929
(3)	Polydor	67246	78, 1936
A. B. Michelangeli	Telefunken	SKB 3289	78, 1943
H. Neuhaus	USSR	5938/9	*e* 1950s
R. Pugno	Rococo	2009	1903, from 78 ac. G & T 35540
A. Reisenauer	Welte	–	PR, 1905
M. Rosenthal (1)	Odeon	173164	78, 1929
(2)	Telefunken	F 429	78, 1931
E. Sauer	Vox	06253	78, n.d.
Solomon	HMV	C 3308	78, 1942

Bolero in C major, Op. 19

J. Károlyi	DG	135 013	*e* 1950s, reissue
T. Nikolayeva	USSR	D 01190	*e* 1950s
A. Schnabel	Hupfeld	12456	PR, pre-1912

Piano Concerto No. 1 in E minor, Op. 11

M. Argerich (1) Rowicki	Muza	X 0261	p.p., 1965
(2) Abbado	DG	SLPM 139 383	1969
C. Arrau (1) Klemperer	Cetra	LO 507	p.p., 1954
(2) Inbal	Philips	6747 003	1972
S. Askenase/Otterloo	DG	2548 066	1960, reissue
P. Badura-Skoda/Rodzinski	Westminster	18288	1955
A. Brailowsky (1) Prüwer	Polydor	66753–6	78s, 1928
(2) Steinberg	HMV	ALP 1015	*e* 1950s
(3) Ormandy	CBS Odyssey	Y-31533	*m* 1960s, a reissue
H. Czerny-Stefańska/ Smetáček	Supraphon	SUA 10130	*e* 1950s
B. Davidovitch/Yansons	CFP	40285	1961, from Melodya
S. Falvai/Korody	Hungaroton	LPX 11654	*m* 1970s
E. Gilels/Kondrashin (1)	Ariola Eurodisc	XH 27349 K	p.p., n.d.
/Ormandy (2)	CBS	61931	1965
F. Gulda/Boult	Decca	LXT 2925	1954
A. Harasiewicz/Hollreiser	Fontana	SCFL 101	*l* 1950s
J. Hofmann (1)	Duo-Art	6915–18	PR, for solo piano
J. Hofmann/Barbirolli (2)	IPL	502	p.p., 1938

M. Horszowski/Swarowsky	Vox	SVBX 5402E	1953, reissue
J. Karólyi/Schuchter	EMI	IC 047—29 146	n.d., reissue
E. Kilenyi/Mitropoulos	Columbia	MM–515,	78s, 1942
		1184–7D	
		Tape 774	
R. Lhévinne/Bernstein	BIRS	W & R	p.p., 1963
D. Lipatti/unknown	Seraphim	60007	p.p., 1948, reissue
H. Neuhaus/Gauk	USSR	022732–41 &	78s & LP, 1950
		D 01103/4	
G. Novaës/Perlea	Vox	51070	e 1950s
G. Ohlsson/Rowicki (1)	Muza	SX 06781	p.p., 1970
/Maksymiuk (2)	HMV	SLS 5043	1974
(3)	Desmar	DSM 1005	p.p., 1974 slow movt
			solo
F. Planté	Hupfeld	13601 a & b–	PR, pre-1912
		13664	for solo piano
M. Pollini/Kletzki	HMV	SXLP 30160	1960, reissue
M. Pressler/Josefowicz	Concert Hall	SMSA 2408	1966
M. Rosenthal/Weissmann	Discocorp	RR 409	1930, from 78s
			Parlophone
			9558–9/B 12451 &
			Parlophone
			E 11113–4/R 902–4
A. Rubinstein/Barbirolli	Electrola	C 053–01172M	1937, from 78s HMV
			DB 3201–4
E. Wild/Sargent	Reader's Digest	RDM 1020	1963, a reissue
K. Zimerman (1) Maksymiuk	Muza	SX 1310	p.p., 1975
(2) Giulini	DG	2531 125	1978

Piano Concerto No. 2 in F minor, Op. 21

C. Arrau/Inbal	Philips	6747 003	1972
V. Ashkenazy/Gorzyński	DG	89 671	1955, reissue
S. Askenase/Ludwig	DG	2548 124	1960, a reissue
E. Ax/Ormandy	RCA	RL 12868	1978
P. Badura-Skoda/	Westminster	18288	1955
Rodzinski			
A. Cortot/Barbirolli	Discocorp	RR 409	1936, from 78s
			HMV DB 2612–5
B. Davidovitch/Kondrashin	USSR	D 1087/8	e 1950s
O. Frugoni/Gielen	Vox	PL/D 11460	m 1950s
L. Godowsky	Hupfeld	12740–42	PR, pre-1912, for
			solo piano
C. Haskil/Markevitch	Philips	ABL 3340	l 1950s
J. Hofmann/Barbirolli	IPL	501	p.p., 1936
J. Karólyi/Schuchter	EMI	IC 047–29 146	n.d., reissue
A. de Larrocha/Comissiona	Decca	SXL 6528	1972
M. Long (1) Gaubert	Columbia	D 15236–39	78s, 1930
(2) Cluytens	EMI Japan	GR–2216	e 1950s, reissue
W. Małcużyński/Susskind	CFP	40215	1960, reissue
G. Novaës/Klemperer	Vox	PL 7100	e 1950s
G. Ohlsson/Maksymiuk	HMV	HQS SLS 5043	1974
F. Rauch/Smetáček	Rediffusion	LGD 006	e 1960s, reissue
	Legend		

C. Rosen/Pritchard	Columbia Epic	CX 5273	1966
A. Rubinstein/Barbirolli	Electrola	053–01172M	1931, from 78s HMV DB 1494–97
A. Simon/Beissel	Decca Turnabout	QTV 34602	1972
T. Vásáry/Kulka	DG	136452	1964

Twenty-four Etudes, Opp. 10 and 25 (Collections)

C. Arrau	Columbia	33CX 1443–4	*l* 1950s
V. Ashkenazy	Saga	5293	n.d.
P. Badura-Skoda	Westminster	1811	*m* 1950s
A. Cortot	HMV France	W 1531–36	78s, 1942
G. Cziffra	Philips	AL 3427	1960s
R. Lortat	Columbia	LFX 135–42	78s, 1931 + *Trois Nouvelles Etudes*
G. Novaës	Vox	510930E	1954
M. Pollini	DG	2530 291	1972
D. Saperton	IPA	118–9	*e* 1950s, from LPs Command Performance 1201–3, with relevant Godowsky transcriptions
A. Uninsky	Epic	LC–3065	1954
B. Woytowicz	Muza	SX 0063 & 0064	1960

Twelve Etudes, Op. 10

W. Backhaus	HMV	DB 1132–34	78s, 1928
A. Cortot	HMV	DB 2027–29	78s, 1934
R. Goldsand	Nixa	CLP 1132	1954, with *Trois Nouvelles Etudes*
R. Koczalski	Polydor Germany	67262–64	78s, 1936
D. Ranki	Hungaroton	11555	*e* 1970s

Twelve Etudes, Op. 25

W. Backhaus	HMV	DB 1178–80	78s, 1928
A. Cortot	HMV	DB 2308–10	78s, 1934
R. Goldsand	Nixa	CLP 1133	1954
L. Hoffmann	Somerset	631	*e* 1960s
R. Koczalski	Polydor	67242–45	78s, 1936

Etude in C major, Op. 10 No. 1

M. Argerich	Muza	XL 0654–55	p.p., 1965, reissue
E. Gröschel	Oryx	EXP 64	*e* 1970s, on Erard of 1840
S. Richter	DG	2548 223	p.p., 1963
M. Rosenthal (1)	Edison	47004	78, 1927
(2)	Odeon	4356	78, 1930, and on Parlophone

Etude in A minor, Op. 10 No. 2

V. Perlemuter	BBC	REB 153	1972, from radio series

| N. Shtarkman | Monitor Collector | MCS 2135 | n.d., reissue |
| R. Renard | IPA | 120–21 | p.p., 1949, from 78s |

Etude in E major, Op. 10 No. 3

A. Michałowski	HMV	G. C 25632	*l* 1910s
R. Renard	IPA	120–21	p.p., 1949, from 78s
S. Richter	EMI	C 053–97784	n.d., p.p.
E. Sauer	IPL Veritas	VM 114	1928, from 78
			Odeon o–6793

Etude in C sharp minor, Op. 10 No. 4

C. Arrau	Desmar	GHP 4001–2	*e* 1930s, from 78
			Electrola EG 1500
E. Gröschel	Oryx	EXP 64	*e* 1970s, on Erard of
			1840
T. Lerner	Ampico	6854	post-1914
F. Planté	IPL	101	1928, from 78
			Columbia D 15091
R. Renard	IPA	120–21	p.p. 1949, from 78s
V. Sofronitsky	Ariola Eurodisc	85 993 XFK	p.p., 1960

Etude in G flat, Op. 10 No. 5

F. Busoni (1)	IPA	104	1922, 78 ac. from
			Columbia L 1432
(2)	IPA	104	1922, 78 ac. from
			Columbia L 1470
A. Cortot*			
I. Friedman	Muza	XL 0157—60	1928, from 78
			Columbia D 1615
L. Godowsky	Pearl	GEMM 167	1928, from 78
			Brunswick 15123
E. Gröschel	Oryx	EXP 64	*e* 1970s, on Erard of
			1840
M. Hambourg	HMV	D 71	78, ac., 1910
V. Horowitz	CBS	72969	1971
M. Levitzki	IPA	114	1923, from 78 ac.,
			Columbia, n.n.
G. Novaës*			
V. de Pachmann (1)	Pearl	GEM 102	1911, 78, ac. HMV D
			264
(2)	HMV	DA 1302	78, 1927
F. Planté	IPL	101	1928, from 78
			Columbia D 15090
M. Rosenthal	Parlophone	9570 & E 11161	78, 1930
A. Uninsky	Muza	XL 0654–55	*e* 1930s from 78
			Syrena 6917

Etude in E flat minor, Op. 10 No. 6

| L. Oborin | Muza | XL 0654–55 | *l* 1940s, from 78 |
| | | | USSR 17787 |

* See collections of Etudes above.

V. Perlemuter	BBC	REB 153	1972, from radio series
N. Shtarkman	Monitor Collector	MCS 2135	n.d., reissue

Etude in C major, Op. 10 No. 7

I. Friedman	Columbia	7119M	78, *l* 1920s
F. Planté	IPL	101	1928, from 78 Columbia D 13060

Etudes in F minor and A flat major, Op. 10 Nos. 9 and 10

V. Perlemuter	BBC	REB 153	1972, from radio series

Etude in E flat major, Op. 10 No. 11

J. Lhévinne	RCA	VIC 1046	1935, from 78 Victor 8868
A. Michałowski	Syrena	6571	78, *e* 1930s
R. Renard	IPA	120–21	p.p., 1949, from 78s

Etude in C minor, Op. 10 No. 12

I. Friedman	Columbia	7119M	78, *l* 1920s
A. Hoehn	Parlophone	E 10915	78, 1930
V. de Pachmann	HMV	D 835	78 ac., 1909
S. Richter	DG	135013	p.p., n.d.

Etude in A flat, Op. 25 No. 1

C. Arrau	Desmar	GHP 4001–2	1930, from 78 Electrola EG 1500
W. Gieseking	Discocorp	RR 415	1925, from 78 ac., Homocord 1–8614
L. Godowsky	IPL Veritas	VM 103	n.d., from 78 ac., previously unissued
M. Levitzki	IPA	114	1923, from 78 ac., Columbia, n.n.
F. Planté	IPL	101	1928, from 78 Columbia D 15090

Etude in F minor, Op. 25 No. 2

E. d'Albert	Odeon	XX 76939	78 ac., 1910
C. Arrau	Desmar	GHP 4001–2	1930, from 78 Electrola EG 1500
W. Gieseking	Discocorp	RR 415	1925, from 78 ac., Homocord 1–8614
L. Godowsky	Pearl	GEMM 167	1916, from 78 ac., Columbia A 6013
Y. Guller	Nimbus	2106	*m* 1970s
A. Hoehn	Parlophone	E 10915	78, 1930
B. Hungerford	Vanguard	VSD 71214	1975
L. Oborin	Muza	XL 0654–55	*l* 1940s, from 78, n.n.
F. Planté	IPL	101	1928, from 78 Columbia D 13060
R. Renard	IPA	120–21	p.p., 1949, from 78s

M. Rosenthal	Parlophone	EC 59521	78, 1931
A. Schnabel	Hupfeld	12457	PR, pre-1912

Etude in F major, Op. 25 No. 3

L. Godowsky	IPL Veritas	VM 103	n.d., from 78 previously unissued
L. Oborin	Muza	XL 0654–55	*l* 1940s, from 78, n.n.
V. de Pachmann (1)	Columbia	L 1010	78 ac., 1915
(2)	Columbia	L 1112	78 ac., 1916
(3)	HMV	DB 860	78, 1925

Etude in A minor, Op. 25 No. 4

V. Perlemuter	BBC	REB 153	1972, from radio series
R. Renard	IPA	120–21	p.p., 1949, from 78s

Etude in E minor, Op. 25 No. 5

G. Anda	Polydor	68088	78, 1943
F. Busoni	IPA	104	*e* 1920s, from 78 ac., Columbia L 1445
L. Oborin	Muza	XL 0654–55	*l* 1940s, from 78 USSR 17786
V. de Pachmann	Pearl	GEM 103	1911, from 78 ac., HMV D 262
V. Perlemuter	BBC	REB 153	1972, from radio series
R. Renard	IPA	120–21	p.p., 1949, from 78s
S. Richter	EMI	C 053–97784	n.d., a reissue

Etude in G sharp minor, Op. 25 No. 6

J. Lhévinne	RCA	VIC 1046	1935, from 78 Victor 8868
V. Perlemuter	BBC	REB 153	1972, from radio series
M. Rosenthal	Ampico	62961H	PR, post-1918
I. Scharrer	Columbia	DB 1348	78, 1934

Etude in C sharp minor, Op. 25 No. 7

H. Cohen	Columbia	D 1632	78, 1929
I. Moravec	Connoisseur Society	CS-23	1969
V. Perlemuter	BBC	REB 153	1972, from radio series
S. Richter	Rococo	2142	p.p., 1954
E. Sauer	IPL Veritas	VM 114	1928, from 78 Pathé X 5506

Etude in D flat major, Op. 25 No. 8

V. Perlemuter	BBC	REB 153	1972, from radio series
R. Renard	IPA	120–21	p.p., 1949, from 78s

Etude in G flat, Op. 25 No. 9

E. d'Albert	Odeon	XX 76939	78 ac., 1910
L. Godowsky	Pearl	GEMM 167	1928, from 78 Brunswick 15123
J. Hofmann	IPA	5001–2	p.p., 1937
F. Planté	IPL	101	1928, from 78 Columbia D 13059
E. Sauer	Welte	881	PR, 1905

Etude in B minor, Op. 25 No. 10

P. Grainger	Columbia	67 605D	78, 1927
J. Lhévinne	RCA	VIC 1046	1936, from 78 Victor 14024
V. de Pachmann	Pearl	GEM 103	1907, from 78 ac., G & T 3566

Etude in A minor, Op. 25 No. 11

J. Lhévinne	RCA	VIC 1046	1935, from 78 Victor 8868
F. Planté	IPL	101	1928, from Columbia D 15089

Etude in C minor, Op. 25 No. 12

P. Grainger	Columbia	L 1805 or 7109M	78, 1927
E. Sauer	Columbia	LW 38	78, 1939

'Trois Nouvelles Etudes': No. 1 in F minor

H. Cohen	HMV	HLM 7148	1946, from 78 Columbia DX 1231

'Troise Nouvelles Etudes': No. 2 in A flat major

H. Cohen	HMV	HLM 7148	1946, from 78 Columbia DX 1231
M. Rosenthal	Edison	47004	78, 1927

Fantasy on Polish Airs, Op. 13, for piano and orchestra

C. Arrau/Inbal	Philips	6747 003	1972
G. Ohlsson/Maksymiuk	HMV	SLS 5043	1974

Fantasy in F minor, Op. 49

A. Cortot	HMV	DB 2031–32	78s, 1934
P. Frankl	Decca Turnabout	34271	1964
Fou T'song	CBS	61857	*l* 1970s
A. Harasiewicz	Fontana	698 028CL	1960
J. Gimpel	Genesis	GS 1030	1972
J. Károlyi	Polydor	VM 5012	78, n.d.
W. Kempff	Decca Eclipse	ECS 769	1958, a reissue
M. Levitzki	Ampico	63623 & 63633H	PR, post-1918
W. Małcużyński (1)	CFP	40215	1960, a reissue
(2)	Muza	SX 1511–2	1975
H. Neuhaus	USSR	013441/2	*e* 1950s

E. Ney	Colosseum	COL M 2003	*e* 1960s
G. Ohlsson	HMV	HQS 1328	*e* 1970s
A. Rubinstein	RCA	SB 6683	1966
X. Scharwenka	Welte	C241a & b	PR, n.d.
Solomon	HMV	SLS 701	1935, from 78s
			Columbia DX 668–9
B. Vázsonyi	Pye Virtuoso	TPLS 13058	1972

Fugue in A minor, Op. Posth.

N. Janotha	G & T	5561	78 ac., 1904

Four Impromptus (Collections)

S. Askenase	DG	2548 215	1972
G. Casadesus	Polydor	566299–300	78s, 1948
A. Cortot	Electrola	C 047–00889M	1935, from 78s HMV
			DB 2021–22
B. Davidovitch	Melodya	33SM 02421/2	n.d.
M. Horszowski	Vox	SVBX 5402E	*e* 1950s, reissue
J. Karólyi	DG	DGM 18068	1955

Impromptu No. 1 in A flat, Op. 29

L. Godowsky	Pearl	GEMM 167	1921, from 78 ac.,
			Brunswick 50009
L. Kentner	Edison Bell	X 543	78, 1928
R. Koczalski	Polydor	62440	78 ac., 1923
V. de Pachmann	Columbia	L 1009	78 ac., 1915
R. Pugno	Rococo	2009	1903, from 78 ac.,
			G & T 35518

Impromptu No. 2 in F sharp major, Op. 36

R. Koczalski	Polydor	67248	78, 1936
V. de Pachmann	HMV	DB 859	78 ac., 1925
E. Sauer	IPL Veritas	VM 114	1928, from 78 Pathé
			X 5506

Impromptu No. 3 in G flat major, Op. 51

A. Harasiewicz	Muza	XL 0654–55	1955, reissue

Impromptu No. 4 in C sharp minor, Op. Posth. 66 (*Fantaisie-Impromptu*)

A. Fischer	Melodya	33D 06059/60	n.d.
O. Gabrilowitsch	Duo-Art	7074	PR, n.d.
L. Godowsky	Pearl	GEMM 167	1926, from 78
			Brunswick 50070
E. Gröschel	Oryx	EXP 64	*e* 1970s, on Erard of
			1840
L. Kentner (1)	Edison Bell	X 543	78, 1928
(2)	Columbia	DX 997	78, 1939
R. Koczalski	Polydor	67248	78, 1936
X. Scharwenka	Columbia	254	78 ac., 1911

'Krakowiak' Concert Rondo, Op. 14, for piano and orchestra

C. Arrau/Inbal	Philips	6747 003	1972
G. Ohlsson/Maksymiuk	HMV	SLS 5043	*e* 1970s

Mazurkas (Collections and complete recordings)

W. Backhaus	Decca	LX 3044	1953, Nos. 17, 20, 24
I. Friedman	Columbia	LX 99–102	78s, 1930, Nos. 5, 6, 7, 17, 23, 25, 26, 31, 41, 44, 45, 47
O. Frugoni	Vox	VUX 2017/1–2	*l* 1950s, complete but without juvenile Mazurkas
V. Gornostayeva	Melodya	33S10–7775/6	p.p., n.d., Nos. 7, 15, 17, 20, 21, 29, 34, 35, 40, 41, 47, 49, 51
W. Kapell	Victor	LM 1865	*e* 1950s, Nos. 2, 6, 11, 12, 20, 22, 26, 27, 31, 32, 37, 40, 41, 43, 47, 51
W. Małcużyński	CFP	40082	1963, a reissue, Nos. 5, 7, 15, 20–23, 25, 27, 32, 41, 45, 47, 49
N. Milkina	Pye Virtuoso	TPLS 13038	1971, complete
S. Niedzielski	HMV	C 2008–10 & B 3550	78s, 1930, Nos. 6, 9, 10, 17, 19, 23, 30, 38, 41, 44–49
G. Novaës	Vox	57920E	*m* 1950s, Nos. 13, 15, 17, 23–26, 34, 37, 39, 42
R. Smith	HMV	SLS	*m* 1970s, complete
H. Sztompka	Muza	SX 0092–95	1960, complete, but without juvenile Mazurkas

Mazurka in B flat major, Op. 7 No. 1
M. Pressler	Concert Hall	SMSA 2539	1968

Mazurka in A minor, Op. 17 No. 4
N. Shtarkman	Monitor Collector	MCS 2135	n.d., reissue

Mazurka in C major, Op. 24 No. 2
S. Falvai	Hungaroton	LPX 11654	*m* 1970s
A. Szumowska	Ampico	58103H	PR, post-1918

Mazurka in B flat minor, Op. 24 No. 4
V. de Pachmann	HMV	DB 861	78, 1925
M. Pressler	Concert Hall	SMSA 2539	1968
M. Rosenthal	Odeon	171017	78, 1930

Mazurka in C minor, Op. 30 No. 1
J. Zak	Muza	XL 0654–55	n.d., from 78, n.n.

Mazurka in C sharp minor, Op. 30 No. 4
M. Pressler	Concert Hall	SMSA 2539	1968
R. Renard	IPA	120–21	p.p., 1949, from 78s

Mazurka in G sharp minor, Op. 33 No. 1
M. Rosenthal   Parlophone   EC 59521   78, 1931

Mazurka in D major, Op. 33 No. 2
M. Rosenthal   Victor   1951   78, 1931

Mazurka in C major, Op. 33 No. 3
V. de Pachmann   Columbia   L 1112   78ac., 1916

Mazurka in B minor, Op. 33 No. 4
R. Koczalski   Polydor   90031   78, 1927
A. B. Michelangeli (1)   Telefunken   SKB 3289   78, 1943
           (2)   DG   2530 236   1972
V. de Pachmann   Columbia   1102   78ac., 1916
M. Pressler   Concert Hall   SMSA 2539   1968
M. Rosenthal   HMV   DB 2773   78, 1936
C. Zecchi (1)   Ultraphone   BP 1487   78, 1935
         (2)   Cetra   CB 20359   78, 1946

Mazurka in C sharp minor, Op. 41 No. 1
S. Askenase   DG   2530 078   with Nos. 2–4 of
                                                            same opus, 1972
L. Kreutzer   Polydor   90035   78, 1927

Mazurka in A flat major, Op. 50 No. 2
V. de Pachmann (1)   HMV   E 80   78 ac., 1911
           (2)   HMV   DB 861   78, 1925
M. Rosenthal   HMV   DB 2773   78, 1936

Mazurka in C sharp minor, Op. 50 No. 3
R. Etkin   Muza XL   0157–60   e 1930s, from 78, n.n.
                                                            (possibly Tri-Ergon
                                                            label)
V. Horowitz   HMV   DB 2788   78, 1936
W. Małcużyński   Columbia   LX 1028   78, 1947
I. Moravec   Connoisseur   CS–2019   1969
                            Society

Mazurka in C major, Op. 56 No. 2
Z. Rabcewicz   Muza   XL 0157–60   e 1930s, from 78
                                                            Syrena 217129

Mazurka in A flat major, Op. 59 No. 2
I. Paderewski   Muza   XL 0157–60   1925, from 78 ac.,
                                                            HMV DA 633

Mazurka in F sharp minor, Op. 59 No. 3
A. Loesser   IPL   5003–4   p.p., 1967
V. de Pachmann   HMV   E 80   78 ac., 1911
R. Renard   IPA   120–21   p.p., 1949, from 78s

Mazurka in B major, Op. 63 No. 1
M. Rosenthal   Victor   1951   78, 1936

Mazurka in F minor, Op. 63 No. 2

M. Pressler	Concert Hall	SMSA 2539	1968

Mazurka in C sharp minor, Op. 63 No. 3

A. Foldes	Remington	RLP 149–4	*e* 1950s
A. Michałowski	Muza	XL 0157–60	*e* 1930s, from 78 Syrena 6572
V. de Pachmann	HMV	DB 1106	78, 1929
Z. Rabcewicz	Muza	XL 0157–60	*m* 1930s, from 78 Syrena 271488
M. Rosenthal	Parlophone	E 11161	78, 1930
J. Zak	Muza	XL 0654–55	n.d., from 78, n.n.

Mazurka in G major, Op. Posth. 67 No. 1

V. de Pachmann	HMV	DA 1302	78, 1927
M. Rosenthal	Parlophone	E 11161	78, 1930

Mazurka in A minor, Op. Posth. 67 No. 4

G. Anda	Polydor	68088	78, 1943
V. de Pachmann (1)	Columbia	L 1014	78 a.c., 1915
(2)	HMV	DB 1106	78, 1927

Mazurka in A minor, Op. Posth. 68 No. 2

G. Anda	Polydor	68088	78, 1943
R. Koczalski	Polydor	90040	78, 1927
A. B. Michelangeli (1)	HMV	DA 5371	78, 1943
(2)	Discocorp	IGI 350	n.d., from radio
(3)	DG	2530 236	1972

Mazurka in F major, Op. Posth. 68 No. 3

R. Koczalski	HMV	DA 4430	78, 1938
J. Śmidowicz	Muza	XL 0157–60	*l* 1940s, from 78 Muza 1345

Nocturnes (Collections and complete recordings)

C. Arrau	Philips	6747 485	*l* 1970s, Nos. 1–21
A. Brailowsky	RCA	16050–3	*l* 1950s, Nos. 1–19
Fou T'song	CBS	61827–8	*l* 1970s, Nos. 1–21
L. Godowsky	Columbia	L 2164–71	78s, 1928, Nos. 1, 2, 4, 5, 7, 8, 9, 11, 12, 14, 15, 19
I. Haebler	Vox	VUX 2007–1 & 2	*e* 1960s
J. Smeterlin	Philips	A 00256–7L	*m* 1950s, Nos. 1–20
A. Weissenberg	HMV	SLS 838	*e* 1970s, Nos. 1–21

Nocturne in B flat minor, Op. 9 No. 1

J. Karólyi	Polydor	68090	78, 1943
H. Sztompka	Muza	SX 0070	1960

Nocturne in E flat, Op. 9 No. 2

P. Badura-Skoda	Europa Klassik	114040	n.d., reissue

A. Cortot (1)	HMV	DB 1321	78, 1931
(2)	Electrola	C 047–01 400	1949, from 78, n.n.
R. Ganz	Pathé Saphir	9600	78 ac., 1922
L. Godowsky	Pearl	GEMM 167	1913, from 78 ac., Columbia A 5485
M. Hambourg	HMV	C 1416	78, 1927
J. Hofmann	IPA	5001–2	p.p., 1937
R. Koczalski (1)	Polydor	65786	78 ac., 1920
(2)	IPL Veritas	VM 115	1936, from 78 Polydor 67246, with Mikuli variants
A. Lear	Pearl	SHE 544	1978, with Mikuli variants
V. de Pachmann	Columbia	L 1014	78, ac., 1915
M. Rosenthal	Victor	14297	78, 1934
H. Sztompka	Muza	SX 0070	1960

Nocturne in B major, Op. 9 No. 3

W. Gieseking	Discocorp	RR 415	1925, 78 ac., from Homocord 1–8614
J. Hofmann	IPA	5007–8	p.p., 1938
J. Lhévinne	Ampico	62883H	PR, post–1918
A. Loesser	IPL	5003–4	p.p., 1967
H. Sztompka	Muza	SX 0070	1960

Nocturne in F major, Op. 15 No. 1

A. Cortot	Electrola	C 047–01 400	1951, reissue of LP
W. Małcużyński	Muza	SX 1511–12	1975
V. de Pachmann	Pearl	GEM 103	1911, 78 ac., HMV D 263
I. Paderewski	Pearl	GEMM 136	1912, 78 ac., Gram. Co. 056620
A. Schnabel	Hupfeld	12458	PR, pre-1912

Nocturne in F sharp major, Op. 15 No. 2

E. d'Albert	Polydor	65562	78 ac., 1916
F. Busoni	IPA	104	1920, from 78 ac., Columbia L 1432
A. Cortot	Electrola	C 047–01 400	1948, from 78, n.n.
R. Etkin	Muza	XL 0157–60	e 1930s, from 78, n.n., (possibly Tri-Ergon label)
A. de Greef	HMV	D 1379	78, 1928
M. Hess	Columbia	DB 1232	78, 1935
J. Hofmann (1)	IPA	5001–2	p.p., 1937
(2)	RCA	VIC 1550	p.p., 1938
V. Horowitz	RCA	VH 011	1947, from 78 HMV DB 6627
R. Koczalski (1)	Polydor	65788	78 ac., 1920
(2)	HMV	DA 4430	78, 1938
A. Michałowski	Syrena	6571	78, e 1930s
V. de Pachmann	Duo-Art	013	PR, n.d.

I. Paderewski (1)	Gram. Co.	945538	78 ac., 1911
(2)	Pearl	GEMM 136	1917, from 78 ac., Gram. Co. 0–5616
(3)	HMV	DB 1167	78, 1927
(4)	HMV	DB 3711	78, 1937
R. Pugno (1)	Welte	C 548	PR, 1905
(2)	Rococo	2009	1903, from 78 ac., G & T 035500
E. Risler	Pathé Saphir	9530	78 ac., 1917
J. Turczyński	Syrena	6561	78, *e* 1930s
A. Uninsky	Muza	XL 0654–55	1931, from 78 Syrena 6917

Nocturne in C sharp minor, Op. 27 No. 1
C. Arrau*

A. Cortot	Electrola	C 047–01 400	1951, reissue of LP
V. de Pachmann	Duo-Art	6795	PR, n.d.
H. Sztompka	Muza	SX 0070	1960

Nocturne in D flat major, Op. 27 No. 2
C. Arrau*

L. Diémer	G & T	35544	78 ac., 1904
J. Hofmann	RCA	VIC 1550	1935, from unissued 78
R. Koczalski (1)	Polydor	65786	78 ac., 1920
(2)	Polydor	95172	78, 1928
T. Leschetizky	Welte	1194	PR, 1906
V. de Pachmann (1)	Columbia	L 1124	78 ac., 1921
(2)	HMV	DB 860	78, 1925
E. Petri	Encore	PHS 1278	p.p., n.d.
M. Rosenthal	Victor	14297	78, 1936
E. Sauer	Welte	879	PR, 1905
Solomon	HMV	SLS 701	1942, from 78 HMV C 3308

Nocturne in B major, Op. 32 No. 1

R. Koczalski	Polydor	67534	78, 1938
A. de Larrocha	IPA	109	1932, from 78 Odeon 183480
V. de Pachmann	HMV	DB 859	78 ac., 1925
H. Sztompka	Muza	SX 0070	1960

Nocturne in A flat, Op. 32 No. 2

| F. Lamond | HMV | D 1871 | 78, 1928 |

Nocturne in G minor, Op. 37 No. 1

| R. Pugno | Hupfeld | 13732 | PR, pre-1912 |

Nocturne in G major, Op. 37 No. 2

| V. de Pachmann | Pearl | GEM 103 | 1912, from 78 ac., HMV D 263 |

* See collections of Nocturnes.

Nocturne in C minor, Op. 48 No. 1

T. Carreño	Welte	366	PR, 1905
A. Grünfeld	Welte	X 174	PR, n.d.
R. Koczalski	Polydor	67534	78, 1938
M. Levitzki	IPA	114	1929, from HMV 78, n.n.

Nocturne in F minor, Op. 55 No. 1

A. Cortot	HMV	DB 6730	78, 1949
M. Levitzki	Ampico	58486H	PR, post-1918
V. de Pachmann	IPA	117	1912, from 78 ac., previously unissued

Nocturne in E flat major, Op. 55 No. 2

A. Cortot	HMV	DB 6730	78, 1949
I. Friedman	Muza	0157–60	1937, from 78 Columbia DX 781

Nocturne in B major, Op. 62 No. 1

A. Harasiewicz	DG	89646	1955, from Muza LP
R. Koczalski	Polydor	95172	78, 1928

Nocturne in E major, Op. 62 No. 2

A. Dorfmann	Columbia	DX 803	78, 1938

Nocturne in E minor, Op. Posth. 72 No. 1

V. de Pachmann	HMV	DB 1106	78, 1927

Nocturne in C sharp minor, 'Lento con gran espressione', Op. Posth.

S. Falvai	Hungaroton	LPX 11654	m 1970s

Polonaises (Collections)

L. Berman	DG	2531 094	1979, Nos. 1–6
P. Frankl	Decca Turnabout	TV 342545	1964, Nos. 1–16
W. Małcużyński	Angel	S–35728	e 1960s, reissue
G. Ohlsson	HMV	SLS 843	1972, Nos. 1–16
M. Pollini	DG	2530 659	1975, Nos. 1–7

Polonaise in C sharp minor, Op. 26 No. 1

Y. Bowen	Vocalion	K 05261	78, 1926
Z. Drzewiecki	Muza	XL 0117	m 1950s
L. Godowsky	IPL Veritas	VM 103	n.d., from unissued 78
M. Pressler	Concert Hall	SMSA 2539	1968
S. Richter	EMI	C 053–97784	n.d., reissue

Polonaise in E flat minor, Op. 26 No. 2

Z. Drzewiecki	Muza	XL 0117	m 1950s
J. Flier	Melodya	33SM 03265/6	n.d.
J. Hofmann	IPA	5007–8	p.p., 1938
M. Pressler	Concert Hall	SMSA 2539	1968
J. Żurawlew	Muza	XL 0373	e 1950s

Polonaise in A major, Op. 40 No. 1

L. Godowsky	Pearl	GEMM 167	1922, from 78 ac., Brunswick 50015
J. Hofmann	RCA	VIC 1550	1935, from originally unissued Victor 78
R. Koczalski	Polydor	90031	78, 1927
A. Michałowski	Muza	XL 0157–60	1907 (?), from 78 ac., n.n.

Polonaise in C minor, Op. 40 No. 2

A. Brendel	Vanguard	VCS 10058	1969
H. Czerny-Stefańska	Supraphon	SUA 10012	1960s
E. Gilels	DG	2531 099	1979

Polonaise in F sharp minor, Op. 44

D. Bashkirov	Melodya	SM 03931/2	p.p., 1971 or 72
A. Brendel	Vanguard	VCS 10058	1969
L. Godowsky	Hupfeld	12705	PR, pre-1912
V. Horowitz	CBS	72720	p.p., 1968
T. Nikolayeva	USSR	D 01190	e 1950s
M. Pollini	Muza	XL 0654–55	p.p., 1960, reissue
V. Sofronitsky	Melodya	33D 015001/2	p.p., 1948

Polonaise in A flat major, Op. 53

G. Anda	DG	LPM 18604	n.d.
W. Backhaus	HMV	D 888	78 ac., 1924
A. Brendel	Vanguard	VCS 10058	1969
F. Busoni	Welte	C 440	PR, pre-1910
A. Cortot	HMV	DB 2014	78, 1934
I. Friedman	Columbia L	1990	78, 1927
L. Godowsky (1)	Ampico	56336H	PR, post-1918
(2)	Polydor	A 73065	78 ac., 1925
(3)	Brunswick	50024	78 ac., 1925
P. Grainger	Pearl	GEMM 143	1918, from 78 ac., Columbia A 6027 & L 1352
J. Iturbi	Turia	101M	1950s
R. Koczalski (1)	Polydor	62441	78 ac., 1923
(2)	HMV	DA 4431	78, 1938
M. Levitzki	HMV	DA 1316	78, 1933
J. Lhévinne	RCA	VIC 1046	1936, from 78 Victor 1765
J. da Motta	IPL	108	1928, from 78 Pathé X 5452
K. Müller	Coliseum	No. 91	78 ac., 1918
E. Petri	Columbia	17377D	78, 1947
Solomon	HMV	SLS 701	1934, from 78 Columbia LX 1314
A. Verne	Columbia	L 1213	78 ac., 1917

'Polonaise-Fantaisie' in A flat, Op. 61

A. Brendel	Vanguard	VCS 10058	1969

V. Horowitz (1)	RCA	VH 008	p.p., 1951, reissue
(2)	CBS	72969	p.p., 1966
H. Neuhaus	USSR	5938/9	*e* 1950s
L. Pouishnoff	Saga	XID 5013	*l* 1950s
M. Pressler	Concert Hall	SMSA 2539	1968
S. Richter (1)	Rococo	2142	p.p., 1954
(2)	DG	2548 223	p.p., 1963
I. Zaritskaya	Muza	L 0308	p.p., 1960

Polonaise in D minor, Op. Posth. 71 No. 1

H. Czerny-Stefańska	Supraphon	SUA 10012	1960s

Polonaise in B flat, Op. Posth. 71 No. 2

M. Hambourg	HMV	C 1451	78, 1928

'Chants polonais' No. 1, 'The Maiden's Wish', arr. Liszt

M. Rosenthal	Victor	14300	78, 1936

'Chants polonais' No. 12, 'My Joys', arr. Liszt

C. Ansorge	Parlophone	E 10975	78, 1929
M. Rosenthal	Odeon	132587	78, 1930

Twenty-four Preludes, Op. 28 (Collections, some including Preludes in C sharp minor, Op. 45, and A flat, Op. Posth.)

M. Argerich	DG	2530 721	1977, Nos. 1–26
G. Anda	DG	LPM 18604	n.d.
S. Askenase	DG	DGM 19002	*m* 1950s
A. Cortot (1)	HMV	DB 957–60	78s, 1926
(2)	Electrola	C 047–00 889M	1933, from 78s HMV DB 2015–18
(3)	HMV	W 1541–44	78s, 1943
J.-M. Darré	Vanguard	VCS 71151	1965
C. Eschenbach	DG	2530 231	1973, Nos. 1–26
A. de Larrocha	Decca	SXL 6733	1975
R. Lortat	Columbia	D 15036–39	78s, 1928
V. Merzhanov	Melodya	D 04996/7	*m* 1950s
G. Novaës	Vox	SVBX 5401E	*e* 1950s, reissue
M. Perahia	CBS	76422	1975, Nos. 1–26
E. Petri	Columbia	71402-5D	78s, 1943
M. Pollini	DG	2530 550	1975
A. Rubinstein (1)	Victor	12–0564–67	78s, 1949
(2)	RCA	LM 1163	*m* 1950s
P. Yegorov	Melodya	33S10–06691/2	*e* 1970s

Prelude in G major, Op. 28 No. 3

Y. Bowen	Vocalion	K 05275	78, 1927
V. de Pachmann	HMV	DA 927	78, 1927
M. Rosenthal	HMV	DB 2772	78, 1936

Prelude in B minor, Op. 28 No. 6

V. de Pachmann (1)	HMV	DA 927	78, 1927
(2)	HMV	DA 1302	78, 1927

M. Rosenthal (1)	Edison	47004	78, 1927
(2)	HMV	DB 2772	78, 1936
A. Szumowska	Ampico	57675H	PR, post-1918

Prelude in A major, Op. 28 No. 7
F. Busoni	IPA	104	1920, from 78 ac., Columbia L 1470
R. Koczalski	Odeon	0–4761	78, 1930
M. Rosenthal (1)	Edison	47004	78, 1927
(2)	HMV	DB 2772	78, 1936

Preludes in E major, C sharp minor and B major, Op. 28 Nos. 9, 10 & 11
R. Koczalski (1)	Polydor	90038	78, 1927
(2)	Polydor	67506	78, 1938

Prelude in B major, Op. 28 No. 11
M. Rosenthal	Edison Bell	47004	78, 1927

Prelude in G sharp minor, Op. 28 No. 12
R. Koczalski (1)	Polydor	90030	78, 1927
(2)	Polydor	67506	78, 1936

Preludes in F sharp major and E flat minor, Op. 28 Nos. 13 & 14
R. Koczalski	Polydor	67506	78, 1938

Prelude in D flat major, Op. 28 No. 15
V. Sofronitsky	Melodya	33D 015001/2	p.p., 1949

Prelude in B flat minor, Op. 28 No. 16
J. Lhévinne	RCA	VIC 1046	1936, from 78 Victor 14024
A. Michałowski	Syrena	6571	78, *e* 1930s
V. de Pachmann	Columbia	L 1010	78, ac., 1915

Prelude in A flat major, Op. 28 No. 17
P. Grainger	Pearl	GEMM 143	1918, from 78, ac., Columbia L 1352
R. Koczalski	Polydor	95174	78, 1929
J. Lhévinne	RCA	VIC 1046	1936, from 78 Victor 14024

Prelude in C minor, Op. 28 No. 20
Y. Bowen	Vocalion	K 05275	78, 1927
R. Koczalski	Polydor	90030	78, 1928

Prelude in B flat major, Op. 28 No. 21
A. Szumowska	Ampico	57675H	PR, post-1918

Prelude in F major, Op. 28 No. 23
C. Arrau	Desmar	GHP 4001–2	1930, from 78 Electrola EG 1500
Y. Bowen	Vocalion	K 05275	78, 1927
V. de Pachmann	Columbia	L 1014	78 ac., 1915
M. Rosenthal	Edison	47004	78, 1927

| A. Schnabel | Hupfeld | 12459 | PR, pre-1912 |
| A. Szumowska | Ampico | 57675H | PR, post-1918 |

Prelude in D minor, Op. 28 No. 24

F. Busoni	Duo-Art	040	PR
V. de Pachmann (1)	Pearl	GEM 103	1911, from 78 ac., HMV D 264
(2)	Columbia	L 1009	78 ac., 1915

M. Pollini (see Collections)

Prelude in C sharp minor, Op. 45

| A Harasiewicz | Muza | X 0654–55 | 1955, a reissue |
| R. Koczalski | Polydor | 95174 | 78, 1929 |

Rondo in E flat, Op. 16

V. Horowitz	CBS	72969	1971
H. Neuhaus	USSR	013029/30	e 1950s
L. Pouishnoff	Saga	XID 5013	l 1950s

Four Scherzos (Collections)

C. Arrau	Brunswick	AXTL 1043–34	1954
V. Ashkenazy	Decca	SXL 6334	1968
J. Bolet	Remington	199–161	e 1950s
J.-M. Darré	Vanguard	VCS 10122	m 1970s
G. Ohlsson	HMV	HQS 1328	e 1970s
D. Ranki	Hungaroton	SLPX 11773	e 1970s
S. Richter	Ariola Eurodisc	25068MK	1977
A. Simon	Decca Turnabout	TVS 34460	n.d.

Scherzo No. 1 in B minor, Op. 20

J. Hofmann (1)	Duo-Art	6992	PR, n.d.
(2)	Muza	XL 0157–60	1923, from 78 ac., Brunswick 50044
V. Horowitz (1)	RCA	VH 011	1950, from Victor LM 1707
(2)	RCA	LM 6014	p.p., 1953
(3)	CBS	72180	1964
A. Michałowski	Syrena	6579	78, e 1930s
B. Moiseiwitsch	HMV	HQM 1153	1949, from unissued 78, n.n.
I. Moravec	Connoisseur Society	CS–2019	1969
S. Szpinalski	CIW	Tape 201	n.d.
J. Turczyński	Syrena	6560	78, e 1930s
A. Weissenberg	RCA	SB 6743	1967

Scherzo No. 2 in B flat minor, Op. 31

Y. Bowen	Vocalion	K 05237	78, 1926
L. Godowsky	IPA	117	1924, from 78 ac., previously unissued
L. Hoffmann	Europa Klassik	1140175	n.d.
J. Hofmann	Duo-Art	6118	PR, n.d.
R. Koczalski	Electrola	DB 4474	78, 1938

A. B. Michelangeli	DG	2530 236	1972
B. Moiseiwitsch	HMV	D 1065	78, 1926
I. Scharrer	Columbia	DX 433	78, 1935
A. Weissenberg	RCA	SB 6743	1967

Scherzo No. 3 in C sharp minor, Op. 39

C. Arrau	Parlophone	R 20469	78, 1932
S. Barer	Varese	VC 81045	1950, from Remington REP 2
V. Cliburn	RCA	LSB 4092	e 1960s
L. Godowsky	Hupfeld	12708	PR, pre-1912
J. Hofmann	Duo-Art	8007	PR, n.d.
M. Levitzki	HMV	D 1814	78, 1931
W. Małcużyński	Columbia	LX 1173	78, 1949
S. Rachmaninov	Melodya	033755–60	1924, 78 ac., from unissued disc

Scherzo No. 4 in E major, Op. 54

B. Davidovitch	Muza	XL 0564–55	1950, from 78 Muza 1387/8
L. Godowsky	IPL Veritas	VM 103	n.d., from 78 unissued disc
V. Horowitz	RCA	VH 008	1937, from 78 HMV DB 3205

Sonata No. 2 in B flat minor, Op. 35 (the 'Funeral March')

M. Argerich	DG	2530 530	1975
S. Askenase	DG	DGM 18349	m 1950s
W. Backhaus	Decca	LXT 2535	m 1950s
A. Barbosa	Connoisseur Society	CS–2026	1970
D. Barenboim	HMV	ASD 3064	e 1970s
R. Casadesus	Columbia	ML 2025	e 1950s
A. Cortot (1)	HMV	DB 1250–51	78s, 1929
(2)	HMV	DB 2019–20	78s, 1934
(3)	Electrola	C 047–01 400	1953, from LP Victor LHMV 18
J. Ekier	Muza	SX 0059	1960
J. Flier	Melodya export	MK 1548	n.d.
Fou T'song	CBS	61857	1978
E. Gilels	USSR	D 012277–80	e 1950s
L. Godowsky	IPA	113	1930, from Columbia LX 124–26
P. Grainger	Columbia	M-116, 67 603–5D	78s, 1927
A. de Greef	HMV	D 1220–22	78s, 1927, 5 sides
J. Hofmann	Duo-Art	6239, 6258	PR, n.d.
V. Horowitz	CBS	72067	1962
W. Kapell	Opus	83	p.p., 1953
W. Kempff	Decca Eclipse	ECS 770	1958, reissue
V. Kraiynev	Melodya/Chant du monde	LDX 78518	e 1970s
R. Lortat	Columbia	D 15092–3	78s, 1928

W. Małcużyński	CFP	40095	1962, a reissue
S. Niedzielski	Ducretet-Thomson	320 C 024	*m* 1950s
G. Novaës	Vox	SVBX 5401E	*e* 1950s, a reissue
M. Perahia	CBS	76242	1974
V. Perlemuter	Nimbus	2109	*m* 1970s
S. Rachmaninov	RCA	VIC 1534	1930, from 78s
			HMV DA 1186–89
F. Rauch	Supraphon	SUA 50893	1967
B. Vázsonyi	Pye Virtuoso	TPLS 13053	1972

'Funeral March' alone

A. Friedheim	Columbia	335	78, 1928
V. de Pachmann	Pearl	GEM 103	1912, from 78 ac.,
			HMV D 264
R. Pugno	Rococo	2009	1903, from 78 ac.,
			G & T 035505

Sonata No. 3 in B minor, Op. 58

M. Argerich	DG	2542 110	1967, reissue
S. Askenase	DG	DGM 18349	*m* 1950s
E. Ax	RCA	ARL 1 1030	1975
P. Badura-Skoda	Discocorp	AUDAX 761	n.d., from radio
A. Barbosa	Connoisseur Society	CS–2026	1970
D. Barenboim	HMV	ASD 3064	*e* 1970s
O. Bochnyakovitch	Melodya	S10 06479/80	n.d.
A. Cortot (1)	HMV	DA 1209–12	78s, 1931
(2)	Seraphim	60241	1933, from 78s
			HMV DA 1333–36
J. Ekier	Muza	SX 0059	1960
R. Firkušný	Capitol	8526	1950s
Fou T'song	CBS	61866	1978
E. Gilels	DG	2531 099	1979
P. Grainger	Columbia	L 1695–97	78s, 1926
J. Hofmann	RCA	VIC 1550	1935, from 78, originally unissued, n.n., first movt
W. Kapell	RCA	SB 6743	*e* 1950s
D. Lipatti	HMV	HQM 1163	1947, from 78s
			Columbia LX 994–96
H. Neuhaus	USSR	013441/2	*e* 1950s
G. Novaës	Vox	PL 7360	*e* 1950s
V. de Pachmann	Columbia	L 1131	78 ac., 1921, second movt
M. Perahia	CBS	76242	1974
V. Perlemuter	Nimbus	2109	*m* 1970s
F. Rauch	Supraphon	SUA 50893	1967
M. Rosenthal	RCA	VIC 1209	1939, from 78s, originally unissued
O. Samaroff	Victrola	6419A	78, n.d., fourth movt
M. Tagliaferro	Angel Brazil	n.n.	1972
A. Weissenberg	RCA	SB 6743	1967
I. Zhukov	Melodya	33S 10–07033/4	n.d.

'Tarantelle' in A flat, Op. 43

C. Arrau	Desmar	GHP 4001–2	1932, from 78 Parlophone R 2588
A. Cortot (1)	Gram. Co.	7–65501	78 ac., 1910
(2)	HMV	DA 1213	78, 1932
(3)	HMV	DB 2032	78, 1934
(4)	Electrola	C 047–01 400	1953, a reissue from LP
A. Dorfmann	Columbia	DB 1724	78, 1938
R. Koczalski	Polydor	65787	78 ac., 1925
M. Rosenthal	RCA	VIC 1209	1942, from originally unissued 78

Variations on Mozart's 'Là ci darem la mano', Op. 2, for piano and orchestra

C. Arrau/Inbal	Philips	6500 422	1972
W. Kędra/Rowicki	Muza	SX 0076	1960
A. Weissenberg/Skrowac-zewski	HMV	ASD 2371	1968

Variations on Hérold's 'Je vends des scapulaires', Op. 12, for solo piano

R. Goldsand	Nixa	CLP 1133	1954
T. Nikolayeva	USSR	M. D 400	e 1950s

Waltzes, Nos. 1–14 (unless otherwise stated)

S. Askenase	DG	2548 146	1964, reissue
A. Barbosa	Connoisseur Society	CS–2036	e 1970s
A. Brailowsky	Columbia	MS 6228	e 1960s
A. Cortot (1)	Seraphim	60127	1934, from 78s HMV DB 2311–16
(2)	HMV	W 1603–05 & DA 4962–64	78s, 1943
B. Davidovitch	Melodya	D 011653/4	e 1960s
A. Dorfmann	Victor 'Bluebird'	LBC 1050	e 1950s
P. Entremont	Seraphim	S–60252	m 1960s, reissue
I. Haebler	Vox	GBY 11970	e 1960s
D. Lipatti (1)	HMV	HLM 7075	1950, from 78s Columbia LX 1341–46
(2)	Columbia	33CX 1500	p.p., 1950, Nos. 1 and 3–14
R. Lortat	Columbia	LFX 214–18	78s, 1931
G. Novaës	Vox	58170E	e 1950s, Nos. 1–15
V. Perlemuter	Concert Hall	SMS 2337	e 1960s
A. Simon	Decca Turnabout	TV 34580S	1974, Nos. 1–19
K. Zimerman	DG	2530 965	1977

Waltz in E flat, Op. 18

L. Godowsky	Pearl	GEMM 167	1922, from 78 ac., Brunswick 50015
J. Hofmann	IPA	5007–8	p.p., 1938
R. Koczalski (1)	Polydor	95201	78, 1929
(2)	Polydor	67515	78, 1939

Discography

Waltz in A flat, Op. 34 No. 1

R. Ganz	Victor	7290	78, 1931
R. Koczalski	Polydor	67247	78, 1939
R. Pugno	Rococo	2009	1903, from 78 ac., G & T 35503
S. Richter	Rococo	2142	p.p., 1954
X. Scharwenka	Columbia	30609	78 ac., 1905

Waltz in A minor, Op. 34 No. 2

V. Horowitz	CBS	72969	1972
R. Koczalski (1)	Polydor	95201	78, 1929
(2)	Polydor	67515	78, 1939
A. de Larrocha	IPA	109	1932, from 78 Odeon 183480
S. Richter	Rococo	2142	p.p., 1954
I. Vered	Decca Phase 4	PFS 4313	1974

Waltz in F major, Op. 34 No. 3

C. Arrau	Desmar	GHP 4001–2	1930, from 78 Electrola EG 833
J. Familier-Hepnerowa	Muza	XL 0157–60	e 1930s, from 78 Syrena 8313
R. Koczalski	Polydor	67533	78, 1938
S. Rachmaninov	RCA	VIC 1534	1920, from 78 ac., originally unissued
S. Richter	Rococo	2142	p.p., 1954
E. Sauer	Columbia	LW 38	78, 1939
J. Zak	Muza	XL 0654–55	n.d., from 78 USSR **20437**

Waltz in A flat, Op. 42

E. d'Albert	Polydor	65562	78 ac., 1923
W. Backhaus	HMV	D 888	78 ac., 1924
S. Barer (1)	Parlophone	R 1144	78, 1928
(2)	HMV	DB 2166	78, 1934
L. Godowsky	Pearl	GEMM 167	1916, from 78 ac., Columbia L 1069
P. Grainger	Columbia	A 6027 & 7000M	78 ac., 1922
A. de Greef	HMV	D 1379	78, 1928
M. Hambourg	HMV	D 71	78 ac., 1910
J. Hofmann (1)	RCA	VIC 1550	1935, from 78, originally unissued
(2)	IPA	5001–2	p.p., 1937
R. Koczalski	Polydor	65789	78 ac., 1920
E. Petri	Electrola	B 3791	78, 1931
M. Rosenthal	HMV	DB 2772	78, 1936
E. Sauer	IPL Veritas	VM 114	1930, from 78 Odeon o–6817 or o–7835
X. Scharwenka	Welte	X 245	PR, pre-1910
J. Weiss	Anker	E 9597	78 ac., n.d.

Waltz in D flat, Op. 64 No. 1

M. Hambourg	HMV	C 2579	78, 1933

L. Hoffmann	Europa Klassik	114 0175	n.d.
J. Hofmann (1)	IPA	5001–2	p.p., 1937
(2)	RCA	VIC 1550	p.p., 1938
R. Koczalski (1)	Polydor	65789	78 ac., 1920
(2)	Polydor	90030	78, 1927
(3)	Odeon	0–4761	78, 1930
(4)	Polydor	67533	78, 1938
A. Michałowski (1)	IPL Veritas	VM 115	1905, from 78 ac., G & T 25601, arr. by pianist
(2)	IPL Veritas	VM 115	n.d., 78, arr. by pianist, recorded later than (1)
(3)	Syrena	6578	e 1930s, 78, original version
V. de Pachmann (1)	G & T	5566	78 ac., 1907
(2)	HMV	DA 761	78, 1926
S. Rachmaninov	RCA	VIC 1534	1923, from 78, ac., n.n.

Waltz in C sharp minor, Op. 64 No. 2

L. Godowsky (1)	Columbia	L 1095	78 ac., m 1910s
(2)	Pearl	GEMM 167	1928, from 78 Brunswick 15124
R. Koczalski (1)	Polydor	62440	78 ac., 1923
(2)	Polydor	90038	78, 1927
J. Malats	IPA	109	1903, from cylinder
A. Michałowski	Muza	XL 0157–60	n.d., from 78, Gramophone Co. G.C 2563
G. Novaës*			
M. Novello	Edison Bell	3479	78 ac., 1924
V. de Pachmann (1)	Pearl	GEM 103	1907, from 78 ac., G & T 5568
(2)	HMV	DB 860	78, 1925, n.d. arr. by pianist recorded later than (1)
Z. Rabcewicz	Syrena	271488	78, e 1930s
E. Risler	Pathé Saphir	9530	78 ac., 1917
M. Rosenthal (1)	Parlophone	9520	78, 1930
(2)	Victor	14299	78, 1936

Waltz in A flat, Op. 64 No. 3

R. Koczalski	Polydor	67533	78, 1938
V. de Pachmann	HMV	DB 931	78, 1926

Waltz in A flat, Op. Posth, 69 No. 1

R. Koczalski	Polydor	67247	78, 1939
A. B. Michelangeli (1)	HMV	DA 5371	78, 1943
(2)	Discocorp	IGI 350	n.d., from radio

* See collections of Waltzes.

Waltz in B minor, Op. Posth. 69 No. 2

S. Rachmaninov	HMV	DA 593	78 ac., 1923
J. Zak	Muza	XL 0654–55	n.d., from 78, n.n.

Waltz in G flat, Op. Posth. 70 No. 1

M. Hambourg	HMV	C 2579	78, 1933
R. Koczalski (1)	Polydor	65789	78 ac., 1920
(2)	Polydor	90029	78, 1927
V. de Pachmann (1)	Columbia	L 1103	78 ac., *l* 1910s
(2)	HMV	DA 761	78, 1926
S. Rachmaninov	RCA	VIC 1534	1921, from 78 ac., originally unissued

Waltz in E minor, Op. Posth.

R. Ganz	Pathé	10216	78 ac., 1910
R. Koczalski (1)	Polydor	65790	78 ac., 1925
(2)	Polydor	90029	78, 1927
M. Rosenthal	Parlophone	9520	78, 1929
I. Scharrer	HMV	E 255	78 ac., 1920

Complete Collections of piano works

A. Harasiewicz	Philips	6747 017	1960s, on 14 LPs
N. Magaloff	Philips	6708067	1970s, 16 LPs, excluding concerted works

Miscellaneous Anthologies

A. Rubinstein *Rubinstein Plays Chopin*	RCA	SER 5692	1960s, 11 record set, with majority of solo piano works
G. Bánhalmi *Chopin Cameos*	Vox	PL 10370	*l* 1950s, miscellaneous lesser-known works
R. Smith *Chopin Rarities*	HMV	HQS 1290	1973, lesser-known works
J. Smeterlin	Mace	MCS 9079	*l* 1960s, miscellaneous Waltzes and Mazurkas
Various pianists *The Lost Art of Chopin Interpretation*	IPL Veritas	VM 115	historical discs by pianists such as Koczalski, Hofmann, Michałowski, etc., from 78s

BIBLIOGRAPHY

ALLINÓWNA, STEFANIA, 'Aleksander Michałowski', *Zeszyty naukowe*, No. 10, Państwowa wyższa szkoła muzyczna w Katowicach, 1969.

ANDERSON, HARRY L., 'Josef Lhévinne Discography', *Recorded Sound*, No. 44, October 1971.

BACHE, CONSTANCE, *Brother Musicians*, Methuen & Co., London, 1901.

BADURA-SKODA, PAUL, 'Schlanker, meine Herren!', *Chopin Jahrbuch*, No. 1, Vienna, 1956.

—— (ed.) *Chopin Etudes Opp. 10 and 25 and Trois Nouvelles Etudes* (2 vols), Wiener Urtext, 1973.

BAKER, THEODORE, *Biographical Dictionary of Musicians* (5th edition ed. N. Slonimsky, with 1971 supplement), G. Schirmer, New York, 1971.

BENOIST, ANDRÉ, *The Accompanist: an Autobiography* (ed. J. A. Maltese), Paganiniana Publications, New Jersey, 1978.

BERGER, FRANCESCO, *Reminiscences, Impressions and Anecdotes*, Sampson Low, Marston & Co., London, 1913.

BERTENSSON, SERGEI and LEIJDA, JAY, *Sergei Rachmaninoff*, New York University Press, 1956.

BESCOMBY-CHAMBERS, J., *The Archives of Sound*, Oakwood Press, Surrey, 1964.

BIDOU, HENRI, *Chopin*, F. Alcan, Paris, 1925.

BIE, OSCAR, *A History of the Pianoforte and Pianoforte Players* (tr. and revised by E. Kallet and E. Naylor), J. Dent & Sons, London, 1899, reprinted Da Capo Press, New York, 1966.

BLOCK, MAXINE (ed.), *Current Biography 1940*, H. W. Wilson Co., New York.

BONE, AUDREY EVELYN, *Jane Wilhelmina Stirling*, published privately under the auspices of the Chopin Institute, Warsaw, 1960.

BOWEN, CATHERINE DRINKER, *Free Artist: The Story of Anton and Nicholas Rubinstein*, Random House, New York, 1939.

BRONARSKI, LUDWIK, 'Les élèves de Chopin', *Annales Chopin* (Journal of the Chopin Institute, Warsaw), VI, 1961.

BROOK, DONALD, *Masters of the Keyboard*, Barrie & Rockliff, London, 1946.

BROWN, JAMES D. and STRATTON, STEPHEN S., *British Musical Biography*, S. S. Stratton, Birmingham, 1897.

BROWN, MAURICE J. E., *Chopin: an Index of his Works*, Macmillan, London, 1960.

BÜLOW, HANS GUIDO VON, *Early Correspondence of Hans Guido von Bülow* (tr. Constance Bache), T. Fisher Unwin, London, 1896.

BUSONI, FERRUCCIO, *Letters to his Wife* (tr. Rosamond Ley), Edward Arnold & Co., London, 1938.

CANDEE, MARJORIE D. (ed.), *Current Biography 1956*, H. W. Wilson Co., New York.

CAPES, S. J., 'Early Pianoforte Records', *Journal of the British Institute of Recorded Sound*, No. 3, 1956.

CASELLA, ALFREDO, *Music in My Time* (tr. and ed. Spencer Norton), University of Oklahoma Press, 1955.

CERNIKOFF, VLADIMIR, 'Pianists: some Memories and Reflections', *Music and Letters*, Vol. LXIII, February 1933.

CHASINS, ABRAM, *Speaking of Pianists* (2nd edition), Alfred A. Knopf, New York, 1961. *Clavier*.

CLOUGH, F. and CUMING, G. J., *The World's Encyclopaedia of Recorded Music* (with three subsequent supplements), Sidgwick & Jackson, London, 1952.

COHEN, HARRIET, *A Bundle of Time*, Faber, London, 1969.

COOKE, JAMES FRANCIS, *Great Pianists on Piano-Playing*, Theo. Presser & Co., Philadelphia, 1917.

CORTOT, ALFRED, *Aspects de Chopin*, A Michel, Paris, 1949, tr. by Cyril and Rena Clarke as *In Search of Chopin*, P. Neville, London, 1951.

DANDELOT, A., *Francis Planté : une belle vie d'artiste*, Edouard Dupont, Paris, 1921.

DAVISON, HENRY, *From Mendelssohn to Wagner* (based on the writings of his father, J. W. Davison, music critic of *The Times*), Wm. Reeves, London, 1912.

DAVISON, J. W., *Frederic Chopin: a Critical and Appreciative Essay*, Wm. Reeves, London, 1913.

DENT, EDWARD J., *Ferruccio Busoni*, Oxford University Press, 1932.

Dictionary of American Biography.

Dictionary of National Biography.

DIEHL-MANGOLD, ALICE, *Musical Memories*, Richard Bentley & Son, London, 1897.

DRZEWIECKI, ZBIGNIEW, article accompanying *The Golden Pages of Polish Pianistic Art*, Muza Records XL 0157–60 (early 1960s).

DUNSTAN, RALPH (ed.), *A Cyclopaedic Dictionary of Music* (4th edition), Curwen, London, 1925.

EAGLEFIELD-HULL, A. (ed.), *A Dictionary of Modern Music and Muscians*, J. M. Dent & Sons, London, 1924.

EHRLICH, A., *Celebrated Pianists of the Past and Present Time* (tr. A. H. Payne), Leipzig, 1894.

EIGELDINGER, JEAN-JACQUES, *Chopin vu par ses élèves* (2nd edition), la Baconnière, Neuchatel, 1979.

EKIERT, JAN, 'Tradition, ˙mythe et réalité: comment les pianistes polonaises jouent-ils Chopin en 1960', *Peuples Amis* (Special Number), Paris, 1960.

EWEN, DAVID, *Living Musicians* (with supplement), H. W. Wilson Co., New York, 1940.

FAY, AMY, *Music Study in Germany*, A. C. McClurg & Co., Chicago, 1880, reprinted with introduction by Frances Dillon, Dover Publications Inc., New York, 1965.

FERRIS, GEORGE T., *The Great Pianists and Violinists* (3rd edition), Wm. Reeves, London, n.d.

FEUCHTWANGER, PETER, 'Clara Haskil', *Recorded Sound*, Nos. 63 and 64, July and October 1976.

FRIEDHEIM, ARTHUR, Introduction and Notes for *Chopin Etudes*, Schirmer, New York, 1916.

GAISBERG, FRED W., *Music on Record*, Robert Hale Ltd, London, 1946.

GANCHE, EDOUARD, *Dans le souvenir de Frédéric Chopin*, Mercure de France, Paris, 1925.

—— *Voyages avec Frédéric Chopin*, Mercure de France, 1934.

GANZ, WILHELM, *Memories of a Musician*, John Murray, London, 1913.

GARDEN, EDWARD, *Balakirev: a Critical Study of his Life and Music,* Faber, London, 1967.

GAVOTY, BERNARD, *Alfred Cortot*, Editions Buchet/Chastel, Paris, 1977.

GERIG, REGINALD R., *Famous Pianists and their Techniques*, David & Charles Ltd, Newton Abbot, 1976.

Gramophone, The.

GROVE, SIR GEORGE, *Dictionary of Music and Musicians* (2nd edition), ed. J. A. Fuller-Maitland (4 vols), 1900, and 5th edition ed. Eric Bloom (9 vols), Macmillan Press, London, 1954 with 1961 supplement.

HALLÉ, CHARLES, *Autobiography*, first published 1896, reprinted by Paul Elek, 1972.

HAMBOURG, MARK, *From Piano to Forte*, Cassell & Co., London, 1931.

HARASOWSKI, ADAM, *The Skein of Legends around Chopin*, Wm. Maclellan, Glasgow, 1967.

HAWEIS, H. R., *My Musical Life*, Longmans, Green & Co., London, 1912.

HEDLEY, ARTHUR, *Chopin* (Master Musicians series), J. Dent & Sons Ltd, London 1947, revised 1974.

—— *Selected Correspondence of Fryderyk Chopin*, Heinemann, London, 1962.

—— 'Some Observations on the Autograph Sources of Chopin's Works', *Book of the First International Musicological Congress devoted to the works of F. Chopin, Warsaw, 16–22 February 1960*, Warsaw, 1963.

HENSCHEL, GEORGE, *Musings and Memories*, Macmillan & Co., London, 1918.

HIPKINS, EDITH, *How Chopin Played*, J. M. Dent, London, 1937.

HOFFMAN, RICHARD, *Some Musical Recollections of Fifty Years*, Scribner, New York, 1910, reprinted Information Coordinators, Detroit, 1976.

HOFMANN, JOSEF, *Piano Playing with Piano Questions Answered*, reprinted Dover Books Inc., New York, 1976.

HOLCMAN, JAN, *The Legacy of Chopin*, Philosophical Library Inc., New York, 1954.

HOLLAND, JEANNE, 'Chopin's Teaching and his Students', doctoral thesis, University of North Carolina, 1973 (microfilm 73–26 183).

HUNEKER, JAMES G., *Chopin: the Man and his Music*, Charles Scribner's Sons, New York, 1900, reprinted Dover Publications Inc., New York, 1966.

—— *Letters of James Gibbons Huneker* (ed. Josephine Huneker), T. Werner Laurie Ltd, London, 1922.

—— Preface to *The Piano Works of Chopin*, Schirmer, New York, 1916.

—— *Steeplejack: an Autobiography* (2 vols), C. Scribner's Sons, New York, 1921.

JAEGER, BERTRAND, 'Quelques nouveaux noms d'élèves de Chopin', *Revue de Musicologie*, Vol. LXIV, Paris, 1978.

JOHNSON, H. EARLE, *First Performances in America to 1900: works with orchestra*, American Music, No. 4, College Music Society, Detroit, 1979.

JONSON, E. ASHTON, *Handbook to Chopin's Works*, Wm. Reeves, London, 1905.

KAISER, JOACHIM, *Great Pianists of our Time* (tr. David Wooldridge and George Unwin), George Allen & Unwin, 1971.

KLECZYŃSKI, J., *Frédéric Chopin: de l'interprétation de ses oeuvres*, Mackar, Paris, 1880.

KOBYLAŃSKA, KRYSTYNA, *Rękopisy utworów Chopina: Katalog* (Catalogue of manuscripts of Chopin's works) (2 vols), PWM, Warsaw, 1977.

—— 'Zofia z Poznańskich Rabcewiczowa', *Ruch Muzyczny*, Vol. XVII, No. 3, Warsaw, 1973.

KUHE, WILLIAM, *My Musical Recollections*, R. Bentley & Son, London, 1896.

LAMOND, FREDERIC, 'Memories of Anton Rubinstein', *Recorded Sound*, No. 65, January 1977.

LANDAU, ROM, *Paderewski*, Ivor Nicholson & Watson Ltd, London, 1934.

LANDOWSKA, WANDA, *Landowska on Music* (ed. and tr. D. Restout and Robert Hawkins), Secker & Warburg, London, 1965.

LARA, ADELINA DE, *Finale*, Burke, London, 1955.

LASSIMONNE, DENISE and FERGUSON, HOWARD (eds.), *Myra Hess by her Friends*, Hamish Hamilton, London, 1966.

LENZ, WILHELM VON, *Great Piano Virtuosos of our Time*, first published in Germany 1872, English tr. published by Schirmer 1899, repr. Regency Press, London, 1971.

LHÉVINNE, JOSEF, *Basic Principles of Piano Playing*, Dover Publications Inc., New York, 1972.

LOESSER, ARTHUR, *Men, Women and Pianos*, Simon & Schuster, New York, 1954.

LONG, MARGUERITE, *Au piano avec Claude Debussy*, Julliard, Paris, 1960 (tr. Olive Senior-Ellis, J. M. Dent, London, 1972).

McARTHUR, ALEXANDER, *Anton Rubinstein*, Adam and Charles Black, Edinburgh, 1889.

MACIEJEWSKI, B. and ABRAHAMIAN, F. (eds), *Karol Szymanowski and Jan Smeterlin*, Allegro Press, London, *c.* 1970.

MARMONTEL, ANTOINE FRANÇOIS, *Les Pianistes célèbres*, A. Chaix & Son, Paris, 1878.

MASON, DANIEL GREGORY, *Music in My Time and Other Reminiscences*, Macmillan & Co., New York, 1938.

MERRICK, FRANK, *Practising the Piano*, Barrie & Jenkins, London, 1958.

MICHAŁOWSKI, ALEKSANDER, 'Jak grał Fryderyk Szopen?', *Muzyka*, Vol. IX/7–9, Warsaw, 1932.

MICHAŁOWSKI, KORNEL, *Bibiliografia Chopinowska*, PWM, Warsaw, 1970.

Bibliography

MIKULI, KAROL, Preface to *Complete Edition of Chopin's Works*, Kistner, Leipzig, 1880, and Schirmer, New York.

MILHAUD, DARIUS, *Notes without Music*, Alfred A. Knopf, New York, 1953.

MILINOWSKI, MARTÁ, *Teresa Carreño*, Yale University Press, New Haven, 1940.

Monthly Musical Record.

MOSCHELES, CHARLOTTE, *Aus Moscheles' Leben: nach Briefen und Tagebüchern* (2 vols), Duncker & Humbolt, Leipzig, 1872–3.

MURDOCH, WILLIAM, *Chopin: his Life*, Murray, London, 1938.

Music Quarterly, The.

Musical Times, The.

NEUHAUS, HEINRICH [HARRY], *The Art of Piano Playing*, Praeger Publications, New York, 1973

NEWCOMB, ETHEL, *Leschetizky as I knew him*, repr. Da Capo Press, New York, 1967.

NIECKS, FREDERICK, *Frederick Chopin as a Man and Musician* (2 vols), Novello Ewer & Co., London, 1888.

OPIEŃSKI, HENRYK, *Chopin's Letters*, Alfred A. Knopf Inc., New York 1931, reprinted Vienna House, New York, 1973.

——*I.J. Paderewski*, Editions Spes, Lausanne, 1948.

OSTRZYŃSKA, LUDWIKA,*Wspomnienia o F. Chopinie i uczniu jego F.-H. Péru*, Warsaw, 1927.

PADEREWSKI, IGNACY JAN and LAWTON, MARY, *The Paderewski Memoirs*, Collins, London, 1939.

PANIGEL, ARMAND, *L'oeuvre de Frédéric Chopin: discographie générale*, Editions de la Revue Disques, Paris, 1949.

PAUER, ERNST, *The Pianist's Dictionary*, Novello, Ewer & Co., London, 1895.

PHILIPP, ISIDORE, *Exercices quotidiens tirés des oeuvres de Chopin* with preface by Georges Mathias, Hamelle, Paris, 1897.

PLANTÉ, FRANCIS and others, 'Lettres sur Chopin', *Courrier musical*, Vol. XIII/Paris, 1910.

PORTE, JOHN F., *Chopin: the Composer and his Music*, Wm. Reeves, London, 1935.

POTOCKA, ANGÈLE, *Theodore Leschetizky*, Century Co., New York, 1903.

PRATT, WALDO SELDEN (ed.), *New Encyclopaedia of Music and Musicians*, Macmillan & Co., London, 1924.

PROSNAK, JAN, *The Frederic Chopin International Piano Competitions*, Frédéric Chopin Society, Warsaw, 1970.

PUGNO, RAOUL, *Leçons écrites de Raoul Pugno*, Libraire des Annales, Paris, 1909.

RAYSON, E., *Polish Music and Chopin its Laureate*, Charles Scribner, New York, 1916.

Records and Recording.

REID, ROBERT H., *The Gramophone Shop Encyclopaedia of Recorded Music*, Crown Publishers, New York, 1948.

RIEMANN, HUGO (ed.), *Dictionary of Music* (tr. J. Shedlock), Augener & Co., London, 1908.

ROTHE, ANNA (ed.), *Current Biography 1945*, H. W. Wilson Co., New York.

RUBINSTEIN, ARTUR, *My Young Years*, Jonathan Cape, London, 1973.

RUST, BRIAN, *Gramophone Records of the First World War*, David & Charles, London, 1975.

SACKVILLE-WEST, E. and SHAWE-TAYLOR, D., *The Record Year* (2 vols), Collins, London, 1952 and 1954.

SAERCHINGER, CESAR, *Artur Schnabel*, Cassell & Co., London, 1957.

SALESKI, GDAL, *Famous Musicians of Jewish Origin*, Bloch Publishing Co., New York, 1949.

SAMAROFF-STOKOWSKI, OLGA, *An American Musician's Story*, W. W. Norton & Co. Inc., New York, 1939.

SCHELLING, ERNEST, 'Chez un élève de Chopin', *Revue musicale*, Vol. XII/121, Paris, 1931.

SCHONBERG, HAROLD C., 'Frédéric Chopin: a Discography', *High Fidelity*, Vol. 5 No. 4, 1955.

——*The Great Pianists*, Victor Gollancz, London, 1965.

SCHWERKÉ, IRVING, 'Francis Planté, Patriarch of the Piano', *Recorded Sound,* No. 35, July 1969.

SHAW, GEORGE BERNARD, *London Music in 1888–89 as heard by Corno di Bassetto,* Constable & Co., London, 1937.

—— *Music in London, 1890–94* (3 vols), Constable & Co., London, 1932.

SHERMAN, GLEN, 'Josef Lhévinne', *Recorded Sound,* No. 44, October 1971.

SILOTI, ALEXANDER, *Meine Erinnerungen an Franz Liszt,* Herman, 1913, tr. as *My Memories of Liszt,* Methven Simpson Ltd, Edinburgh, 1913.

SITWELL, SACHEVERELL, *Liszt,* Cassell & Co. Ltd, 1955, revised edition Dover Publications, New York, 1967.

SMITH, JULIA, *Master Pianist: the Career and Teaching of Carl Friedberg,* Philosophical Library, New York, 1963.

SMITH, RONALD, *Alkan,* Vol. I: 'The Enigma', Kahn & Averill, London, 1976.

SOWIŃSKI, ALBERT, *Les Musiciens polonais,* Le Clère, Paris, 1857.

STUCKENSCHMIDT, H. H., *Ferruccio Busoni,* Calder & Boyars, London, 1970.

THOMPSON, OSCAR (ed.), *International Cyclopedia of Music and Musicians* (9th edition ed. Robert Sabin), Dodd, Mead & Co., New York, 1964.

VERNE, MATHILDE, *Chords of Remembrance,* Hutchinson, London, 1936.

WALKER, ALAN (ed.), *Frédéric Chopin: Profiles of the Man and the Musician,* Barrie & Rockliff, London, 1966.

WALKER, BETTINA, *My Musical Experiences,* R. Bentley & Son/Novello, Ewer & Co., London and New York, 1892.

WEILL, JANINE, *Marguerite Long: une vie fascinante,* Julliard, Paris, 1969.

WILLEBY, CHARLES, *Frédéric François Chopin,* Sampson Low, Marston & Co., London, 1892.

WOODHOUSE, GEORGE, 'How Leschetizky Taught', *Music and Letters,* Vol. XXXV, 1954.

Index

Index

275

Index

Index

Index